D0824648

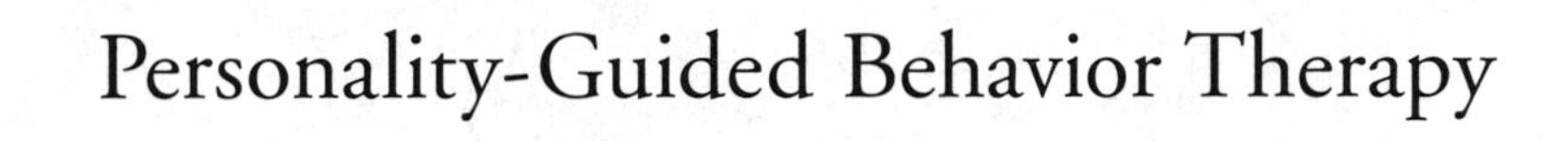

Personality-Guided Behavior Therapy

Personality-Guided Behavior Therapy

Richard F. Farmer
Rosmery O. Nelson-Gray

Series Editor Theodore Millon

AMERICAN PSYCHOLOGICAL ASSOCIATION
WASHINGTON, DC

Published by
American Psychological Association
750 First Street, NE
Washington, DC 20002
www.apa.org

To order
APA Order Department
P.O. Box 92984
Washington, DC 20090-2984
Tel: (800) 374-2721; Direct: (202) 336-5510
Fax: (202) 336-5502; TDD/TTY: (202) 336-6123
Online: www.apa.org/books/
E-mail: order@apa.org

In the U.K., Europe, Africa, and the Middle East, copies may be ordered from
American Psychological Association
3 Henrietta Street
Covent Garden, London
WC2E 8LU England

Typeset in Goudy by Stephen McDougal, Mechanicsville, MD

Printer: Data Reproductions, Auburn Hills, MI
Cover Designer: Berg Design, Albany, NY
Technical/Production Editor: Gail B. Munroe

Library of Congress Cataloging-in-Publication Data

Farmer, Richard F.
Personality-guided behavior therapy / by Richard F. Farmer and Rosemery O. Nelson-Gray. — 1st ed.
p. cm.
Includes bibliographical references and index.
ISBN 1-59147-272-5
1. Psychotherapy. 2. Personality disorders—Treatment. 3. Behavior therapy.
I. Nelson-Gray, Rosemery O. II. Title.

RC480.5.F325 2004
616.89'14—dc22 2004028065

British Library Cataloguing-in-Publication Data
A CIP record is available from the British Library.

Printed in the United States of America
First Edition

To my two wonderful parents, Roy and Emily
Richard F. Farmer

To my two fine sons, Joseph Benjamin Gray and Jeffrey Brendt Gray
Rosemery O. Nelson-Gray

CONTENTS

SERIES FOREWORD

The turn of the 20th century saw the emergence of psychological interest in the concept of individual differences, the recognition that the many realms of scientific study then in vogue displayed considerable variability among "laboratory subjects." Sir Francis Galton in Great Britain and many of his disciples, notably Charles Spearman in England, Alfred Binet in France, and James McKeen Cattell in the United States, laid the groundwork for recognizing that intelligence was a major element of import in what came to be called *differential psychology*. Largely through the influence of psychoanalytic thought, and then only indirectly, did this new field expand the topic of individual differences in the direction of character and personality.

And so here we are at the dawn of the 21st century, ready to focus our attentions ever more seriously on the subject of personality trait differences and their impact on a wide variety of psychological subjects—how they impinge on behavioral medicine outcomes, alter gerontological and adolescent treatment, regulate residential care programs, affect the management of depressive and PTSD patients, transform the style of cognitive–behavioral and interpersonal therapies, guide sophisticated forensic and correctional assessments—a whole bevy of important themes that typify where psychologists center their scientific and applied efforts today.

It is toward the end of alerting psychologists who work in diverse areas of study and practice that the present series, entitled *Personality-Guided Psychology*, has been developed for publication by the American Psychological Association. The originating concept underlying the series may be traced to Henry Murray's seminal proposal in his 1938 volume, *Explorations in Personality*, in which he advanced a new field of study termed *personology*. It took its contemporary form in a work of mine, published in 1999 under the title *Personality-Guided Therapy*.

The utility and relevance of personality as a variable is spreading in all directions, and the series sets out to illustrate where things stand today. As will be evident as the series' publication progresses, the most prominent work at present is found with creative thinkers whose efforts are directed toward enhancing a more efficacious treatment of patients. We hope to demonstrate, further, some of the newer realms of application and research that lie just at the edge of scientific advances in our field. Thus, we trust that the volumes included in this series will help us look beyond the threshold of the present and toward the vast horizon that represents all of psychology. Fortunately, there is a growing awareness that personality variables can be a guiding factor in all spheres of study. We trust the series will provide a map of an open country that encourages innovative ventures and provides a foundation for investigators who wish to locate directions in which they themselves can assume leading roles.

Theodore Millon, PhD, DSc
Series Editor

ACKNOWLEDGMENTS

The authors acknowledge the valuable input provided by Janice Howard, William Baum, Alexander Chapman, Bruce Ellis, Randolph Grace, Janet Latner, Kathryn Whitehead, and the Nelson-Gray lab group, especially Ruth Hurst, on draft portions of this book. Thanks also to John Mitchell for his dedicated and timely assistance. We also wish to express our appreciation and gratitude to Theodore Millon as well as Susan Reynolds, Judy Nemes, Gail Munroe, and Elizabeth Budd from the American Psychological Association for their editorial support and assistance.

Personality-Guided Behavior Therapy

1

PERSONALITY AND BEHAVIOR THEORY: TOWARD THE RECONCILIATION OF AN APPARENT INCOMPATIBILITY

Upon telling our colleagues about a new book we were writing on personality-guided behavior therapy, we were often met with a variety of curious responses, among them: "Isn't that an oxymoron?" "Finally decided to jump the behaviorist ship, eh?" And, less charitably, "So, you've finally lost it, huh?"

Indeed, there is something a bit oxymoronic about the title of this book. Behavior therapists who are true to their theory have an active aversion to attributing behavior to presumed internal entities or "mentalisms." As is apparent in the pages that follow, however, there is room for the concept of personality within a behavior therapy framework. The way in which personality is conceptualized and treated within a behavior therapy perspective, though, differs substantially from more traditional approaches.

In this first chapter, we provide an outline of the main philosophical, theoretical, and conceptual foundations for the overall therapeutic approach described in this book. We first provide an overview of behavior therapy and how this therapy differs from other approaches. Next, we discuss the unifying theoretical principle of this book, selection by consequences, and how this principle is relevant at three levels of analysis of human behavior: phylogenetic, ontogenetic, and cultural. We then note some philosophical assumptions that underlie selectionist accounts of human behavior, including those associated with behavior theory. Finally, we embark on a discussion of how personality is viewed within a behavioral context and provide an overview of "personality-guided" approaches to assessment and treatment from a behavioral perspective.

OVERVIEW OF BEHAVIOR THERAPY

Contemporary behavior therapy has been influenced by a variety of behavioral theories or behaviorisms. Dominant behavior theories from the last century, many of which continue to be highly influential today, include the instrumental–operant paradigm most strongly associated with E. Thorndike (1911) and B. F. Skinner (1953, 1974), the theory of classical conditioning illuminated by I. Pavlov (1927) and subsequently applied to human problems by J. B. Watson (1925) and O. H. Mowrer (Mowrer & Mowrer, 1938), the stimulus–response behaviorism of C. Hull (1943), the neobehavioral movement associated with H. J. Eysenck and the Maudsley group (Eysenck, 1957, 1967), the theory of reciprocal inhibition advanced by J. Wolpe (1958), the paradigmatic behaviorism–psychological behaviorism of A. Staats (1963, 1996), and the social learning perspective associated with A. Bandura (1977). The last few decades have witnessed the emergence of other influential behavioral accounts, such as functionalism–contextualism (e.g., Hayes, Hayes, Reese, & Sarbin, 1993), interbehaviorism (Kantor, 1958), biological behaviorism (Timberlake, 1999), and teleological behaviorism (Rachlin, 1999), as well as the emergence of new applied paradigms such as cognitive–behavioral therapy (e.g., Beck, Rush, Shaw, & Emery, 1979; Mahoney, 1974; Meichenbaum & Cameron, 1982).

The theoretical roots of contemporary behavior therapy are as diverse as they are deep. Similarly, behavior change techniques and applications that have emerged from these theoretical perspectives are likewise distinct and diverse. Given the heterogeneity within the behavior therapy movement, it is perhaps more accurate to use the term "behavior therapies" rather than simply "behavior therapy." Nonetheless, the varieties of theories and applications that underlie the behavior therapies share a number of commonalities that, in the aggregate, distinguish the general field of behavior therapy from other schools of psychotherapy. Several of the features and theoretical perspectives common to the various forms and manifestations of behavior therapy are described below. In chapter 2, we highlight many of the historical milestones of the behavior therapy movement.

Behavior Therapy: Basic Tenants and Fundamentals of the Therapeutic Approach

At the most basic level, behavior therapy represents the application of learning theory and principles to the enhancement of human well-being and the amelioration of human suffering. The form of behavior therapy emphasized in this book is largely influenced by the behavior analytic tradition known variously as *radical behaviorism*, *Skinnerian behaviorism*, or *operant theory*. Principles central to this form of behavior theory include reinforcement, shaping, stimulus control of behavior, modeling, and imitation. This theory is also tied to a number of assumptions about the causes of human behavior, including environmental determinism and functionalism. Behavior therapy, as derived from this theoretical framework, is primarily concerned with what a person *does*, not what a person *has* (Nelson & Hayes, 1986; Spiegler & Guevremont, 2003). That is, the focus is on the behavior of the person, not on presumed underlying traits or inner entities (e.g., ego, will, schema). Simply put, from the behavioral perspective on human psychological functioning, people *are* what they *do*.

Spiegler (1983) and O'Leary and Wilson (1987) have delineated a number of features, listed below, that distinguish behavior therapy from other forms of therapy:

- Clients are best described in terms of what they think, feel, and do in specific life situations.
- In behavior therapy, the client is an active collaborator in decisions that involve therapy, including therapeutic goals and methods.
- In behavior therapy, the client is an active participant in the therapeutic process. That is, the therapy is not administered to the client as much as the client carries out the therapy.
- In the view of behavior therapists, most abnormal or clinically relevant behavior is acquired and maintained according to the same principles as normal behavior.
- Behavior therapy deals with client behavior that is observable by at least one person, including the client.
- In behavior therapy, the therapeutic approach is largely educational in nature, whereby the client is taught new behavior, instructed in methods for changing environmental situations that influence behavior, or both.
- The focus of behavior therapy is on the current situation, which includes the client's current behaviors and the environmental influences that occasion or maintain them.
- Behavior therapy may take place in the environments where the problem behavior actually occurs.

- Behavior therapy integrates the scientific method into the therapeutic framework. This is evident in the reliance on empirically supported principles of behavior and therapeutic strategies, objective evaluation of therapy programs, and the clear identification of treatment targets and goals.
- Behavior therapy is more about doing than talking—it is action oriented.
- Behavior therapy approaches are individualized to the client's specific needs or unique problem areas.
- Behavior therapy involves the continuous assessment or measurement of target behaviors and the conditions that influence them. As a consequence, the effectiveness of a therapy program is monitored in an ongoing fashion.
- In behavior therapy, extensive use is made of psychological assistants, such as parents and teachers, to modify problem behavior in the settings in which it occurs.

In addition, behavior therapy does not hold the view that people who come for therapy are "sick" or "disordered" or that the clinically relevant behaviors that clients display represent symptoms of an underlying disease process. In a similar way, the theory behind behavior therapy does not attribute the source of a person's problematic behavior to inner causes, nor does it assume that the person must change something "abnormal" within him or her if therapeutic progress is to occur. Rather, behavior therapists see problematic behavior as the problem. Because problematic behaviors are viewed as arising from the same processes that result in nonproblematic or normal behavior, a primary focus of behavior therapy is on the development of new behavior patterns or the refinement of existing ones, often through altering the context within which such behavior occurs.

From the behavioral perspective, when behavior is regarded as abnormal, it is typically done so with reference to the social context. That is, the social context provides a frame of reference for the determination of which forms of behavior are acceptable or appropriate. Because social contexts vary significantly across different settings, cultures, or subcultures, general guidelines as to what defines normal or abnormal behavior are difficult to offer. From a behavioral perspective, the labeling of a behavior as either normal or abnormal ultimately reflects a value judgment of the person who is applying the label. The application of the label itself, however, does not explain the behavior, at least not from a behavioral perspective.

Operant Theory of Behavior: A Theoretical Foundation of Behavior Therapy

An operant theory of behavior is primarily concerned with the causal or functional relationships that exist between the behavior of a person and the environment that establishes the context for such behavior. Skinner (1953, p. 65) defined an *operant* as a class of behavior that operates on the environment by producing consequences. In this definition, operant learning is evident when the probability of a behavior class is altered (i.e., becomes more or less likely) in association with the consequences that follow behavior.

Within operant theory, the *three-term contingency* constitutes the fundamental unit of analysis. Skinner (1969, p. 7) summarized the three-term contingency as follows:

> An adequate formulation of the interaction between an organism and its environment must always specify three things: (1) the occasion upon which a response occurs, (2) the response itself, and (3) the reinforcing consequences. The interrelationships among them are the "contingencies of reinforcement."

As a result, when behavior therapists seek to develop hypotheses about behavior, they will often do so within the three-term contingency framework. *Antecedent conditions* (or *stimuli*) set the occasion for behavior to occur. This means that whether a given behavior occurs in the presence of these conditions is directly related to the person's history of behaving in the presence of similar conditions in the past. If a particular form of behavior was enacted in the presence of these stimulus features in the past *and* resulted in a reinforcing outcome, then the presence of similar conditions in the current environment increases the likelihood that these behaviors will be enacted again. Conversely, if a particular form of behavior was enacted in the presence of such stimulus cues in the past *and* followed by a punishing outcome, it would then be unlikely that the individual would enact that form of behavior in the current context.

As we describe in greater detail in chapter 3, a *response* can be anything that a person does. This includes overt behaviors that involve some form of muscle activity (i.e., behaviors that involve physical movement, including speech that is spoken aloud) or covert responses that occur within the person (e.g., thoughts, feelings, physical sensations).

When a response occurs, *consequences* associated with that response often follow. These consequences may be reinforcing or punishing. By definition, a response is *reinforced* if the consequences that follow result in an *increase* in the probability or frequency of that response on future occasions. In a similar way, a response is *punished* if the consequences that follow result in a *decrease* in the probability or frequency of that response in the future. Alternatively, an absence of consequences may follow a behavior, as is the case in behavioral *extinction*. Under conditions of extinction, behavior would eventually extinguish or no longer occur if it repeatedly failed to produce any reinforcing consequence.

Also of note in the earlier quoted passage is Skinner's use of the word *organism*. The writings of Skinner and other behavior theorists often use this word to denote the fact that the principles of reinforcement are not species-specific. Rather, in the behavioral framework, many of the same processes that influence human behavior have also been observed to influence the behavior of other organisms. As we discuss later, however, humans' capacity for language and symbolic speech set us apart from other organisms and suggest additional processes that influence behavior.

A common misunderstanding associated with operant theory is that it is a mechanistic stimulus–response theory, whereby a stimulus (S) event elicits a response (R), or S → R. Although this process is central to classical, respondent, or Pavlovian conditioning, Skinner set out an alternative behavioral theory more than 65 years ago (Skinner, 1938). In Skinner's operant model, the centrality of selection by consequence (C) was emphasized, or R → C. (Other common misconceptions about behavior theory and therapy are delineated in Todd & Morris, 1983.) As subsequent sections illustrate, the concept of selection by consequence serves as a unifying principle associated with our personality-guided approach to behavior therapy.

SELECTION BY CONSEQUENCES: EVOLUTIONARY THEORY AS A FRAMEWORK

> There are remarkable similarities in natural selection, operant conditioning, and the evolution of social environments. Not only do all three dispense with a prior creative design and a prior purpose, they invoke the notion of survival as a value. What is good for the species is what makes for its survival. What is good for the individual is what promotes his well-being. What is good for a culture is what permits it to solve its problems.
>
> —B. F. Skinner (1974, pp. 225–226)

> [H]uman behavior is the joint product of (i) the contingencies of survival responsible for the natural selection of the species and (ii) the contingencies of reinforcement responsible for the repertoires acquired by its members, including (iii) the special contingencies maintained by an evolved social environment. (Ultimately, of course, it is all a matter of natural selection, since operant conditioning is an evolved process, of which cultural practices are special applications).
>
> —B. F. Skinner (1981, p. 502)

Selection by consequences is the means by which the environment determines outcomes among individual organisms and living systems (Delprato & Midgley, 1992). As applied to everyday human behavior, the thesis of selection by consequences suggests that behavior is a function of, or is influenced by, the effects it produces.

Skinner (1981) suggested that human behavior is the result of three forms of selection by consequences: phylogenetic selection (also known as *natural selection* or *Darwinian selection*), ontogenetic selection (or the environmental selection of behavior over one's lifetime), and cultural selection (or the selection of cultural practices based on their associated consequences). Skinner noted that each of these forms of selection is the focus of different disciplines, namely, biology, psychology, and anthropology, respectively. Even though these three forms of selection may be studied by different disciplines, a common core foundation associated with these selection models is that each can be conceptualized within the broader framework of evolutionary theory (e.g., Alessi, 1992; Skinner, 1981). A unifying principle that underlies the theory and approach to therapy that we outline in this book is selection by consequence and the potential functional role that selection in these three areas (phylogeny, ontogeny, and culture) may have in relation to human behavior.

To some, the suggestion that Skinner's radical behaviorism or operant psychology is theoretically consistent with evolutionary theory may come as a surprise, particularly because one popular misconception of behavioral theories is that they discount the influence that heritable factors have on behavior. However, as Skinner (1971, p. 101) himself noted, "a person's behavior is determined by a genetic endowment traceable to the evolutionary history of the species and by the environmental circumstances to which as an individual he has been exposed" (Skinner, 1971, p. 101).

Phylogenetic (or Natural) Selection

In phylogenetic (Darwinian) selection, the environment selects variations among individuals within a species on the basis of the survival and reproductive values associated with those variations. That is, the environment selects individuals who possess the most adaptive variations for the environments in which they live. In turn, those individuals with the more adaptive variations have a greater likelihood of procreating and passing their adaptive variations on to their offspring. Notions of what the units of selection are in Darwinian theory vary among theorists; some suggest that the unit of selection is the gene, whereas others suggest that it is the organism in interaction with the environment (Hull, Langman, & Glenn, 2001).

Selection processes in evolutionary theory involve three components (Baum, 1994). First, environmental factors that result in an advantageous population variation must be present over an extended period of time. Second, there must be a genetic basis for the population variation in question that can, in turn, be passed on to successive generations (i.e., reproduction and genetic transmission, or *genetic inheritance*). Third, competition for resources results in those organisms with the advantageous variant having greater success in producing offspring to whom the variant is passed on (i.e., differential reproductive success, or *fitness*). In the event environmental factors that selected the genetic variation, or *genotype*, continue to persist over an extended time, then one would expect that the selected genotype would become more predominant over successive generations.

Phylogenetic Selection and the Effects on Species Behavior

A critical element associated with the selection processes in evolutionary theory is the notion that individual organisms within a species interact with the environment through the organisms' behavior (Baum, 1994). Examples of such behavior would include fighting, fleeing, hunting, finding or producing shelter, mating, and caring for offspring. Those organisms that are more efficient and effective in their behavior are likely to have greater fitness in relation to their environment.

From a behavioral perspective, Baum (1994, pp. 62–63) suggested five ways that the process of natural selection has influenced the behavior of organisms, including people:

1. Natural selection has resulted in the emergence of reliable patterns of behavior that contribute to survival and reproduction. Examples of these patterns include reflexes (i.e., unconditional or unlearned behaviors elicited by an unconditional stimulus) and fixed action patterns (i.e., instinctual behavior).
2. Natural selection has resulted in the capacity for respondent (or classical or Pavlovian) conditioning, whereby unconditional and conditional stimuli come to evoke unconditional and conditional responses, respectively. These unlearned and learned responses to unconditional and conditional stimuli, respectively, are similar to reflexes or fixed action patterns.
3. Natural selection may have favored the selection of genotypes associated with sensitivity to the effects of reinforcement and punishment, or *operant conditioning*. Sensitivity to the consequences of behavior may favor the refinement, efficiency, and effectiveness of behavior. As a result, operant learning likely had a role in the enhancement of the fitness of genes over evolutionary history.
4. Natural selection has resulted in physiological mechanisms and processes associated with a general sensitivity to the effects of environmental factors that influence the efficacy of reinforcers and punishers. Deprivation and satiation are two such examples. If an individual is deprived of water for a prolonged period, for example, the reinforcement qualities associated with drinking water will be enhanced. Conversely, if an individual is satiated on water, then the reinforcement qualities associated with drinking water will be diminished.
5. Natural selection has resulted in some forms of behavior (e.g., those most strongly associated with survival and reproductive

value over the history of the species, such as hunting or fleeing) to be more readily influenced by both respondent and operant conditioning processes than others.

The range of potential behavior that an organism within a particular lineage can produce is also the result of phylogenetic selection (Hull et al., 2001). In a similar way, susceptibility to the effects of reinforcement and punishment, at least in relation to primary reinforcers and punishers (e.g., food, sex, physical pain), is the product of the evolution of the species. Sensitivities in these areas may vary across individuals, however, and some have analogously suggested that varying sensitivities to these and other forms of consequent stimuli are related to variations in temperament (e.g., Cloninger, 1987; Gray, 1987a). The association of temperament to sensitivity to behavioral consequences are reviewed later in this book (see chap. 4).

Natural selection also has likely played a role in determining which types of events function as reinforcers or punishers and has resulted in certain consequences becoming associated with either a greater or lesser likelihood for reproductive success (Baum, 1994; see also Millon, 1990; Millon & Davis, 1996). That is, the selection of genes that associated extreme temperatures, nausea, threatening events, and pain with aversion or punishment likely increased the fitness of organisms that had such genes. Similarly, the selection of genes that associated sexual intercourse, shelter, food, and water with reinforcement increased the fitness of organisms that had the associated genotypes. Those who were the most highly reinforced for escaping or avoiding dangerous situations had obvious fitness advantages over those who were not (Skinner, 1971). As Skinner (1971, pp. 104–105) concluded, all reinforcers, both learned and unlearned, ultimately produce their effects as a result of natural section.

Ontogenetic Selection and Operant Theory

The idea that phylogenetic selection operates on variations associated with effective behavior in relation to environmental demands is fully consistent with behavioral notions of ontogenetic selection of behavior. Skinner, however, viewed the notion that genes cause behavior as overly simplistic. He further suggested that behavior per se is not inherited because even behavior that is under some degree of genetic control is influenced by the environmental context within which it occurs (Hull et al., 2001; Skinner, 1989, pp. 49–50). Put even more succinctly, behavior does not and cannot occur in a vacuum—it occurs in a context.

In ontogenetic or operant selection, the environment selects behavior of an organism within the lifetime of the individual. Behaviors operate on the environment by producing effects or consequences. Those behaviors that are instrumental in producing successful or effective outcomes, or that are more efficient, tend to be selected on the basis of the principle of reinforcement. Conversely, those behaviors that are instrumental in producing unsuccessful or ineffective outcomes, or are not efficient, tend to be punished or fail to produce reinforcement and become less probable over time.

Just as natural selection operates on variations by repeatedly selecting among variable morphological features of organisms, selection in operant theory operates on behavioral variations that are the most effective or "fit" for the environments in which they occur. In ontogenetic selection, however, behavior is not necessarily selected because of its associated reproductive and survival value for the species. Rather, behavior is selected because it is effective within the environmental context in which it occurs, which may or may not have associated reproductive or survival value (Hull et al., 2001).

Furthermore, and as noted by Alessi (1992), ontogenetic selection allows the organism to adjust to changing environmental contexts and situations during its lifetime, whereas phylogenetic selection, which often requires hundreds of generations to occur for complex organisms (Ayala, 1985), does not allow for such adjustments.

Ontogenetic Selection and the Effect on the Behavior of the Individual

In the course of an individual's lifetime, the environment selects behavior on the basis of the consequences that they produce. As Baum noted (1994), behaviorally oriented theorists and therapists tend to view *behavioral shaping* over one's lifetime as analogous to evolutionary processes that occur within species over successive generations:

> Just as differences in reproductive success (fitness) shape the composition of a population of genotypes, so reinforcement and punishment shape the composition of an individual's behavior. . . . Just as with evolution, behavior shaping operates on the population and on the average . . . Not every action of a type need be reinforced or punished for the type to be strengthened or suppressed; the type only need be reinforced or punished more *on the average* over time. (Baum, 1994, pp. 64–65, emphasis in original)

Whereas natural selection involves variation, reproduction, and differential success, so, too, does the process of behavioral shaping. As Baum (1994) noted, we rarely if ever produce the exact same form of behavior on more than one occasion. That is, there is some natural variation in our behavior, and some of these variations may prove to be more successful than others. In a similar way, for shaping processes to occur, there must be some reproduction of the form of behavior over time. Different forms of behavior are associated with different degrees of success, and those that are most successful are selected and become an established part of the individual's behavior repertoire.

From the process of environmental shaping, behavioral repertoires are established and refined. As the individual matures, these repertoires become more complex and varied (Staats, 1996). Staats, for example, outlined the cumulative and hierarchical development of one behavioral repertoire, mathematics skills, as follows:

> The child . . . learns a language repertoire. . . . This repertoire will then provide the basis for the child learning to count . . . And these repertoires will provide the basis for the child learning the number operations of adding, subtracting, multiplying, and dividing. These repertoires (and others), in turn, will be basic to learning algebra, which is requisite to learning more advanced mathematics, which is requisite to learning physics. Decades may be involved in such extended learning. (p. 80)

We see much of human behavior as the result of extended shaping processes that take place over the individual's lifetime. Before more complex forms of behavior can become established, more basic or elemental forms must be selected, strengthened, and refined. In this regard, environmental selection of behavior is a centrally important concept because selection of behavior is the first step in this complex learning process.

Cultural Selection

Cultural evolution as used here refers to the development, maintenance, and modification of the behavior of a group. The transmission of cultural practices or customs occurs through (a) genetic inheritance or (b) behavioral transfer processes within groups, most notably though the processes of modeling and imitation, rule provision, and reinforcement for rule following, or a combination of these.

In the case of genetic inheritance, certain genetic variations may become predominant among members of a population that, in turn, affect cultural practices. For example, the predominance of a genetic variation within a culture related to hypersensitivity to the effects of punishment may result in cultural practices that protect against potential threats or dangers, and the promotion of rules or modeled behavior that emphasize punishment contingencies or the avoidance of punishment.

The selection of genes for culture, just like the selection of genes for learning, might represent a mechanism that functions to enhance the fitness of the organism. For example, the ability to learn from others' experiences or through rules passed down from previous generations may provide for more effective and efficient forms of learning (Baum, 1994). If culturally transmitted traits enhanced the fitness of genes shared among persons within a culture, then the genes that contributed to those traits will be selected by the environment and become more predominant within the culture over time (Baum, 1994). Examples of culturally transmitted traits might include *sensitivity* to particular forms of environmental stimuli (e.g., speech sounds, cues that signal threat or danger, cues that signal the availability of reward, stimuli that precede illness) and the *capacity* for imitation, instruction, and responsiveness to social reinforcement contingencies (Baum, 1994; Skinner, 1989).

In the case of *behavioral transfer processes*, cultural selection involves the process of selection acting on variation and the transfer of selected behavior of one organism to another (Baum, 1994). That is, behavior can continue to exist apart from the individual organism that acquired it during its own lifetime (i.e., after the organism dies) provided that the social environment selects the behavior. If the behavior is subsequently passed on, then it continues to exist through its enactment by others (i.e., it is shared among members of a group). Common behavioral transfer processes involved in cultural selection include verbal behavior, rule-governed behavior, observational learning, imitation, and the arrangement of social contingencies (Catania, 1994).

The Role of Language

Skinner (1957, 1981, 1984) noted that the evolved capacity for language has resulted in more and varied forms of social behavior in humans and has resulted in a class of behaviors (i.e., verbal behaviors) that can come under operant control. Language, both spoken (e.g., oral traditions) and written (e.g., in published works), also allows for individuals within a culture to transmit behavior to others, either within the span of a brief period of time or across several generations (Alessi, 1992).

As part of culture, perhaps the most important forms of speech are known as *rules*. Rules include instructions, moral injunctions, commands, propositions (i.e., "if–then" statements), advice, demands, knowledge of behavior–environment relations, oral traditions (e.g., stories, myths), and modeled behavior (Baum, 1994). At the most basic level, a rule specifies consequences or outcomes associated with acting in particular ways. Rules may also alter the functions of the environment (e.g., by either strengthening or weakening its influence) and promote the enactment of behavioral sequences over extended periods with reference to possible distal consequences (Barnes-Holmes et al., 2001). *Rule-governed behavior* constitutes a unique form of behavior that is under the influence of verbal stimuli (i.e., rules).

Why do people generally follow rules? Rule-governed behavior, technically speaking, has its roots in contingency-shaped behavior. That is, the very act of rule-following is shaped at an early age by more proximate contingencies (e.g., the provision of tangible reinforcers such as food or a favored toy or verbal praise for rule following). The degree to which an individual complies with rules is influenced, in part, by the extent to which rule-following has been reinforced in the past. As Baum (1994, p. 140) has noted, rule-following constitutes a functional category or class of behavior. Once this response class is established, it becomes generalized to different forms and varieties of rules.

Individuals are more likely to imitate and follow the rules of persons whose behavior has been successful (e.g., those who show signs that their behavior has been reinforced, such as through apparent wealth, status, appearance, and roles; Baum, 1994). The degrees to which rule generation, rule adherence, and a concept we discuss later, *imitation of modeled behavior*, occur ultimately depends on the extent to which doing so enhances fitness (Baum, 1994).

Imitation, Modeling, and Observational Learning

Imitation, modeling, and observational learning are other means by which cultural practices may be passed on or transferred. In these forms of learning, observers discriminate the behavior displayed by others (models). The selection of modeled behavior to imitate subsequently by observers is, in turn, influenced by the consequences that follow instances of modeled behavior (Catania, 1994; Malott, Malott, & Trojan, 2000). When a model is reinforced for behaving in a certain way, the likelihood that an observer will imitate modeled behavior is greater. On the other hand, when a model's behavior is punished, then the observer is less likely to imitate the modeled behavior. When behavior patterns become acquired by the process of imitation, they can be further shaped and modified (e.g., reinforced and punished) by the environment and, as a result, become more highly evolved and efficient forms of behavior (Baum, 1994).

One can easily see how imitation might enhance the fitness of an organism that has such a capacity. If one has the capacity to imitate, one does not need to experience several learning trials to acquire a particular form of behavior. Those who cannot imitate would be less likely to acquire adaptive behavior or behavior necessary for reproduction and survival.

Cultural Selection and the Effect on the Practices of a Culture

The degree of genetic modification among humans over the last 50,000 years is likely quite small. As a result, the changes that we see in cultural practices among humans within this time (e.g., the development and refinement of written language, the emergence of various technologies, the appearance of vast cities, the establishment of laws and codes of conduct) are likely the result of the evolution of cultural practices, not the evolution of the species (Gould, 1980).

Cultures are, in part, defined by shared rules, mores, values, practices, social contingencies, and customs. All of these are expressed in the form of action or behavior, or *cultural practices* (sometimes also referred to as *cultural replicators*). As Alessi (1992) noted, cultural practices often come about as ways to solve societal problems or to maintain societal functions. Alessi (1992, p. 1364) further suggested that the distinctiveness of cultures is a direct result of a given society's history of problem-solving practices, the effectiveness of which are directly contingent on the nature of the problems encountered by a culture and the sequences within which they emerged and were addressed.

Rules are also used to institute practices of restraint (Alessi, 1992). Laws are examples of rules that function to restrain behavior by the suggestion of distal aversive consequences (e.g., a fine, jail time) for rule infractions. Value, mores, warnings, admonishments, and taboos may also have a similar restraining function and are maintained by more proximate factors such as immediate negative social consequences that follow instances of compliance or noncompliance (Alessi, 1992).

As noted by Baum (1994), *values* held by a culture connote what is good or bad, right or wrong, acceptable or nonacceptable, moral or immoral. Values exist as forms of verbal behavior that take the form of rules that specify the contingencies of a behavior. That is, activities deemed "bad" are likely to be punished by members of a culture, whereas activities regarded as "good" are likely to be reinforced if enacted (Skinner, 1971). The labels "good" and "bad" associated with various forms of behavior exist through social arrangement (Baum, 1994) and hence represent value judgments made by the larger culture. Values are also often expressed as rules in the form of "should," "ought," "must," or "have to" statements, such as in the statement, "I must lead a virtuous life." In this example, punishment is implied in the event one fails to comply with the demands of the rule.

Summary

Selection by consequence provides a compelling and unifying framework for the conceptualization of processes involved in the influence of human behavior. Table 1.1 provides a comparative summary of these processes with reference to phylogenetic, ontogenetic, and cultural selection. In the next section, we extend the analysis of selection by consequence by specifying the underlying philosophical assumptions associated with this approach.

PHILOSOPHICAL PERSPECTIVES ON THEORIES OF SELECTION BY CONSEQUENCE

Although the theories that underlie the various behavior therapies demonstrate diversity in basic assumptions and emphases, there is nonetheless a good deal of common philosophical ground shared by these theories. In the sections that follow, we highlight some of the core philosophical assumptions of behavior theory and therapy and distinguish these from those found in other related accounts of human behavior, such as evolutionary psychology.

TABLE 1.1
Processes of Natural Selection, Operant Selection, Cultural Selection Contrasted

Process	History	Variation	Replication/ transmission	Selection process	Units of selection
Natural selection	Phylogeny (evolutionary history of the species)	Genotypes within species populations (genetic mutations)	Genetic inheritance	Differential fitness (selection pressures determine which variations survive and reproduce)	Genes and phenotypic traits
Operant selection	Ontogeny (reinforcement and punishment history of the individual organism)	Behavioral forms of topographies	Modifications in the central nervous system and behavior recurrence	Differential environmental consequences of behavior (reinforcement and punishment)	Operants (units of behavior)
Cultural practices	Phylogeny, ontogeny (evolutionary history, cultural practices)	Genotypes, cultural replicators (e.g., customs, rules, practices, values, social contingencies)	Genetic inheritance, behavioral transfer among group members	Differential fitness, consequences associated with imitated behavior, rule-governed, verbal behavior, and behavior under the influence of social contingencies	Cultural selection

Note. From *Understanding Behaviorism: Science, Behavior, Culture* (p. 67), by W. M. Baum, 1994, New York: HarperCollins. Copyright 1994 by W. M. Baum. Adapted with permission.

Philosophical Dimensions of Behavior Theory and Therapy

The various levels of selection by consequence delineated in the previous section all have in common a number of philosophical assumptions. Some of the main theoretical views that distinguish this perspective are described here.

Monism (or Materialism) Versus Dualism (or Mentalism)

Whereas *monism* is the philosophical view that mind and body are the same (i.e., the only substance is matter), the *dualistic* view holds that the mind is nonphysical and transcends time and space. In Cartesian dualism, thoughts were considered to be causal and mental (nonphysical), whereas nonreflexive motor behaviors were viewed as the effects of mental processes executed through sequences of physical processes (Nelson & Hayes, 1986).

Darwinian or selectionist views on the mind–body issue tend to be monistic and hold that humans' origins and fundamental nature can be explained by the laws of physics and natural selection (Richards, 2000). Philosophically, behavioral theorists also tend to fall on the side of monism and believe that our origins are wholly the product of natural selection. Skinner is clear in his assertion that mind and body are the same: "[W]hat is felt or introspectively observed is not some nonphysical world of consciousness, mind or mental life but the observer's own body" (Skinner, 1974, pp. 18–19).

In everyday language, causes for human action are often attributed to the mind. As Baum (1994) noted, however, the mind is a problematic concept for a science of human behavior because "mind" is not a part of nature. That is, when regarded as a nonphysical entity or conceptualized as a psychological construct, the concept of mind has none of the properties of natural objects—that is, no mass, weight, volume, or physical form. Nonetheless, the concept of mind is often used as a causal determinant, grammatically as a noun, as if the mind had some sort of "thing-ness."

Behaviorism can address concepts such as thoughts, memories, sensations, dreams, images, and the like as private events, or naturally occurring events that are observable by the individual within whom they occur (Baum, 1994). In so doing, behavioral accounts avoid *mentalism*, or the invoking of mental concepts to explain behavior. Furthermore, as Baum (1994) noted, there are other problems associated with mentalistic concepts. First, they are often proposed to have autonomous properties. In the case of the mind, it is sometimes suggested that the mind has autonomous control over behavior, or that the mind has special properties that place it outside the realm of scientific study. For example, consider the following typical passage from an introductory psychology text:

> psychology is the scientific study of behavior and mind . . . . By *mind*, psychologists usually mean the contents and processes of subjective ex-

perience: sensations, thoughts, and emotions. Behavior and mind are kept separate in the definition because only behavior can be directly measured by the scientific observer. (Narine, 2000, pp. 6–7, emphasis in original)

Baum (1994) has also suggested that mentalistic accounts often suffer from circular reasoning or reification processes. That is, mentalistic explanations typically involve an inference about the effects of a mentalistic entity from behavior, which is then followed by the assertion that the inferred entity caused the behavior. For example, it not too atypical in psychology to hear one claim that "a harsh superego resulted in a person's feelings of guilt and subsequent engagement in self-injurious behavior," and later, "we know this person has a harsh superego because of this person's propensity to feel guilt and habitually engage in self-injury."

This same process of circular reasoning or reification can be illustrated with reference to the concept of intelligence. Some infer presence of intelligence by the display of intelligent behavior (e.g., "her strong performance on the IQ test is the result of her superior intelligence"). The inference that intelligence is the cause of intelligent behavior is, however, the same as attributing intelligent behavior to a fictional "thing" (i.e., intelligence). When one views the relationship between intelligence and intelligent behavior as causal and unidirectional, or that these two exist at different levels of analysis or causality, then a logical error is made (Baum, 1994). Behaviorally oriented psychologists tend to escape these processes of circular reasoning and reification through the assertion that intelligence is the same as intelligent behavior.

At the cultural level of analysis, Baum (1994, p. 221) suggested that to construe cultural values as beliefs or ideas that are passed along to group members also conveys a type of mentalism. Such a process implies that variations selected in the evolution of a culture are mental entities rather than behavior (for a particularly egregious example of this, the "meme" concept, see Blackmore, 1999; Dawkins, 1976). As a result, when behavior theorists discuss the evolution of culture, they emphasize the behavior of group members that define a culture, not invented mentalistic entities such as memes.

From a behavioral perspective, the science of behavior cannot proceed if the supposed cause of behavior is some hidden, inner, autonomously functioning entity that cannot be observed by anyone, yet requires scientific inquiry and exploration if the effects of the entity—namely, behavior—are to be explained. Rather, explanations for human action are to be found in the natural world. In the radical behavioral view, private events (e.g., thoughts, feelings, sensations, memories) take place in the natural world. Viewed in this way, private events are subject to the same influences as public behavior (i.e., that behavior directly observable by others). Therefore, in behavior theory, references to the controlling functions of invented mental entities such as schemas, will, and ego are avoided.

From a radical behavioral perspective, then, the only meaningful difference between public and private events is the number of people who can observe them (Baum, 1994). Apart from this, public and private events are subject to the same influences and are the same types of events.

Determinism Versus Free Will

Assumptions of determinism generally follow from monistic or materialistic stances. That is, from the position of monism or materialism, the argument is often put forth that (a) human origins are entirely material, and (b) given that matter is deterministic, and (c) that determinism is incompatible with free will, (d) free will, therefore, cannot be possible (Richards, 2000, p. 135).

The corresponding bipolar opposite of determinism is free will. The concept of free will suggests that individuals freely choose to act and can do so without the influence of other factors (e.g., biological, environmental). That is, if one's actions are not determined by any prior condition, and if one could have just as easily acted in a different way if he or she had *chosen* or *wanted* to, then it is said that one acted freely. If actions are determined by prior conditions or events, however, then it is said that we do not act freely. Strictly speaking, free will can only exist in the absence of determinism.

Within selectionist accounts of human behavior, behavior is largely, if not exclusively, determined. As Hull et al. (2001) noted, in all selectionist models, variation is an essential element. If there is no variation, then there is no basis for differential selection. Furthermore, as noted by Hull et al., variations involved in selection processes must be caused.

Determinism is central to any form of science that has as its overarching goals the prediction and influence of some phenomenon. In psychology, this phenomenon would be behavior. Within psychology, however, various forms of determinism have been proposed. For example, some biological psychiatrists, trait theorists, and evolutionary psychologists embrace the concept of genetic determinism. Cognitive psychologists often attribute the causality of human behavior and experience to mental processes and structures. Those from the traditional psychoanalytic perspective and many adherents from the psychodynamic school tend to embrace the concept of psychic determinism. In behavior theory, environmental determinism is used to explain behavior (Skinner, 1971, 1981).

Functionalism Versus Structuralism

As currently applied in the field of psychology, *structuralism* refers to the study of *how* people behave, or the form of behavior. Response–response relationships (or response covariations) might be studied to make inferences about the structure of behavior or personality (e.g., Goldberg, 1993). In contrast, *functionalism* is associated with the study of *why* people behave the way that they do (Nelson & Hayes, 1986; Skinner, 1974).

Historically within psychology, structuralism assumed that the repeated pairing of stimuli caused elements to become bounded together that, in turn, resulted in the emergence of compounds. Pavlov, the father of classical or respondent conditioning, is an example of a structuralist; he proposed that complex behavior is mechanical and the result of a combination of simple elements, namely, reflexes (Rachlin, 1976). To Pavlov, more complex forms of behavior are the result of a combination of several, more elemental forms of reflex.

Functionalism, on the other hand, is based on Darwinian evolutionary principles (Rachlin, 1976). Darwin proposed that the physical structure of a given species was determined by its associated function. Natural selection selects physical structure according to functional properties associated with that structure, namely, those associated with the enhancement of gene fitness.

Radical behaviorism and behavior therapy traditionally have been more strongly associated with the functionalism than structuralism. In radical behaviorism, behavior that is functional in particular environmental contexts is selected (or made more probable) whereas behavior that is not functional (i.e., does not produce reinforcing consequences) dies out or becomes extinguished. Other forms of behavior theory, however, such as those based on stimulus–response models of behavior (e.g., respondent, classical or Pavlovian conditioning), come from the structuralistic tradition.

Contemporary investigations into response structure or response covariation within a behavioral framework (e.g., Evans, 1986; Lang, 1968; Staats, 1986) are more consistent with the structuralistic than the functionalistic perspective. In a similar way, aspects of psychometric theory and its application are consistent with the structuralistic position, as is evident among those behaviorally oriented therapists who argue for the use of psychometric principles in the evaluation of the utility of behavioral assessment devices (e.g., Barrios & Hartmann, 1986). The extent to which the study of behavioral form or covariation in addition to function has utility for behavior theory, assessment, and therapy has been the object of growing debate in recent years (e.g., Bissett & Hayes, 1999; Farmer & Nelson-Gray, 1999; Nelson-Gray & Farmer, 1999; Staats, 1999). As we discuss in greater detail throughout this book, we see distinct advantages for behavior therapists to consider both the function and form of behavior patterns in client assessment and treatment.

Contextualism Versus Mechanism

The form of behaviorism affiliated with the respondent (or Pavlovian) tradition is aligned with the mechanistic view of behavior. Much of the activity of those who studied respondent conditioning was geared toward the development of mechanistic explanations for behavior. As a rule, the *mechanist* is a structuralist and seeks to explain behavior through the identification of structural elements and the associated effects that they produce (Nelson & Hayes, 1986). For example, in contemporary cognitive psychology, structural concepts such as *short-term storage*, *buffers*, *filters*, *comparators*, *processors*, and *schemas* are used to explain how the mind evaluates information.

Contextual approaches to the study of behavior found in radical (or Skinnerian) behaviorism are associated with descriptions of how events, including behavior, are organized and linked together in a meaningful way (i.e., "the act in context"). To this end, contextualism is concerned with the context in which a behavior occurs, or how behavior fits into its associated contextual flow.

Selection by Consequences, Not Evolutionary Psychology

As the preceding discussions have suggested, Skinner's radical behaviorism has many parallels to Darwinian evolutionary principles, most notably the notion of selection by consequence. There are a number of similarities from a philosophical perspective as well. Both radical behaviorism and Darwinian theories of selection are grounded in similar underlying philosophical assumptions, and both lean more toward monism or materialism (vs. dualism or mentalism), environmental determinism (vs. free will), functionalism (vs. structuralism), and contextualism (vs. mechanism).

Within the last 2 decades, a new paradigm has emerged that has claimed to be the heir of Darwinian theory as it is applied in psychology, named *evolutionary psychology* by its adherents. Because some readers may be familiar with this emerging field, and because we wish to avoid confusion between these two distinctly different perspectives, we differentiate in this section the selectionist evolutionary account presented here from that associated with this relatively new theoretical approach.

At the most basic level, contemporary evolutionary psychology is an attempt to integrate Darwinian evolutionary concepts and cognitive psychology (e.g., Buss, 1999; Cosmides & Tooby, 1992; Kirkpatrick, 1999). This field is the most recent descendant of the highly controversial area known as *sociobiology* (e.g., Dawkins, 1976; Howe & Lyne, 1992; Segerstråle, 2000). This resultant "new science of the mind" (e.g., Buss, 1999) has produced a theoretical approach that is, at times, far removed from basic Darwinian theoretical assumptions (Rose & Rose, 2000).

Because evolutionary psychology is relatively new on the scene, it is still a young science undergoing a continual process of development and revision. Yet even at this early stage, there are obvious differences apparent in this approach compared with the selectionist accounts presented thus far. Three areas in particular standout as noteworthy: the acceptance of mentalism, the emphasis on phylogentic contingencies in accounts of human behavior, and species-centrism.

The Acceptance of Mentalism

Evolutionary psychologists propose the existence of an inherited mind with innate ideas and reasoning abilities that directs nonreflexive behavior

(Buss, 1999). Mental structures are proposed, termed *evolved psychological mechanisms*. Evolved psychological mechanisms in the form of sophisticated evolved cognitive modules are proposed to be domain-specific and geared toward the detection, analysis, and resolution of reoccurring problems encountered within the history of the species. These modules are conceived as special-purpose entities encapsulated within the brain system that contain phylogenetically derived information about situations or scenarios and associated adaptive responses. Such mental structures are also viewed as the source of new or novel behavioral skills that emerged over successive generations: "[W]e have a collection of evolved mechanisms that are reasonably good at solving problems efficiently" (Buss, 1999, p. 21) and "With each new mechanism that is added to the mind, an organism can perform a new task" (Buss, 1999, p. 53). Notably absent in this account is any description of a learning process that serves as the foundation of this problem-solving approach.

In evolutionary psychology, then, there is emphasis on mentalism (rather than monism or materialism), structuralism (vs. functionalism), mechanism (vs. contextualism), and the acceptance of a strong form of nativism (i.e., the notion that many of our basic ideas about the world are innate and that knowledge of the world is something that is possessed, not gained as a result of experience). These differences in philosophical perspective distinguish the evolutionary psychology account from the evolutionary accounts emphasized here.

Emphasis on Phylogenetic Contingencies in Accounts of Human Behavior

Although proponents of evolutionary psychology claim their theory recognizes that behavior arises from the interaction of genes and the environment (Buss, 1999), emphasis is nonetheless placed on phylogenetic selection processes and evolved adaptations in accounts of human behavior, and the influence of environments during one's lifetime is downplayed. As a result, it is not difficult to understand why some might regard evolutionary psychology as grounded in genetic determinism, or as a "gene-machine" form of psychology (Richards, 2000; see also Panksepp & Panksepp, 2000). Furthermore, and consistent with other cognitive accounts of human behavior generally, evolutionary psychology proposes mechanisms for the phylogenetic selection of behavior but does not propose selection mechanisms at the ontogenetic level (Palmer & Donahoe, 1992). Thus, evolutionary psychology, at present, cannot provide a complete and integrated account of the factors that influence human behavior.

Species-Centrism

In addition to its seeming departure from basic Darwinian assumptions, concepts, and principles (Rose & Rose, 2000), some have suggested that evolutionary psychology's inclusion of a cognitive framework (and the "computer metaphor") has resulted in overzealous claims and "creative excesses" concerning the role of human history on brain and behavior functions (e.g., Panksepp & Panksepp, 2000). Furthermore, claims by evolutionary psychologists are often in stark conflict with known structural and functional aspects of the mammalian brain (Panksepp & Panksepp, 2000), existent neuropsychological research on humans (Panksepp & Panksepp, 2000, 2001), and recent developments in the biological sciences (Lickliter & Honeycutt, 2003a, 2003b; Segerstråle, 2001). For this and other reasons, commentators on evolutionary psychology have been critical of the "species-centrism" present within this model (Mealey, 2001; Panksepp & Panksepp, 2000, 2001), a feature absent in behavior theory, which is notably cross-species general in scope.

"PERSONALITY-GUIDED" FROM A BEHAVIORAL PERSPECTIVE: AN OVERVIEW

As is apparent from the previous discussions, behaviorally oriented theorists and therapists tend to avoid explaining behavior with reference to a person's personality. Just as the popular concepts of mind, will, ego, and schema are regarded as fictional concepts in behavior theory, so, too, is the concept of personality as an inner structural entity that causes or guides behavior. From a behavioral perspective, however, three central concepts are somewhat analogous to the concept of "personality": (a) organismic variables (i.e., the effects of historical influences on behavior that have become part of the individual's physiological makeup, such as inherited attributes or traits and the learning history of the individual); (b) functional response classes; and (c) behavior patterns, repertoires, or topographies. These concepts are elaborated in detail in later portions of this book. In the sections that follow, we briefly summarize these centrally important concepts for a personality-guided behavior therapy.

Organismic Variables

The behavioral theoretical framework that we emphasize throughout this book is Goldfried and Sprafkin's (1976) functional analytic SORC model, which stands for *Stimuli–Organism–Response–Consequence*. As is further elaborated in chapter 3, the S and C in this model refer to the environmental determinants of behavior, that is, the stimulus (S) conditions that set the occasion for a behavior to occur and the consequences (C) that follow responses (R) and influence their future probability. Organismic variables (O) include both learning history and biological factors that either mediate or moderate the relationships among S, R, C, or a combination of these. As such, the O in the SORC model reflects the influence of selected phylogenetic characteristics (e.g., genotypes, temperament, physiology), other biological variables (e.g., physiology, natural effects of aging, disease processes), and environmental shaping over one's lifetime (ontogenetic selection), including behavior that has been shaped and influenced by culturally mediated rules or social contingencies (cultural selection).

Functional Response Classes

Functional response classes represent a second behavioral analogy to the personality concept. These consist of groups of behavior that, although possibly different in form or topography, are alike in that they produce the same or similar outcomes across a number of response domains (Follette, Naugle, & Linnerooth, 2000; Lubinski & Thompson, 1986; Malott et al., 2000). For example, Hayes, Wilson, Gifford, Follette, and Strosahl (1996) delineated several examples of the experiential-avoidance functional response class (defined by behaviors that function to avoid or terminate contact with aversive internal events such as unpleasant thoughts, feelings, and sensations), as well as factors that support and maintain behaviors that belong to this class.

Behaviorally oriented theorists have made some attempts to link functional response classes to traditional personality concepts. Lubinski and Thompson (1986), for example, have suggested that behaviors influenced and maintained by social events could, collectively, be labeled *extraverted*. Furthermore, behavior covariations (or behavioral traits) associated with the extraversion concept may, in part, be influenced by phylogenetically selected predispositions associated with positive mood (D. Watson, 2000), enhanced sensitivity to rewarding stimuli (Gray, 1987a), and enhanced reactivity to the effects of socially mediated consequences of behavior (Cloninger, 1987).

Whereas traditional forms of assessment might seek to group behaviors according to similar topographies or behavioral features that reliably covary, behavioral assessors are more inclined to group behaviors in terms of the functional similarity they have in different contexts. Examples of functional response classes and the domains within which they are likely to be expressed are described in greater detail in chapter 5.

Behavior Patterns, Repertoires, and Topographies

Behavioral theories and therapies have traditionally emphasized the functional properties of clinically relevant behavior and de-emphasized behavior patterns, forms, or topographies as a means of conceptualizing behavior (e.g., Bissett & Hayes, 1999; Skinner, 1981). From a client assessment and therapy perspective, we find it valuable to consider behavior patterns as well, including diagnostic classes (Farmer & Nelson-Gray, 1999; Nelson & Barlow, 1981; Nelson-Gray & Farmer, 1999). Consideration of behavioral topography and response covariations and repertoires has the potential to inform a traditional behavioral assessment and formulation, and as such this consideration can

- provide a framework that acknowledges commonalities among groups of persons;
- provide a method of client description that can facilitate communication and scientific inquiry among researchers and clinicians;
- suggest possible additional relevant response classes, as sets of response classes are known to covary with each other (Kazdin, 1982);
- suggest nomothetic controlling variables, as some nomothetic response classes are often influenced by a limited number of such controlling variables across persons (e.g., Brown, Comtois, & Linehan, 2002);
- inform target behavior selection and, relatedly, suggest dependent measures to index therapeutic change, because diagnostic or construct labels are often defined by specific problematic behaviors that can be targeted in treatment; and
- suggest effective modes of treatment, because both psychologists and psychiatrists have developed and evaluated therapies based on the identification of groups of individuals who have similar experiences or who display similar forms of behavior (e.g., Barlow, 2001; Chambless et al., 1998).

We also suggest, however, that a client assessment and formulation influenced by a consideration of response forms or covariations complement but do not substitute for an idiographically based functional analysis and behavioral assessment. Therefore, in addition to noting the importance of concepts such as response covariation, topographical response classes, and behavioral repertoires in later sections of this book, we also emphasize the need to consider contextual factors and behavior function in client assessment and therapy.

Respondent Conditioning and Personality

Although our focus is on selectionist accounts of the development and maintenance of behavior, as well as the application of operant principles to the process of behavior change in therapy, we do not mean to imply that other forms of learning, such as respondent forms of conditioning, are unimportant. In respondent (or classical or Pavlovian) conditioning, responses are prepared in advance (i.e., *unconditional responses*) to a narrow range of stimuli (i.e., *unconditional stimuli*) as a result of the natural selection process (Skinner, 1981; see also Rescorla, 1988). The range of possible *conditional stimuli* that may become associated with these unconditional stimuli is likewise narrow. Once a conditional stimulus is established through its association with an unconditional stimulus, however, the presence of a conditional stimulus will elicit a topographically similar *conditional response* to the unconditional response.

As Glenn, Ellis, and Greenspoon (1992) noted, Pavlov's work on conditional reflexes on dogs illustrated how a conditional reflex can be acquired during an individual's lifetime. The development of a learned conditional reflex requires an unconditional (or phylogenetic) behavioral unit of responding as a prerequisite. That is, the learned (conditional) response is acquired through the establishment of a contingency between a neutral stimulus and a reflex relationship previously established through the process of natural selection. In the case of Pavlov's demonstration of classical conditioning in dogs, the unconditional behavioral unit of salivation in response to food presentation was paired with a previously neutral stimulus (i.e., the sound of a metronome), which eventually resulted in the conditional (learned) response of salivation to conditional stimuli (i.e., the ticking of the metronome).

Although learning processes associated with respondent conditioning are not a central focus of this book, we do acknowledge that such forms of learning have been emphasized in some behavioral theories of personality (e.g., Eysenck, 1957; Staats, 1996), particularly in relation to the respondent conditioning of emotional responses to a variety of stimuli.

BEHAVIOR THEORY AND THERAPY CONTRASTED WITH PERSONALITY-GUIDED THEORETICAL AND THERAPEUTIC FRAMEWORKS: COMPATIBILITIES AND POTENTIALLY RECONCILABLE DIFFERENCES

Theodore Millon (1999) proposed that aspects of a client's personality have relevance for the selection of therapeutic interventions and how such interventions are organized and administered within a course of treatment. This proposition is central to his personality-guided therapy approach. We strongly concur with this proposal given our behavioral conceptualization of personality delineated earlier. As behaviorists, however, we additionally emphasize the relevance of environmental factors in association with clinically relevant behaviors in the formulation of treatment approaches and applications. The main objective of this book, then, is to outline behavioral therapy approaches that are based on consideration of personality from a behavioral perspective. Relevant personality concepts as used here include response structure (i.e., behavior patterns, form, or topography), response function, and the contextual domains within which clinically relevant behavior occurs. It is our view that simultaneous consideration of these factors will result in a synergistic and potentially effective approach to therapy.

The theory behind Millon's personality-guided therapy approach is both eclectic and integrative. That is, Millon (e.g., Millon, 1999; Millon & Davis, 1996) has incorporated theoretical principles, philosophical assumptions, and therapeutic techniques from psychodynamic, interpersonal, cognitive, behavioral, biophysical, and humanistic perspectives into his theory of psychopathology and approach to therapy. As a consequence, there are natural areas of both compatibility and incompatibility between Millon's approach and traditional behavioral approaches. The most significant compatibilities and potentially reconcilable differences are enumerated in the following sections.

Compatibilities

Perhaps the areas of greatest compatibility between the behavioral approach presented here and Millon's approach are found in the following areas: (a) appreciation of environmental influences on behavior, (b) acknowledgment of the relevance of evolutionary development on human capacities and functioning, and (c) recognition of the association that temperament factors have with sensitivity and responsiveness to certain environmental contingencies.

The Influence of One's Environment

Millon and colleagues (e.g., Millon, 1969, 1981, 1999; Millon & Davis, 1996; Millon & Everly, 1985) have discussed the organization of clinical and personality disorders in terms of three intuitively derived polarities or bipolar dimensions: pleasure–pain, active–passive, and self–other. Millon (1969, 1981, 1986; Millon & Everly, 1985) historically referenced these polarities to variations in responsiveness to environmental consequences (e.g., rewards, punishments), sources of reinforcement, and the forms of instrumental behavior used to obtain certain environmental outcomes. Although many of the details of Millon's selectionist account in relation to the polarities differ from those presented here, there is common recognition of the instrumental nature of behavior and individual differences in reward and punishment sensitivity.

The Relevance of Evolutionary Development of Human Capacities and Functioning

In more recent writings, Millon's (1990, 1999; Millon & Davis, 1996) emphasis on presumed guiding influences associated with these three organizing polarities has shifted away from reinforcement contingencies (ontogenetic selection) to evolutionary concepts and principles (phylogenetic selection). Even still, Millon (1999, pp. 96–99) has acknowledged the importance of both phylogenetic and ontogenetic influences on human behavior. Such an evolutionary account of behavior is similarly compatible with the framework described here, although there are some important differences among the details of our accounts within this framework.

The Association of Temperament With Sensitivity to Environmental Contingencies

Millon (1969, 1999, pp. 97–98) also noted the association that temperament may have with variations in sensitivity to reinforcing and punishing consequences and further suggested that temperament, in conjunction with environmental factors, shapes response patterns and repertoires. As is apparent in chapter 4, we also comment on the association between temperament and sensitivity to various behavioral contingencies and the effect that such individual differences may have on the development of response patterns and repertoires.

Other Compatible Perspectives

We concur with Millon on a number of more minor philosophical stances. For example, Millon (e.g., Millon, 1999, p. ix; Millon & Davis, 1996) rejected the notion that abnormal forms of behavior result from physical diseases or manifestations of discrete syndromes. Like Millon (1999, p. ix), we agree that individuals are diverse and that therapy should therefore be geared toward the individual needs of the client. Finally, we adopt a similar holistic view of the person as Millon proposed (1999, p. xi). In particular, our primary frame of reference is on the actions of persons within the contexts in which they live.

Potentially Reconcilable Differences

As the above review suggests, there are a number of areas of compatibility between Millon's personality-guided therapy and behavior therapy. However, there are some areas of divergence that are more difficult to reconcile. These include aspects of underlying theory as well as therapeutic approaches and goals.

Emphasis on Inner Personality Structure and Mentalistic Concepts

As noted, Millon's theory is eclectic and integrative. One consequence of this is that Millon has attributed causality of behavior to variables that behaviorists would eschew. For example, he has placed causal emphasis on "structural attributes" that "guide the experience and transform the nature of ongoing life events" (Millon & Davis, 1996, p. 323). In so doing, he attributes the cause of behavior to hypothesized internal structures or constructs. Traditional behavior theorists and therapists, however, reject the notion that personality exists as an internal entity or structure or that such hypothetical structures can cause or guide behavior. From a behavioral perspective, such an account would be regarded as mentalistic. The avoidance of mentalistic explanations of behavior is a unique and defining feature of traditional behavioral approaches.

Unlike some of our behavioral counterparts, we do see value in the consideration of the structural organization, or topography, of behavior in the assessment and therapy of persons. Our reasons associated with this view were enumerated earlier in this chapter. Viewed from this perspective, we share with Millon interest in the "structure of personality." The main difference is that Millon is primarily concerned with inner structural attributes that are presumed to guide behavior, whereas we are primarily concerned with the observable structure of overt and covert behaviors that are influenced by environmental events.

Personality Change and the Realization of Balance Among the Polarities

Another significant incompatibility between Millon's approach and traditional behavioral approaches involves the goals for therapy. Millon's personologic therapy is geared toward the goal of personality restructuring—specifically, the promotion of internal balance along a number of bipolar organizational continua. Millon's emphasis on the promotion of polarity balance through therapy is likely reflective of influences during his career, such as neo-Freudian perspectives related to the reconciliation of opposites and the striving for self-actualization (Millon & Davis, 1996, p. 294). In contrast, the therapeutic goals of behavior therapy are to reduce suffering and promote effective functioning in current environments, typically by teaching new behavior or modifying existing environments that support problematic behavior (or both).

We note, however, that the polarity framework and the goal of finding balance among antithetical response tendencies has become a central feature of some contemporary behavior therapies. For example, a central guiding framework within Linehan's (1993a) dialectical behavior therapy (DBT) is dialectics. *Dialectics* refers to the process of synthesizing opposing elements, ideas, or events into more integrated, cohesive, or balanced wholes. The inclusion of this philosophical influence in DBT came, in part, from Linehan's observation that some personality-disordered individuals, particularly those with borderline personality disorder, are often highly polarized in their thoughts, actions, and emotional experiences. In this respect, behavior therapy has similar objectives as Millon's personality-guided approach to therapy. The main difference is that from the behavioral perspective, response tendencies are the object of synthesis, whereas in Millon's framework, emphasis is placed on the synthesis of the guiding influences of inner structural attributes and functions.

OVERVIEW OF THE BOOK

This chapter has detailed the theoretical and philosophical foundations that distinguish behavioral from other approaches. In so doing, we have established a framework for many of the therapeutic principles, concepts, and practices that we subsequently review.

After a review of the history of behavior therapy (chap. 2), we discuss an overarching perspective on client assessment and formulation from the behavioral perspective, namely, the functional–analytic approach (chap. 3). Discussion then turns to the concept of personality from a behavioral perspective, which includes a delineation of common behavior patterns, topographical response classes, and associated relationships with sensitivity and responsiveness to various environmental consequences (chap. 4) as well as functional response classes and the contextual domains within which they are likely to be exhibited (chap. 5). After a review of basic behavior therapy techniques (chap. 6), we then provide overviews of behavioral therapy approaches for Axis I (chap. 7) and Axis II (chap. 8) conditions.

2

THE HISTORY OF BEHAVIOR THERAPY

This chapter describes the history of behavior therapy, from its beginnings to its middle stages to its contemporary developments. During much of its history, behavior therapy focused on the specific problems of individual clients. There was little recognition of the commonalities across individuals, in terms of both problematic syndromes or diagnoses and personality characteristics. Also, there was much more emphasis on present environmental controlling variables, with little emphasis on historical determinants of behavior or temperamental or physiological differences across people. There were exceptions, however, because some behaviorists, namely, Hans Eysenck, Jeffrey Gray, and Arthur Staats, did develop theories of personality that were consistent with behavioral principles.

THE BEGINNINGS OF BEHAVIOR THERAPY

There were several main backdrops for the early beginnings of behavior therapy. These and other historical developments are exquisitely detailed in a book on the history of behavior modification by Kazdin (1978). One backdrop was developments in learning theory: for example, the experiments on conditioning and reflexology by Sechenov, Pavlov, and Bechterev in Russia, followed by elaborations of learning theory in the United States by Thorndike, Guthrie, Tolman, Hull, Mowrer, and Skinner. Another backdrop was the growing dissatisfaction in some circles with the effectiveness, or lack thereof, of traditional psychotherapy. Eysenck (1952), for example, examined several outcome studies that evaluated primarily the treatment of neurotic patients. He concluded that psychotherapy was no more effective than spontaneous remission (with 67% of neurotic patients recovering over 2 years, even in the absence of formal psychotherapy). A third and final backdrop was the development of the theory of behaviorism by J. B. Watson (e.g., 1919), who espoused that the proper subject matter for the science of psychology was not consciousness but rather overt behavior and that the proper scientific method for psychology was not introspection but rather observation of behavior. Before the formal development of behavior therapy, there were a few isolated instances of the application of learning theory to clinical problems: Watson and Raynor (1920) demonstrated that a fear could be classically conditioned in a young child named Albert; Mary Cover Jones (1924) demonstrated in another child, Peter, that a fear of rabbits could be decreased by gradually presenting the rabbit while Peter was eating a favorite food; and the Mowrers (Mowrer & Mowrer, 1938) demonstrated that nocturnal enuresis could be treated with the bell-and-pad method that associated urination with awakening.

The formal beginnings of behavior therapy, however, began in the 1950s with simultaneous developments in three English-speaking countries. These developments are detailed by Kazdin (1978) and are summarized here. Joseph Wolpe was a psychiatrist working in South Africa who developed the first manualized treatment, that is, systematic desensitization (Wolpe, 1958). Wolpe began research on the production and elimination of experimental neuroses in cats. He produced neurotic reactions in cats by shocking them and then demonstrated that such reactions could be diminished by feeding the animal in the gradual presence of stimuli associated with shock. Wolpe accounted for the success of this procedure by formulating a principle called *reciprocal inhibition:*

> If a response antagonistic to anxiety can be made to occur in the presence of anxiety-evoking stimuli so that it is accompanied by a complete or partial suppression of the anxiety responses, the bond between these stimuli and the anxiety responses will be weakened. (p. 71)

Wolpe then extended the principle of reciprocal inhibition to treat neurotic reactions in humans: Fearful stimuli were gradually presented in the patient's imagination by means of a fear hierarchy progressing from least to most fearful, and anxiety was suppressed by progressive muscle relaxation. In his book, Wolpe (1958) claimed that psychotherapy by reciprocal inhibition cured about 90% of 210 patients. Two of Wolpe's students who later became very influential in the development of behavior therapy were Arnold Lazarus and Stanley Rachman. The importance of Wolpe's contributions to behavior therapy cannot be overemphasized. Systematic desensitization was the first manualized treatment and hence could be replicated worldwide. It was therefore possible to subject systematic desensitization to experimental evaluations, both in terms of its therapeutic outcomes and in terms of the processes claimed to underlie its effectiveness (Paul, 1969a, 1969b).

England was the second English-speaking country in which behavior therapy developed, through the work of Hans Eysenck and his colleagues. Eysenck was trained as an experimental psychologist and was head of the department of psychology at the Institute of Psychiatry at the Maudsley Hospital in London. In 1959, Eysenck published the first paper that introduced the term *behavior therapy* in England. In this paper, Eysenck provided an explicit comparison between psychotherapy and behavior therapy and criticized psychoanalytic theory and the disease model. In 1960, Eysenck edited a book that was a compilation of various treatment methods applied to neurotic patients, such as desensitization, negative practice, and aversion therapy. This book was the first to bring together diverse treatment applications under the name *behavior therapy* (Eysenck, 1960).

The third English-speaking country where behavior therapy developed was the United States, where the flavor of behavior therapy was quite different from that of South Africa and England. The names given to this new therapy were *behavior modification* or *applied behavior analysis*. The techniques were derived largely from Skinnerian principles of operant conditioning, and the clinical populations were more likely to be developmentally disabled children (e.g., Bijou, Birnbrauer, Kidder, & Tague, 1966), institutionalized psychotic adults (e.g., Ayllon, 1963; Ayllon & Michael, 1959), or autistic children (e.g., Lovaas, Freitag, Gold, & Kassorla, 1965).

Because of the movement of influential individuals across national boundaries (e.g., Wolpe moved to the United States, first to University of Virginia School of Medicine and then to Temple University Medical School) and because of publications, there was cross-fertilization across these three original branches of behavior therapy.

THE MIDDLE STAGES OF BEHAVIOR THERAPY

During the 1970s and 1980s, behavior therapy evolved into several distinct branches or varieties that are summarized by O'Leary and Wilson (1987). One type of behavior therapy is known as *applied behavior analysis*, which is philosophically consistent with Skinner's (1953) radical behaviorism and emphasizes the principles and procedures of operant conditioning. Applied behavior analysis espouses environmental determinism, noting that the main causes of behavior lie in the environment. Private events, such as thoughts and feelings, are included in the study of human behavior (Skinner, 1957) but are not given causal properties. In terms of methodology, applied behavior analysis uses primarily a single-subject experimental design (Hayes, Barlow, & Nelson-Gray, 1999). Techniques based on operant conditioning have been successfully applied to a wide range of populations and to a wide range of problems. The *Journal of Applied Behavior Analysis* is an excellent source describing the successes of operant conditioning.

A second type of behavior therapy is what O'Leary and Wilson (1987) termed *the neobehavioristic stimulus–response approach*. The evolution of Wolpe's and Eysenck's work, this approach involves the application of learning theory principles to the treatment of clinical problems. Techniques such as systematic desensitization, negative practice, and aversion therapy were used to treat the problems of clinical outpatients. Both Wolpe and Eysenck, unlike applied behavior analysts, used hypothetical constructs in their explanatory systems. For example, Wolpe (1958) explained the efficacy of systematic desensitization by the construct of reciprocal inhibition. Eysenck (e.g., 1970) developed a model of personality that explained personality as the result of the interaction between constitution and environment. Constitution consisted of three orthogonal variables: neuroticism–normalcy, psychoticism–normalcy, and introversion–extraversion.

A third type of behavior therapy is *cognitive–behavioral therapy*. A central difference in cognitive–behavioral therapy from other types of behavior therapy is the important mediational role given to thoughts and perceptions. The assumption is that there is an activating event in the environment that produces certain beliefs (thoughts, perceptions) that then produce feelings and behavioral reactions. Cognitions are the direct target of modification in cognitive therapy. Persons associated with early developments in cognitive–behavioral therapy include Mahoney (e.g., 1974) and Meichenbaum (e.g., Meichenbaum & Cameron, 1982). Today, the persons most frequently associated with cognitive–behavioral therapy are Aaron Beck (e.g., Beck, Rush, Shaw, & Emery, 1979) and Judith Beck (e.g., Beck, 1995). Behavioral techniques, such as behavioral activation and guided mastery, are often used in conjunction with cognitive techniques; hence, the term cognitive–behavioral therapy.

A fourth type of behavior therapy is *social learning theory* (or, more recently, *social cognitive theory*), associated with Bandura (1969, 1986). A basic principle of social learning theory is *reciprocal determinism*, which holds that there is interplay among behavior, cognitive factors, and environmental influences. Note the contrast with *environmental determinism*, which emphasizes the influence of the environment on the organism. In social learning theory, the person is not only subjected to environmental control, but is also capable of self-control. Similar to cognitive behavior therapy, cognitions are given causal properties. In social learning theory, cognitions include not only specific beliefs and automatic thoughts, but also representations of environmental events, expectations and self-efficacy, and motivation and incentives.

The main therapy technique derived from social learning theory is modeling, both in vivo and symbolic. Bandura (1969) viewed modeling as a third way of learning, in addition to classical and operant conditioning.

COMMONALITIES AMONG BEHAVIOR THERAPISTS

With all these different varieties of behavior therapists, what do they have in common? Why are they all called "behavior therapists"? In chapter 1, we presented several features that distinguish behavior therapy from other forms of therapy. Even though there are many versions or types of behavior therapy, a sufficient common basis exists to label them all behavior therapy.

CONTEMPORARY TRENDS IN BEHAVIOR THERAPY

Behavior therapy remains a vital and evolving approach for addressing clinical problems. A few of the trends that characterize contemporary behavior therapy are (a) acculturation into mainstream clinical psychology, (b) cognitive additions to behavior therapy, (c) development of additional behavior therapy techniques based on learning theory, and (d) acceptance as a principle, in addition to change. Each of these trends is elaborated in the following sections.

Acculturation of Behavior Therapy Into Mainstream Clinical Psychology

One of the characteristics of contemporary behavior therapy is that it has become acculturated into mainstream clinical psychology (Nelson-Gray, Gaynor, & Korotitsch, 1997). As described in greater detail in chapter 7, Division 12 of the American Psychological Association created the Task Force on Psychological Interventions. Members of the task force have published a series of papers that list therapies found to be "well established" or "probably efficacious" for producing therapeutic change among persons with particular diagnoses (Chambless & Ollendick, 2001; Chambless et al., 1996, 1998). One good illustration of the acculturation of behavior therapy is that the majority of techniques on the list of empirically supported or empirically validated techniques (EVTs) are behavioral or cognitive–behavioral techniques. Division 12 represents clinical psychologists of various theoretical orientations and includes both academicians and service providers. The inclusion of a great number of behavioral or cognitive–behavioral techniques among these EVTs designated by a Division 12 Task Force could be taken as an indication of the acceptance of behavioral approaches among clinical psychologists.

As will be described in chapter 3, characteristic objectives of behavioral assessment include the identification of target behaviors (also known as *treatment goals*), the selection of a treatment strategy that is likely to address the treatment goals, and the designation of outcome measures likely to track changes in the treatment goals. In the age of managed care, these objectives are no longer unique to behavioral assessment. In the United States, an example of the requirements of managed care is the Medicaid service plan. Essential components of this service plan include specification of treatment goals. A way to measure the goals is also mandated by the phrase "as evidenced by." For example, in the case of a child diagnosed with oppositional–defiant disorder, one goal might be, "The child will comply with at least 80% of the requests made of him at home, as evidenced by parent recording of compliance within 2 minutes divided by number of requests." This statement includes not only a treatment goal of increasing compliance, but also a way to measure changes in compliance, that is, by a percentage of the requests to which the child complied. The Medicaid service plan also requires specification of the service or intervention that will be provided, including the provider and frequency of that service. As can be seen, the traditional objectives of behavioral assessment are compatible with the requirements of managed care, and this fact is another illustration of the mainstreaming of behavioral assessment and therapy.

This acculturation of behavior therapy is different from its early history, when it was seen as a contentious outlier, a maverick among more traditional approaches to therapy. In its early days, behavior therapy was sometimes pugnacious. For example, in addressing psychoanalysis, Eysenck wrote the following:

> Analysts often seem to be more concerned with these nebulous, ill-understood and poorly defined changes than with relief from those symptoms which originally caused the patient to seek help. It is indeed curious that those who cannot *even* cure the patient of his symptoms criticize others for *only* curing him of his symptoms! (1964, p. 7, emphasis in original)

Although behavior therapy has become more tolerant of and more tolerated by other theoretical viewpoints, it has nonetheless remained distinct, focusing on its origins in learning theory and experimental psychology (Nelson-Gray et al., 1997). In contrast, there is a movement called *integrationism* that calls for the integration of therapies developed from different theoretical perspectives and the identification of the common factors that make them effective (e.g., Beitman, Goldfried, & Norcross, 1989; Goldfried & Castonguay, 1992; Wachtel, 1977). Some behavior therapists do indeed espouse integrationism. For example, Powell (1996) discussed the importance of insights that occur during the application of behavior therapy techniques. In one example, Powell presented a case of a woman who had

Raynaud disease. While she was treated with biofeedback and autogenic training for hand warming, she had the insight that she was angry about her brother's "nervous breakdown," which had occurred when she was 16 and drew the attention and concern of the family away from the woman to the brother. After she vented these feelings, the woman reported feeling much better, and her Raynaud symptoms gradually abated. Most behavior therapists, however, are still traditional in the sense that they focus on behavioral techniques and the new learning that they produce.

Cognitive Additions to Behavior Therapy

Another contemporary trend in behavior therapy is the use of cognitive therapy techniques in addition to behavior techniques. One example is A. T. Beck's cognitive therapy for depression (Beck, 1995; Beck et al., 1979). The premise of cognitive therapy is that there is an activating event in the environment that produces automatic thoughts (activates cognitive schema) and then produces emotional and behavioral reactions. Although cognitive therapy initially focused on the treatment of depression, its scope has widened to the treatment of anxiety disorders including panic attacks and panic disorder, phobias, and obsessive–compulsive disorder, personality disorders, marital distress, anger, suicidal behaviors, anorexia, bulimia, obesity, and schizophrenia (Spiegler & Guevremont, 2003).

The growth of cognitive therapy has been so powerful that there is even discussion about changing the name of the chief professional association of behavior therapists. Recently there has been a controversial proposal to change the name of the AABT, or Association for Advancement of Behavior Therapy, to the Association for Behavioral and Cognitive Therapies. The proposal was made by AABT President Jacqueline Persons (Persons, 2003) and was hotly debated in the October 2003 issue of *Behavior Therapist*.

Despite the demonstrated efficacy of cognitive therapy or cognitive–behavioral therapy for many disorders, both practical and theoretical issues mar the homage to cognitive therapy. In practical terms, both of the Beck books that narrate cognitive therapy for depression describe not only the cognitive components, but also more behavioral components. One of these components is activity scheduling or activity monitoring, during which clients schedule and carry out specific activities each day or week. These activities are given mastery and pleasure ratings. Another component is graded task assignments that encourage a client to perform small sequential steps that lead to a goal. Thus, because cognitive therapy includes both cognitive and behavioral components, it is difficult to attribute the efficacy data for cognitive therapy (e.g., Dobson, 1989) solely to its cognitive components.

On another practical note, some studies that have used a dismantling strategy have found that the behavioral components of cognitive therapy are more useful than the cognitive components. For example, Jacobson et al.

(1996) found that the behavioral activation component of cognitive therapy is the most effective ingredient in the treatment. In another example, on the basis of a literature review, Latimer and Sweet concluded,

> In summary, the efficacy of cognitive therapy (excluding behavioral components) has not been demonstrated in clinical populations and what evidence there is suggests that the "cognitive" procedural component of the cognitive therapies is less potent than established behavioral methods such as exposure in vivo. (1984, p. 14)

In a later review, Sweet and Loizeaux (1991, p. 159) reached a similar conclusion:

> Most studies reflected an equivalence in outcome between cognitive–behavioral therapy (CBT) procedures and behavioral procedures alone. Behavior therapy was superior in two studies to treatments with a cognitive component. One finding was that cognitive therapy has shown promise in the areas of social anxiety. The behavioral aspect of CBT seemed central to its effectiveness, while the same cannot be said for the cognitive components. (1991, p. 159)

On a more theoretical note, there are many arguments against giving causal properties to cognitions (and other explanatory fictions). Skinner (1953) expanded on the importance of cognitions as private events that are dependent variables, controlled by the independent variables in the environment. The so-called mediationalists hold that giving causal properties to cognitive events expands the science of psychology. The nonmediationalists conversely hold that, although cognitions are important behaviors, causality properly lies in the environment. The proponents and opponents of the cognitive revolution and their arguments are outlined in Sweet and Loizeaux (1991). An opponent view is that both cognitions and motor behaviors are behaviors and that no further explanation is provided by identifying one behavior (i.e., cognitions) as a cause of another behavior (i.e., motor behavior; Hayes & Brownstein, 1986).

Combining both these practical and theoretical concerns, Hawkins (1997) held that cognitive conceptualizations have limited the progress of behavior therapy:

> The fact that cognitive conceptualizations have become popular in behavior therapy and replaced conceptions in which the influence of the environment—which is where therapists are and the only place where they can manipulate independent variables (Dougher, 1993)—has resulted in a slowing of behavior therapy's progress toward greater and greater effectiveness with a greater and greater range of problems. (p. 641)

On the positive side, the cognitive revolution within behavior therapy has forced nonmediational behaviorists to consider and elaborate the theoretical role of cognitions and other verbal behavior in both behavior theory and behavior therapy. The efficacy of cognitive–behavioral therapy across many disorders is incontrovertible. Cognitive–behavioral therapy presents an attractive therapeutic package to clients and therapists alike. This package may keep some clients in therapy, whereas less attractive packages may not. Also, some therapists may be willing to be labeled "cognitive–behavioral therapists," while eschewing the label "behavior therapists."

Nonetheless, although there may be a cognitive revolution within behavior therapy, there are concerns expressed about how effective cognitive techniques are apart from behavioral techniques with which they are usually combined. There are also concerns regarding whether it is useful and proper to attribute causal properties to cognitions as opposed to the environment.

Development of New Behavior Therapy Techniques Based on Learning Theory

As previously summarized by Nelson-Gray et al. (1997), there are three relatively newly developed therapy approaches for adults that are based on learning theory, at least in good part. One treatment approach is *functional analytic psychotherapy* (FAP), developed by Kohlenberg and Tsai (1991). In FAP, there is emphasis on the clinically relevant behaviors that are likely to occur not only in the client's daily life, but also within therapy sessions. These clinically relevant behaviors include interpersonal behaviors between the client and therapist. The therapeutic relationship is used to comment on and change such behaviors as they occur in the here and now of the therapeutic session. The primary role of the therapist is as a contingent responder, responsible for recognizing, evoking, interpreting, and consequating such behaviors in session.

A second treatment approach is *acceptance and commitment therapy* (ACT), developed by Hayes, Strosahl, and Wilson (1999). ACT begins with the assumption that experiential and emotional avoidance in clients is largely the result of excessive control by private events (e.g., thoughts, feelings, sensations). It is designed to restructure and extinguish attempts at controlling private events. The therapist uses paradox, metaphor, modeling, illustrations, and in-session exercise to accomplish this. The client is then helped to identify areas in the domain of action that are possible to change. The client makes a commitment to change in the domain of action. Standard behavior therapy techniques, such as scheduling of pleasant events, exposure, and homework assignments, are then used to facilitate this change.

A third treatment approach is *dialectical behavior therapy* (DBT), developed by Linehan (1993a). DBT is recognized as an empirically validated treatment for a personality disorder (i.e., borderline personality disorder [BPD]). The dysfunctional behaviors that characterize persons diagnosed with BPD are viewed as maladaptive and ineffective attempts to regulate emotion. DBT focuses on training and maintaining more effective skills, using both specific skills training sessions (Linehan, 1993b) and the context of a validating therapeutic relationship.

Acceptance as a Principle Within Behavior Therapy

Some of the more recently developed behavior therapy techniques have included acceptance as a principle underlying techniques, in addition to change. Over many years, the main focus of behavior therapy was on changing problematic behavior, including both decreasing unwanted behaviors and increasing replacement or alternative behaviors. More recently, some techniques have developed that include acceptance of the current state of affairs as an underlying principle.

> For example, in DBT, one of the dialectics of therapy is the thesis of acceptance versus the antithesis of change: "At each moment, there is a temporary balance between the patient's attempt to maintain herself as she is without changing, and her attempts to change herself regardless of the constraints of her history and current situation." (Linehan, 1993a, p. 34)

Also,

> By "acceptance" here, I mean something quite radical—namely acceptance of both the patient and the therapist, of both the therapeutic relationship and the therapeutic process, exactly as all of these are in the moment. This is not an acceptance in order to bring about change; otherwise, it would be a change strategy. (p. 109)

In the DBT skills training manual (Linehan, 1993b), there are four components. Two are directed at acceptance: mindfulness training and distress tolerance. Two others are directed at change: emotion regulation and interpersonal effectiveness. According to Linehan (1993b, p. 63), "Mindfulness skills are the vehicles for balancing 'emotion mind' and 'reasonable mind' to achieve 'wise mind.' " The other acceptance skill is distress tolerance:

> "Distress tolerance skills . . . have to do with the ability to accept, in a nonevaluative and nonjudgmental fashion, both oneself and the current situation. . . . Although the stance advocated here is a nonjudgmental one, this should be understood to mean that it is one of approval. It is especially important that this distinction be made clear to clients: Acceptance of reality is not equivalent to approval of reality. . . . The distress tolerance behaviors targeted in DBT skills training are concerned with tolerating and surviving crises and with accepting life as it is in the moment. Four sets of crisis survival strategies are taught: distracting, self-soothing, improving the moment, and thinking of pros and cons. (Linehan, 1993b, p. 96)

One of the two DBT skills that emphasize change is interpersonal effectiveness training. This includes effective strategies for asking for what one needs, saying no, and coping with interpersonal conflicts. The other DBT skill that emphasizes change is emotion regulation. This includes identifying and labeling emotions, identifying obstacles to changing emotions, reducing vulnerability to "emotion mind," increasing positive emotional events, increasing mindfulness to current emotions, taking opposite action, and applying distress tolerance techniques.

In ACT, the client is encouraged and taught how to change actions while accepting negative emotions. The premise in ACT is that experiential and emotional avoidance seen in clients is the result of excessive control by private events, which is the result of long social and verbal histories emphasizing this control. ACT is designed to restructure and extinguish attempts at controlling private events and to make changes in the domain of action. Clients learn to accept private events that have been feared and avoided. Clients also develop greater clarity about personal values and then commit to behavior change.

A third new behavior therapy approach that includes acceptance is *integrative behavioral couple therapy* (Jacobson & Christensen, 1996). One goal for distressed couples is to enhance the ability of both partners to accept their partner's upsetting behaviors. In some cases, partners have limitations that are unchangeable, such as physical conditions. In other cases, partners are not willing to change particular behaviors that are upsetting to their partner, such as cigarette smoking or frequent late nights out with friends. Last, partners always have individual differences, acceptance of which may be a requirement for long-term and satisfactory relationship.

ROLE OF PERSONALITY VARIABLES AND DIAGNOSIS IN BEHAVIOR THERAPY

Behavior therapists have traditionally eschewed the use of constructs, which they have considered to be too inferential and too easily reified (i.e., given causal properties). In reification, for example, a list of behaviors (e.g., behaviors listed in the diagnostic criteria in *DSM–IV–TR* (for major depressive disorder; American Psychiatric Association, 2000) is summarized by means of a diagnosis (e.g., major depressive disorder), and then that diagnosis is used to explain the behaviors (e.g., the person is fatigued and sad because she has major depressive disorder). In a statement that typified many behavior therapists, Kozak and Miller (1982, p. 350) wrote, "More generally, it could be claimed that all hypothetical constructs (with their associated spectre, reification) should be barred from behavioral science entirely." Both diagnoses and personality traits are examples of constructs that summarize or are inferred from behavior.

Behavior therapists avoid constructs and instead generally work at the level of behavior. In terms of behavioral assessment, Goldfried and Kent (1972) borrowed Goodenough's (1949) distinction between sign and sample approaches to assessment. Behavior assessors and therapists prefer a "sample" approach. Behavioral assessment techniques are thought to provide a sample of the person's behavior in specific situations, for example, through self-monitoring or through role-playing. Behavior is thought to be situation- and response-mode-specific, so inferences are not made to other situations or to other response modes without evidence. Even more absolutely, inferences are not made to hypothesized entities purporting to cause or underlie behavior (Goldfried & Kent, 1972). Conversely, traditional assessment focuses more on a "sign" approach, interpreting behavior as a sign of an underlying personality trait or form of psychopathology. The sign approach is more inferential than the sample approach. Behavior assessors and therapists prefer a sample approach to a sign approach.

Recent Acceptance of Diagnosis by Some Behavior Therapists

In earlier days, behavioral clinicians avoided the use of diagnostic categories, one reason being that diagnoses were too inferential. Kazdin (1983) drew parallels between *DSM–III* (American Psychiatric Association, 1980) concepts (the diagnostic classification system in place in 1983, which is in most ways similar to the current diagnostic system of *DSM–IV–TR*) and behavioral concepts in the following ways. On a first level, *symptom* in psychiatric parlance refers to a particular overt behavior, affect, cognition, or perception. In behavioral terms, the symptom corresponds closely to a target behavior or treatment goal. A second level is a *syndrome*. In psychiatric terms, a syndrome is a constellation of symptoms occurring together and covarying over time. In behavioral terms, a syndrome might refer to response covariation. A third level is *disorder*. For a syndrome to be considered a disorder in psychiatry, more information is needed than merely the clustering of symptoms, such as the natural course of the disorder, family history, possible biological correlates, and response to treatment. Kazdin noted, "In behavior therapy, there is no clear analogue to the concept of disorder. Indeed few proponents of behavior modification might even agree that this level of concept would be useful" (1983, p. 86). A fourth level of conceptualization is *disease*. In psychiatric terms, the notion of disease is invoked for a disorder when there is a specific known etiology and an identifiable underlying pathophysiological process. Kazdin commented, "Needless to say, the notion of disease is not embraced in describing behavioral dysfunctions in behavior therapy. However, neither is the concept of great use in the classification of mental disorders . . . *DSM–III* focuses on syndromes and disorders" (1983, pp. 86–87).

In more recent years, behavioral clinicians have come to appreciate the advantages of diagnosis. As mainstream scientist–practitioners, behavior therapists have much to gain by using *DSM* diagnoses. Communication functions are greatly simplified by the use of a well-agreed-on classification system. It would be virtually impossible to contribute to or access the clinical research literature without the use of diagnostic labels. In a similar way, there could no clinical science without recognizing the commonalities across individuals. In chapter 5, we consider in greater detail the utility of diagnostic concepts in behavioral assessment and therapy, as well as some related disadvantages associated with their use.

We note here, however, that the use of *DSM* diagnoses can also be considered in some ways to be theoretically consistent with a behavioral framework. Nelson-Gray and Paulson (2003) described in detail the relationship between behavioral assessment and diagnoses. Using Kazdin's (1983) concept of a syndrome, the *DSM–IV–TR* (American Psychiatric Association, 2000) specifies a class of covarying behaviors in the set of operational criteria of each diagnosis (Nelson & Barlow, 1981). When the clinician observes a criterion that, in part, characterizes a disorder, he or she is provided with a ready-made list of likely concomitants that can be targeted and observed in greater detail. For example, if a person complains of depressed mood and insomnia, the behavioral assessor should inquire about all nine symptoms or behaviors that constitute a major depressive episode. Thus, when an individual reports some of the responses within a diagnostic category, there is sufficient probability of his or her manifesting other responses within this same category to warrant assessment of these additional responses.

In addition to suggesting covarying responses, the *DSM* suggests environmental and organismic controlling variables for each disorder (Nelson & Barlow, 1981). Environmental and organismic variables may commonly occur across individuals with a particular set of covarying behaviors, that is, with a particular diagnosis. A too obvious example is the trauma that precipitates posttraumatic stress disorder. *DSM–IV–TR* describes the nature of the trauma as

> an extreme traumatic stressor involving direct personal experience of an event that involves actual or threatened death or serious injury, or other threat to one's physical integrity; or witnessing an event that involves death, injury, or a threat to the physical integrity of another person; or learning about unexpected or violent death, serious harm, or threat of death or injury experienced by a family member or other close associate. (American Psychiatric Association, 2000, p. 463)

Despite these various advantages to behavioral assessors of using a *DSM* diagnosis, a diagnosis is an adjunct to and not a replacement for behavioral assessment. The main reasons diagnosis must be supplemented by behavioral assessment are elaborated by Nelson-Gray and Paulson (2003) and are summarized here. The main reason is that the *DSM* is nomothetic (i.e., group or variable centered), and behavioral assessment is idiographic (i.e., centered on the unique aspects of the individual). Each of the contributions made by *DSM* to behavioral assessors consists of nomothetic suggestions that must be tailored to the individual client through behavioral assessment. Behavioral assessment is necessary to make an idiographic determination of specific symptoms, controlling variables, treatment choice, and treatment outcome measures for an individual client. Individual treatment goals and appropriate treatment outcome measures must be established in the context of the client's presenting problems, covarying responses, and values. Even though the *DSM* does indeed suggest environmental and organismic controlling variables for each disorder, a behavioral assessment must be conducted to determine which of these additional controlling variables is applicable for the specific client. Also, the list of empirically validated treatments, although a great contribution to clinical science, is far from being an easy blue print for treatment selection for all clients, as elaborated in chapter 7 of this book on the treatment of Axis I disorders.

Use of Personality Theories to Recognize Commonalities Across Individuals

In the early decades of behavior therapy, the focus of behavioral assessment was highly idiographic. Commonalities that existed across individuals with and without psychopathology were not recognized. Diagnosis is one way of recognizing the commonalities in covarying behavior patterns (syndromes) and in possible controlling variables (environmental and organismic) that contribute to various forms of psychopathology.

Another way to recognize the commonalities that exist across individuals is by the construction and description of personality theories. In his detailed history of behavior therapy, Kazdin (1978, p. 316) noted that, "Personality theory has had little direct impact on the development of behavior modification." There were some exceptions, however. Within a behavioral framework, personality theories were developed that included both organismic (biological or constitutional) and environmental variables. Eysenck, Gray, and others have emphasized that personality or behavior patterns result from both biological and environmental factors (Eysenck & Rachman, 1965; Gray, 1987a). Eysenck's personality theory, for example, stressed two constitutional or innate factors. One factor was introversion–extraversion, which was thought to be related to activity of the central nervous system. The other factor was neuroticism–stability, thought to be related to the activity of the autonomic nervous system. Personality theories that have potential relevance for behavior therapy, such as Eysenck and Gray's theories, are described in detail in chapter 4 of this book.

Meyer (1960) demonstrated the treatment utility of Eysenck's theory of personality in two cases with agoraphobia. The first case was readily treated by gradual in vivo exposure, going on longer and longer walks and other trips, first with the therapist and then alone. The second case was more recalcitrant. On the basis of an eye-blink conditionability measure and the Maudsley Personality Inventory, it was determined that the second case had personality features of a neurotic extravert. In Eysenck's model, extraverts were hypothesized to be especially poor at forming conditioned associations due to relatively attenuated levels of cortical arousal. The patient was administered Dexedrine, which was thought to improve his conditionability by increasing cortical arousal. The in vivo exposure continued, this time with much greater success.

Another personality theory that incorporates both biological and environmental variables was developed by Jeffrey Gray. Gray (e.g., 1987a) rotated Eysenck's two axes 45 degrees and relabeled them *impulsivity* and *anxiety*. He proposed that the biological mechanisms underlying these two axes were the Behavioral Inhibition System (BIS), which contributed to the level of anxiety, and the Behavioral Activation System (BAS), which contributed to the level of impulsivity. Gray's system has been helpful in understanding some of the *DSM* disorders. Farmer and Nelson-Gray (1995) assessed persons for personality disorders and found that those with Cluster B personality disorders (erratic–dramatic) were high in impulsivity, whereas those with Cluster C personality disorders (anxious–fearful) were high in anxiety. Kepley (2003) assessed persons diagnosed with attention-deficit/hyperactivity disorder (ADHD) with and without co-occurring anxiety and depression. Within Gray's model, the combined ADHD subtype with co-occurring disorders was high in both anxiety and impulsivity. Conversely, the inattentive subtype with co-occurring disorders was low on Gray's impulsivity but high on anxiety.

Other descriptive models of personality, including several that emphasize biological variables, are described in chapter 4 of this book. For behavioral clinicians, sometimes these models add to our understanding or conceptualization of clinical problems. At other times, these models may have treatment implications, as noted with Meyer's (1960) case studies.

Staats described another type of personality theory (Staats, 1963, 1971, 1996). This model is different from those described earlier in this chapter and in chapter 4 in that the theory does not result in either a dimensional or categorical typology of persons. Staats's theory does not label the commonalities that exist across persons, but focuses on the commonalities in behavioral processes that produce individual personalities. The theory emphasizes the behavioral learning processes and the resultant behavioral repertoires that they produce in an individual. Staats noted that personality consists of different strands of behavior in the cognitive, emotional, and social domains that develop across time through behavioral processes. One of the interesting aspects of Staats's theory of personality (Staats, 1971) is the concept of cumulative and hierarchical learning within each of these strands. In hierarchical learning, the view is that the child is involved in a progression of learning that moves from the acquisition of basic repertoires of skill to the acquisition of more advanced skills based on earlier learning. There is a cumulative effect of behavior development. Personality, then, is an effect of past learning. According to Staats, however, personality is also a cause of future learning and future behavior. The individual continues to receive reinforcement for skillful repertoires and then becomes more skillful, producing an upward spiral in that repertoire. Conversely, an individual with a poor repertoire in a particular arena will continue to be punished, and that arena may be avoided, thus producing a downward spiral in that arena. Skillful repertoires also produce exposure to other skillful models and further contact with opportunities to practice and further enhance those skills. Staats uses the example of academically successful versus unsuccessful children. The academically successful child develops an upward spiral, having contact with other successful children and increased opportunities to enhance an academic repertoire. Conversely, the academically unsuccessful child develops a downward spiral, having contact with other unsuccessful children and decreased opportunities to develop academically. A more clinical example might be a person with conduct disorder or antisocial personality disorder. Acts of crime are likely to lead to prison sentences, exposure to similar models, and a return to crime upon release.

SUMMARY

The history of behavior therapy is reviewed in this chapter. Behavior therapy developed simultaneously in three English-speaking countries: South Africa, England, and the United States. Each country had its own type of behavior therapy. These types evolved into four styles or types of behavior therapy: applied behavior analysis, the neobehavioristic stimulus–response approach, cognitive–behavioral therapy, and social learning theory. Despite differences in these four approaches, there are also commonalities that make them all behavior therapy.

Behavior therapy remains a vital and evolving approach to addressing clinical problems. A few of the trends that characterize contemporary behavior therapy are the following: (a) acculturation into mainstream clinical psychology, (b) cognitive additions to behavior therapy, (c) development of additional behavior therapy techniques based on learning theory, and (d) acceptance as a principle, in addition to change. Each of these trends is elaborated in this chapter.

Behavioral assessment and behavior therapy have historically viewed each client from an idiographic perspective. Many behavioral clinicians eventually came to appreciate the benefits of recognizing commonalities across individuals. Organism variables—namely, the history and physiological makeup of the person—can be described in terms of these commonalities.

Often, these commonalities are described using constructs such as personality traits or diagnostic categories. The benefits of using such constructs are that they sometimes add to the understanding and conceptualization of a particular case, and sometimes they contribute to the treatment of the individual. The latter has been termed the "treatment utility" of assessment (Hayes, Nelson, & Jarrett, 1987).

The potential usefulness of diagnostic labels is exemplified by its communication function and the associated recognition of commonalities across individuals. Recognition and use of commonalities across clients is a nomothetic approach and will always need to be supplemented by the idiographic approach that characterizes behavioral assessment and behavior therapy, as described in subsequent chapters of this volume.

3

CHARACTERISTICS OF BEHAVIORAL ASSESSMENTS AND TREATMENT FORMULATIONS

Regardless of theoretical orientation, a therapist often begins a course of therapy with client interviews and formal assessments. From initial assessments, observations, and client statements, the therapist goes on to generate a formulation of the client's problem behaviors. From this formulation and in collaboration with the client, the therapist then devises an intervention strategy. Although this general approach may be commonly used among a wide range of practitioners, how this approach is carried out often varies considerably in accordance with a therapist's theoretical orientation. For example, the types of information that a therapist attends to in the development of a client formulation often differ as a function of the theory that guides the therapist's work. The assessment methods used and how the data from these assessments are used in informing treatment decisions also vary among therapists who work within different theoretical frameworks.

This chapter begins with an overview of theoretical assumptions associated with behavioral approaches to client assessment, formulation, and therapy and how such assumptions differ from those commonly associated with traditional nonbehavioral approaches. Discussion then turns to how client formulations are linked to interventions within the behavioral therapy approach. Following a description of behavioral assessment and formulation methods, we outline a personality-guided approach to behavioral assessment.

CONCEPTUAL FOUNDATIONS OF BEHAVIORAL ASSESSMENT AND CLIENT FORMULATION

In behavioral assessment and therapy, functional analysis has long been a central component and distinguishing feature (e.g., Ferster, 1973; Kanfer & Saslow, 1969). The functional analytic approach, influenced by Darwinian principles of adaptability, involves the identification of functional relationships between clinically relevant behaviors and the environmental variables that select, influence, and maintain them (Dougher & Hayes, 2000; Haynes & O'Brien, 1990; Kirk, 1999; Sturmey, 1996). As becomes apparent later in this chapter, the behavioral functional analytical approach is geared toward the development of a hypothetical model about problematic behavior. The resultant model, in turn, is used to inform the selection and design of therapy interventions. Before outlining the general procedure used to develop a functional understanding of a client's problem areas, we first enumerate and contrast the theoretical assumptions of the functional analytic approach with those associated with more traditional forms of assessment and formulation.

Theoretical Assumptions of Behavioral Functional Analysis Contrasted With Those of Traditional (Nonbehavioral) Analytic Approaches

The behavioral functional analytic approach to clinical assessment differs in many important respects from more traditional approaches. Dougher and Hayes (2000), Follette et al. (2000), Goldfried and Kent (1972), and Nelson and Hayes (1986) have highlighted several of these differences. A summary of the main distinguishing features follows.

Behavior Function Versus Topography

A behavioral approach to assessment and treatment involves a distinction between the *topography* of behavior and its associated *function*. Topography refers to the form or descriptive features of a behavior, independent of the consequences that follow a behavior. "Combing one's hair," "running out of the mall," "exaggerating one's accomplishments," "taking someone else's money," and "cutting one's arm" are examples of different behavioral topographies. In contrast, a functional understanding of behavior involves an analysis of the antecedent conditions that set the occasion for a behavior to occur, as well as the consequences that a behavior produces. Examples of behavioral topographies and associated functions might be "combing one's hair *to receive attention from others*," "running out of the mall *to escape a threatening environment*," "exaggerating one's accomplishments *to elicit admiration from others*," "taking someone else's money *in order to buy drugs*," and "cutting one's arm *to communicate to others one's emotional pain*." If the form of a given behavior is effective in producing desired consequences, then that behavior will likely become more frequent in the future as a means of producing these desired outcomes.

Perhaps the most salient example of a traditional approach to client assessment and formulation based on behavior topography is the *Diagnostic and Statistical Manual of Mental Disorders*, now in its fourth edition, revised (*DSM–IV–TR*; American Psychiatric Association, 2000). In the *DSM*, syndromal and personality disorders are specified according to a constellation of covarying behaviors (i.e., behavioral topographies). If an individual displays the threshold number of requisite behaviors for a diagnostic concept within a specified period of time, then the diagnostic label is applied to the individual's behavior. The *DSM* assessment approach, then, is largely a similarity-based system of classification that is limited to the description of concepts and their association features (Morey, 1991). From a behavioral perspective, systems defined exclusively by behavioral topographies are limited in their theoretical and clinical utility, because behavioral descriptions alone do not explain these concepts. Whereas topographical classification methods such as *DSM* are primarily concerned with *how* people behave, behavioral functional analysis is primarily concerned about a behavior's purpose with reference to the consequences it produces, or *why* people behave as they do (Nelson & Hayes, 1986; Skinner, 1974).

Functionalism Versus Structuralism

Contemporary *DSM* classification has as its roots the methodological work of the Washington University–St. Louis group, who in the 1970s developed an approach to classification based on the proposal of discrete syndromes, the delineation of operational criteria that defined these syndromes, standardized interview techniques for assessing the criteria that define syndromes, and the development of statistical tests to evaluate the reliability of diagnostic judgments (Klerman, 1986). This group was also central to the development of what would be eventually referred to as the *neo-Kraepelinian* movement, which consisted largely of psychiatrists who believed that mental disorders could be accounted for by biological or genetic etiologies and that such disorders are best classified within a categorical framework (Klerman, 1986; Morey, Skinner, & Blashfield, 1986). Because the leading architects of *DSM* viewed symptoms of the various psychological disorders as indicators of the influence of associated biological or genetic etiologies, the *DSM* approach to assessment and classification was based on *structural assumptions* concerning causal entities that, in turn, give rise to problematic behavioral topographies. Medical-model structural assumptions of psychological disorders are similarly evident in presumptions of strong linkages between diagnosis and treatment intervention. As an example, Sturmey (1996) offered a structualistic–diagnostic model as applied to a simple illness, meningitis. *Meningitis* is a diagnostic label that may be applied to a collection of covarying symptom features (e.g., headache, neck stiffness or soreness, progressive fever, convulsions, coma) with known etiology (i.e., bacterial infection of the meninges) as well as a known effective treatment (i.e., antibiotics). Thus, the diagnostic label, in addition to summarizing a collection of covarying symptoms, also encompasses presumed etiology and treatment recommendations.

Psychometric assessment also has roots in the structural tradition (Nelson & Hayes, 1986). In an elaboration of this approach, Harkness and Hogan (1995) distinguished three related concepts: traits, constructs, and trait indicators. *Traits* are presumed to exist as biological structures or systems within persons that give rise to behavioral predispositions. When behavioral consistency across time and situations is observed, trait theorists assume that this consistency is largely the result of personality traits. Because traits at present are not directly knowable or observable, however, *construct* labels are used to refer to collections of covarying behaviors, cognitions, emotions, and physiological responses. Constructs are not the same as traits because constructs are not presumed to be real "things" like traits but are instead conceptualized as theoretical models of traits. Examples of constructs include terms such as *depression*, *schizophrenia*, *anxiety*, *extraversion*, and *borderline personality disorder*. *Trait indicators* refer to specific test and nontest behaviors, cognitions, emotions, and physiological responses that are presumed to arise from biologically based traits. Collections of trait indicators are used to define specific constructs. To the extent that constructs represent accurate models of traits, assumptions concerning the presence and strength of a trait may be inferred by "how much" of a construct a person possesses. Thus, traditional forms of psychological assessment are concerned about structural elements (traits) and associated behavioral topographies (trait indicators) that, when accurately measured and appropriately aggregated, provide a theoretical representation of the trait and its hypothesized degree of influence (constructs).

Another related example is evident in how the quality of traditional assessment devices is evaluated, that is, in terms of its associated response–response relations (Nelson & Hayes, 1986). In the case of the reliability of an assessment measure, indicators such as test–retest reliability, internal consistency, parallel forms reliability, and interobserver agreement are considered. All of these forms of reliability are concerned with how one set of responses, either measured or observed, relates to another set of responses associated with the same assessment measure. In the case of the validity of an assessment device, responses from a given measure are evaluated in relation to those assessed by an external measure of topographically similar (e.g., convergent validity) or dissimilar (e.g., discriminant validity) behaviors. In the case of both reliability and validity, then, temporal stability and cross-situational generalizability of behavior are assumed. In contrast, the traditional behavioral model suggests that behavior is situation-specific (Nelson & Hayes, 1986), and the extent to which behavior is temporally stable may depend on the breadth of an individual's behavioral repertoire and the degree to which environmental contingencies (i.e., the antecedents and consequences of behavior) remain constant across diverse contexts over time.

Unit of Analysis: Person in Context Versus Characteristics of Person

The principle unit of analysis in a behavioral functional assessment is the whole person in interaction with environmental contexts. That is, to comprehend the context within which a person's behavior occurs, the conditions under which the behavior was first established and how it has since been maintained must be understood. As such, a full understanding of the individual's actions requires recognition of the interdependence of such acts in conjunction with the contexts in which they occur (Follette et al., 2000).

In contrast, traditional forms of assessment, such as self-report measures, are largely geared toward the identification of behavior patterns or symptom features, with little regard for the context in which they occur. This is perhaps most evident in how questions within such measures are structured (e.g., "Have you ever . . . ," "How many times . . . ," or "Did you experience _______ within the past week?"). With such measures, emphasis is placed on characteristics of those sampled (largely the display of a particular form of behavior or behavioral topography), not the contexts in which the behaviors in question occurred.

Distinction Between Behavioral Topography and Etiology

In clinical behavioral assessment, there is a distinction between behavior topography and etiology. In some traditions of psychology, certain behaviors are viewed as *pathagnomic*, or definitive, indicators of that behavior's etiology. As Follette et al. (2000, p. 102) have noted, however, it would often be inappropriate to conclude that a 25-year-old woman's fear and avoidance of the dark are pathagnomic indicators of a childhood history of sexual abuse. This is because such behaviors (fear response and avoidance behaviors) in such environmental contexts (dark places) can have a potentially infinite number of etiologies across persons. How a person responds to certain environmental events (i.e., the topography of behavior) will depend on the person's history in relation to those events (i.e., the effects that such responses historically had on the environments in which they occurred). Given the multiple functions that specific forms of behavior often serve, no single form of behavior could possibly be the result of a single environmental antecedent across all persons.

Behavior as a Sample Versus Sign

Some traditional approaches to assessment are premised on the assumption that clinically relevant behavior is often an indicator or *sign* of an underlying problem that gave rise to the behavior in question. In behavioral assessment, however, behavior is viewed as a *sample* of responding in a particular environmental context (Goldfried & Kent, 1972; Nelson & Hayes, 1986). The emphasis of assessment is on what the person *does* (Mischel, 1968). In contrast, diagnostic and traditional assessment is consistent with *personologism*, the view that psychopathology or individual differences are the result of relatively stable intraorganismic variables that reside within the individual. Thus, such an approach views behavior as a potential *sign* of these underlying variables, or what one *has* (Loevinger, 1957; Mischel, 1968). Consistent with this view, behavior is an indicator of an underlying problem, and not viewed as the problem in itself.

To further distinguish sign versus sample conceptualizations of behavior, Follette et al. (2000) offer the example of self-injury. In theories of behavior consistent with traditional forms of assessment, self-injury might be viewed as a sign of underlying anger associated with an external person. Because this anger is experienced as psychologically threatening in some way, the individual reduces the threat by redirecting the anger toward the self as expressed in the form of self-injurious behavior. Therefore, the focus of therapy might not be on the behavior itself (i.e., self-injury), but rather on what the behavior is presumed to be a sign of (e.g., difficulties in tolerating ambivalently experienced anger toward another). In the behavioral approach, the self-injurious behavior is itself viewed as a sample of a problematic response class. Acts of self-mutilation and similar forms of behavior would be of interest themselves, as well as an understanding of the contexts in which they occur, the typical responses from the social environment that such behaviors evoke, and other behaviors in the person's repertoire that may have similar functions as self-injurious acts (Follette et al., 2000).

Idiographic Versus Nomothetic Approaches to Assessment and Conceptualization

In clinical behavioral assessment, the focus is on the individual in his or her context. For each client, clinically relevant target behaviors are identified, as well as the contexts in which they occur and the consequences that typically follow their display. As such, behavioral assessment is often based on the *idiographic* approach, that is, focused at the level of the individual.

DSM and traditional psychometric assessment, in contrast, have a *nomothetic* focus; that is, based on groupings of individuals (Nelson & Hayes, 1986). In the case of *DSM* assessment, the basis for classification is on the commonalities within groups of individuals (within-group homogeneity) and the differences that exist across persons (between-group heterogeneity). In the case of psychometric assessments, variability in performance within a group of persons (as indexed by test scores and their variability) forms the foundation of an individual-difference perspective that underlies this approach to assessment.

COMPONENTS AND PROCESSES ASSOCIATED WITH A CLINICAL FUNCTIONAL ANALYSIS

Functional analyses are often useful for developing a description and understanding of the client's current behavioral patterns and repertoires. The behavioral assessment framework used within this section and throughout the book is Goldfried and Sprafkin's (1976) SORC model. SORC is an acronym for Stimuli–Organism variables–Responses–Consequences. In this model, an individual's responses (physiological, emotional, verbal, cognitive, overt motor) are thought to be a joint function of immediate environmental variables (stimuli and consequences) and organism variables (aspects of a person's physiological makeup, as influenced by heritable biological characteristics, other physiological variables, and past learning history) that the individual brings to a situation (Figure 3.1). Additional goals of a functional analysis include the selection of an appropriate intervention, the provision of means to monitor treatment progress, and the identification of methods to evaluate the effectiveness of an intervention (Follette et al., 2000). In the following sections, each of the components of a clinical functional analysis is described in detail.

The Context of Behavior: Antecedent Conditions and Behavioral Consequences

A basic assumption of behavioral theories is the notion that behavior varies according to the antecedent stimuli that precede it and consequences that follow it.

Consequences of Behavior

In discussions of the effects that a behavior has on the environment, the terms *reinforcement* and *punishment* are frequently used. A *reinforcer* is any event that follows a behavior that has the effect of increasing the future probability of that behavior under similar stimulus conditions. A *punisher*, conversely, is any event that follows a behavior that has the effect of reducing the future probability of that behavior under similar stimulus conditions. Therefore, whether an event that follows a behavior serves as a reinforcer or punisher is determined by the effect that the consequent event has on the frequency of behavior over time.

Reinforcers and punishers can be further distinguished on the basis of whether the consequent event is associated with the provision or application

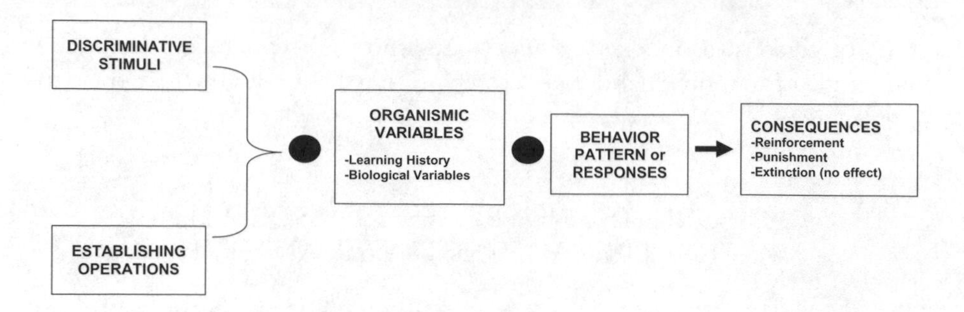

Figure 3.1. Components of a clinical functional analysis. Discriminative Stimuli and Establishing Operations represent environmental events that are to be considered simultaneously in this analysis. The dots in between components in the sequence represent probability functions. The dot between the Discriminative Stimuli and Establishing Operations boxes and the Organismic Variables box indicates that in a given environmental context, there is a probability that an individual is sensitive to the environment's influence based on his or her learning history, relevant biological factors, or both. The dot between the Organismic Variables and Behavior Pattern/Responses box indicates that in a certain environmental context and in conjunction with past learning history and biological factors, there is a probability that that behavior will follow. The Behavior Pattern/Responses box indicates problematic behaviors targeted for change in behavior therapy. The arrow between the Behavior Pattern/Responses and Consequences boxes indicates the effect that behavior has on the environment. From "Functional Alternatives to Traditional Assessment and Diagnosis," by W. C. Follette, A. E. Naugle, and P. J. N. Linnerooth. In M. J. Dougher (Ed.), 2000, *Clinical Behavior Analysis* (pp. 99–125). Reno, NV: Context Press. Copyright 2000 by Context Press. Adapted with permission.

of an event or the removal or termination of an event. The designation "positive" in conjunction with either reinforcement or punishment concepts refers to the provision or application of a consequent event contingent on behavior. The term "negative" in relation to reinforcement and punishment refers to the removal or termination of an event following behavior. As such, the following classes of behavioral consequation can be defined:

- *Positive Reinforcement*: Occurs when behavior results in the application or provision of a reinforcing event, which increases the probability of that behavior on future occasions.

  Possible examples: The awarding of money following work; getting attention for one's provocative or dramatic behavior; receiving praise for one's accomplishments; obtaining support or nurturance from others as a result of volunteering to do things that are personally experienced as unpleasant.
- *Negative Reinforcement*: Occurs when behavior results in the removal or termination of an aversive event or condition, which increases the probability of that behavior on future occasions.

  Possible examples: Avoidance of places where negative evaluation from the social environment is possible; avoidance of situations that topographically resemble a past environment where a traumatic event occurred; frantic efforts to avoid abandonment that are successful.

- *Positive Punishment*: Occurs when behavior results in the application or provision of an aversive event or condition, which decreases the probability of that behavior on future occasions.
  Possible examples: Receiving verbal disapproval following a display of affection; being ridiculed by others as a result of not doing something skillfully; receiving a painful burn as a result of placing one's hand on a hot stove.
- *Negative Punishment*: Occurs when behavior results in the removal or termination of a reinforcing event or condition, which decreases the probability of that behavior on future occasions.
  Possible examples: Placement in timeout following misbehavior; being grounded for 3 days for staying out too late the night before; being charged $1 for returning a library book late; loss of social support following a period of "acting out."

In relation to the examples of behavioral consequences offered here, we cannot assume the function of a consequence simply on the basis of its topography or surface features. For example, some persons might experience verbal praise following behavior as aversive. As a consequence, such an individual would be less likely to enact the behavior that was praised in the future. In this instance, verbal praise would function as a positive punisher, not as a positive reinforcer. Judgments as to whether events following behavior function as reinforcers or punishers can only be inferred according to the observed effect that such consequences have on future behavior.

In addition to reinforcement and punishment, *extinction* represents another form of behavioral consequation that affects the subsequent rate of behavior. Extinction, or the reduction or elimination of behavior, may occur when behavior is reliably enacted without being followed by a reinforcing consequence. For example, a person may display a particular form of behavior (e.g., boasting) to produce a particular response from the social environment (e.g., admiration). If the behavior fails to produce the desired response from the social environment, then the behavior of boasting will likely extinguish over time. The relations and distinguishing features among these various environmental consequences are further illustrated in Table 3.1.

Another consideration in relation to the consequences of behavior is whether the consequences are *short-term*, or immediate, versus *long-term*, or delayed. In the case of problematic behaviors, it is often the case that short-term consequences maintain such behaviors, whereas the long-term consequences make them problematic (Nelson-Gray & Farmer, 1999). For example, possible short-term consequences that maintain personality disorder–related behaviors, at least through intermittent positive reinforcement, include attention from significant others for those with dependent

TABLE 3.1
Forms of Behavioral Consequation

Operation	Type of consequence	Effect on behavior	Behavior/ consequence relationship
Positive reinforcement	Rewarding	Increase	Behavior → receive rewarding event
Negative reinforcement	Relieving	Increase	Behavior → remove aversive event
Extinction	Frustrating	Decrease	Behavior → no outcome
Positive punishment	Aversive	Decrease	Behavior → receive aversive event
Negative punishment	Penalizing	Decrease	Behavior → remove rewarding event

personality disorder and attention from others more generally for those with histrionic personality disorder. Although the short-term consequences that follow problematic behavior may have a behavior-maintaining function, it is the long-term consequences of these behaviors that are, by definition, problematic for the individual. As such, when conducting a functional analysis, the behavioral assessor should attend to both the short- and long-term consequences of problematic behavior.

It is also important to note that when we speak of behavior, we are referring to *overt* behavior (i.e., publicly observable behaviors, such as motor and verbal behavior) as well as *covert,* or private behavior (i.e., behavior that is not observable to outside observers, such as thinking, feeling, physiological responding, imagining, visualizing, etc.). From a behavioral perspective, reinforcement and punishment processes affect covert behavior in a manner similar to how they affect overt behavior. The contingencies associated with covert behavior (i.e., reinforcers or punishers) can also be external or internal. For example, an individual might imagine a sequence of behaviors associated with an upcoming performance, such as a football play (see Malott et al., 2000, pp. 384–385). A player can, for instance, visualize himself throwing a block for a particular play, and discriminate within the imagery behaviors that were effective in producing a successful block and those that were not. While visualizing himself throwing a block, a person might privately state to himself, "A block executed like that isn't going to work. I'm going to need to bend down a little lower and throw my shoulder up a little higher," and after visualizing the modified blocking style and its imagined consequences, "Yes, that will work!" In relation to this example, the visualization of analog behavior and its associated consequences is not the same as the actual motor behavior and the tangible consequences associated with it, however. Rather, covert reinforcement of covert behaviors leads to the establishment of covert behaviors that, when initially translated to overt behaviors, results in behaviors that are in the first instance under rule control. These overt behaviors under rule control can, in turn, be shifted to direct contingency control once the behavior has been enacted and the environmental consequences that follow those behaviors are experienced.

Until such time that overt behavior comes under direct environmental control, covert processes can lead to displays of overt behavior in naturalistic contexts that are *rule-governed.* A *rule* is a verbal description of a behavioral contingency that specifies a response or behavior, an outcome or consequence associated with that behavior, an antecedent condition in the presence of which the behavior will produce the specified outcome, or any combination of these (Anderson, Hawkins, Freeman, & Scotti, 2000; Malott, 1989). Examples of rules might be, "If you smoke cigarettes for a long period of time, you will develop lung cancer" or "If you touch the gas stove flame, you will be burned." *Rule-governed behavior*, then, is a term used to denote those behaviors that are influenced by verbal statements (i.e., rules) that specify the operating contingencies associated with a behavior and is usually used to account for behavior that is influenced by consequences that follow behavior after a delayed interval of time (Malott et al., 2000). The concept of rule-following or rule-governed behavior can also provide a framework for the conceptualization of how thoughts or self-talk function to influence goal-oriented behaviors (Malott, 1989).

The distinction between rule-governed and contingency-shaped behavior can be illustrated though the example of the processes involved in learning to use cars with manual transmission (Malott et al., 2000, p. 385). At first, the use of a manual transmission might be under the influence of rules imparted by an instructor: "With your left foot, first push in the clutch. Then, while holding down the clutch, begin to gradually shift the gear. Then, just at the right moment, begin to accelerate, and then gradually release the clutch." When first enacting this behavioral sequence, the individual may follow the rules that he or she had been told for using the manual transmission. Over time, though, the behavior becomes less influenced by the rule and more influenced by the direct consequences of the behavior, namely, the sounds and feel associated with shifting the gears properly. In a similar way, the behavior may eventually become "automatic," and the person may produce the behavior without first verbalizing the rules. In fact, this behavior may eventually become under such strong stimulus control (based on the revving of the engine or other contextual factors, such as traffic slowing or a red light) that it eventually requires little effort to perform. As noted by Malott et al. (2000, p. 386), with response repetition, the influence of behavior often shifts from a rule that describes a direct acting contingency to the direct acting contingency itself. The influence that rules can have on behavior is further discussed in the following section.

Antecedent Conditions

Antecedent stimuli include two general classes of stimuli: discriminative stimuli and establishing operations. *Discriminative stimuli* (S^D) signal to the individual the likelihood of reinforcement or punishment following some type of response. An *S-delta* (S^{Δ}) is a stimulus that, when present, indicates that reinforcement or punishment will not likely follow behavior. The informational value associated with an S^D or S^{Δ} is based on the person's previous experiences in the presence of those stimuli or related stimuli. For example, a young boy has a particular fondness for chocolate-chip cookies. In fact, if he had his way, chocolate-chip cookies would constitute the vast majority of his diet. Within his home, chocolate-chip cookies are stored in a cookie jar (an S^D that indicates the availability of reinforcement, namely, cookies) in the kitchen. The child has learned, however, that his mother has a tendency to restrict his access to chocolate-chip cookies to the period immediately following dinner (and only if he has finished his dinner). That is, the child has learned that if he attempts to take a cookie from the jar at any other time *while his mother is present in the kitchen*, his mother (an S^{Δ} in this situation) would stop him and prevent him from having a cookie. The child has also learned that when his mother is not present in the kitchen (S^{Δ} is absent), he can open the cookie jar, grab a cookie, and subsequently take pleasure in the joys (or reinforcing properties) that eating chocolate-chip cookies bring. In this example, then, the presence of the cookie jar and the absence of mother served as antecedent conditions for cookie-stealing behavior. We might further conclude that the behavior of cookie stealing is under *stimulus control;* that is, the behavior reliably occurs in the presence of an S^D (i.e., cookie jar) except when the S^{Δ} (i.e., mother) is present at any time other than after dinner.

From a cultural perspective, a wedding band might act as a discriminative stimulus for intimate affiliative behavior, most typically as an S^{Δ} for the reinforcement for such behavior (and possibility an S^D for punishment following behavior). That is, if one is looking for a short- or long-term mate, one is less likely to pursue others who wear a wedding band on the ring finger because the likelihood for reward is lower from such individuals (and the probability of punishment in the form of rejection is much higher).

In the case of behavior that is rule-governed, rules are often considered to function as reinforcement- or punishment-based S^Ds (Malott et al., 2000; Skinner, 1969). In this sense, rules are regarded as stimuli that, in the presence of which, a response specified by the rule will be either reinforced or punished. The extent to which an individual follows rules can only be determined with respect to the individual's history of rule following (Skinner, 1969), that is, whether the class of behaviors called *rule following* has been consistently reinforced.

Establishing operations (or motivational operations) represent a second class of antecedent stimuli and refer to the impact that environmental events, operations, or conditions have on behavior by altering the reinforcing or punishing properties of other environmental events (Laraway, Snycerski, Michael, & Poling, 2003; Michael, 1982, 1993, 2000). For example, if a person is deprived of water for a substantial length of time, this deprivation (an establishing operation) can increase the reinforcing value of other relevant environmental stimuli (e.g., water, grape juice, soda) and likewise increase the frequency or intensity of behaviors that have been previously reinforced by the stimulus that has been deprived. Someone who has been deprived of water for some time, then, will be more inclined to display behaviors that have been previously successful in obtaining water because the reinforcing properties of water have become greater as a result of the deprivation.

In relation to the cookie-stealing example, the boy might be substantially less inclined to steal cookies from the jar even in his mother's absence if he has already eaten a box of chocolate-chip cookies earlier in the day. This is because satiation on cookies serves as an establishing operation that, in this case, is associated with a decrease in the value of cookies as reinforcers.

Michael (1982, 1993) further noted that emotional states can often serve as establishing operations for various behaviors. For example, most persons would experience anger toward those who intentionally cause physical pain. Anger in conjunction with the painful stimulation may serve as an establishing operation for forms of aggressive behavior (e.g., striking, biting, scratching, yelling) that may subsequently be negatively reinforced in the event the behavior is effective in reducing or eliminating such stimulation.

In another example, Michael (2000) proposed that deprivation of attention may serve as an establishing operation that increases the effectiveness of attention from the social environment as a reinforcer. If a person lives in an environment that is generally devoid of attention, then he or she is likely to display attention-seeking behaviors in social environments where such behaviors are likely to be consequated, even if these behaviors are in some way inappropriate or problematic in such environments. Consistent with the establishing operations concept, one might seek to reduce inappropriate attention-seeking behavior by modifying the individual's living conditions whereby attention is offered with greater frequency and noncontingently in relation to inappropriate behaviors.

Substance use or abuse might also be understood in the context of establishing operations. People with substance abuse problems are often more likely to consume substances when aversive conditions are experienced. These establishing operations might include physical pain, impoverished environments, or physiological withdrawal due to deprivation of the substance from the body (Malott et al., 2000). The behavior of drug consumption, in turn, produces effects that often function to alter the establishing operation that gave rise to drug consumption in the first place. A drug-induced state itself can be an establishing operation. For example, some studies have indicated that benzodiazepines, barbiturates, and opiates can increase the reinforcing qualities of some environmental events or decrease associated punishing qualities (e.g., Gray, 1987a). Stimulant medications have been known to reduce the effectiveness of food reinforcers (Laraway et al., 2003), which likely accounts for why many persons seek to lose weight through stimulant drug consumption.

Organismic Variables: Biological Characteristics and Learning History

Within the SORC model, organism variables include both biological characteristics and the effects of past learning and constitute part of the person's physiological makeup.

Biological Differences

Biological characteristics include genetic predispositions, physiological correlates of a condition (e.g., psychophysiological, neurotransmitter, and hormonal activity), temperament-related factors, physical appearance, and other physiological characteristics (e.g., the effect of disease or aging), all of which can influence behaviors associated with various psychological disorders. It is beyond the scope of this chapter to review all possible relevant biological differences that may mediate or moderate environment–behavior relations. Thus, the overview that follows is selective, and illustrative of some of the types of biological differences that might be relevant for a clinical functional analysis.

In the case of syndromal disorders, some evidence indicates a genetic contribution for many conditions, including schizophrenia (and related spectrum disorders), some developmental disorders (attention-deficit/hyperactivity disorder, oppositional–defiant disorder), mood disorders, and anxiety disorders (for a review, see Rhee, Feigon, Bar, Hadeishi, & Waldman, 2001). Some evidence also suggests a genetic influence on some forms of personality disorder pathology. For example, schizotypal personality disorder has been observed to be more prevalent among families in which schizophrenia is present (Kendler, McGuire, Gruenberg, & Walsh, 1995), with schizophrenia suspected of having a heritable component (Rhee et al., 2001; Schneider & Deldin, 2001). Scores on measures of novelty seeking, a construct similar to that of impulsivity (Gray, 1987c), have been associated with structural variations in DNA, specifically, the gene codes for the dopamine D4 receptor (Pickering & Gray, 1999). Both novelty seeking (Svrakic, Whitehead, Przybeck, & Cloninger, 1993) and impulsivity (Farmer et al., 2004; Farmer & Nelson-Gray, 1995) have been strongly associated with symptom features of the Cluster B (erratic–dramatic cluster) of *DSM* personality disorders (i.e., histrionic, narcissistic, borderline, and antisocial).

Closely tied to genetic theories of personality are those grounded in the temperament concept. Research by Kagan and colleagues on infant temperament (e.g., Kagan, Reznick, Clarke, Snidman, & Garcia-Coll, 1984; Kagan & Snidman, 1991) suggests that some infants as young as 9 months reliably display behavior patterns characterized by behavioral inhibition or disinhibition. *Behaviorally uninhibited* in this context refers to thrill- and adventure-seeking behavior patterns, similar to those patterns used to define the novelty-seeking or impulsivity constructs (see also Rothbart, Ahadi, & Evans, 2000). *Behaviorally inhibited* refers to a tendency to avoid new or unfamiliar situations or objects, including those of a social nature (i.e., interpersonal shyness). Both inhibited and uninhibited behavioral tendencies have been observed to be temporally stable and associated with distinct physiological profiles (Kagan & Snidman, 1991). Relatedly, and in support of the intergenerational transmission of temperament, children of parents with anxiety disorders are at greater risk to be behaviorally inhibited (Rosenbaum et al., 1988), whereas mothers of children with anxiety disorders often have histories of anxiety disorders themselves (Last, Hersen, Kazdin, Francis, & Grubb, 1987; Reeves, Werry, Elkind, & Zametkin, 1987). Given these patterns of observations and because behavioral inhibition and anxiety seem to have similar biological underpinnings (e.g., Fowles, 2001), there is some indirect evidence to support the notion that behavioral inhibition and anxiety may have a biological or genetic foundation. There is also evidence that uninhibited tendencies tend to run in families (Eysenck, 1983) and, as noted earlier, that a specific genetic risk factor exists for uninhibited (impulsive) behavior (Pickering & Gray, 1999).

Another relevant example is linked to research on the superordinate dimensions of personality, specifically the five-factor model (FFM) of personality. The independent dimensions of personality description that define this model (i.e., extraversion, neuroticism, agreeableness, conscientiousness, and openness) have a moderate degree of cross-cultural commonality (McCrae & Costa, 1997). These dimensions also demonstrate varying degrees of association with personality disorder pathology (Costa & Widiger, 2002). In particular, high neuroticism and low agreeableness are common features of most of the personality disorders. The dimension of introversion extraversion also appears to differentiate some forms of personality disorder pathology from others (Costa & Widiger, 2002; Farmer et al., 2004; Farmer & Nelson-Gray, 1995).

Positive and negative affect, broadly defined, represent uncorrelated dimensions of mood that also have a number of features that suggest an association with temperament. First, there is some evidence that proneness to positive or negative affect is, at least in part, heritable and present at birth and associated with a number of broad dispositional tendencies (Watson, 2000). Positive moods are more frequently experienced among those who are extraverted (Watson, 2000; Zelenski & Larsen, 1999). Those who are especially vulnerable to negative moods tend to be high in neuroticism (Watson, 2000; Zelenski & Larsen, 1999). Negative emotion or neuroticism is common among those with various forms of psychopathology (e.g., Brown, Chorpita, & Barlow, 1998; Eysenck & Rachman, 1965), including many of the personality disorders (Costa, McCrae, & Siegler, 1999; Farmer et al.,

2004; Farmer & Nelson-Gray, 1995). In the social domain, positive affect–extraversion and negative affect–neuroticism are associated with different forms of social behavior. Extraverted individuals, or those high in positive affect, tend to be socially outgoing, friendly, assertive, and gregarious, whereas introverts, or those low in positive affect, tend to be more reserved, isolative, and aloof. In a similar way, those high in negative affect or neuroticism tend to overexaggerate the degree of threat or danger present in a variety of situations and tend to have negative views of themselves or others. In contrast, those low in negative affect or neuroticism tend to be secure, satisfied, and content (Watson, 2000).

Finally, we acknowledge that one's physical appearance also evokes particular reactions from the environment that, in turn, lead to particular forms of behavior (Nelson-Gray & Farmer, 1999). For example, histrionic men and women may be more attractive than average and have learned that they can use their physical appearance to draw attention to themselves. Such attention must be experienced as positive if the individual consistently seeks to produce this reaction from the social environment.

Past Learning History

A comprehensive and thorough functional analysis should attempt to delineate relevant historical factors that shaped the behavior into its present form. From a behavioral perspective, several factors related to learning history can result in behavior patterns that appear temporally and cross-situationally consistent (Nelson & Hayes, 1986, pp. 19–20), examples of which follow.

- *Behavior may be temporally consistent because environments are functionally the same over time, even if they appear to have differences.* From a behavior analytic perspective, it is not necessarily the topographical features of an environment that exert influence on behavior. Rather, the nature of the consequences historically associated with those features exerts the most influence over one's current behaviors. Thus, a thorough assessment of a problematic behavior will include a historical analysis of the types of environments where problematic behavior has been displayed as a way to better understand how current environmental features influence such behavior.
- *Behavior that is intermittently reinforced in given contexts is resistant to extinction.* A well-supported principle is that intermittently reinforced behavior persists longer once reinforcement has been withdrawn than behavior that was established with a more continuous reinforcement schedule (e.g., Pittenger, Pavlik, Flora, & Kontos, 1988). There is also a suggestion that some temperament concepts such as low anxiety or a weak behav-

ioral inhibition system (BIS) are associated with heightened resistance to extinction (e.g., Gray, 1987a). Ineffective or inappropriate perseveration of previously reinforced behaviors has similarly been hypothesized to be at the root of some forms of pathology, such as aggressive or antisocial behavioral patterns (e.g., Newman, Patterson, & Kosson, 1987; Shapiro, Quay, Hogan, & Schwartz, 1988).

- *Trait or role labels may contribute to behavioral stability.* There is some indication that persons who strongly identify themselves in terms of trait concepts (e.g., extraverted, anxious, conscientious) or role labels (e.g., university professor, mother, military personnel) are more likely to exhibit behaviors that conform with those concepts or labels (e.g., Harter, 1999; Markus, 1977). Thus, adoption of these concepts and labels through environmental learning may contribute to behavioral stability and consistency.
- *A narrow or impoverished behavioral repertoire may result in greater consistency.* Behavior theorists and therapists have long recognized that the extent and breadth of one's behavioral repertoire is largely determined by one's environmental learning history. Because many forms of psychopathology are often characterized by skill deficits (e.g., Dow, 1994; Lewinsohn & Gotlib, 1995; Linehan, 1993a), many behavior therapies include a skills training component in an effort to expand the client's behavioral repertoire. A greater behavioral repertoire allows for greater flexibility in responding to events and situations and, as a consequence, increases the likelihood of effective action.

In addition to these, a fair amount of recent evidence suggests that environmental events may affect brain structure and function, and possibly gene expressions (e.g., Fowles, 2001; Kandel, 1998; Schwartz, Stoessel, Baxter, Martin, & Phelps, 1996). One consequence of such observations is a blurring of the distinction between what constitutes biological–genetic versus environmental influences on behavior. Biological theories that posit unidirectional causal chains that omit environmental influences (e.g., genes → brain structure and function → vulnerability or predisposition to psychopathology) become somewhat tenuous in light of such data (Fowles, 2001). Of note, Skinner (1969, p. 274; 1974, p. 237) previously suggested that contingencies of reinforcement change the physiology of the organism in some way, and accumulating evidence is now beginning to support aspects of that view.

Finally, the theoretical and research literature is filled with hypotheses about prototypical histories that lead to the development of particular forms of pathology. For example, in the case of depression, Lewinsohn (e.g.,

Lewinsohn & Gotlib, 1995) has proposed that depressive symptoms are the result of a low rate of response-contingent positive reinforcement. That is, the depressed person is thought to receive little reinforcement contingent on his or her behavior, particularly reinforcement from the social environment. As a result, the depressed person's behavior is on a reinforcement schedule that facilitates the extinction of responses that have the potential for being reinforced (and maintained). The net result of this pattern is that as the person behaves less, he or she becomes more depressed as opportunities to derive pleasure from one's actions become similarly reduced. In the case of anxiety disorders, avoidance of situations or events that evoke anxiety or somatic sensations has been implicated in the maintenance of these conditions (Rapee & Barlow, 2001). For this reason, many behavioral therapies for anxiety disorders involve graded exposure to stimuli that elicit anxiety and avoidance. With regard to borderline personality disorder, Linehan (1993a) suggested that invalidating environments are etiologically significant in the development of this condition: "An invalidating environment is one in which communication of private experience is met by erratic, inappropriate, and extreme responses. In other words, the expression of private experience is not validated; instead, it is often punished, and/or trivialized" (Linehan, 1993a, p. 49). Readers interested in a detailed example of how an understanding of one's learning history may reveal the functional development of clinically relevant behaviors are referred to Gresswell and Hollin's (1992) account of a person who attempted serial murder.

Responses

In the sections that follow, we discuss behaviors or responses from several different perspectives. We begin by discussing an approach for conceptualizing responses based on the form of the response or the systems involved, and how responses from each of the response domains relate to the definition of psychological or personality constructs. This is followed by a description of an approach for conceptualizing the co-occurrence or covariation of behaviors based on their shared functional properties. Finally, we discuss responses that occur within the skin (e.g., thoughts, feelings, sensations), collectively referred to as *private events*, and how such events are conceptualized within a behavioral framework.

Triple Response System

Responses to events may involve one or more response systems. For example, if a person experiences anxiety or fear in certain social settings, he or she may emit responses consistent with these constructs in any or all of three response domains: overt motor, cognitive–verbal, and physiological–emotional–somatic (Lang, 1968; see also Evans, 1986; Nelson & Hayes, 1986; Nelson-Gray & Farmer, 1999; Rachman & Hodgson, 1974). Overt motor behaviors include those behaviors that involve the use of skeletal muscle systems. Cognitive–verbal behaviors include verbal expressions of thoughts, attitudes, or beliefs "in which the expression is the content, that is, it is not a report of something, rather the report *is* the something" (Evans, 1986, p. 142). Verbal reports of both verifiable and unverifiable private events are included here. An example of the former is a report of a behavior that can be objectively observed by others (e.g., "I had three binge eating episodes last night"), whereas an example of the latter is cognitive self-statements (e.g., "When I walk into a room with a lot of people, I tell myself that everyone is looking at me because I'm such a loser"). Physiological–emotional–somatic responses, most broadly, involve activities of hormonal systems and the autonomic nervous system.

As Lang (1968) noted, we often cannot assume strong covariations of behaviors across response modes linked to a single construct. For many constructs, no evidence indicates that one response mode is more definitive or central to the larger response class than others. Evans (1986, p. 139) has further suggested that "behavioral constructs are best understood by examining the organization of behaviors, or their interrelationships." He goes on to suggest that "[c]orrelations among behavioral indices across individuals provide little information about response organization." As such, a functional analytic accounting for behavior must describe the variety of behavioral topographies across response modes that define a given treatment target domain, and how such behavioral topographies may relate to each other in the context of the functional system in which they are embedded for a given person. Although this tripartite organizational schema of response modes does have some limitations (e.g., Evans, 1986; Forsyth & Eifert, 1996), it challenges the behavioral assessor to think beyond the global construct label and to focus instead on the specific behaviors that define the label and how and to what degree these are expressed for the individual in question.

To illustrate this, the behavioral topographies that define the borderline personality disorder (BPD) diagnostic concept can be described in terms of their associated response modes. Examples of BPD diagnostic criteria that include motoric responses are "recurrent suicidal behavior, gestures, or threats, or self-mutilating behavior" and "impulsivity in at least two areas that are potentially self-damaging"; diagnostic criteria that are physiological–emotional responses are "affective instability due to a marked reactivity of mood" and "chronic feelings of emptiness"; and BPD criteria that are cognitive responses include "identity disturbance: markedly and persistently unstable self-image or sense of self" and "transient, stress-related paranoid ideation" (American Psychiatric Association, 2000, p. 710). For a given individual who exhibits such symptoms, we might subsequently discover that some behavioral responses across response modes share similar functional relations. For example, impulsive self-damaging acts (e.g., promiscuous sex, substance abuse) and recurrent suicidal behavior or self-mutilating behavior might be functionally similar behaviors if they have in common the effect of experiential avoidance or the avoidance of aversive thoughts, feelings, and somatic sensations. If such behavior is successful in terminating these aversive events and negatively reinforced behavior is the result, such behavior will likely again be used in the future when similar aversive events arise.

Response Classes and Response Chains

Sets of behaviors that are functionally related constitute a *response class*. These behaviors may be topographically diverse or dissimilar, yet functionally related in terms of either (a) the consequences that they produce or (b) the antecedent conditions that occasion their production. In an example of the former, a set of behaviors such as dissociative-type behaviors, substance abuse, and self-injury may be functionally related in that they produce similar consequences (e.g., experiential avoidance). In an example of the latter, it may be the case that a variety of trauma-related environmental stimuli might evoke a set of escape-related behaviors that were initially neutral cues but, through their association with the traumatic event, have become conditioned stimuli linked to the traumatic event.

Some behaviors may also be linked together in an orderly sequence, or *response chain*. A response chain is a sequence of behaviors whereby a given behavior within the chain can serve as discriminative stimuli for the next response in the sequence. A response within a chain of behaviors can similarly serve as a secondary reinforcer for the behavior that immediately preceded it (Frankel, 1975). In the case of response chains, it is important to identify the order in which the sequence of behaviors occur and subsequently to identify the terminal (environmental) reinforcer that functions to maintain the chain of behaviors.

Private Events

Private events refer to those behaviors that are experienced covertly or within the skin (e.g., thoughts, emotions, memories, images, sensations). A widely held misconception is that behaviorists view private events as unimportant. Although it is true that methodological behaviorists have argued that the only legitimate data for a science of psychology are those behaviors that can be objectively measured and directly observed by external observers, this has not been the view of radical (Skinnerian) behaviorism (Skinner, 1969, pp. 226–230; 1989, p. 3).

Although private events are important in behavior analysis, the notion of where they fit into such an analysis has been a matter of debate (Anderson et al., 2000; Anderson, Hawkins, & Scotti, 1999). At a broad level of analysis, private events can be distinguished between *private responses* and *private stimuli* (Anderson et al., 2000). In relation to private events as private responses or behaviors, radical behaviorists historically have made no distinction between motoric responses and those responses that occur within the body. Rather, they have asserted that the distinction between the world outside the skin and the world within the skin is not particularly useful (Skinner, 1969) because both overt and private responses are natural, observable, physical events that operate according to the same principles as overt behaviors (Anderson, Hawkins, & Scotti, 1997). Thus, the notion that people can and do have internal responses to external events and that such internal responses have the same status in a behavioral analysis as overt responses, is relatively noncontroversial within a radical behavioral framework. Difficulties associated with private responses in the context of a functional analysis, however, are related to the fact that they are difficult to measure objectively and reliably because private events are only directly accessible to the person who experienced them.

In relation to private events as private stimuli, a theoretical tenant held by many radical behaviorists is that the environment for behavior includes not only the external physical world but also the physical events that occur within the skin (Johnston & Pennypacker, 1993). Within this framework, however, private events are not given special status as a sole cause of behavior. Rather, like other behaviors, private events are ultimately under environmental control. Such an analysis suggests that private events reflect an effect of the environment that may, in the case of private events as private stimuli, influence overt behavior. Private stimuli may have at least two roles in this regard: (a) as discriminative stimuli that exert control over subsequent responses and (b) as contingency-specifying stimuli (Anderson et al., 2000). As discriminative stimuli, private events may set the occasion for other responses to occur according to either their previous association with overt responses that were reinforced or their equivalence relations with external stimuli that have discriminative control over overt behavior (Anderson et al., 2000). As contingency-specifying stimuli, private events take the form of rules that describe relations between antecedent conditions, behavior, and the consequences of behavior. Such rules indicate what behavior should be enacted in the presence of an environmental (antecedent) event that will result in the most desirable or effective outcome (Anderson et al., 2000). In either case, a complete account of private stimuli would include the identification of environmental antecedents of private stimuli, as well as an identification of the environmental consequences that have resulted in these private stimuli having influence over overt behavior (Anderson et al., 1997). Consider the following example in which S = the discriminative stimulus from the environment, r/s = a private response with stimulus properties, R = overt response, and C = consequence:

> [W]hen driving in heavy traffic (S), a woman feels light headed (r/s), notices this and thinks, "I am going to faint and wreck the car" (r/s) and, as a result, pulls over and asks the passenger to drive (R). This chain would not continue to occur unless it was somehow being reinforced (C), in this case by removal of the demands of driving in heavy traffic

and perhaps the sensations of light-headedness. (Anderson et al., 1997, p. 165)

This example illustrates that a private response with stimulus properties can occasion other private events (also with stimulus properties) that set the occasion for overt behavior. Furthermore, these private events are likely to become more probable in the future under similar stimulus conditions as a result of their association with an overt response that was reinforced by the environment.

TREATMENT FORMULATION BASED ON A CLINICAL FUNCTIONAL ANALYSIS

A clinical functional analysis will often result in a set of scientific hypotheses about the behavior under study (Sturmey, 1996), the validity of which rests on systematic tests of associated underlying assumptions. Often, the findings from such an analysis will result in the design of an intervention that is conceptually linked to the assessment findings. The goals of such an intervention will generally involve the modification of existing behavior by (a) instruction in and development of new behavioral skills, (b) modification of the environment such that it no longer supports problematic behaviors, or (c) alteration of inappropriate or faulty rule statements that influence problematic behavior, or a combination of these. In addition, Kirk (1999) noted the intervention should also attempt to identify and strengthen (reinforce) an appropriate behavioral repertoire that can produce outcomes similar to the inappropriate behaviors targeted for reduction or elimination. Once a therapy program is implemented, the target behavior(s) should be continually assessed to detect any change in frequency, intensity, or duration. In the event that the intervention is not successful in producing desirable behavior change, it might be because the original hypotheses that resulted from the functional analysis were incorrect, or that the intervention was inappropriate given factors that functioned to establish and maintain the target behavior (Hayes & Follette, 1992).

To illustrate many of the concepts and principles described within this chapter, an example of a functional analysis for a client with an eating disorder follows. One goal of this analysis was to develop hypotheses about antecedent conditions that reliably set the occasion for binge and purge behaviors. Another goal of this analysis was to generate hypotheses about the consequences of binge and purge behaviors instrumental in their maintenance.

Case Example: Intervention Strategies Suggested From a Clinical Functional Analysis

During an initial assessment phase, a 24-year-old female client with a 6-year history of frequent bingeing and purging was asked to self-monitor each occurrence of these behaviors. That is, each time the client engaged in a target behavior (binged or purged), she was asked to record the antecedent conditions that immediately preceded the behavior, the form of the target behavior and other behaviors that followed the antecedent condition (these included motor, cognitive–verbal, and physiological–emotional responses), and the consequences associated with the engagement in these behaviors (both positive and negative, immediate and delayed).

These functional analyses, collected over multiple episodes, revealed a common pattern whereby binge episodes (target behavior) were often preceded by periods of severe dietary restraint, specifically no food intake during a 24-hour period (antecedent condition, namely, an establishing operation that increased the reinforcement value of food). The analysis also indicated that binge episodes occurred in situational contexts in which large amounts of foods, specifically cakes and other high-carbohydrate foods, were readily available (antecedent condition, an S^D, that indicated reinforcement for bingeing behavior was available). Typical short-term consequences of binge eating were satiation, or the removal of the aversive state of hunger (immediate negative reinforcement); the taste of the desired food (immediate positive reinforcement); and feelings of fullness after the binge episode, which for this individual were experienced as aversive (slightly delayed positive punishment).

Purge episodes in the form of vomiting (target behavior) were almost always preceded by feelings of fullness after binge-eating episodes (antecedent condition, namely, an establishing operation that increased the reinforcement value of purging). Before purging and immediately after experiencing feelings of fullness, the client often reported the experience of depressed and anxious moods as well as thoughts such as, "Now I'm going to gain 5 pounds," and "I've failed again," and "Everybody's going to think I'm a fat pig" (negative moods and co-occurring thoughts might be viewed as clinically relevant behaviors that also have some stimulus properties that contribute to the occasion for purging). After purging, the client characteristically reported the attenuation or termination of negative moods and thoughts (immediate negative reinforcement) and a sense of relief for having escaped the aversive weight-related consequences of the binge (immediate negative reinforcement).

Because purges almost always followed binge episodes for this client, the therapist speculated that the binge–purge behavior pattern constituted a response chain. The first link in the chain was hypothesized to be self-starvation. For this client, the act of self-starvation appeared to be under rule control, or a form of rule-governed behavior. Recall that a *rule* is a verbal description that specifies a response, a consequence associated with that response, or the antecedent condition that sets the occasion for the behavior to produce the specified outcome, or a combination of these. The basis for this assumption came from several statements the client made that often took the form of contingency-specifying rules (e.g., "If I am thin, people will like me better. Not eating is a way to remain thin" and "If I don't eat, I'll be more attractive, and more likely to be asked out on dates"). Taken together, these rules likely functioned to influence the client's self-starvation because they specified reinforcement contingencies associated with engagement in this behavior, namely, social approval.

The therapist went on to speculate that the next link in the chain was the binge episode. Severe dietary restraint produced a strong establishing operation for the client, namely, intense hunger. When the client binged, the aversive state of hunger was immediately terminated. As such, the act of bingeing was a negatively reinforced behavior because it functioned to eliminate an unpleasant state condition (i.e., hunger). However, the binge episode also had another slightly delayed consequence, namely, the production of another aversive state, feelings of excessive fullness. For this client, feelings of fullness subsequently served as discriminative stimuli for negative moods and negative thoughts. In turn, these negative moods and thoughts along with feelings of fullness set the occasion (i.e., acted as S^Ds) for the next link in the chain, purging behavior. Purging, in turn, resulted in the attenuation or elimination of the aversive S^Ds. Viewed in this way, all behaviors in the chain were ultimately maintained by the terminal reinforcers at the end of this behavioral sequence (i.e., attenuation or termination of feelings of fullness, negative moods, and negative thoughts). Furthermore, each S^D in the sequence acted as a secondary reinforcer for the behavior that immediately preceded it in the chain.

This analysis suggested several therapeutic approaches designed to reduce or eliminate the target behaviors. For example, several effective approaches to the treatment of bulimia place strong emphasis on the elimination of self-starvation practices and the subsequent normalization of eating habits and behavior (e.g., Agras, Schneider, Arnow, Raeburn, & Telch, 1989). For the client in this example, self-starvation was her first link in the binge–purge behavior chain. Elimination or reduction of the establishing operations that often set the occasion for a binge episode may result in a corresponding reduction in all behaviors that would normally follow in the sequence, including purging. In fact, the likelihood for a full-blown binge episode would probably be significantly reduced if the establishing operation that set the occasion for bingeing (i.e., food deprivation and associated hunger) was substituted with a reliable eating pattern that consisted of three meals each day plus planned snacks.

Additional areas for intervention would include other behaviors in the chain that have stimulus properties and, as such, set the occasion for other behaviors in the sequence. One such behavioral target might be feelings of fullness following a binge episode, which for this client set the occasion for the experience of negative mood and thoughts that collectively acted as establishing operations for purge episodes that functioned to terminate these aversive experiences. Some approaches to treatment for bulimia seek simultaneously to expose clients to feelings of fullness while blocking the purge response (e.g., Leitenberg, Rosen, Gross, Nudelman, & Vara, 1988). These approaches are premised on the notion that purging following eating is partly responsible for the maintenance of binge eating because purging is conceptualized as a form of escape response maintained by the relief from discomfort that it provides. In this context, feelings of fullness following binge-eating episodes may act as triggers for thoughts and fears concerning weight gain and that purging functions to provide relief from these thoughts and feelings (Rosen & Leitenberg, 1988). By challenging the client to focus on feelings of fullness and other clinically relevant private behaviors that fullness occasions (e.g., associated negative mood, negative thoughts about the self) and not to escape these experiences, the expectation is that the client's negative reactions to fullness will be subsequently extinguished as a result of nonreinforced exposure. Furthermore, habituation to feelings of fullness during the exposure process is thought to extend to the client's natural environment, whereby the client would be less likely to experience intense negative emotions and thoughts following the experience of fullness and would be less likely to purge as a result.

Another possible treatment target would be purge behaviors, because several therapists and theorists have speculated that many persons with bulimia would be less likely to engage in binge episodes if the act of purging were subsequently viewed as undesirable or ineffective for reducing calorie intake. In fact, studies on the effectiveness of vomiting and laxative use as forms of purging indicate these acts only eliminate a modest to moderate amount of calories consumed during a typical binge episode. In the case of laxatives, only about 12% of consumed calories are eliminated through this process (Bo-Linn, Santa Ana, Morawski, & Fordtran, 1983), and less than 50% of calories consumed during a binge, on average, are expelled as a result of self-induced vomiting (Kaye, Weltzin, Hsu, McConaha, & Bolton, 1993). Given that the binge episodes often involve the consumption of more than 2,000 calories, the use of purging as a form of self-regulation may be maintained, in part, by inaccurate rules that suggest greater effectiveness of this behavior than is actually the case. The substitution of erroneous rules that imply purging to be an effective behavior with more accurate rules that indicate it is, at best, modestly to moderately effective, may result in a reduction in these behaviors.

Therapy might also target the apparent overall function of the binge–purge behavioral sequence, as evident in the apparent terminal reinforcers, namely, the reduction or elimination of aversive states and experiences through engagement in bingeing and purging (negative reinforcement; for similar formulations, see Heatherton & Baumeister, 1991; McManus & Waller, 1995), or the sight of food remnants in the toilet following purging (negative reinforcement), which indicates the removal of something experienced as aversive from the body. Preliminary evidence indicates that a modified form of dialectical behavior therapy for bulimia that focuses on the development and use of alternative emotion regulation skills is effective in decreasing the frequency of binge and purge behavior (Safer, Telch, & Agras, 2001).

Finally, as is apparent in the analysis for the client described here, behavioral elements within the chain were apparently maintained by the immediate or short-term reinforcing consequences associated with their enactment. A number of longer-term consequences associated bingeing and purging make these behaviors problematic, however, most notable of which are associated health-related problems (e.g., electrolyte abnormalities, low potassium levels, renal damage or failure, tooth enamel erosion, chronic diarrhea or constipation, severe dehydration, and stretching, weakening and tearing of the esophageal wall; delayed positive punishment). As such, intervention components that increase the salience of the longer-term punishing consequences of binge and purge behaviors might be included in treatment. A goal associated with this approach would be that binge and purge behaviors eventually come under the control of rules that link these behaviors to more distal negative consequences and that these rules exert greater influence on binge and purge behaviors than the more immediate reinforcing consequences. Motivational interviewing techniques (Miller & Rollnick, 1991) might be especially well suited for this purpose.

TOWARD A PERSONALITY-GUIDED BEHAVIOR THERAPY

In our approach to a personality-guided behavior therapy, the term *personality* is used to refer to (a) stable patterns of behavior that are the product of past environmental learning (i.e., learning history) and (b) biologically based individual differences (e.g., genetic endowment, temperament, physical appearance) that mediate or moderate the relationships between environmental events and behavior. Taken together, these two domains define the "O" component of the SORC model detailed earlier. In addition, and as discussed in chapter 1, (c) functional response classes and (d) behavior patterns, repertoires, and topographies also have relevance for the definition of the personality concept as applied in behavior theory and therapy.

In the example of the woman with a 6-year history of bulimia, the analysis of her repetitive binge and purge behavior (i.e., problematic behavioral repertoire) can be further extended by a consideration of both past learning history and individual-difference variables (i.e., organismic variables). In relation to this woman's past learning history, several contextual factors operated to shape these behaviors, some of which continued to exert a maintaining function for these behaviors. For example, an analysis of historical contingencies for this client revealed that as an adolescent she was exposed to several contingency-specifying rules by her parents, such as, "Don't eat so much. You'll get fat, and then no man will want you." As a result of exposure to rules such as these, the client's behavior of self-starvation had come under rule control whereby these rules implied that a fat body is an S^{Δ} for social approval (whereas a thin body is an S^{D} for social approval). Therapy, perhaps in the form of cognitive therapy for bulimia (e.g., Wilson, Fairburn, & Agras, 1997), may be used to substitute these maladaptive rules with more adaptive or accurate rules. A historical analysis of this client's binge and purge behavior revealed that the physical absence of other people was an antecedent condition for eating because the client was often teased by family members as a child and adolescent for having a "non-ladylike" appetite. As a result, the presence of others had historically been an antecedent condition associated with subsequent punishment for eating, whereas the absence of people in current environments signaled that punishment would not follow eating behavior. To overcome the effects of this early learning and to facilitate social eating, exposure sessions could be conducted within sessions that involved eating in the presence of others (Hoage, 1989).

The research literature is ripe with suggestions of possible mediating or moderating individual-difference variables that may influence the frequency of binge and purge behavior. For example, studies of temperament suggest that relatively high levels of anxiety are common among those with eating disorders (Schwalberg, Barlow, Alger, & Howard, 1992). A subset of persons with eating disorders also report impulsive tendencies (e.g., DaCosta & Halmi, 1992; Lilenfeld et al., 1997; Lowe & Eldredge, 1993). Highly impulsive persons with eating disorders may represent an important subtype (Lacey & Evans, 1986), because the frequent engagement in impulsive acts has been associated with poorer treatment outcome (Lacey, 1992), greater chronicity of disordered eating behavior (Keel & Mitchell, 1997), and greater overall psychopathology (Lilenfeld et al., 1997), including comorbid Cluster B personality disorders (Rossiter, Agras, Telch, & Schneider, 1993). Both anorexia and bulimia nervosa have also been associated with reduced central nervous system serotonin activity (Weltzin, Fernstrom, & Kaye, 1994).

These nomothetic findings based on samples of persons with eating disorders may suggest possible mediators or moderators that warrant assessment or consideration in relation to the individual therapy of a person with an eating disorder. For example, the use of experiential avoidance coping strategies (i.e., a functional response class) appears to be pervasive among those who experience higher levels of anxiety. Thus, if anxiety is a concomitant feature for someone with an eating disorder, the function of various coping behaviors (including eating disorder–related behaviors) might be assessed, particularly in relation to a possible experiential avoidance function. If relevant, therapies that include an exposure component to block experiential avoidance tendencies might be considered, such as dialectal behavior therapy (Linehan, 1993a; Safer et al., 2001) or exposure and response prevention (Rosen & Leitenberg, 1988). If an individual with an eating disorder demonstrates impulsive or disinhibited patterns of behavior, then intervention strategies that facilitate the development of self-control strategies might be contemplated (e.g., Baumeister, Heatherton, & Tice, 1994; Linehan, 1993a; Rachlin, 2000). Finally, if serotonin dysregulation is a likely mediator or moderator of disordered eating behavior and associated mood disturbance and impulsive tendencies, pharmacological interventions that target this neurochemical might be considered (Jimerson et al., 1997; Stunkard, Berkowitz, Tanrikut, Reiss, & Young, 1996).

Future chapters of this book further develop the notion of a personality-guided or informed approach to behavior assessment and therapy.

4

TOPOGRAPHICALLY DEFINED BEHAVIOR PATTERNS IMPORTANT TO BEHAVIORAL ASSESSMENT AND THERAPY

The main focus of this chapter is on commonly observed and topographically defined behavior patterns that are potentially important to a behavioral assessment and approach to therapy. *Nomothetic topographical response classes* refer to patterns of behavior that tend to moderately or highly covary among a broad range of persons or specific subsets of persons. Admittedly, from a behavioral perspective, a chapter on topographically defined behavior patterns is a bit unusual. This is because behavior theory and therapy have largely focused on the proximate functional properties of behavior (Skinner, 1981), or the immediate purpose that a behavior serves or the outcome that it produces. Less emphasis has historically been placed on forms of behavior out of recognition that the principle variables that influence behavior are those associated with behavior consequence.

Consistent with behavior theory, however, we acknowledge that some forms of behavior are, in part, influenced by heritable biological endowments that have been intergenerationally transmitted through phylogenetic selection processes. At the most basic level, the susceptibility to response consequences is inherited (Skinner, 1971, 1981). Just as there are individual differences in a variety of human physical attributes as a result of natural selection processes, so, too, are there individual differences in the susceptibility to the effects of particular environmental events or consequences. That is, the behavior of some individuals is generally more sensitive to the effects of reinforcement or punishment than others, as supported in studies on the association between learning and temperament (Gray, 1987a). There is also evidence for individual differences in the sensitivity to consequences that follow more specific forms of behavior. One such behavior is alcohol consumption, which is experienced as more rewarding among some individuals than others (Tabakoff & Hoffman, 1988).

From such observations, we offer a primary thesis that is central to this chapter: Some forms of behavior that demonstrate reliable patterns of covariation across persons may, in part, reflect the influence of phylogenetic selection contingencies associated with fitness or survival over successive generations. These heritable individual differences, in turn, manifest themselves as variability in sensitivity to the effects of rewarding or punishing consequences and are subsumed under the broader concept of temperament.

For illustrative purposes, in this chapter we limit the discussion to temperament concepts that (a) have been reliably identified through multivariate correlational methods across a diverse range of persons and (b) have demonstrated associations to individual differences in reward and punishment sensitivity and responsiveness. We also briefly touch on major diagnostic categories of the *Diagnostic and Statistical Manual of Mental Disorders* (*DSM*; American Psychiatric Association, 1980), which are defined in accordance with the presence of symptom features that covary. Later in the book, we provide a more detailed account of the possible functional properties associated with behaviors that define specific *DSM* diagnostic concepts and how recognition of such properties may inform client formulation and treatment selection. Before embarking on a review of specific behavior patterns important to behavioral assessment and therapy, we first briefly discuss the concepts of response class and temperament.

THE RESPONSE CLASS CONCEPT

Response classes are sets of behaviors that are similar on at least one response dimension (e.g., form of behaviors within a set) or are similar in terms of the types of outcomes they produce from the environment (i.e., the function of behavior; Malott et al., 2000). The terms *topographical response class* and *functional response class* are often used to denote these two types of response classes, respectively.

Topographical Response Classes

Topographical response classes, or behavior patterns defined by their surface-level or descriptive features, constitute one behavioral analogy to the concept of personality. Diagnostic categories (or symptom constellations) in *DSM* and the features that define psychological constructs are largely based on specific forms of behavior, or behavior topography. Topographical response classes can be temporally and cross-situationally consistent and are often maintained by discriminative stimuli and reinforcing consequences that share similar functional relations (Koerner, Kohlenberg, & Parker, 1996).

From a behavior-analytic view, exclusive emphasis on topographically defined behavior patterns or response–response relations has limited value, particularly when it comes to the modification of behaviors (Naugle & Follette, 1998). Because behavior therapists are primarily concerned with the modification of behavior, one must first alter the conditions under which it does or does not occur in order to change behavior. A focus on response–response relationships, then, does not inform us about the circumstances associated with a behavior's occurrence and, consequently, does not give us any guidance to determine how behavior came about or what maintains it.

Emerging research suggests, however, that certain behavior patterns, namely, those associated with temperament concepts, often indicate the presence of individual differences in responsiveness to environmental events and behavioral consequences. As such, physiological properties associated with temperament constructs may mediate or moderate the relationship between current environmental events and behavior. The focus of this chapter, then, is on nomothetic topographical behavior patterns that have been associated with individual differences in learning and responsiveness to environmental consequences.

Functional Response Classes

Functional response classes represent another behavioral analogy to the personality concept. These response classes consist of a group of behaviors that are similar in that they produce the same or similar outcomes, even though they may be quite different in form or topography (Follette et al., 2000; Lubinski & Thompson, 1986; Malott et al., 2000). When behavioral assessors classify or group behaviors, they typically do so according to the similarity of functions they serve across contexts. This is in contrast to more traditional approaches to assessment in which behaviors are classified or grouped according to the similarity of topographical features or the degree of covariation they exhibit across persons. Functional response classes and the domains within which they are likely to be displayed are reviewed in the next chapter.

Response Classes and Personality

Because topographical and functional response class concepts can be considered behavioral analogies to the concept of personality, personality in behavior theory is regarded quite differently when contrasted with more traditional approaches. As we noted in chapter 1, traditional approaches tend to view observed behavior as the result of underlying variables that are not observable to anyone, including to the individual within whom these structural variables are purported to reside. Within such traditional approaches, behavior is often regarded as a sign of these underlying structures, and behavior itself is viewed as relatively unimportant except for the suggestive role it may serve as a sign of these unobservable determinants. In contrast, the behavioral perspective asserts that personality is reflected by what one does, not what one supposedly has, even if behavior is influenced by biological variables such as genes or temperament.

TEMPERAMENT

Temperament is widely regarded as arising from heritable genetic endowments. The response patterns associated with individual differences in temperament are similarly considered to affect environments in which they are expressed, and such environments, in turn, reciprocally affect future displays of temperamentally influenced behavior (e.g., Rothbart et al., 2000). Although temperament has been conceptualized in various ways, our notion of temperament is most consistent with that proposed by Derryberry and Rothbart (1984, p. 132, italics added):

> We have defined temperament as constitutional differences in reactivity and self-regulation, with "*constitutional*" referring to the relatively enduring biological makeup of the individual, influenced over time by heredity, maturation, and experience. . . . By *reactivity* we mean the functional state of the somatic, endocrine, autonomic, and central nervous systems as reflected in the response parameters of threshold, latency, intensity, rising time, and recovery time. By *self-regulation* we mean higher level processes functioning to modulate (enhance or inhibit) the reactive state of these systems . . . Self-regulatory processes are best approached in terms of emotions or affective–motivational processes.

Various studies tend to converge on three basic types of childhood temperament: (a) self-controlled, well-adjusted, or "easy"; (b) undercontrolled, impulsive, or restless; and (c) inhibited, shy, or anxious. These basic temperaments have been reliably noted among infants and children from a variety of Western cultures (Caspi, 2000). There is also an emerging consensus that these temperament patterns observed in infancy and childhood subsequently demonstrate strong associations with adult personality (Caspi, 2000). It is interesting that, as studies reviewed in this chapter illustrate, these three basic temperament types are also associated with individual differences in reactivity to various environmental events and sensitivity to response consequences.

MODELS OF TEMPERAMENT

Within psychology and psychiatry, several models of temperament have been proposed and evaluated. In this section, we review several major models of temperament that have relevance for behavioral assessment and therapy.

Eysenck's Model of Personality and Conditionability

Eysenck's 1957 Theory of Personality

Eysenck's early theoretical writings, which eventually gave rise to his 1967 theory of personality (reviewed subsequently), had as its foundations the theoretical ideas advanced by Jung, Pavlov, Hull, and Yerkes and Dodson (Eysenck, 1957). Drawing from predictions from these theories and from empirical findings reported in the literature, Eysenck (1957, p. 114) advanced two postulates for integrating findings from learning theory and personality research: (a) the postulate of individual differences and (b) the typological postulate.

The *individual-differences postulate* suggests that the relative balance of two psychophysiological constructs, excitatory and inhibitory processes, were instrumental in accounting for differences in behavior among persons. The *typological postulate* specifies the relationship between differences in the balance of excitation and inhibition processes by specifying a predominant personality type (i.e., *introversion* or *extraversion*). When combined, these two postulates suggest that introverts' excitatory potentials are generated quickly and are relatively strong, whereas reactive inhibitions are developed slowly and weakly and, once developed, dissipate quickly. For extraverts, the combination of the two postulates suggests that excitatory potentials are generated slowly and are relatively weak, whereas reactive inhibitions are developed quickly and are strong, and once developed, dissipate slowly.

Eysenck (1957, p. 115) went on to hypothesize individual differences in learning between introverts and extraverts based on these differences in excitation and inhibition processes. Eysenck suggested that introverts should form conditioned responses quickly and strongly, whereas extraverts should form conditioned responses slowly and weakly. Eysenck further suggested that *neuroticism* (which, in his model, is analogous to emotionality) should have no association with conditionability. Thus, according to this model, there should be no differences in conditionability between neurotic introverts (e.g., anxious types and reactive depressives) and normal introverts or differences in conditionability between neurotic extraverts (e.g., hysterics and psychopaths) and normal extraverts (Eysenck, 1957, p. 115).

Eysenck's 1967 Arousal Theory

Whereas Eysenck's 1957 theory is one of differences in inhibition and excitation, his 1967 theory is primarily concerned with differences in cortical arousal (specifically, arousal of the ascending reticular activating system [ARAS]) and the effects that differences in arousal have on conditionability. The concept of arousal as described in this theory is a unitary one; that is, arousal is viewed as a unidimensional construct.

As applied to personality, Eysenck (1967) suggested that introverts are, in general, more cortically aroused than extraverts. Furthermore, Eysenck (1967) equated degree of baseline cortical arousal with conditionability, whereby higher levels of arousal usually enhanced conditioning. Introverts, because of their higher cortical arousal, are hypothesized generally to form conditioned responses with greater ease compared with extraverts. The superiority in conditionability for introverts is hypothesized to be invariant across different types of response consequation (i.e., punishment and reward; Eysenck & Eysenck, 1985).

Neuroticism, as in the 1957 theory, is hypothesized to have little influence on conditioning. Rather, Eysenck (1967) conceptualized neuroticism as a motivational variable (pp. 131–132) associated with the level of autonomic arousal (pp. 231–242). The critical brain structures thought to underlie neuroticism are the limbic system and hypothalamus. Eysenck (1967) further hypothesized that the autonomic and cortical arousal systems were partially independent of one another. The relative independence of these two systems breaks down when persons become extremely emotional. That is, Eysenck (1967) postulated that significant autonomic activation (neuroticism or emotionality) could potentially increase cortical arousal. As related to learning, Eysenck (1967) speculated that high neuroticism could interfere with learning because it impairs attention and "the higher nervous process," but that such interference is relatively rare because one is only infrequently highly emotionally aroused. As such, in this theory, neuroticism is thought to have little effect on conditionability in general. Under highly arousing conditions, however, Eysenck's theory predicted that introverts would perform at a suboptimal level because of overarousal, whereas extraverts' performance would be optimal under highly arousing conditions relative to low arousing conditions.

One implication from Eysenck's arousal theory is that introverts, relative to extraverts, would be more likely to show greater fear conditioning because of their stronger autonomic reactivity to a greater variety of stimuli and, as a result, more inclined to develop fears and phobias (Eysenck, 1969a). Extraverts, conversely, are regarded as less likely to develop fear conditioning and consequently more likely to demonstrate impulsive, self-gratifying, and psychopathic behavior (Eysenck, 1969a). Thus, in both the 1967 theory and the 1957 theory, introverts were regarded to be neurotically predisposed to experience dysthymia (anxiety and reactive depression) and extraverts to experience hysteria and psychopathy.

In the mid-1970s, Eysenck and Eysenck (1975) introduced a third dimension, called *psychoticism*. The measurement of this dimension in the Eysenck Personality Questionnaire (EPQ; Eysenck & Eysenck, 1975), an updated revision of the Eysenck Personality Inventory (EPI; Eysenck & Eysenck, 1968), includes impulsivity items previously included within the Extraversion scale. Other items in the Psychoticism scale assess socially deviant acts and unusual experiences. Traits associated with psychoticism include aggressive, cold, egocentric, impersonal, impulsive, and antisocial behavior. Subsequent research on the EPQ Psychoticism scale, however, indicates that items on this scale primarily inquire about behaviors associated with the psychopathy construct. Furthermore, Psychoticism scale scores demonstrate poor psychometric qualities (e.g., skewed distribution, poor reliability) and fail to discriminate psychotic individuals from nonpsychotic persons (Block, 1977a, 1977b). These findings eventually resulted in a revision of that scale. Perhaps for these reasons, the psychoticism dimension never acquired the same theoretical and empirical status as the introversion–extraversion and neuroticism–stability dimensions that were the centerpieces of Eysenck's earlier models.

Summary

In both the 1957 and 1967 theories, emphasis is placed on two causal, but uncorrelated, dimensions of personality: introversion–extraversion and neuroticism–stability. In both of these theories, greater emphasis is placed on the introversion–extraversion dimension for explaining differences in learning. In the 1957 theory, this difference is accounted for by unspecified central processes responsible for the excitation or inhibition of cortical functioning, with introverts hypothesized to have quicker and stronger excitatory potentials and extraverts hypothesized to have quicker and stronger inhibitory potentials. The 1967 theory hypothesizes that the underlying physical substrate responsible for individual differences in personality (i.e., introversion and extraversion) is cortical arousal (Eysenck, 1967), with introverts hypothesized to be more aroused generally than extraverts, and thus more conditionable.

Difficulties With Eysenck's (1967) Theory

Several research findings presented some difficulties for Eysenck's (1967) model of personality. For example, a number of studies (e.g., Blake, 1967; M. W. Eysenck & Folkard, 1980; Revelle, Humphreys, Simon, & Gilliland, 1980; Zuber & Ekehammar, 1988) suggest that levels of arousal are not consistently higher for introverts compared with extraverts, a finding inconsistent with Eysenck's (1967) theory that postulated chronically higher arousal levels among introverts relative to extraverts. Furthermore, these and other studies suggest that impulsivity and sociability (or, analogously, low anxiety), regarded by Eysenck to be subfactors of extraversion, are better conceived as two separate constructs associated with different responses to a variety of independent variables. In particular, subsequent findings indicate that anxiety and impulsivity, and not introversion–extraversion, are generally better predictors of conditionability and that anxiety and impulsivity are associated with greater sensitivities to the effects of punishment and rewarding consequences, respectively. Because these latter findings are more consistent with Gray's modification of Eysenck's model, they are reviewed in the next section.

Gray's Modifications of the Eysenck Model

Gray (1970, 1973, 1981, 1987a, 1987b, 1999; Gray & McNaughton, 1996; McNaughton & Gray, 2000) has proposed a modification of Eysenck's theory, one that emphasizes the dimensions of anxiety and impulsivity rather than introversion–extraversion as causal determinants of differences in conditionability and sensitivity and responsiveness to varying environmental cues. In contrast to Eysenck's (1957, 1967) proposition that introverts are superior in conditionability than extraverts under all types of contingencies, Gray (1970, 1987a) proposed that introverts are more susceptible to contingencies of punishment and frustrative nonreward (the omission or termination of a reward that eventually leads to extinction) and more responsive to novel stimuli and innate fear stimuli (e.g., snakes). In support of these views, Gray (1970) reviewed findings on anxiety in relation to the behavioral effects of drugs, specifically animal studies that examined the effect of amytal (a barbiturate and central nervous system depressant) on learning under various reinforcement contingencies. Gray's (1970) review suggested that amytal attenuated the influences of punishment and frustrative nonreward on behavior, ostensibly because the drug reduced arousal. Although amytal affected learning under punishment and nonreward contingencies, it had no effect on learning under reward contingencies. Gray went on to conclude from his review that the function of amytal on behavior was to reduce the sensitivity of an endogenous punishment mechanism, later termed the *behavioral inhibition system* (BIS; Gray, 1981).

In Gray's model, the activities of the BIS, from which states of anxiety arise, function to (a) inhibit behavior in situations in which cues associated with punishment, novel, or innate fear stimuli are present; (b) increase arousal to energize subsequent behavior; and (c) increase attentional resources to novel or threatening stimuli (Corr, Pickering, & Gray, 1997). In recent accounts, Gray (1999, p. 86) has associated BIS activity with "a widely distributed brain system . . . centering upon the hippocampal formation and related

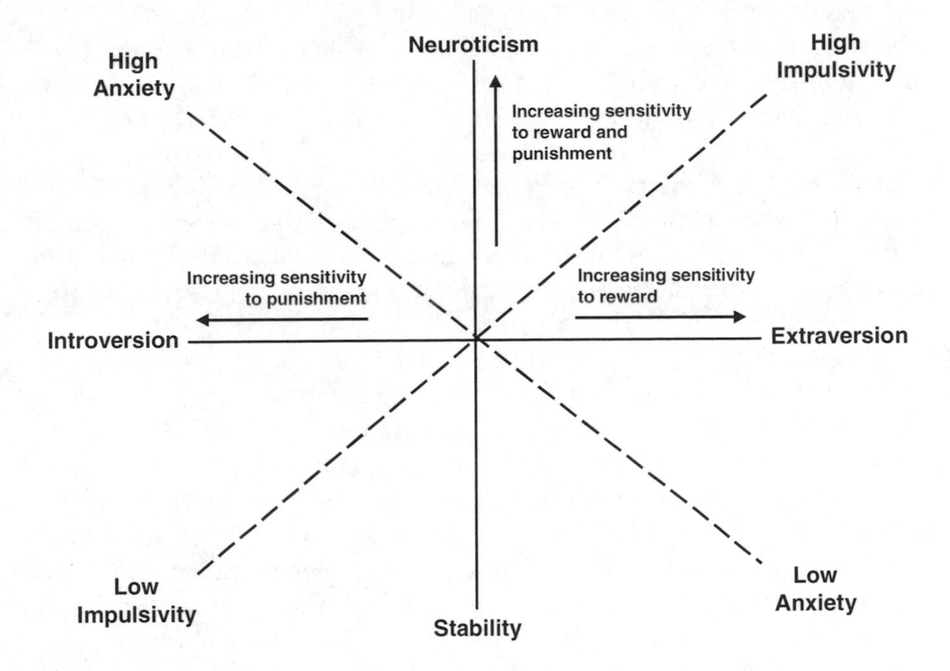

Figure 4.1. Representation of Gray's theoretical model within Eysenck's two-dimensional space.

structures in the temporal and frontal cortex, thalamus and hypothalamus, as well as associating monoaminergic pathways innervating these structures."

As will be recalled, Eysenck (1957, 1967) de-emphasized the role that neuroticism (emotionality) played in learning. He further conceived of neuroticism as a drive or motivational variable (Eysenck, 1957, p. 115; 1967, p. 132, pp. 182–183). Gray (1970), in contrast, conceptualized neuroticism principally as emotional reactivity to various forms of external stimuli. In an extension of this assumption, Gray suggested that level of neuroticism (or emotionality) served as an index of susceptibility to the effects of both reward and punishment. As individuals move from stability to high neuroticism along the stability–neuroticism dimension in Eysenck's two-dimensional space, they become increasingly more sensitive to both rewarding and punishing consequences (Figure 4.1). There is also an additive effect for personality type (introversion–extraversion) in relation to susceptibility to reward or punishment specifically by which introverts relative to extraverts tend to be more sensitive to the effects of punishment and extraverts are more sensitive to the effects of reward.

Gray (1970) further suggested that the relationship between susceptibility to punishment, introversion–extraversion, and neuroticism could be illustrated by a diagonal dimension that runs from the introversion–neurotic quadrant (high anxiety) at approximately 45 degrees through the extraverted–stability quadrant (low anxiety; Figure 4.1). In Gray's model, this dimension describes one's level of anxiety as well as sensitivity to punishment. Those most sensitive or reactive to the effects of punishment would be those highest on the anxiety dimension. Those least sensitive or reactive to punishment, conversely, would be those who are at the low end of the anxiety pole. The placement of the anxiety dimension within two-dimensional space is consistent with Eysenck's (1967, p. 167) proposition that anxiety is a combination of neuroticism and introversion and is consistent with findings from descriptive (Farmer & Nelson-Gray, 1995) and factor analytic studies (see, for example, Eysenck, 1969b; Eysenck & Rachman, 1965).

Gray (1973) proposed a second causal dimension of behavior orthogonal to that of anxiety, labeled *impulsivity*, which extends at an approximate 45-degree angle from the extravert–neurotic quadrant (high impulsivity) through the introvert–stability quadrant (low impulsivity). In speculating about sensitivity to the effects of particular contingencies, Gray (1973) proposed that as one's level of impulsivity increases, one becomes increasingly more susceptible to the effects of reward and relieving nonpunishment (or the nonoccurrence of an anticipated punishment). Those lowest on this dimension (i.e., the stable introvert) would be the least sensitive or reactive to the effects of reward and nonpunishment. The function of this system, later termed the *behavioral approach (or activation) system* (BAS; Fowles, 1980; Gray, 1987a), is to activate behavior in situations in which cues associated with reward or nonpunishment are present. Both descriptive and factor analytic research support the placement of this dimension within Eysenck's two-dimensional space as proposed by Gray; however, the actual angle of the dimension appears to be less than 45 degrees and is perhaps closer to 30 degrees (Farmer & Nelson-Gray, 1995).

Gray has not developed the physiological basis of the BAS to the same degree that he has the BIS. Nevertheless, he (1987a) previously suggested that the activities of this system are linked to the dopaminergic pathways of the ventral tegmental area, the nucleus accumbens, and the ventral striatum.

Gray has also theorized about the neuropsychological basis of psychotic disorders. He (1987a) proposed the *fight–flight system* that mediates responses to unconditioned aversive stimuli and unconditioned frustrative nonreward. This third dimension has been conceptually linked to Eysenck and Eysenck's (1975) psychoticism dimension. As noted earlier, however, scores on Eysenck's psychoticism dimension are more strongly associated with the concept of psychopathy than psychosis. In Gray's model, emotional states that most commonly arise from this system are panic (which is distinguished from anxiety or fear) and rage. Behavioral tendencies most strongly associated with the activation of this system are escape and defensive aggression. Gray (1987a) has further proposed that the major neural pathways associated with this system are the central gray of the midbrain, the ventromedial nucleus of the hypothalamus, and the amygdala. There is also an indication that persons high on Eysenck's psychoticism dimension demonstrate impairments in learning through punishment during both operant (Corr et al., 1997) and classical conditioning (Beyts, Frcka, Martin, & Levey, 1983) tasks.

In more recent writings, Gray (1999) has suggested that positive psychotic symptoms (e.g., hallucinations, delusions, disorganized speech) are associated with communication disruptions or failures between the hippocampal system and the nucleus accumbens, which thus results in dopaminergic overactivity. Associated with this and other biological events is a failure of cognitive processes to integrate past regularities of experience with current percepts and actions.

Empirical Evaluation of Gray's Model

A good deal of support exists for Gray's observations and predictions related to the neurophysiological processes hypothesized to underlie his systems, as well as the personality and behavioral predictions that arise from his theoretical model (reviewed in Corr et al., 1997; Gray & McNaughton, 1996; McNaughton & Gray, 2000; Pickering et al., 1997; Pickering, Díaz, & Gray, 1995; Pickering & Gray, 1999; Rothbart et al., 2000). Observed findings across studies are not invariant or uniformly supportive, however, and suggest that additional refinement and elaboration of this rich, detailed, and multileveled model is indicated.

Newman's Further Elaborations

Extensions of Gray's theory have been proposed, such as those suggested by Newman. Citing his laboratory's research as examples, Newman (1987) proposed that extraverts display a general tendency toward disinhibition, as evidenced by faster responses following punishment and failures to withhold responses that typically result in punishment (i.e., passive avoidance errors, or PAEs). Introverts, conversely, who slow down following punishment, are thought to be more reflective and thus better able to learn from their experiences with punishment.

A series of studies in Newman's laboratory suggest that, relative to introverts and control participants, extraverts and persons with psychopathic personality traits (who are presumed to be extraverted or disinhibited) more frequently fail to withhold responses previously associated with punishment (PAEs) when simultaneously responding for reward. In one such study, Newman, Widom, and Nathan (1985) found that extraverted college students, relative to introverts, were unable to avoid punishment (i.e., the loss of money) when avoidance of punishment required the inhibition of a previously rewarded response (for similar findings, see also Patterson, Kosson, & Newman, 1987; Newman et al., 1987). In another experiment reported in that paper, Newman et al. (1987) compared the performance of primary psychopaths (defined in this study by elevated psychopathic deviate, or *Pd*, scale scores on the Minnesota Multiphasic Personality Inventory [MMPI; Hathaway & McKinley, 1943] plus low scores on the Welsh Anxiety Scale [Welsh, 1956]) and secondary psychopaths (defined by elevated *Pd* scale scores and high scores on the Welsh Anxiety Scale). Results from this comparison indicated that primary psychopaths made significantly more PAEs than secondary psychopaths. Newman and Kosson (1986) also found that psychopaths (undifferentiated) made more PAEs than nonpsychopath control participants.

Newman's (Newman & Kosson, 1986; Newman et al., 1985) findings are largely consistent with the theorizing of Gray (see Gray, 1987b, for his discussion of these experiments). According to Gray's model, extraverts would be more sensitive to signals of reward relative to signals of punishment. Newman et al. (1985) observed that extraverts, relative to introverts, tended to learn from punishment except when punishment occurred when participants were also responding for reward. BIS activation in introverts to signals of punishment and nonreward would account for their response inhibition, whereas BAS activation among extraverts in response to signals of reward would result in responding that was relatively uninfluenced by punishment signals.

The differences in performance between primary and secondary psychopaths in Newman et al. (1985) are also consistent with Gray's theorizing. Primary psychopaths would fall within the stable–extravert quadrant, and thus would be insensitive to the effects of punishment and moderately sensitive to the effects of reward. Because of their elevated levels of anxiety, secondary psychopaths would fall within the neurotic–extravert quadrant, and thus would be highly sensitive to reward and moderately sensitive to the effects of punishment. The observation that primary psychopaths would make more PAEs than secondary psychopaths would be expected according to Gray's model, because primary psychopaths are largely insensitive to punishment cues (i.e., they are low in BIS activation), whereas secondary psychopaths are moderately sensitive to such cues.

Newman (e.g., 1987) further suggested that disinhibited behavior is largely a consequence of BAS hyperactivity among extraverts, specifically in response to reward cues when both reward and punishment contingencies are operative. In this instance, the tendency to respond for reward is stronger than the tendency to inhibit responding that may lead to punishment, which results in a PAE. Thus, among impulsive or extraverted individuals, there is a greater tendency to make PAEs when simultaneously responding for reward.

Newman and colleagues (e.g., Patterson & Newman, 1993; Wallace & Newman, 1990, 1997), in the context of their *response modulation hypothesis*, have extended their theoretical formulations to encompass the predisposing role that neuroticism has in relation to the speed, force, and intensity of responding and on the automatic orienting of attention. That is, responses among neurotic individuals are hypothesized to be more rapid and vigorous and potentially result in less evaluation of response effectiveness and less reflection on the consequences associated with behavior. Disinhibited behavior, in turn, is the hypothesized result of these tendencies. When attention is oriented and allocated to a stimulus (either a stimulus associated with threat or punishment in the case of BIS activation or a stimulus associated with reward in the case of BAS activation), attentional resources necessary for controlled self-regulatory processes become less available and thus increase the probability of unregulated behavior. As a result, in a mixed incentive context in which both rewards and punishments are operative and contingent on behavior, neurotic extraverts would be expected to (a) be oriented and responsive to rewarding stimuli, (b) respond rapidly and vigorously to such stimuli and reflect less on performance feedback, and (c) allocate disproportionately more ongoing attention to reward cues, thus resulting in fewer attentional resources allocated to punishment cues.

Although Newman's formulation and research findings are generally not inconsistent with the theorizing of Gray (see Gray, 1987b), Newman's theory does place greater emphasis on the role of reflectivity, response perseveration, and passive avoidance failure in accounting for performance differences, whereas Gray's theory principally emphasizes differing sensitivities to signals of reward and punishment. In fact, in some of Newman's research, PAEs appear to be more commonly experienced among those psychopathic individuals who are low, not high, in anxiety (Newman, Patterson, Howland, & Nichols, 1990; Newman & Schmitt, 1998; see also Lykken, 1957). These particular findings seem counter to some of the assumptions of the response modulation hypothesis, although they can be viewed as at least partially consistent with Gray's theory. Somewhat problematic for Gray's theory, but consistent with Newman's response modulation hypothesis, are findings by Newman and others (e.g., Avila, Moltó, Segarra, & Torrubia, 1995; Patterson et al., 1987) that suggest extraversion or impulsivity in combination with neuroticism among men is associated with more PAEs than extraversion in combination with low neuroticism. Also difficult to reconcile with Gray's views are findings obtained by Thornquist and Zuckerman (1995) that associate impulsivity and psychopathy (but not anxiety or neuroticism) with the frequency of PAEs among male inmates. Finally, Gray's theory may require some modifications because passive avoidance learning seems to be affected by several moderator variables, such as race of the participants (Gremore, Chapman, & Farmer, in press; Kosson, Smith, & Newman, 1990; Newman & Schmitt, 1998; Thornquist & Zuckerman, 1995) and whether the experimental context includes both rewards and punishments (mixed incentives) versus only punishments contingent on behavior (Avila et al., 1995; Newman, 1987). Pickering et al. (1995) have also suggested differences in the controlling effects of a variety of reinforcers as a function of sex. Specifically, they proposed that monetary rewards could exert stronger reinforcing properties among men, whereas intrinsic interests or social incentives may serve as stronger incentives among women.

Cloninger's Model of Temperament

Cloninger (1986, 1987, 2003; Cloninger, Svrakic, & Przybeck, 1993) has also delineated a typology of temperament styles to account for individual differences in reactivity to an array of conditioned and unconditioned stimuli. Similar to Gray's BIS, Cloninger has proposed the temperament dimension of *harm avoidance* (HA), which is characterized by a heritable susceptibility to anxiety and behavioral inhibition to punishment cues and heightened reactivity to novel cues and frustrative nonreward (behavioral extinction). Persons who are high in HA are also described as particularly adept with passive avoidance learning (Cloninger, 1987). Cloninger has suggested that serotonin concentrations underlie HA and that common personality traits associated with HA include passive–aggressive, explosive (traits of schizoid and paranoid personality coupled with rage), obsessional, and passive–dependent.

Similar to Gray and Fowles's BAS, Cloninger has also proposed a *novelty-seeking* (NS) dimension, characterized by an increased sensitivity and responsiveness to reward cues as well as cues that signal relief from punishment. The principal neurochemical proposed to be associated with NS is dopamine, and related behavioral trends include reward seeking and punishment avoidance. Personality traits associated with high levels of NS include antisocial, histrionic, passive–aggressive, and explosive.

Reward dependence (RD), a third temperament dimension proposed by Cloninger, is associated with sensitivity to conditioned reward cues, particularly social incentives (e.g., social approval), as well as to socially mediated signals that suggest relief from punishment (or negative reinforcement). Cloninger suggested that norepinephrine concentrations are related to this temperament dimension and that persons high on RD are particularly resistant to extinction of previously rewarded behavior. Personality traits associated with RD include histrionic, passive–aggressive, cyclothymic, and passive–dependent personality traits. Cloninger (1987) has further associated low RD with antisocial and psychopathic personality traits, among others.

Persistence (Per), originally regarded by Cloninger as a subfactor of RD, has been proposed as a fourth independent temperament dimension as scores on this subscale have been repeatedly observed to singly load on a separate fourth factor. There are, however, many theoretical and psychometric concerns associated with Per as a separate dimension of temperament (Chapman, Mayer, Specht, Farmer, & Field, 2003; Farmer et al., 2003), and this seeming statistical artifact has not had a prominent feature in Cloninger typology.

Little research has examined Cloninger's behavioral predictions in relation to his theory and measure of temperament (the Temperament and Character Inventory; Cloninger, 1992). Given the great similarity to Gray's theory, it is likely that future tests of his behavioral predictions will demonstrate similar findings to those based on Gray's model. Of the existent research, Farmer et al. (2003) examined passive avoidance learning as a function of Cloninger's temperament dimensions. They found that among women, HA alone was not significantly associated with the number of PAEs committed in a mixed incentive (reward + punishment) context, as would have been predicted by Cloninger's model. Rather, HA in interaction with NS emerged as the only significant predictor of PAEs, whereby PAE frequency was most strongly associated with high NS and low HA. This finding suggests that impulsive women may have difficulty inhibiting previously punished behavior, overrespond for reward, or have a weak sensitivity to punishment cues only if they are also low in HA. As such, disinhibited responding among women may reflect the influence of a strong approach (BAS) and weak inhibition (BIS) system, which would be consistent with predictions arising from Arnett's (1997) *motivational imbalance model.* This model suggests that a weak inhibitory system in combination with a strong activation system are most strongly linked to tendencies toward disinhibited behavior. A subsequent evaluation of this model with men (Chapman et al., 2003) failed to replicate the significant interaction effect observed for women, however. In fact, and somewhat paradoxically, even though men were higher than women on NS and both groups were similar in level of HA, women made significantly more PAEs than men (Chapman et al., 2003), which further supports the notion that learning processes in relation to temperament may show sex differences.

In Farmer et al. (2003) but not in Chapman et al. (2003), reflection on response-contingent feedback immediately following the commission of PAEs demonstrated a significant negative association with the frequency of PAEs ($r = -.44$), thus indicating that those who spent more time reflecting on the punishment errors were less likely to make such errors across trials. Others have reliably obtained this finding (Patterson & Newman, 1993), suggesting that reflection on performance may itself be an important individual-difference variable associated with effective behavior. Of the temperament dimensions examined in Farmer et al. (2003), only NS was significantly correlated with the amount of time spent viewing response-contingent feedback following PAEs, whereby those who had higher NS scores tended to reflect less on this feedback. This finding supports the notion that disinhibited individuals are less likely to reflect on their situation, particularly when it involves punishment for ongoing behavior (Patterson & Newman, 1993) and suggests that this assertion holds true for nonpathological women. This finding is also consistent with Cloninger's (1987, p. 581) proposal that low NS individuals engage in "methodical reflection."

Five Factor Model of Personality

The five factor model (FFM) of personality is a widely accepted taxonomy of personality (John & Srivastava, 1999) that demonstrates a fair

TABLE 4.1
Principle Attributes Associated With the Dimensions of the Five Factor Model

Factor dimension	Corresponding attributes
Extraversion–surgency	Sociable, talkative, assertive, energetic, positive moods, adventurous, enthusiastic, outgoing
Agreeableness	Good-natured, cooperative, trustful, warm, sympathetic, compliant, kind
Conscientiousness	Dependable, responsible, orderly, organized, deliberate, disciplined, persevering, not impulsive
Neuroticism (versus emotional stability)	Easily upset, not calm, excitable, tense, self-doubts, negative moods, low self-esteem
Cultural (or intellect or openness to experience)	Intellectual, cultured, polished, independent minded, creative, artistically inclined, curious, imaginative, unconventional

degree of generalizability across cultures (McCrae & Costa, 1997). The FFM has evolved as a joint result of statistical procedures used to identify uncorrelated dimensions of personality description that maximally accounted for variation among sets of items or scores (factor analysis) and an approach to personality classification proposing that important socially relevant behavior and personality descriptors have become encoded into the natural language (i.e., the lexical approach to personality classification).

The FFM personality dimensions consist of superordinate factors that have traditionally been labeled *extraversion* (or surgency), *agreeableness*, *conscientiousness*, *neuroticism* (versus emotional stability), and *culture* (or intellect or openness to experience; Costa & McCrae, 1992; Goldberg, 1993). Primary attributes associated with these factor dimensions are listed in Table 4.1.

Some theories of the FFM traits have suggested that these personality dimensions are associated with underlying causal personality dispositions (McCrae & Costa, 1996) that are genetically based (Loehlin, McCrae, Costa, & John, 1998) and strongly intertwined with the concept of temperament (Digman & Shmelyov, 1996; Rothbart et al., 2000). Indeed, existent research supports the notion that when factor analyzed, variables typically regarded as measures of temperament constructs result in a factor solution that resembles the FFM (e.g., Angleitner & Ostendorf, 1994). There is an indication, too, that the models of temperament described earlier also map onto elements of the FFM. Central dimensions in Eysenck's model are extraversion and neuroticism. Gray, in his BIS/BAS model, redefined the causal dimensions of description as impulsivity and anxiety, which are graphically represented as 45-degree rotations of Eysenck's dimensions in two-dimensional space. Others (e.g., Rothbart et al., 2000) have organized infant and childhood temperament in relation to Gray's tridimensional model and the FFM. Finally, there is an indication that Cloninger's temperament and character dimensions also display good correspondence to the FFM (De Fruyt, Van De Wiele, & Van Heeringen, 2000; McDonald & Holland, 2002; Ramanaiah, Rielage, & Cheng, 2002).

Summary

As evident in the temperament models reviewed, there is growing convergence among researchers as to what represents the primary dimensions of temperament. Furthermore, there is a substantial body of literature that implicates two dimensions of temperament as important predictors of individual differences in reward and punishment sensitivity: impulsivity–extraversion–positive affect and anxiety–neuroticism–negative affect, respectively. There is some indication, too, that Gray's fight–flight system may be associated with individual differences in learning under conditions of punishment (Beyts et al., 1983; Corr et al., 1997). Taken together, these patterns of findings lend support for the notion that variations in at least some forms of temperament may have been phylogenetically selected on the basis of their associated functional properties in relation to the environment.

DIAGNOSTIC AND STATISTICAL MANUAL OF MENTAL DISORDERS (DSM) DIAGNOSTIC CLASSES

DSM diagnostic concepts are specified through a delineation of collections of signs and symptoms. Signs and symptoms that define disorder concepts in *DSM* are typically behaviors (motor, cognitive–verbal, emotional–physiological–motivational) that are presumed to covary among positive cases and to be minimally expressed or absent among negative cases. As such, *DSM* is a topographically based descriptive system whereby diagnostic judgments are based on the extent to which a given person's experience and behavior matches those listed within specific diagnostic categories.

Psychiatric Diagnoses From a Behavioral Perspective

The *DSM* system is purported to be an atheoretical classification scheme. Yet it retains many features of the medical model, such as reference to psychological conditions as "syndromes" or "disorders," the use of categorical rather than dimensional representation of psychological conditions, and the practice of diagnosis based on clinical signs and symptoms.

From a behavioral perspective, *DSM* has failed to realize the goals of traditional syndrome classification. That is, in traditional syndrome classification within the medical model, collections of signs and symptoms were identified that commonly appeared among persons who hypothetically had the same underlying disease process. Given that the diagnosis itself specified a presumed underlying etiology (a disease) that accounted for signs and symptoms and indicated a potentially effective treatment (if one was known), the diagnosis itself represented a meaningful functional unit (Hayes et al., 1996). A classical example in this regard is the diagnosis of syphilis. Syphilis (initially termed "general paresis") was diagnosed on the basis of the presence of a collection of signs and symptoms commonly experienced among positive cases. A sexually transmitted bacterium that gave rise to the signs and symptoms of this disease was eventually identified. Later still, an effective therapy was identified to rid the body of this bacterium. As such, the diagnostic label "syphilis" encompassed a collection of signs and symptoms, a known etiology (a bacterium) associated with these signs and symptoms, and an effective treatment (penicillin). As such, the diagnosis of syphilis served as a meaningful functional response unit.

As Hayes et al. (1996) noted, however, psychiatric concepts over the last 100 years have failed to link syndromes (collections of signs and symptoms) to specific disease processes. Physiological markers (specific signs and symptoms) of psychiatric disorder concepts are rarely sensitive or specific to particular diagnostic concepts (Hoes, 1986). Behavioral, cognitive, and emotional signs or symptoms that define psychiatric diagnostic concepts are also not particularly sensitive or specific in relation to the very diagnostic concept to which they belong (Farmer & Chapman, 2002; Trull, Widiger, & Frances, 1987). Therefore, from a behavioral perspective, all that remains are psychiatric syndromes with no functional properties and questionable utility.

Syndrome classification can potentially have utility from a behavior therapy perspective, however. This would be the case in the event patterns of responses that nomothetically covary across persons or subgroups of persons reveal the presence of functional response classes, treatment-relevant target behaviors (Nelson & Barlow, 1981), or biologically influenced response predispositions that mediate or moderate environment–behavior relations. As such, topographical response classes such as those specified in *DSM* diagnostic concepts may not necessarily be in conflict with behavioral assessment and therapy approaches (Nelson & Barlow, 1981).

Syndromal Disorders of the *DSM*

DSM–IV (American Psychiatric Association, 1994) contains more than 800 diagnostic labels (Follette & Houts, 1996), most of which are coded on Axis I (syndromal disorders) of this system. Thus, it is difficult to offer general summaries about such a vast number of conditions, many of which are little researched. Nonetheless, there is evidence that many of these conditions are related to temperament or biological differences (Claridge & Davis, 2003). In particular, neuroticism–negative affect appears to be a common feature among the vast majority of psychological disorders (and, by association, anxiety and impulsivity–low conscientiousness). Excesses and deficits in extraversion and deficits in agreeableness likely constitute common features across a wide spectrum of psychological conditions.

In offering these observations, we do not mean to imply that all psychological disorders are reducible or best described as variations in temperament or a set number of descriptive dimensions. This would be too simplistic a conclusion. It does suggest, however, the possibility that the 800 or so diagnostic labels in *DSM* can be organized conceptually within the body of existent psychological knowledge.

Many of the critics of *DSM* classification (e.g., Farmer, 2000; Follette & Houts, 1996) have noted the limits of atheoretical descriptive classification schemes and have proposed instead the development of theoretically driven taxonomies. From our vantage point, such a goal seems possible, and perhaps the first step is to identify the commonalities as well as the discriminative features among diagnostic concepts. A resultant product may be a more conceptual model of psychopathology that has embedded within it specific diagnostic concepts. Temperament constructs may represent useful foundations for such a conceptual model.

Personality Disorders of the *DSM*

With the introduction of the third edition of the *DSM* (*DSM–III*; American Psychiatric Association, 1980) and its subsequent revisions came formal recognition that personality disorders are differentiable from other psychological disorders. The 10 personality disorders described in this classification scheme, coded on Axis II of this system, are divided into three symptomatological clusters: the odd–eccentric cluster (paranoid, schizoid, schizotypal personality disorders), the anxious–fearful cluster (dependent, avoidant, obsessive–compulsive personality disorders), and the erratic–dramatic cluster (histrionic, narcissistic, borderline, antisocial personality disorders).

Overall, there appears to be moderate empirical support for aspects of the *DSM* personality disorder clustering scheme. The greatest support comes from factor analytic studies that examined the factor structure of the personality disorder categories (Farmer et al., 2004; Farmer & Nelson-Gray, 1995; Hyler & Lyons, 1988; Kass, Skodol, Charles, Spitzer, & Williams, 1985). These studies, however, displayed some inconsistencies in findings, perhaps because of differences in participant composition (i.e., patients versus nonpatients) or other methodological differences. Morey's (1988) cluster analysis of the personality disorders also lends some support to the proposed clusters, although the odd–eccentric cluster was found to be largely undefined in this study, perhaps because of low frequency of these disorders observed in the sample studied. Perhaps the least support for the *DSM* clustering scheme is found when individual symptom criteria associated with the personality disorders are factor analyzed (Hyler et al., 1990; Livesley & Jackson, 1986; Livesley, Jackson, & Schroeder, 1989).

Other conceptual frameworks might eventually be shown to do a better job of accurately organizing the variability among the individual *DSM* personality disorder concepts. For example, the FFM has been investigated as an alternative organizing schema for the personality disorders. Available research, however, suggests an absence of unique FFM profiles for individual personality disorder concepts (Widiger, Trull, Clarkin, Sanderson, & Costa, 2002). Nonetheless, the FFM model accounts well for the breadth of personality disorder pathology (O'Connor & Dyce, 1998; although see Svrakic et al., 1993, and Yeung, Lyons, Waternaux, Faraone, & Tsuang, 1993). In general, studies that have examined FFM dimensions in relation to personality disorders have indicated that neuroticism is central to personality disorder pathology, with the possible exception of antisocial personality disorder (e.g., Blais, 1997; Costa & Widiger, 2002; Duijsens & Diekstra, 1996; O'Connor & Dyce, 1998). Excesses (histrionic and narcissistic) and deficits (avoidant, schizoid, schizotypal) in extraversion are often observed, as are excesses (obsessive–compulsive) or deficits (antisocial, borderline, histrionic, narcissistic paranoid) in conscientiousness, which interestingly has as an opposite end pole, the impulsivity construct. Agreeableness is often low among those with personality disorders, with the exception of those who are high in dependent personality disorder traits. Openness to experience appears to be only minimally related to personality disorder pathology and perhaps is most evident among those with schizotypal traits.

There is an indication, too, that *DSM* personality disorder concepts fit into the models of Eysenck, Gray, and Cloninger. Eysenck (1987), for example, has speculated that the odd–eccentric personality disorders correspond to the psychoticism factor, the erratic–dramatic personality disorders are associated with the extraversion factor, and the anxious–fearful personality disorders are linked to the neuroticism factor. Existent research also suggests that many of the *DSM* personality disorders can be incorporated into Gray's descriptive framework. The anxious–fearful and erratic–dramatic personality disorders, respectively, are well positioned on the dimensions of anxiety and impulsivity, respectively (Farmer et al., 2004; Farmer & Nelson-Gray, 1995). Those persons who display symptoms associated with the odd–eccentric cluster often show significant elevations on anxiety, impulsivity, or both (Farmer et al., 2004), which is consistent with Fowles's (2001) suggestion that combinations of BIS and BAS activation can further account for the variability observed among individuals with various psychotic features or disorders.

Research has further suggested that Cloninger's temperament dimensions account for variations in personality disorder features subsumed within the *DSM* personality disorder cluster scheme. Specifically, Svrakic et al. (1993)

have empirically associated the odd–eccentric, erratic–dramatic, and anxious–fearful personality disorders with low RD, high NS, and high HA, respectively.

SUMMARY

As this brief review has suggested, variations in temperament appear to account well for the variability seen among a variety of psychological conditions. Because temperament is regarded as arising from heritable genetic endowments and linked to individual differences in sensitivity or responsiveness to environmental contingencies, it might be the case that variations in temperament were selected on the basis of associated survival and fitness value. Such a notion is fully consistent with behavior theory and lends support for the notion that biologically based individual differences may mediate or moderate the association between environmental influences and behavior.

5

FUNCTIONAL RESPONSE DOMAINS

In the preceding chapter, we discussed traditional personality dimensions and diagnostic categories that have potential relevance for a behavioral assessment and approach to therapy. One conclusion from that chapter was that patterns of behavior that nomothetically covary across persons or subgroups of persons might suggest the presence of biologically influenced response predispositions that mediate or moderate environment–behavior relations. Indicators of such predispositions, if observed, could suggest hypotheses about sensitivities or responsiveness to various environmental contingencies and, correspondingly, potential maintaining factors for problematic behavior.

In this chapter, we discuss and provide examples of a different type of response class, the *functional response class*. Functional response classes are groupings of behavior that often vary in form but are functional in producing similar outcomes. We discuss such classes of behavior because they provide an alternative approach to behavioral classification, one that emphasizes the conditions under which problematic behavior is most likely to occur or the purpose that such behavior serves. Thinking about behavior in this way can suggest hypotheses as to why people act in the way that they do and aid our understanding as to why some individuals engage in multiple kinds of problematic behavior (e.g., agoraphobic avoidance, obsessive thinking, substance abuse, dissociation, and self-harm). Such behaviors, although vastly different in form, might perform the same or similar functions for the individual (e.g., escape and avoidance). Knowledge of the conditions that facilitate problematic behavior and the functions that such behavior serve can, in turn, be used in the design of intervention strategies that specifically target the contextual factors in which behavior is embedded.

In the latter portion of this chapter, we offer examples of how functional and topographical classification schemes can be integrated to provide what might be regarded as an optimal formulation of the client's problematic behaviors and factors that may maintain them. First, however, we discuss how nomothetic or general principles and observations can usefully inform the idiographic or individual assessment and treatment of the person.

THE APPLICATION OF BOTH IDIOGRAPHIC AND NOMOTHETIC APPROACHES TO ASSESSMENT, CONCEPTUALIZATION, AND TREATMENT OF THE INDIVIDUAL'S BEHAVIOR

In behavior therapy, client assessments and treatment formulations are based on an idiographic or individual assessment. This is done in the recognition that each individual is distinctly different from any other in terms of learning history and physiological makeup. In the same way, each person exists in a unique context. Given the uniqueness of individuals in these areas, behavior therapists enter into therapeutic work with recognition and appreciation of the diversity among persons, and accordingly tailor their assessment and treatment approaches to the strengths and needs of each client.

In their initial assessments and formulation of a given client's problem areas, behavior therapists also consider the relevance of general principles of human behavior as well as what is generally known about response patterns similar to those displayed by the client. The use of relevant nomothetic principles and observations as guides in the assessment and formulation of the individual case is an efficient way to proceed because the therapist does not need to start from scratch for each new client. Rather, such an approach can suggest ideas about possible variables that influence the client's behavior as well as possible therapeutic strategies could be particularly effective, ideas that can subsequently be evaluated in the context of an ongoing idiographic assessment of the client. In a way, attention to nomothetic principles and observations in the context of behavior therapy is like rule-governed behavior. That is, the therapist might have certain rules that are something like, "If the client displays substance abuse patterns, then these behaviors are likely maintained through both positive and negative reinforcement functions," or, "if the client displays obsessive–compulsive tendencies, then a therapy program based on exposure and response prevention will likely be the most efficacious treatment approach." These nomothetically derived rules, when followed, will often result in positive therapeutic effects (Tarrier & Calam, 2002). A behavior therapist will likely seek to establish the relevance of these nomothetic rules for a given client before undertaking a given course of therapy, however.

For example, from a behavioral perspective, a good deal is known about phobic behavior. Common nomothetic vulnerability factors among persons who display such behavior include elevated autonomic reactivity and the tendency to view the experience of anxiety as harmful, dangerous, or threatening. Furthermore, there is some evidence to suggest that these vulnerability factors are influenced by a combination of biological endowments (e.g., temperament) and early learning experiences (Craske & Barlow, 2001). Other relevant nomothetic principles and observations suggest that people who display phobic behavior tend to avoid situations or objects that evoke marked physiological reactions (e.g., elevated heart rate, increased respiration rate, dizziness) and associated feelings of anxiety or panic. If a situation or object is encountered that results in such physiological states and emotions, a phobic person often will actively seek to get away from these sources in the presence of which fear and aversive physiological sensations are felt. As the phobic individual is able to establish physical distance between himself or herself and the object or situation, relief from unpleasant physiological and emotional states is typically experienced. The anxiety-reduction function of avoidance behaviors is often viewed within behavior therapy as a maintaining factor for phobic anxiety and avoidance through the process of negative reinforcement. Furthermore, as a result of the effects of escape and avoidance, the individual learns that such behavior can have relieving effects and are hence effective means of short-term coping. Overreliance on escape and avoidance as a method of coping is often ultimately detrimental, however, because it almost inevitably results in the avoidance of an increasingly wider range of situations or contexts over time. On the basis of such formulations of phobia, exposure therapy is typically undertaken, whereby the individual is gradually and systematically exposed to aversive physiological sensations and feared objects or situations, during which engagement in escape coping responses is discouraged. As a result of such exposure, the client learns that his or her unpleasant internal reactions will subside in time and that presumed negative consequences associated with remaining in the situation do not occur.

Studies that have evaluated the effectiveness of exposure therapy for phobic behavior typically involve the assignment of phobic clients to one or more treatment conditions. Treatment assignment is often either random or prescribed, and not based on an individualized functional assessment. That is, clients who display a topographical response class (phobic behavior) are assigned to receive a treatment that is thought, on the basis of general (nomothetic) principles or observations, to be potentially efficacious for the majority of individuals who display such behavior patterns. When cognitive–behavioral therapies that include exposure components are applied in this manner, they are strikingly effective for the vast majority individuals (Craske & Barlow, 2001). Even though associated success rates are high, not all individuals who display phobic behaviors benefit equally from therapy, a finding that suggests the need for the development of individualized treatment strategies (Craske & Barlow, 2001). Although nomothetic treatment guides or rules often work for many individuals who display similar topographical and functional response classes, the applicability of these general observations and principles should be evaluated rather than assumed for each individual case.

Functional Responses Classes: A Behavioral Analogy to Personality From a Functional Perspective

As discussed in the previous chapter, topographical response classes or behavior patterns constitute one behavioral analogy to the concept of personality. Likewise, functional response classes represent another behavioral analogy to the personality concept (Lubinski & Thompson, 1986) and consist of a group of behaviors that, although possibly different in form, are alike to the extent that they produce the same or similar outcomes (Follette et al., 2000; Mallot et al., 2000). Just like with topographical response classes, functional response class categories refer to the classification of behaviors, not people (Wulfert, Greenway, & Dougher, 1996).

Functional response classes that produce similar outcomes are often under the influence of the same class of environmental variables. As such, the function of these behaviors can often be understood with reference to the three-term contingency described in chapter 1, that is, the antecedent conditions that set the occasion for a behavior to occur (i.e., establishing operations and environmental cues or events), the behavior itself, and the consequences that follow the behavior (i.e., reinforcers, punishers). To this we would also add biological endowments (including heritable predispositions), other biological variables (e.g., natural effects of aging, onset of disease processes, change in biological systems or structures due to accident or injury), and the effects learning history on one's physiological makeup, collectively defined as *organismic variables* (or the "O" in the SORC model described in chap. 3), which mediate or moderate the association between environmental events and responses.

The Context of Functional Response Classes: Relationships Among Stimulus Events, Response Topographies, and Response Functions

Like other forms of behavior, behaviors that define functional response classes occur within a context and are often enacted to produce a particular outcome. Naugle and Follette (1998) described the varied associations that stimulus events, behavior topography, and behavior function may share. Consideration of the nature of these relationships is potentially important in the assessment of the client and in the development of a therapy plan based on assessment information. Following is a summary of their conceptual framework.

The Same Stimulus Conditions Can Lead to the Development of Different Response Forms or Topographies

Individuals who are exposed to similar events may demonstrate vastly different behavioral outcomes following these events. For example, it has been repeatedly observed that persons who have been exposed to the same traumatic event are often affected in different ways and that factors that predate trauma exposure often predict variability in outcomes. Research has identified a number of pretrauma risk factors for the subsequent development of posttraumatic stress disorder (PTSD), and these include the experience of negative affect or neuroticism, a preexisting psychological disorder, family history of psychological disorders, family instability, and lower levels of social support (McNally, 1999). Responses a person displays during exposure to a traumatic event, particularly dissociative behaviors, are also associated with the persistence of PTSD-related symptoms over time (McFarlane & Yehuda, 1996; McNally, 1999). For such individuals, the possibility exists that dissociative reactions to acute stressors may have been previously established in other contexts and maintained through their associated negative reinforcement (escape, avoidance) function. Dissociative reactions observed during a given traumatic event might simply be an extension of this response pattern or an alternative expression of a functional response class of avoidant behaviors. Given that dissociative tendencies are often associated with broader experiential avoidance repertoires (Wagner & Linehan, 1998), it follows that individuals who already have such functional response classes firmly established before trauma exposure would be more vulnerable to the subsequent development of PTSD, particularly because this condition has also been suggested to be maintained, in part, by experiential avoidance (Walser & Hayes, 1998).

Different Stimulus Conditions Can Result in the Establishment of Similar Response Topographies

Different causal factors, or stimulus conditions, can result in displays of similar forms or manifestations of behavior across persons. Research on the etiology of psychological disorders suggests that several factors can, singly or in combination, give rise to signs of symptoms consistent with a given diagnostic concept or problematic behavior pattern (Adams & Sutker, 2001; Barlow & Durand, 2002). Consequently in the assessment of persons and in the development of a client formulation, it is important to consider that common forms of behavioral expression seen in clinical settings may have different and unique origins across persons and may similarly be maintained by varied and unique current contextual factors.

Behaviors That Are Similar in Response Topography Can Have Different Associated Functions

Several studies converge on the observation that behaviors that appear similar in form often have widely different functions across persons or different functions for the same person dependent on other contextual factors (Brown et al., 2002; Wulfert et al., 1996). This may explain why there is often a great deal of heterogeneity observed among members of a diagnostic category or among persons who are of a similar "personality type." For example, Wulfert et al. (1996) noted that a variety of theorists who have developed taxonomies of problem drinkers tend to converge on two subtypes: those with anxious–dependent traits and those with a more chronic abuse pattern coupled with antisocial traits. Such within-group heterogeneity may account for why personality constructs account for only a limited amount of variation in specific construct-related behaviors (Mischel, 1968). Considerable within-group heterogeneity presents problems for constructs or diagnostic concepts that are strictly defined according to response topography. That is, if responses that appear similar are actually associated with different etiologies or maintaining factors, then it is possible that treatments may be offered according to topographical considerations that have no bearing on the associated function of the behavior targeted for treatment.

Behaviors With Different Forms or Topographies May Have Similar Functions

Many clinicians and researchers have observed that behavioral topographies that have vastly different structural characteristics (e.g., alcoholism, self-injury, binge eating, behavioral avoidance) may serve similar functions for the individual (e.g., attenuate or alleviate aversive internal states, such as unpleasant emotions or physiological sensations). From a behavioral perspective, understanding the function of a behavior is a requirement if one is to facilitate behavior change through either an alteration of the context in which it occurs or by teaching alternative and healthier forms of behavior that produce similar effects.

Our discussion of functional response classes in the pages that follow go into greater depth about the characteristics of such classes and provide relevant examples of different categories of functional response classes and the domains within which they are likely to be expressed.

Goals Associated With Functional Response Class Assessment

A primary goal associated with the assessment of functional behaviors, including functional response classes, is to identify modifiable internal and external antecedents and consequences associated with maintenance of problematic behavior targeted for treatment (Follette et al., 2000). As suggested by Follette et al., the success of an assessment based on the functional properties of behavior depends, in part, on the clinicians' ability to modify those antecedent and consequent events that maintain problematic behaviors.

An understanding of the types of *antecedent conditions* associated with an increased likelihood of problematic behaviors being displayed is critical for understanding the context that occasions those behaviors. Generally speaking, any situational context (e.g., specific person, place, object, event; establishing operations or motivational states; content of verbal statements that convey rules for behavior, such as in the form of beliefs or expectancies) that has been present in the past when the problematic behavior patterns have occurred can subsequently serve as a salient cue that increases the likelihood that behaviors within the class will be displayed. The identification of these cues and their association with problematic behavior is often one of the first considerations in the development of a functional understanding of a client's behavior.

In addition to an assessment of possible environmental antecedent conditions that may influence behavior, we suggest, too, that attention be given to the possibility that *verbal rules* may serve as an antecedent influence on behavior in certain contexts. Such rules, if present and influential, can themselves be targeted for treatment in an effort to modify behavior. Examples of verbal rules that may influence behavior include, "Why should I try? I never get what I want"; "Live for today, because who knows what tomorrow might bring"; "If I make myself vomit, I won't get fat"; "Cutting myself is the only way that I can make myself feel real"; and "Every time I open up to someone, I get hurt." Often, such rule or expectancy statements reveal the nature of factors that influence behavior. That is, rules reveal whether behavioral displays will be more or less likely under certain circumstances, according to the consequences associated with actions referred to in the rule statements.

In the assessment of *consequences* associated with behavior, it is often useful to distinguish among short- and long-term consequences. Behavior influenced by immediate consequences tends to be controlled by reinforcers or punishers that immediately follow behavior. Behavior under the influence of more distal consequences, in contrast, is often under rule control. A useful pretreatment assessment goal is to evaluate whether problematic response classes are primarily maintained by positive or negative reinforcement processes (or both), because these different consequent events have implications for the nature of the therapy that might be most beneficial for the client concerned (Wulfert et al., 1996). In general, behavior maintained through the process of positive reinforcement is influenced by the pleasure-enhancing function it serves, whereas behavior maintained by negative reinforcement is often influenced by the cessation of aversive states or conditions that it provides (Wulfert et al., 1996).

Finally, during the assessment of functional response classes relevant for treatment, it is often useful to evaluate other behavioral repertoires (e.g., coping skills, social skills, problem-solving skills) that can be used to counteract or substitute for the problematic response class (Wulfert et al., 1996).

EXAMPLES OF FUNCTIONAL BEHAVIORS AND THEIR RESPONSE DOMAINS

William Follette and colleagues have written extensively on functional response domains (see Follette, Bach, & Follette, 1993; Follette & Hayes, 2000, pp. 393–398; Follette et al., 2000; Hayes & Follette, 1992; Naugle & Follette, 1998), and much of the discussion that follows is influenced by their work. Within this section, a number of functional response domains under the influence of various environmental contingencies are reviewed. The list provided is not exhaustive, nor is it suggested that these response domains are independent of one another. Indeed, in many instances, there will be a variety of stimulus situations, response repertoire problems, and reinforcement factors that, in combination, result in problematic forms of behavior.

Within this section, we note the various influences that give rise to different response classes and the various forms such classes may take. We begin our discussion with response classes associated with antecedent conditions that may set the occasion for problematic behaviors, namely, discriminative stimuli and establishing operations. This is then followed by a discussion of response problems that are often associated with relatively ineffective or unhealthy forms of behavior across many situational contexts. Finally, we discuss reinforcement factors that may make problematic behaviors more likely and more adaptive or healthy responses less likely.

Problems With Stimulus Control and the Problematic Influence of Establishing Operations

In this section, antecedent conditions are discussed that set the occasion for particular forms of problematic behavior to occur. In chapter 3, we differentiated between two types of antecedent conditions: (a) discriminative stimuli and (b) establishing operations. *Discriminative stimuli* were described as events or cues that indicated the likelihood that reinforcement or punishment would follow displays of particular forms of behavior. These events or cues can take place in the external environment, or, alternatively, they may take place in the internal environment (i.e., private events that take place under the skin). Discriminative stimuli, then, are informational signals that, as a result of a person's learning history, indicate whether certain behaviors are likely to be reinforced or punished.

In contrast, *establishing operations* refer to the motivational influence that certain environmental conditions have on behavior by altering the reinforcing or punishing qualities of some events. That is, environmental events that produce states of satiation, deprivation, aversive arousal, or other physiological events can, in turn, alter the reinforcing qualities that may follow behavior. Consideration of possible establishing operations for problematic behavior is important because the reduction or elimination of such conditions will often decrease the likelihood that such behavior will be reinforced.

Inappropriate Stimulus Control

As discussed in chapter 3, stimulus control of behavior is evident when a given response is more likely to occur if one class of stimuli is present and less likely to occur in the presence of another stimulus class. The probability that a behavior will occur in the presence of a class of stimuli will be a direct function of the individual's learning history in relation to those stimuli, that is, whether behavior has been reinforced or punished in the presence of those stimuli.

In the case of inappropriate stimulus control, a response is emitted that is not appropriate for the stimulus conditions within which it occurs. Whereas the form of the response itself may be appropriate and effective in some contexts, the context in which it is emitted is neither appropriate nor effective.

An example of this response class offered by Follette and Hayes (2000) is the disclosure of too much personal information given the nature of the occasion. That is, it is often regarded as inappropriate for persons to disclose highly personal or intimate aspects of themselves to relative strangers. Others often experience such actions as unpleasant, and often avoid individuals who inappropriately self-disclose as a result.

Another example is the act of complaining in certain contexts. Coyne (1989) and others have suggested that among some persons, the social environment may have initially reinforced acts of complaining though the provision of attention, reassurance, and advice and consequently established the social environment as a cue that signals reinforcement for complaining behavior. Over time, however, the social environment will often seek to avoid individuals who constantly complain in their presence. Perhaps because of learning experiences that associated the social environment with reinforcement for complaining, individuals may continue to complain in an effort to receive attention or reassurance, even though the consequences of such behavior have shifted, and the social environment is no longer acting as a discriminative stimulus that signals reinforcement for such behavior.

For individuals who inappropriately self-disclose or complain, social skills training that seeks to substitute positive interpersonal behaviors for inappropriate complaints or disclosures may be indicated. As an alternative, a therapeutic goal might be to shift the expression of such behaviors to more appropriate contexts, such as to therapeutic settings (Naugle & Follette, 1998).

Discrimination Deficits of Private Events (or Inappropriate Self-Generated Stimulus Control)

The primary problem associated with this response class is that the individual displays difficulty discriminating among private events (e.g., different emotional states) or accurately labeling such events (i.e., applying a word label that accurately describes the pattern of emotional arousal experienced). For example, an individual may have difficulty differentiating between anxious arousal and angry arousal and as a result may mislabel his or her feeling state. Such mislabeling may, in turn, contribute to behavior that is incongruent with the actual arousal state experienced but congruent with the misapplied label (e.g., the person may verbally attack another when feeling anxious).

The ability to discriminate among private events is a complex skill that is often dependent on an attentive and empathic social environment during early development. For example, when it comes to reinforcing a child for attaching an appropriate verbal label to public events, the task of doing so is fairly straightforward. If a child points to an object and exclaims "apple!" the child might be told something like, "no, that is an orange." In the future, if a child points to an apple and exclaims "apple!" the child is more likely to be reinforced for this response when made in the presence of the apple. When it comes to reinforcing the application of labels to private events such as feelings, however, the process is more difficult. For example, a child may say, "I feel sad," when he or she actually has a feeling of anger. Should the social environment reinforce the use of the word "sad" in the presence of anger, then faulty learning occurs, and the child is less likely to discriminate his or her experience accurately.

Clinically, some populations of clients seem to have greater difficulty in identifying and labeling private events, particularly emotions. This difficulty or inability has sometimes been labeled *alexithymia*. Individuals who have childhood histories of abuse or neglect are among those individuals who more commonly report difficulties in discriminating and accurately labeling varying states of emotional arousal (Cloitre, Scarvalone, & Difede, 1997). As noted by Follette et al. (2000), difficulty in accurately labeling one's emotions can pose several problems. For one, clients who have such difficulties may not be able to respond emotionally to events or people in their social environment. Second, such clients may have difficulty expressing to others the impact that their actions are having. Therapeutic interventions for such deficits may include discrimination training among emotional states and training in self-labeling in which feeling-state words are taught and applied to various emotional experiences. (These and other therapeutic techniques mentioned in this chapter are more fully described in chap. 6.)

In a broader application of problems in self-generated stimulus control, we note that in everyday language, private events are often conceptualized as experiences of the self. Consistent with the approach taken thus far, when we speak of "self," we are not speaking of some entity, trait, or cognitive structure that causes or guides behavior. Rather, like other behaviorists (e.g., Koerner et al., 1996; Kohlenberg & Tsai, 1991), we consider the experience of self as the result of processes involved in the identification and description of events that are experienced. Many of these experiences involve private experiences, or those that occur under the skin and are not directly observable to persons other than the person within whom they occur. The processes involved in self-experience also include a combination of both private and public events (Koerner et al., 1996). In short, from a behavioral view, to understand the development and experience of the concept of self is to understand the learning history and maintenance factors that specify the stimulus events that influence or evoke the verbal response "I" (Kohlenberg & Tsai, 1991).

As described by Koerner et al. (1996), much of what we regard as self-experience begins to develop in early childhood and coincides with the emergence of language abilities. Soon after the emergence of such abilities, the social environment prompts, models, and shapes the appropriate use of self-referent terms, such as "I" or "me," as in "I want a cookie," "I am cold," or "I see the car." The social environment also typically assists the developing child to discriminate private experience from experiences or events that involve others (e.g., "I am cold. Are you cold?").

Koerner et al. (1996) went on to suggest that once this basic repertoire of verbalizing concrete self-experiences has been established, more abstract forms of self-referent statements are modeled and shaped by the social environment, such as "I feel . . . ," "I think . . . ," "I remember . . . ," or "I believe . . . ." Throughout this process, the concept of "I" or "me" becomes repeatedly associated with private experience. The word "I" eventually emerges as a single functional unit that has independent meaning (Kohlenberg & Tsai, 1991).

In the course of typical development, then, the concept of "I" or "me" becomes less context dependent (e.g., "I want cookie" → "I want" → "I") and correspondingly becomes more strongly associated with private experience. That is, after a child learns several larger functional units (e.g., "I want cookie," "I want doggie,", "I want mommy"), somewhat smaller functional unit emerge (e.g., "I want"), which can then be combined with almost any other verbal label that has become a part of the child's language repertoire. As a result, the child can construct unique or novel statements that combine "I want" with other verbal labels present in the language repertoire.

Once a large number of "I ______" statements have been learned (e.g., "I want," "I see," "I am," "I feel"), then the possibility exists for a smaller functional unit to emerge, "I." The perspective of "I" remains constant across all contexts where "I want," "I see," "I am," and "I feel" statements are overtly or covertly made. That is, the concept of "I" or "me" in relation to private experiences remains a constant, even though the nature of the experiences (e.g., content of thoughts, nature of emotional experiences) changes within brief time spans or over extended periods. Similarly, the concept of "I" or "me" typically remains constant over extended periods even though the very body within which these experiences are observed undergoes change (e.g., gets taller, fatter, older; Kohlenberg & Tsai, 1991).

The concept of "I," then, is a functional unit that is under the stimulus influence of a particular locus, namely, the nature of the environment where the experiences in question take place—the environment within the skin. The concept of "I" or "me," however, can become uncertain, vague, or paradoxical in the event that there are failures associated with the previously mentioned learning sequences. A more significant example of such a failure may occur when self-referential statements (e.g., "I want," "I feel") remain largely under the influence of public stimuli, or other persons in one's social environment. For example, a child who is told "No, you don't want a cookie" following the child's accurate verbal statement of "I want a cookie" can become somewhat confused about how the term "I" actually relates to private experiences. Such improper responding by the social environment may result in the relative disconnection between private events and the context in which they occur (i.e., under one's skin). As suggested by Koerner et al. (1996), those parents who are distracted or otherwise unavailable, emotionally chaotic, or thought-disordered are perhaps among those who are most vulnerable to failures in assisting their children make accurate discriminations of private experiences and linking such experiences to the concept of "I" or "me."

In another example of an outcome associated with a failure in this process, consider individuals who report difficulty discriminating the locus of their own private experiences. Statements that may reveal this discrimination problem may take the form of "I don't know who I am," or "I feel differently when I am around different people," or "Who I think myself to be changes so dramatically at times." In such instances, it may be the case that "I" statements are not evoked by private stimuli or events as much as by external social stimulus events (i.e., other people to whom these private events have been associated with). That is, such individuals may have a learning history whereby statements such as "I want" or "I feel" are under the influence of others whereby the presence of certain others acts as a discriminative stimulus for such reports. As a result, private experiences become partially or completely under the influence of others, and, similarly, the experience of self will be partially or completely under the influence of others.

A less severe example of a failure in this process may be evident among individuals who have difficulty expressing their preferences across different contexts because the verbalization of such preferences is often not the result of one's own learning history but is instead affected by the preferences of others in the immediate social environment (Naugle & Follette, 1998). The degree of difficulty a person may encounter in relation to the experience of the self is in direct proportion to the degree to which "I" statements are under the influence of private events relative to the social (public) environment (Kohlenberg & Tsai, 1991).

Discrimination Difficulties Among Environmental Contexts

A principal characteristic of this functional problem is evident when the individual experiences different environmental features as functionally similar when they are not and responds in a rigid and inflexible manner as a result. In one example of this, data are accumulating that suggest some individuals with PTSD demonstrate certain learning, habituation, and stimulus discrimination impairments, all of which may be related to the physiological effects of excessive stimulation of the central nervous system during exposure to trauma (McFarlane, Weber, & Clark, 1993; van der Kolk, 1996). Among people with PTSD, problems in stimulus discrimination may be evident in a variety of ways. For example, stimuli that are topographically similar to stimuli present when the trauma originally occurred can be experienced as threatening or dangerous, even though such stimuli in nontraumatic contexts might be quite innocuous. In a possible manifestation of this, a traumatized war veteran in a noncombat context may experience pronounced fear and panic at the sounds of a helicopter overhead, particularly if helicopter sounds were a part of the larger environment in which traumatizing events occurred. Another possible manifestation of such deficits may be evident in the pronounced acoustic startle response among traumatized persons. Such observations may suggest that a subset of persons with PTSD has greater difficulty in both evaluating some forms of sensory stimulation and responding with appropriate levels of sensory stimulation. To facilitate discrimination when impairments are noted, discrimination training or exposure-based procedures might be used.

Overly Rigid Rule Governance

Rules function in a manner similar to discriminative stimuli because rules often suggest response–consequence relations when certain stimuli are present. Sometimes, as a result of similar past experiences, people verbalize rules about potential behavioral contingencies. Often, such rules may be accurate. On such occasions, behavior guided by rules may result in more efficient forms of behavior because the individual does not need to go through several trial-and-error tests to discern which behavior works in a given context (Follette et al., 2000). Other times, however, rules may not accurately state the true relations between behavior and consequence. Such instances can be particularly problematic because rules, once formed, are often resistant to change (Hayes, Brownstein, Zettle, Rosenfarb, & Korn, 1986).

With this type of functional problem, the individual may fail to discriminate accurately the actual relationship between behavior and consequence as a result of rigid adherence to rules that inaccurately describe the contingencies associated with behavior. Such an absence of flexibility may lead to the display of behaviors that result in ineffective or aversive outcomes, consequences that could have been avoided if the person's behavior were affected more by the actual contingencies associated with behavior than rigid adherence to inaccurate rules.

As an example of rigid rule adherence incompatible with actual behavioral contingencies, we previously noted the example in which some persons with bulimia engage in purge behavior based on a rule that suggests such actions will effectively eliminate calories consumed during a binge episode. Research on the effectiveness of purging indicates, however, that such a rule is often inaccurate, particularly when one considers the number of calories consumed during an episode of binge eating (Bo-Linn et al., 1983; Kaye et al., 1993). A person with anorexia nervosa may similarly be operating under a rule that implies that control of eating will enhance self-control and mastery and result in a more attractive appearance.

Therapeutic techniques that might be used in such circumstances would be those that challenge rigid rule following and seek to bring behavior more in line with actual contingencies. Techniques of traditional cognitive therapy can be applied to this end, as could behavior interventions such as hypothesis testing or those that seek to alter verbal rules and functions that dominate behavior regulation.

Ineffective Arrangement of Contingencies

With this functional problem, problematic behavior is the result of immediate environmental features that either fail to influence behavior appropriately or set the occasion for more problematic forms of behavior to occur. In an example, a parent may use sugary, sweet snacks to stop a child from throwing a tantrum in a public context. That is, when the child throws a tantrum, the parent may try to stop the behavior by giving the child a cookie. In the short term, this works. The parent's behavior of giving a child a cookie while the child is in the throes of a tantrum functions to terminate various aversive aspects of the environment (e.g., the child's shrills, unwanted stares from others) and is hence negatively reinforced. In a similar way, the child's tantrum behavior is positively reinforced, as he received a cookie from his parent as a result of it. As a consequence, the child has learned that when he wants a cookie in a public setting, an effective way to experience this outcome is to scream, yell, stomp, and say "no!"

In another example, sweet and highly caloric snacks brought into the home and left on countertops would often not be particularly helpful for someone who is dieting, because the presence of these food items in observable locations around the house sets the occasion for their consumption. That is, if a person comes home from a difficult day at work and sees a box of doughnuts on the kitchen counter and no other foods, what do you think that person will do?

To modify behaviors that are maintained by the ineffective arrangement of contingencies, contingency management procedures may be used. Stimulus control procedures might similarly be applied by which stimulus events that set the occasion for problematic behavior to occur are reduced or eliminated.

Substance Intoxication

Intoxication as a result of substance use, misuse, or abuse can act as a form of establishing operation for behavior. Recall that establishing operations (or motivational events), in general, have a potentiating effect on the reinforcing quality of events that follow behavior. For example, deprivation of alcohol for an alcohol-dependent individual will facilitate physiological withdrawal and potentiate the negative reinforcing qualities of alcohol consumption. It has been demonstrated that a variety of drugs can alter one's sensitivity and responsiveness to reinforcing or punishing consequences (Gray, 1987a). Often, substance intoxication acts as a disinhibitor for behavior by either attenuating aversive arousal that might otherwise be experienced in some contexts (e.g., social anxiety) or by increasing the salience of potential reinforcers relative to potential punishers, as may be evident in risk-taking behaviors displayed during intoxicated states (Wulfert et al., 1996).

States of Physiological Arousal or Activation

Certain physiological states, when activated or aroused as a result of some environmental event, can alter the reinforcing or punishing consequences associated with particular forms of behavior. For example, among those who experience anxiety acutely or perhaps more chronically in relation to temperament factors, environments where anxious arousal occurs may be experienced as aversive and thus enhance the negative reinforcement function of escape or avoidance behaviors in those environments. Just as the experience of anxiety may potentiate the negative reinforcing qualities of escape or avoidance behaviors, the experience of anger may likewise potentiate the reinforcing qualities associated with verbally or physically aggressive acts directed toward others.

When physiological activation or arousal states accompany problematic behavior, therapeutic interventions that seek to reduce or eliminate these establishing operations may be particularly beneficial. Exposure therapies often result in a reduction in the influence that establishing operations have on behavior (Brondolo, DiGiuseppe, & Tafrate, 1997; Craske & Barlow, 2001). Intervention strategies such as relaxation strategies that seek to produce physiological states incompatible with anxiety, anger, or other aversive emotions (Davis, Eshelman, & McKay, 2000) may similarly be helpful.

Response Problems

In this section, we discuss behavior patterns that are problematic as a result of their inappropriate or excessive display, a likely result of the positively reinforcing consequences associated with such actions. We also delineate examples of behavior classes that either are not displayed or are weakly displayed in appropriate contexts, perhaps as a result of such behaviors not being learned in the first place or not being adequately reinforced during the person's learning history, or because the person has been inappropriately punished in past environments.

Behavioral Deficits

Behavioral deficits may be evident when individuals do not display an adequate range or repertoire of behavior for functioning effectively in a variety of contexts. Such deficits may arise because the environment did not model or shape such behaviors. Alternatively, the environment may have punished such behaviors, thus resulting in behavioral extinction or a low rate of behavior occurrence. Because of absent or underdeveloped behavioral repertoires in particular areas, an individual may be unable to behave effectively in certain environmental contexts and, consequently, may not experience reinforcement of behavior (Naugle & Follette, 1998).

For example, some behavioral theories have suggested that depression may be a consequence of an inability to produce reinforcement from the social environment for one's own behavior (Lewinsohn & Gotlib, 1995). Therapeutic approaches based on such models are likely to include a social skills training component so that such persons can learn more effective forms of social behavior not currently in their repertoire and, as a result, become more likely to experience the range of reinforcing qualities associated with social relationships.

In general, social skills deficits, if present, can result in an absence of reinforcement and perhaps even punishment from the social environment. In the case of children with social skills deficits, for example, group entry skills may be lacking and result in passive isolation from peer groups. Such isolation, in turn, can result in further lags in the development of age-appropriate social skills (Scotti, Morris, McNeil, & Hawkins, 1996). Among adults, social skills deficits can be devastating for the quality of one's social, family, and vocational life.

In general, intervention approaches that are geared toward the development or strengthening of weak behavioral repertoires involve direct instruction, modeling, and behavioral rehearsal. It would also be important, too, for a therapist to establish that apparent behavioral deficits are not instead environmentally suppressed behaviors. In such instances, weakly or nondisplayed behaviors (e.g., deficit assertiveness skills) may exist in one's behavioral repertoire, but suppressed as a result of a current contingencies that punish displays of such behavior (e.g., in the case of a person who may be physically assaulted by a spouse for displays of assertion; Dow, 1994).

Experiential Avoidance

Experiential avoidance as a functional response class can be conceptualized as occurring when "a person is unwilling to remain in contact with particular private experiences (e.g., bodily sensations, emotions, thoughts, memories, behavioral predispositions) and takes steps to alter the form or frequency of these events or contexts that occasion them" (Hayes et al., 1996, p. 1154). That which is avoided is often experienced as bad, threatening, dangerous, overwhelming, unpleasant, aversive, awful, terrible, repulsive, dreadful, and the like by the individual who avoids. Theorists and therapists from a variety of theoretical orientations and therapeutic schools have suggested that many forms or expressions of psychopathology are maintained experiential avoidance processes (Hayes et al., 1996).

Like many forms of unhealthy behavior or psychopathology, behaviors that have an experiential avoidance function are most likely maintained by their short-term effects. Furthermore, the dominant reinforcement process that maintains this class of behaviors is negative reinforcement or rules that specify negative outcomes associated with certain physical states (e.g., "When I'm anxious, I feel like I'm going to go crazy and everyone will look at me and stare") or behaviors ("If I go into the mall, I'll have a panic attack"). Not all forms of experiential avoidance are unhealthy, however. For example, noticing and removing one's hand from a hot surface (e.g., a stove heating element) is often much more desirable than leaving one's hand on the surface and accepting the pain. Experiential avoidance can have a much more malignant quality, of course, as evident in its maintaining function for a variety of anxiety disorders (e.g., phobia, obsessive–compulsive disorder), substance abuse and dependence disorders, and perhaps the most experientially avoidant form of behavior, suicide. Although we acknowledge that not every person who displays behaviors consistent with these conditions does so as a result of experiential avoidance or negative reinforcement processes, we do assume that there is at least a large subset of individuals who meet diagnostic criteria for these conditions whose behavior is maintained by this function.

Because one might experientially avoid for a variety of reasons, it is important for a therapist to assess the context within which avoidance occurs, how avoidance is behaviorally manifested (e.g., behavioral escape, psychological escape in the form of dissociation or numbing, self-injurious behavior, substance misuse), and what other behaviors currently exist in the client's behavioral repertoire that may serve a similar function yet be more adaptive or healthy in form.

Inappropriate Conditioned Emotional Response

Examples of this response class are most likely to be observed in the context of emotional disorders, although it may also been seen in other forms of disorder (e.g., sexual deviations and paraphilias). Many behavioral paradigms suggest that emotions and arousal states can be classically conditioned to a variety of environmental cues. The nature of the emotion or arousal that is elicited by conditional stimuli will subsequently influence whether these stimuli are approached or avoided. In the case of stimuli associated with past trauma, for example, individuals may seek to actively avoid such stimuli because of the unpleasant emotions that such stimuli elicit. Stimuli that elicit pleasant emotional responses may be actively approached.

For conditioned negative emotional responses such as anxiety that lead to avoidance, therapeutic techniques such as exposure, response prevention, and modeling may be appropriate. For inappropriate conditioned positive emotional responses, such as those that accompany arousal to sexually inappropriate stimuli, interventions that involve reconditioning may be appropriate, such as covert conditioning that pairs inappropriate sexual stimuli and arousal with aversive consequences, orgasmic reconditioning, as well as social skills training and relapse prevention strategies.

Behavioral Excesses

Behavioral excesses may be evident when an individual displays particular forms of behavior that are excessive in terms of frequency, intensity, or duration, to the point that such excesses are associated with distress or impairment in functioning in one or more domains (e.g., social, occupational; Naugle & Follette, 1998). In work with clients in the early stages of assessment, it is often useful to ask clients which aspects of their behavior are problematic. One approach that can be used to evaluate this is to ask whether the behavior in question appears to be happening too much, or if it seems too intense or goes on for too long (Follette et al., 2000).

Behavioral excesses may take on a variety of forms. As with any other functional response class, it is important to distinguish among various forms of behavioral excess according to the functions that such behaviors serve. For example, some forms of behavior may be displayed excessively because of their associated reinforcement function. Many forms of behavioral excesses have attention as a maintaining function, particularly in children (Scotti et al., 1996). Other examples of behavioral excesses that have a strong associated reinforcement function include pathological or unhealthy forms of gambling or promiscuous sex, to the point that such behavior has a compulsive-like quality to it and is associated with distress or impairment. Furthermore, as noted by Wulfert et al. (1996), excessive displays of behaviors consistent with such reinforcement-based disorders often occur under inappropriate motivational conditions (or establishing operations) associated with stress, anger, anxiety, or depression. Thus, in assessments of the contexts within which such behavioral excesses occur, it would be useful to examine the possible antecedent influences that such establishing operations may serve.

Another behavioral excess can take the form of excessive self-monitoring of behavior. Here, the individual may be more concerned about getting the form of behavior correct rather than focusing on behavioral effectiveness. Perfectionism that interferes with task completion may be an example of such a response class. For such individuals, response prevention strategies that block engagement in excessive perfectionistic-like behaviors may be a useful form of intervention.

Individuals may also display excessive amounts of aggressive, hostile, or coercive behaviors that are clearly inappropriate for the environmental contexts in which they occur. In such instances, exposure (Brondolo et al., 1997) or self-control forms of therapy (Rachlin, 2000) may be beneficial.

Problems With Reinforcing Contingencies

In this section, we review examples of functional response classes that are primarily affected by reinforcing consequences available for the behaviors in question. As we note subsequently, some of these response classes may be maintained by inappropriate reinforcement from the environment. Other response classes mentioned comprise behaviors that, although potentially effective, become less likely or extinguish because of a failure of environmental support through reinforcement processes. In addition, other classes of behavior may be influenced by aversive consequences, and these consequences, in turn, can result in additional problems.

Behavior Ineffectively Controlled

With this response class, the consequences that follow behavior are not sufficient to affect its future probability. Impulsive forms of behavior, for example, are often not optimally effective in many situational contexts, particularly if such behavior is also associated with aversive outcomes. Mindfulness-based intervention techniques that facilitate awareness within the moment may be especially useful for such individuals, as would be self-control techniques.

Punishment seems to have, at best, a modest influence on the criminal behavior of some individuals who frequently come to the attention of the criminal justice system. Some have suggested that this relative insensitivity to the effects of punishment is mediated or moderated by temperamental factors, such as fearlessness or hypoemotionality (Hare, 1998; Lykken, 1995), high impulsivity in conjunction with low anxiety or fear (Arnett, 1997; Farmer et al., 2003), or high impulsivity in conjunction with high levels of negative affect when the individual receives punishment for behavior while pursuing reward (Wallace & Newman, 1997).

Insufficient Environmental Reinforcement

With this functional domain, reinforcers are generally not available for behavior. As a consequence, behavior is likely to extinguish (become less probable) because the environment fails to maintain it through reinforcement processes. Lewinsohn (Lewinsohn & Gotlib, 1995) speculated that a low rate of response-contingent positive reinforcement (RCPR) is a common environmental feature associated within an increased vulnerability to depression. One aspect of interventions based on the low RCPR model of depression is to involve the client in activity scheduling to facilitate behavioral activation in environmental contexts that are more likely to result in reinforcement. Similar therapies that involve behavioral activation to enhance environmental reinforcement possibilities have recently been proposed (e.g., Martell, Addis, & Jacobson, 2001).

Restricted Range of Reinforcement

Restricted range of reinforcement is evident when the individual's behavior is geared toward the attainment of a narrow range of reinforcing consequences. One example of such a response class is substance abuse. The behavior of substance abusers (e.g., time devoted to getting substance, behaviors displayed to secure funds for purchasing substances, consumption of substances) may, in part, be influenced by both the positive and negative reinforcing qualities that follow substance consumption (Wulfert et al., 1996). As a result, therapy programs for substance abuse may seek to expand the range of reinforcing stimuli that maintain behavior (e.g., participation in pleasant activities that do not involve substances in any way; skills training so other behaviors can be used to produce reinforcing consequences).

Overly Punitive Environment

In these environments, behavior tends to be influenced more by aversive consequences than reinforcing consequences. Such environments are likely to shape and maintain behaviors that are characterized by mistrust, anger, fear, avoidance, and caution. In instances such as these, therapeutic approaches might in the first instance target the environment for change. For example, parents who rely solely on aversive or punitive strategies (i.e., positive punishment strategies) may benefit from learning parent training skills (Clark, 1985).

Excessively Stringent Self-Reinforcement Strategies

With this functional domain, an individual may have excessively high and unrealistic standards or rules for behavior. As a result, the individual may be unlikely to evaluate his or her behavior as worthy of reward even if reward is forthcoming. Thus, the effectiveness of potential reinforcers in such circumstances would likely be diminished. For individuals with unrealistically high standards, therapy may target the relaxation of self-generated rules that contribute to the maintenance of perfectionistic behavior. Therapy might also place emphasis on the effectiveness (i.e., consequences) of behavior rather than the form of behavior in evaluations of behavior.

Excessive Schedule Dependence

With excessive schedule dependence, an individual's behavior may be especially sensitive to the rate of reinforcement that follows behavior. For example, some people might be especially sensitive to occasions when previously reinforced behavior is not reinforced at the rate it once was. That is, such individuals may be especially sensitive to the emergence of an extinction schedule or, at least, a reduced rate of contingent positive reinforcement. As a result, such individuals may not persist in their behavior and may be more easily frustrated or prone to feelings of insecurity or self-doubt. Behavioral interventions, such as acceptance and commitment therapy (Hayes, Strosahl, & Wilson, 1999), that shift the focus of behavior away from immediate consequences to more distal outcomes associated with values and longer term goals may be particularly useful. Behavioral activation approaches may similarly be useful for expanding the breadth of potential reinforcers. A greater range of potential reinforcers will likely attenuate the effects of extinction in a given area on overall behavior rate or frequency.

FUNCTIONAL RESPONSE CLASSES: A CLINICAL EXAMPLE

In this section, we present a hypothetical client to illustrate some of the features of a functional response class analysis of a client's problem areas. The client in this scenario is an 18-year-old woman who has been previously seen in therapy by three therapists for depressed mood, parasuicidal behavior (specifically self-cutting on the arm with a razor), interpersonal difficulties, and anger problems. The time frame of therapy covered in this example includes only the early assessment period.

During the first meeting with this client, the therapist assessed current suicidal and homicidal intent. The client denied any current ideation associated with either of these areas. An assessment of her history in relation to these areas revealed an absence of past homicidal behavior or inclination. The client did report a period of strong suicidal ideation approximately 18 months earlier, however, that followed the death of her mother, which culminated in a suicide attempt by hanging that was subsequently abandoned when the client was unable to configure the rope in a manner that would allow her to hang herself. In her comment on this experience, the client stated that she has not since had suicidal thoughts to the degree that she did then. Furthermore, she indicated that when such thoughts had subsequently emerged, they were typically accompanied by angry mood and tended to subside as her angry mood returned to baseline levels. The client indicated that she has not had suicidal thoughts that were frequent, intense, or long-lasting since this period 18 months earlier.

Given the nature of the client's problem areas and the absence of current suicidal behavior, intent, or planning, early assessments emphasized her nonsuicidal self-injurious acts. In particular, the therapist, who was familiar with and practiced in accordance with the theory, strategies, and interventions associated with dialectical behavior therapy (Linehan, 1993a), sought to gain a contextual–functional understanding of the client's recent parasuicidal behavior. As noted by Brown et al. (2002), it is often important to understand the function of parasuicidal behavior as a precursor to the development of therapeutic strategies or instruction in skills that seek to reduce and eliminate such behavior. A functional assessment of such behavior typically includes an evaluation of its topography, frequency, intensity, duration, and medical severity.

A thorough assessment of previous instances of parasuicidal behavior (i.e., target response) revealed the following. First, parasuicidal acts were fairly frequent (about two to three times per week on average), although they tended to be mild to moderate in intensity and relatively brief in duration. That is, the client would typically cut herself with a razor until which time blood would begin to flow from her injuries. Self-cutting was restricted to her arms in each instance, and the client's report indicated that on only four or five occasions had she previously received stitches for her injuries, and even then never required more than 10 stitches on any single occasion. An examination of the client's arms revealed several healed yet noticeable scars, as well as some relatively recent injuries that did not appear to be overly deep and in the process of healing. All cuts ran across the width of her arm; none ran the length of the arm. The client was adamant in her assertions that when she cuts, she is not suicidal and that cutting is primarily done to "feel better." She also indicated that she very much wanted to stop this behavior.

The therapist's assessments of the *antecedent conditions* that set the occasion for self-injurious behaviors revealed the following. One of two common antecedent conditions for such behavior was disagreeableness and hostility displayed by the client's boyfriend toward the client, usually in the context of an argument between the two. These arguments invariantly evoked feelings of self- and other (partner)-directed rage within the client. The therapist's additional assessments indicated that intense anger in such situations acted as an establishing operation for acts of self-injury, because anger reportedly had a potentiating effect on the reinforcing qualities of self-injury as the client acknowledged that self-injurious acts were experienced as more satisfying in the context of anger than when anger was absent.

The second common context for self-injury was related to occasions where the client was at home alone for extended periods. The client reported that when home alone, she would be more likely to consume excessive amounts of alcohol and review her diary and focus on passages that described life problems or difficult events. According to the client, the review of these passages would often trigger additional thoughts and recollections of past experiences that were associated with a similar negative emotional valence (primarily guilt). The client went on to report that she would then ruminate about these events until she was overwhelmed with negative emotions, at which point she would characteristically dissociate. The client then went on to report that dissociative episodes were initially relieving because they functioned to terminate unpleasant thoughts, recollections, and emotions. After awhile, however, these dissociative states became aversive ("I would feel like I was hollow and filled with cotton, like I wasn't real"), and self-injury through cutting would then be used as a method to terminate this unpleasant state and to restore her to a normal state of consciousness and experience.

A common antecedent to both contexts was the presence of a razor blade. The client disclosed that she often carried a razor with her and that in most of the instances reviewed, she had a razor in either her pocket or purse at the time of the incident. When asked, the client denied that she had a razor blade with her during the therapy session.

Given that acts of self-cutting occurred several times a week, the therapist hypothesized that there was likely some type of *reinforcement function* (i.e., consequences) associated with self-cutting behavior in these two contexts that accounted for its strength and persistence over time. As a result, the therapist set out to assess the function of this behavior within these two situations.

For the first context (boyfriend's hostility and arguments with boyfriend), the client's self-reports suggested several functions associated with self-injurious behavior. A subset of these functions involved short-term and slightly delayed positive reinforcement contingent on self-injury. That is, the client indicated that when she cut in the presence of her boyfriend in the midst of an argument, she was convinced her boyfriend understood that she was feeling angry and hurt. In this respect, the behavior of self-injury appeared to serve an immediate and urgent communication function (i.e., expressions of anger and hurt). She also reported an immediate sense of pleasure or satisfaction, which she would experience almost immediately after the initiation of cutting. The client was unable to link this sense of pleasure and satisfaction to any particular outcome associated with this behavior, although she commented that these feelings were stronger when she observed herself bleed. Typically and shortly after the client self-injured in this context, she also reported that the boyfriend would show affection by hugging her, holding her hands, and by providing reassurance.

The other subset of functions associated with self-injurious behavior in this context appeared to involve negative reinforcement processes. That is, the client noted that when she would begin to cut, the boyfriend would immediately stop his hostile displays and argumentative behavior, something that she experienced as aversive. Also, too, she noted that as she cut, her experience of both inner and outer directed anger would quickly diminish (e.g., "If I cut deep enough and blood flowed, I'd feel better. As it flowed out, it was like my rage was flowing out, too.").

For the second context in which acts of self-injury were more likely to occur (home alone), the client's self-reports suggested three functions associated with self-injurious behavior, all of which appeared to have an associated immediate and slightly delayed negative reinforcement functions. Most immediately, the initial act of self-harm terminated the aversive state of dissociation. The client would often continue to cut for a short while after the dissociative state had ceased, however. As she explained it, she would continue to cut to distract herself from feelings of guilt and painful thoughts about her past and to punish herself for her past mistakes. Regarding the latter, the client reported that she felt and thought better about herself (i.e., less guilty and bad, respectively) when she punished herself by self-cutting. As such, the therapist was able to discern that even though the client conceptualized self-harm in this instance as a form of punishment, it was actually negatively reinforced behavior because it functioned to attenuate or eliminate the negative emotional experience of guilt and the negative self-image of badness (the negative reinforcing aspects of this behavior would also account for the maintenance of this behavior in this context over time). When the client spoke of distracting herself from painful thoughts through self-injury, she indicated that self-injury was relieving (i.e., negatively reinforcing) as it functions to distract her from (or eliminate) painful thoughts and recollections.

Finally, pretreatment assessments revealed the following *organismic information* about the client that may have relevance for her self-harm behavior. First, the client's history of self-harm behavior went back 3 years (onset during the middle of her 15th year). This first instance of self-harm was associated with feelings of guilt and a sense of inner badness in response to some event she could not recall. The client reported that she discovered at the time that cutting herself made these feelings and self-views go away temporarily. The client went on to acknowledge that the functions and triggers for self-harm behavior have been largely consistent over this 3-year period.

Second, on self-report measures, the client's responses indicated high levels of impulsivity and anxiety and high levels of neuroticism. Such standings on these temperament dimensions is common among people who display significant borderline personality disorder pathology (Farmer & Nelson-Gray, 1995) and guilt (Farmer, 1998) and together suggest a more pronounced sensitivity and responsiveness to the effects of positive reinforcement, negative reinforcement, extinction, and punishment contingencies (Gray, 1987a). In addition, the high score on neuroticism may suggest a tendency toward the experience of negative affect (Watson, 2000). High neuroticism scores also suggest a tendency for responses in some contexts to be performed with greater speed and vigor, to be more strongly associated with proximate than distal consequences (i.e., immediate environmental contingencies rather than rules or distal goals), and to be accompanied by a narrowing of the attentional field to certain classes of stimuli, namely, those associated with positive and negative reinforcement (Wallace & Newman, 1997).

Third, the client reported a childhood history of repeated physical abuse in the home at the hands of her father. The main recollections associated with these incidents had to do with the degree of physical and emotional pain she felt both during and after the abuse episodes, her profound experience of powerlessness and vulnerability, her tendency to isolate herself in her room for extended time periods following abuse episodes, and her associated experience of hatred toward her father. In relation to this abuse history, the client reported frequent flashbacks of trauma-related scenes. In general, the client further reported persistent elevated levels of arousal (e.g., difficulty sleeping, exaggerated startle response), vigilance for cues associated with physical threat or danger, and a suggestion of possible difficulty discriminating gradations of emotional experience (e.g., "I go from fine to rage at the drop of a hat"). These responses, in conjunction with her tendency to initially associate all men with violence and abuse potential, are consistent with the presentation of persons with PTSD.

Finally, the client reported that she had not been sleeping well and averaged at most 4 hours of restful sleep each night over the previous 4 days. The client attributed difficultly in sleeping to an inability to "wind down." The therapist's subsequent inquiries revealed that during the last several days, the client had not been sleepy when she went to bed. Rather than get up and participate in some nonarousing activity, the client reported that she tended to lie in bed and ruminate about various current stressors, which she reported made sleep even more unlikely. The client also reported poor eating habits during the last few days, whereby she would often skip several meals, eventually only to have a large binge that consisted of foods with high sugar content and little nutritional value.

From the pretreatment assessment information, two SORC functional analyses can be generated for the two general contexts within which self-injury is most likely to occur. These are displayed in Exhibit 5.1.

Other possible relevant functional domains not indicated for the two situational contexts delineated above include *behavioral deficits*. It may be the case that cutting functions as a behavioral strategy for a variety of purposes for which other behavioral skills are absent or deficit. For example, the communication function that self-injury has in the first context may be an indication of two related skills deficits: the inability to identify and label gradations in emotional experience and to communicate verbally these experiences to others. In both situational contexts, self-cutting may function as the client's primary or only means of emotional arousal modulation or regulation.

EXHIBIT 5.1
SORC Functional Analyses and Response Class Evaluation of Self-Injurious Behavior

SITUATIONAL CONTEXT 1: BOYFRIEND'S EXPRESSIONS OF HOSTILITY AND ARGUMENTS WITH BOYFRIEND

S: Antecedent Conditions

- *Antecedent stimuli*: Verbal and nonverbal expressions of hostility by boyfriend; an argument with boyfriend; presence of razor blade in pocket or purse.
- *Establishing operations*: Environmental events that resulted in intense anger.

O: Organismic Variables

- *Learning history*: Three-year history of self-injurious behavior maintained by positive as well as negative reinforcement processes; early history of physical abuse by father (history of interpersonal violence that involved a man and caretaker) that was associated with both physical and emotional pain, physical isolation from others, feelings of hatred toward her father, and a sense of powerlessness and vulnerability.
- *Physiological–biological factors*: Anxious, impulsive, and negative mood temperaments; possible modifications in brain physiology and processes as a result of past trauma experiences; recent sleep deprivation; poor eating habits within the past few days.

R: Response (Target Behavior)

Self-cutting of arms with a razor (1 to 2 times per week, generally mild to moderate in intensity and of relatively short duration). Behavior would typically persist until either boyfriend responded or blood flowed from injury.

C: Consequences

- *Immediate positively reinforcing consequences*: Nonspecific feelings of pleasure and satisfaction that strengthen in intensity in response to sight of blood.
- *Immediate negatively reinforcing consequences*: Boyfriend's termination of verbal displays of hostility or disagreement; reduction in strength–intensity of self- and other-directed rage.
- *Slightly delayed positive reinforcing consequences*: Communication and expression of anger and hurt to boyfriend, with this communication subsequently acknowledged and responded to by boyfriend through his provision of physical displays of affection and words of reassurance.

Possible Relevant Functional Domains

- *Inappropriate stimulus control:* By carrying a razor blade in her pocket or purse, the client effectively made the presence of the razor a stimulus cue (S^D) for self-injury in the many environmental contexts in which the razor was present. The presence of the razor in any environmental context makes self-injury likely; its absence would probably substantially reduce this likelihood.
- *Ineffective arrangement of contingencies:* The boyfriend's hostile and argumentative behavior served as a trigger (S^D) for self-injurious behavior, with self-injury in this context often followed by a reduction in hostile or aggressive behavior (negative reinforcement) and an increase in affection and reassurance by the boyfriend (positive reinforcement).

continues

- *Discrimination deficits of private events:* As noted by the client, "I go from fine to rage at the drop of a hat." Although this report may accurately describe the client's experience (e.g., the client may be highly emotionally reactive), the therapist should evaluate the possible presence of discrimination deficits associated with the identification of gradations of irritation or anger, because it is quite possible that the client experiences more subtle or less intense forms of anger prior to the experience of rage. Furthermore, there may be other emotional experiences that occur during these occasions that are inappropriately labeled by the client as rage experiences, such as anxiety.
- *Discrimination difficulties among environmental contexts:* The client's engagement in self-injury and experience of rage are strong reactions to verbal hostility displayed by her boyfriend. Such reactions are nonnormative in form and intensity and may have grounding in the client's learning history. As noted earlier, the client indicated that she typically experiences all men initially as potentially violent and abusive. Therefore, there is some suggestion of stimulus generalization, whereby persons who are topographically similar to her father (i.e., men in a caretaking role) are experienced as having the same stimulus properties as her father. Consistent with this possibility, it may be the case that the client is actually responding to more distal stimuli in her learning history that are topographically similar to current stimuli, but functionally quite different.
- *States of physiological arousal and activation:* Environmental events that trigger client's state of rage prior to the commission of self-injurious acts may serve as establishing operations that potentiate the reinforcing qualities of self-injury. In fact, the client's report that self-injury is more satisfying when she is angry supports this view.
- *Experiential avoidance*: In this situation, it appears that there is an experiential avoidance aspect to self-injurious behavior. That is, one of the functions of this behavior is to terminate unpleasant feelings of anger and hurt.
- *Behavioral excess–inappropriate conditioned emotional response:* Although not clear from the information provided by the client thus far, it is possible that the sudden rage the client feels when her boyfriend behaves in a disagreeable or hostile manner is a conditioned emotional response based on learning experiences that involved her father. In fact, a subsequent assessment by the therapist revealed that prior to physically striking the client, the father would typically argue with her for extended periods. As such, it may be the case that rage became a conditioned emotional response to arguments with her father and that this emotional response occurs in her current environments that are topographically similar (men, like her boyfriend, who are in caretaker or supportive role and who act in a disagreeable, argumentative, or hostile manner).

SITUATIONAL CONTEXT 2: HOME ALONE

S: Antecedent Conditions

- *Antecedent stimuli:* Prolonged absence of other people in the environment; exposure to negative or difficult events described in diary, and associated thoughts and remembrances related to those events; presence of razor blade in pocket or purse.
- *Establishing operations:* Events that have resulted in substance intoxication (alcohol) and a dissociative state.

O: Organismic Variables

(Same as in Situational Context 1)

continues

EXHIBIT 5.1
(Continued)

R: Response (Target Behavior):

- Self-cutting of arms with a razor (1 to 2 times per week, generally mild to moderate in intensity and of relatively short duration). Behavior would typically persist until blood flowed from injury.

C: Consequences

- *Immediate negatively reinforcing consequences:* Termination of dissociative state and restoration of baseline levels of consciousness and experience.
- *Slightly delayed negatively reinforcing consequences:* Reduction or elimination of feelings of guilt and sense of inner badness; reduction or elimination of thoughts and recollections related to past difficult events.

Possible Relevant Functional Domains

- *Inappropriate stimulus control:* As previously noted, the presence of the razor is a potent signal and is a setting condition for acts of self-injury.
- *Ineffective arrangement of environmental contingencies.* Disclosures made by the client indicated that (a) being home alone for extended periods, (b) alcohol intoxication, and (c) the review of her diary are a toxic combination that almost always culminates in an act of self-injury. As such, these antecedent conditions and establishing operations set the occasion for problematic behavior to occur.
- *Substance intoxication:* Not only is substance intoxication a part of the antecedent landscape for self-injurious acts, it likely also functions to (a) influence susceptibility to negative moods, (b) disinhibit behavior, and (c) potentiate the reinforcing qualities of self-injury.
- *State of physiological arousal and activation:* Events that result in dissociation also appear to act as an establishing operation for self-injury because this physiological state appears to enhance the reinforcing properties of self-injury, and self-injury terminates this state when experienced as aversive.
- *Experiential avoidance:* The act of self-injury appears to have an important experiential avoidance function because these acts function to promote escape, avoidance, or the attenuation of unpleasant feeling states, thoughts, and views of self.
- *Insufficient environmental reinforcement:* When home alone for extended periods, reinforcers, particularly social reinforcers, are either less available or unavailable for behavior. In this example, it may be useful for the therapist to assess the circumstances that surround occasions when the client isolates herself at home and to facilitate greater participation in activities that could potentially be reinforcing.

Before embarking on an intervention approach to reduce and subsequently eliminate self-injurious behavior, it would be useful to assess other coping responses that may be a part of the client's behavioral repertoire. Such coping skills, if present, may be used as substitute behaviors for self-injury in situations where coping is difficult. If such response repertoires are deficient, then therapy might include skills training elements that emphasize the development of coping skills that can serve as effective and healthier responses to problematic situations.

This analysis has some therapeutic implications for reducing the client's vulnerability to future acts of self-injury. For both situational contexts, a simple application of a cue-elimination procedure may be a particularly potent intervention. That is, if the client did not have razor blades on her person or did not have them easily available, then it would be considerably more difficult for the client to engage in the form of self-injury that she has performed over the last few years. As such, the therapist might work with the client to bring about a genuine commitment to throw away all razor blades currently available to her and to commit to not purchasing razor blades during the course of therapy (or to call the therapist when coping efforts in relation to the urge to purchase razors have been unsuccessful). As a replacement, the client could use an electric razor for all shaving activities.

In relation to the first situational context (disagreeable or hostile boyfriend), the following intervention strategies may be useful:

- Because the boyfriend's hostility and disagreeableness serve a potent discriminative stimulus function for acts of self-injury, therapy may, in part, target his behavior. That is, in the context of a couples therapy component, the client and her boyfriend could participate in a communication training element that would seek to facilitate modes of communication that are effective and not laden with angry affect.
- The boyfriend's reactions following acts of self-injury function both to negatively reinforce (termination of hostility) and positively reinforce (provision of physical affection and reassurance) self-injurious behavior. Therefore, in therapy sessions jointly attended by the boyfriend and client, the possible maintaining functions that the boyfriend's behavior serves following self-injury could be explored and explained to both parties. The therapist may then seek to strike an agreement that reinforcers for self-injurious behavior need to be removed ("we have to make this behavior less reinforcing if it is to become less frequent and eventually stop"). As part of this strategy, the boyfriend would be encouraged not to provide reassurance and physical displays of affection following self-injurious acts.
- Related to the previous point, the boyfriend would be encouraged to display affection and reassurance at times other than when the client self-injures.
- If additional assessments indicate that the client does have some discrimination deficits related to private events (e.g., difficulty discriminating more subtle and less intense forms of anger; labeling anxious arousal as anger), then discrimination training may be undertaken. As a part of this work, the client may be instructed in different feeling-states words and encouraged to practice applying these word labels to variations in emotional quality and intensity. The client might also be taught to dis-

criminate levels of emotional activation or intensity, or the qualities of mood, that represent "danger zones" associated with an increased likelihood for self-injury. If the client is able to make discriminations among the quality and intensity of her emotional experiences, she can then be taught to use these experiences that fall below this "danger zone" threshold to take action to reduce her vulnerability to self-injurious acts (e.g., engage in some form of coping skill).

- The therapist might also consider other ways to reduce the establishing operation of rage in relation to self-injury. One such method is nonreinforced exposure to this emotional state by recounting rage-related experiences in a therapeutic context and staying with rage feelings without engaging in any concomitant escape or avoidance action—in this case, self-injury (Brondolo et al., 1997). Such an approach may eventuate in the extinction of rage reactions to particular stimulus cues. In suggesting this possibility, we urge caution in the use of any exposure-based treatments among individuals who engage in self-injury, at least in the initial stages of therapy. Such emotionally evocative approaches should only be undertaken if the client's self-injurious behavior is relatively well controlled and the client has learned alternative coping skills that can be applied to occasions when he or she is feeling emotionally overwhelmed. Under such circumstances, therapy sessions could also involve more informal approaches to exposure, whereby the client is encouraged to experience difficult emotions, thoughts, or physical sensations as they arise within session while inhibiting action related to self-harm urges.
- Teaching new behavioral coping skills would likely be indicated as well. For example, if being in the presence of a disagreeable or hostile person is a discriminative stimulus for acts of self-injury, the client could, as an alternative, simply walk away from such persons. Doing so would result in the elimination of that cue from her environment. Other skills can be taught for coping with overwhelming affects, difficult environments, or self-harm urges, several examples of which are offered by Linehan (1993a, 1993b). One such skill is "opposite action," in which the client is taught to act in a manner that is opposite to the urges or emotionally expressive behaviors associated with rage. In addition to taking a time out from the situation by leaving it, other opposite actions for rage might include behaving in an understanding and compassionate manner, slowing down one's breathing, or changing one's facial expressions such that they no longer express anger or rage.

In relation to the second situational context (home alone), the following intervention strategies may be used:

- A number of interventions might be undertaken to reduce the likelihood that the stimulus conditions that set the occasion for acts of self-injury in this context will be present on future occasions. A relatively simple intervention related to this approach would involve the removal of not only all razor blades from the home, but also all alcoholic beverages. The diary may, for a time being, be turned over to a friend or placed somewhere outside of the home where the client would not have immediate access to it.
- If social isolation is a common experience that increases the likelihood of acts of self-injury, intervention strategies that reduce the likelihood of future periods of extended social isolation might be used. One such approach may involve behavioral activation, whereby the client identifies and engages in activities that she finds reinforcing, particularly those that are social in nature. An assumption underlying this approach is that behavior followed by reinforcing consequences will become more probable over time. However, for behavior to be selected by naturally occurring environmental consequences, it must be displayed first. Hence, this approach challenges the client to engage in those behaviors that are most likely to be reinforced as a result of their natural consequences.
- As with the first situation, skills training may be particularly helpful for reducing the client's vulnerability to self-harm behaviors in this context. In particular, mindfulness skills may be particularly helpful because an analysis of this situation suggested that rumination over past environments and behaviors constituted part of the behavioral chain that culminated in acts of self-injury. Mindfulness skills, at the most basic level, involve the ability to fully focus on the moment. "Being here now" or being fully focused on the events that are occurring in the present is incompatible with getting stuck in rumination over environments and behaviors that have long ago ceased to exist. In this scenario, the client would be encouraged to be mindful of current sensory events and emotional experiences and unmindful of worry or ruminative thoughts. In addition, mindfulness related to a current aversive emotion might serve as a nonreinforced exposure that allows for the emotion to habituate over time.
- Perhaps later in therapy, once the client has made progress in reducing the frequency of engagement in acts of self-injury and

has acquired healthier coping skills, consideration might be given to nonreinforced exposure sessions that involve material contained in the diary. The goal associated with such an approach would be to extinguish the various aversive reactions the client has to this material. Such an approach may not be necessary if the client no longer seeks exposure to this previous discriminative stimulus for acts of self-injury.

In addition to these treatment recommendations, the therapist might also consider the use of therapeutic interventions for reducing sleep deprivation and for restoring healthier eating habits. The client's relative lack of sleep coupled with alternating periods of self-starvation and binge episodes that involve high sugar–low nutrition foods likely contributed to the client's vulnerability to negative moods. As such, the therapist might consider providing the client with sleep hygiene procedures (e.g., Morin, 1993) and may work with the client to normalize her eating habits and behavior (e.g., three meals per day, plus a couple of planned snacks) and to make healthier food choices.

In the following three chapters, we discuss in greater detail some of the therapeutic interventions described here, as well as other common intervention strategies and techniques used in behavior therapy.

FUNCTION *AND* FORM RATHER THAN FUNCTION *OR* FORM? TOWARD THE INTEGRATION OF TOPOGRAPHICAL AND FUNCTIONAL RESPONSE CLASS ASSESSMENT INFORMATION INTO CLIENT FORMULATION

Although traditional topographical and functional forms of assessment and client conceptualization are not necessarily in conflict with each other (Nelson & Barlow, 1981), they have historically been associated with different assumptions about human behavior and different assessment goals. Whereas behavioral models have placed the cause outside of the individual, the trait and medical model approaches (including psychiatric diagnosis) have placed the cause inside of the individual (Follette, Houts, & Hayes, 1992). Another factor is that behavior theory and therapy have been less concerned about the form or organization of behavior than the function or effects of behavior (Bissett & Hayes, 1999; Skinner, 1981). Behavior theory and therapy have also been strongly grounded in the scientific method, as evident by the use of empirical methods to evaluate testable concepts and principles. Although this also holds true for the tradition of construct definition and assessment, this is not the case for diagnostic classification, which has largely been the product of truth-by-committee and other political processes (Follette et al., 1992; Millon, 1983; Spitzer, 1991).

When viewed from an integrative perspective, topographical (trait, diagnosis) and functional assessments have associated strengths as well as limitations (see Hayes & Follette, 1992, 1993; Hersen, 1988; Krasner, 1992; Nelson-Gray & Farmer, 1999; Scotti et al., 1996, for further discussions on this topic). Strengths and limitations of both approaches are summarized in Exhibit 5.2. As becomes apparent later, some of the weaknesses of topographical assessment and classification represent the strengths of functional assessments. Conversely, some of the weaknesses of a strictly functional approach to assessment are listed among the strengths of topographical forms of assessment and classification.

Among some nonbehavioral theorists and therapists, the idea of an integration of topographical and functional approaches would likely be regarded as having little value. For example, many adherents to the medical model view of psychological and psychiatric disorders tend to ascribe causality of such conditions to an underlying disease process. As a result, knowledge of the function of a particular behavior or class of behaviors would not be particularly important because the environment has little relevance in the development or maintenance of the associated disease process.

Among behavior theorists and therapists, there is some disagreement as to whether structural representations of response–response relations (e.g., construct assessment, psychiatric diagnoses) can usefully aid in the formulation of client problem areas and associated therapy (e.g., Bissett & Hayes, 1999; Krasner, 1992; Scotti et al., 1996). We (Farmer & Nelson-Gray, 1999; Nelson-Gray & Farmer, 1999), like some other behavior therapists, have suggested that benefits can be gained from an assessment of both the function and form of behavior and by an evaluation of the applicability of general or nomothetic observations and rules to the individual client. Furthermore, because of the wide acceptance and application of syndromal classification systems such as the *Diagnostic and Statistical Manual of Mental Disorders* (*DSM*), some behavior theorists and therapists have acknowledged that the abandonment of *DSM* in favor of alternative functional systems is unlikely (e.g., Follette et al., 1992; Wulfert et al., 1996). As suggested by Wulfert et al. (1996), given the extent to which *DSM* has become widely used, it makes little sense for behavior therapists to abandon completely or refrain from using *DSM* in favor of strictly idiographic approaches to assessment.

Toward the Integration of Topographical and Functional Assessment

A variety of suggestions have been proposed for the integration of topographical and functional analytic strategies (e.g., Hayes & Follette, 1992; Haynes, Kaholokula, & Nelson, 1999; Tarrier & Calam, 2002; Wulfert et al., 1996). Some behavior therapists (e.g., Follette & Hayes, 2000; Scotti et al., 1996) have recommended that behavior topography may serve as a useful starting point for the identification of relevant target behaviors and that topographical assessment should then give way to the identification of the

EXHIBIT 5.2
Strengths and Weaknesses of Topographical and Functional Response Class Assessment

TOPOGRAPHICAL ASSESSMENT AND CLASSIFICATION

Strengths

- Suggests treatments that have the highest likelihood for efficacy given the client's problem area, based on nomothetic (group-based) research findings.
- Suggests response patterns that covary and key responses that define the construct or diagnostic concept that can serve as target behaviors for treatment.
- Facilitates communication with third-party payers (e.g., insurance companies) about the nature of a client's problem areas.
- Facilitates communication among clinicians and researchers.
- Provides hypotheses about the prognosis and course related to a client's presentation.

Weaknesses

- Does not provide clear treatment guidance for the individual (treatment recommendations are based at the nomothetic level rather than the idiographic level).
- Provides no information about other behaviors in the client's repertoire, such as skills, that may potentially offset problematic behaviors.
- Does not suggest behavioral deficits or behaviors that would require strengthening as part of a therapeutic program.
- Diagnostic and trait labels may result in stigmatization.
- Fails to recognize the contextual–functional properties of behavior.
- Diagnostic categories are often reified, or given causal status (e.g., individuals are viewed as sad, have difficulty sleeping, troubled by beliefs about self as worthless, etc., because they are depressed—diagnostic labels are used to explain the very behavior that defines the diagnostic category). They are often regarded not only as descriptions of behavior, but also as explanations for it.
- Shifts research and clinical work away from specific problem behaviors and factors that maintain them to research and therapy focused on constructs, diagnostic labels, or classes of people.
- Blurs distinguishing features among individuals who belong to the same diagnostic class; within class homogeneity is assumed.

FUNCTIONAL ASSESSMENT

Strengths

- Explicitly recognizes the context within which people exist and acknowledges the functions that behaviors perform.
- Can result in a comprehensive case formulation of the client's problem area.
- Implies therapy goals or strategies through an identification of potentially manipulable contextual factors that influence behavior and specific target behaviors for therapy.
- Theory and approach associated with behavioral functional assessments are firmly grounded in empirical research and well-validated theories.
- Does not label or stigmatize persons, because the focus is on behavior and environmental factors that support behavior, not classes of people.

continues

- Some research supports the view that clients who are assigned to treatment conditions that are specifically related to the functional properties of their problematic behavior improve more than those who are arbitrarily assigned to treatment.

Weaknesses

- A strictly functional approach would require the "rediscovery" of behavioral principles with each new client (no nomothetic principles to guide therapist).
- Absence of consensus concerning the methodologies for performing such analyses.
- Within methods of assessment, low reliability of functional formulation across assessors is the norm.
- Absence of clear guidelines for how to proceed from assessment to treatment; not always clear on how to proceed from a functional analysis to treatment recommendations.
- Few guidelines as to what types of problem areas are most suitable for functional assessment, and for what populations such analyses are most appropriate.
- Does not acknowledge and has difficulty accounting for reliable patterns of response covariation among persons with widely divergent learning histories.
- Limited research suggests that functional assessments or idiographically informed treatment selections do not necessarily result in treatments that produce greater therapeutic gains than those administered from standardized treatment package (nomothetically administered therapy based on behavior form).

---

more functional properties of clinically relevant behavior. In so doing, assessment would proceed from information about the general case to information about the specific individual and, in particular, response–environment relations relevant for the individual client's problem behavior.

Similar to Wulfert et al. (1996), in our attempt to reconcile topographical and functional class concepts in the assessment and conceptualization of persons, we are not advocating a form of theoretical or philosophical eclecticism (e.g., the merging of structuralistic and functionalistic models of human behavior). Rather, we do so from the standpoint of behavior theory, although the approach that we are suggesting may be described as technically eclectic (e.g., the use of different approaches that are topographically dissimilar but conceptualized within a unified theoretical framework).

Examples of Approaches for the Integration of Topographical and Functional Assessment Systems

Although it would be beyond the scope of this book to propose a thorough and integrative framework that combines topographical and functional assessment approaches, we do outline in the following section some general strategies that can be used toward this end. Interested readers who wish to learn more about proposals that have been put forth that have integration as a goal are referred to Follette and Hayes (2000), Follette et al. (2000), Naugle and Follette (1998), Scotti et al. (1996), and Wulfert et al. (1996).

Treatment Utility of Assessment: Matching Clients to Effective Treatments on the Basis of Assessment Information

One alternative approach that has features of both traditional and behavioral assessment would be treatment utility–oriented taxonomies (Follette et al., 1992; Hayes et al., 1987; Nelson-Gray, 2003). A feature of such approaches is the use of treatment outcome information for informing the development of diagnostic categories. With this approach, there are two relevant components: (a) the classification of clients according to specific target behaviors and (b) the demonstration that a treatment approach based on target behavior or assessment considerations is more effective than a treatment approach applied without reference to such considerations (i.e., treatments that are arbitrarily applied).

Many of the standardized treatment packages (e.g., Agras & Apple, 1997; Barlow & Craske, 2000) and professional guidelines for treatment (e.g., American Psychiatric Association, 1997, 1998, 2002; Chambless et al., 1998) are based on response topography. That is, such treatment packages are generally based on *DSM* diagnostic concepts that are, in turn, defined by a set of behaviors that presumably covary. One potential problem with assignment to treatment based on response topography, however, is that not all individuals with the same response topographies have their associated behaviors maintained by the same factors (Follette et al., 2000).

Evidence in support of the utility of combining what Scotti et al. (1996) referred to as *deductive* (nomothetic) and *inductive* (idiographic) assessments in the conceptualization and therapy for a variety of problematic behaviors comes from the treatment matching–mismatching literature. For example, in a study by Nelson, Hayes, Jarrett, Sigmon, and McKnight (1987), 9 depressed women each received the same assessment battery. Three women received treatment matched to her main problematic behavioral response class, 3 received treatment that was mismatched to her main problematic behavioral response class, and 3 received a package treatment for depression. The results indicated that both the matched treatments and the package treatment were effective in alleviating depression, more so than the mismatched treatment. This study provides some support for selecting treatment for unipolar depression based on treatment matching—providing treatment that matches a particular client problem.

Iwata et al. (1994) investigated the functional properties of self-injurious behavior among persons with an array of developmental disabilities. Among their findings were that 38% of acts of self-injury were maintained by their escape function, whereas 26% were maintained by positive reinforcement in the form of attention getting, and 26% were maintained by sensory reinforcement. In addition, these researchers compared intervention effectiveness on the basis of whether the interventions applied were arbitrarily assigned or functionally matched to the presumed function of the self-injurious behavior. Functionally matched treatments were found to produce more successful outcomes than interventions that were mismatched to the functional aspects of the client's self-harm behavior. Several other studies have added support to the view that treatments that are conceptually linked to problematic response classes or diagnostic subtypes lead to greater therapeutic gains compared with treatments that are mismatched or arbitrarily assigned (e.g., Chesney & Tasto, 1975; McKnight, Nelson, Hayes, & Jarrett, 1984; Ost, Jerremalm, & Johansson, 1981; Repp, Felce, & Barton, 1988; Trower, Yardley, Bryant, & Shaw, 1978).

Functional Diagnostic Categories

The functional diagnostic category approach can potentially serve as a useful compromise between traditional and behavioral approaches to assessment and conceptualization (Hayes & Follette, 1993). The main feature of this approach is the specification of behavioral topographies that have common functional properties. This is different from the emphasis placed on syndromal classification and construct assessment, in which emphasis is more centrally placed on collections of signs or symptoms or on response–response relations. Here, emphasis is placed on behaviors, singly or in combination with other covarying behaviors, that share similar functions.

For example, Follette and Hayes (Follette et al., 2000; Hayes & Follette, 1993; Hayes et al., 1996) have proposed the concept of an "emotional avoidance disorder," characterized by behaviors that function in the avoidance of intense negative emotions (which would be negatively reinforced behavior if successful). These behaviors that have this function may also be characterized by common topographical elements, such as experiential numbing, distancing, or other forms of avoidance.

Nomothetic Functional Analyses Based on Response Topographies

Another possibility for combining topographical and functional response class information can be found in Wulfert et al. (1996). They suggest that topographically based nosological systems such as *DSM* can be modified to specify common functional properties of behaviors that define structural categories. These authors suggested that within topographically defined diagnostic categories, subtype specifiers should be indicated that signify the functional properties of the topographical response class. An associated benefit of such an approach would be the facilitation of the link between assessment observations and the design of intervention strategies that are particularly appropriate for a given client.

For example, on the basis of a review of the literature, Wulfert et al. (1996) proposed two different subtypes of pedophilia. One of these they termed the *preference type*, characterized as a subgroup of pedophiles that prefer sexual interactions with children rather than adults. Individuals in this functional category often have more extensive histories of child sexual abuse and tend

EXHIBIT 5.3
DSM–IV–TR Diagnostic Criteria for Schizotypal Personality Disorder

1. **Ideas of reference**
2. **Odd beliefs or magical thinking** *that influences behavior and is inconsistent with subcultural norms*
3. **Unusual perceptual experiences, including body illusions**
4. **Odd thinking and speech**
5. **Suspiciousness or paranoid ideation**
6. **Inappropriate or constricted affect**
7. **Behavior or appearance that is odd, eccentric, or peculiar**
8. **Lack of close friends or confidants** *other than first-degree relatives*
9. **Excessive social anxiety** *that does not diminish with familiarity and tends to be associated with paranoid fears rather than negative judgments about self*

Note. Emphasis added. From the *Diagnostic and Statistical Manual of Mental Disorders, Text Revision* (p. 701), American Psychiatric Association, 2000, Washington, DC: American Psychiatric Association. Copyright 2000 by the American Psychiatric Association. Reprinted with permission.

to be more resistant to treatment. The *situational type* is the other proposed subtype, based on the observation that there are a group of pedophiles who prefer sexual interactions with adults but who will sexually abuse children under certain circumstances. Given the proposal of several learning history differences and contextual factors that set the occasion for pedophiliac behavior among members of these two subtypes, Wulfert et al. (1996) proposed various treatment approaches that are tailored to the defining functional and behavioral characteristics of members of these two groups.

Nomothetic functional analyses, founded on empirical data, or rationally derived analyses, based on the experiences of experts in the area, have also been presented for several other topographical response classes. These include eating disorders (Johnson, Schlundt, Barclay, Carr-Nangle, & Engler, 1995), depression (Ferster, 1973), personality disorders (Nelson-Gray & Farmer, 1999; Waltz & Linehan, 1999), suicide attempts and self-injury (Brown et al., 2002; Carr, 1977; Iwata et al., 1994), social skills problems (Hayes & Follette, 1992), and alcoholism (Wulfert et al., 1996). In the view of some behavior analysts (e.g., Sturmey, 1996, p. 30), problems associated with the concept of nomothetic functional analyses include tacit support for the concept of diagnostic categories. Furthermore, such an approach may ultimately be more structural than functional because it suggests a one-to-one mapping of diagnosis to treatment. Such an analysis may fail to recognize the possibility that the functions of behavior for a given individual may change over time.

Modification of Diagnostic Categories Such That Diagnostic Criteria Include Contextual or Functional Features

Most of the diagnostic criteria in *DSM* for Axis I (syndromal) and II (personality) disorders consist of delineations of various forms of response topography, with little attention given to functional or contextual factors

EXHIBIT 5.4
Proposed Topographical and Contextual Criteria for Impulsive Personality Disorder

1. **Commonly responds quickly and without deliberation** *when doing so is not optimal, effective, or beneficial*
2. **Difficulty in inhibiting responding** *for possible rewarding consequences when doing so poses a significant possibility of harm to self or others*; **reckless disregard for self and others** *in the pursuit of pleasure or reward*
3. **Relationship quality tends to be evaluated almost exclusively** *in terms of what others can provide or the use they serve*
4. **Routinely engages in provocative, theatrical, seductive, or outlandish behavior** *primarily to receive recognition or attention from others*
5. **Behavior, in several different forms or expressions,** *is largely influenced by immediate or short-term rewarding consequences rather than more distal goals or outcomes; displays difficulty in delaying immediate gratification or satisfaction.*
6. **Regularly displays exaggerated frustration or irritation** *when actions do not produce desired outcomes*
7. **Displays frequent episodes of behavioral excess in two or more of the following areas: binge eating, alcohol or other drug consumption, gambling, shopping, promiscuous sexual activities, criminal behavior, lying, anger expression, property damage or destruction** (*Note that these behaviors are enacted in relation to their associated rewarding qualities, not because of relief they may provide from aversive inner states, events, or situations.*)
8. **Easily becomes bored, disinterested, restless, or agitated** *in situations that are experienced as routine or nonstimulating*

that may influence their occurrence. A typical example can be seen in the diagnostic criteria for schizotypal personality disorder (SZT) in the *Diagnostic and Statistical Manual of Mental Disorders*, 4th Edition (*DSM–IV–TR* (American Psychiatric Association, 2000, p. 701). For each symptom in Exhibit 5.3, the topography of the behavior that defines the symptom is bolded, whereas the context or possible function of that behavior, when indicated, is italicized. As can be seen, most of the symptoms of SZT make no reference to relevant contexts for behaviors described within symptom criteria, nor is there an indication of what function they may serve.

In Exhibit 5.4, we offer a hypothetical diagnostic concept, impulsive personality disorder, in which criteria systematically incorporate both topographical description and the functional properties associated with the topographical features of behavior. Furthermore, inclusion of behaviors and associated functional features is based on the most recent empirical research available on features of this construct. As with the previous examples, this diagnostic concept is defined in terms of criteria that (a) delineate the form or forms of behavior relevant for the criterion (bolded) and (b) the contextual features or functional properties that influence the behavioral form(s) that are delineated in the diagnostic criterion (italicized).

Regardless of which methods are used, our hope is that the architects of future editions of *DSM* will seek to incorporate more meaningfully the context in which behaviors associated with psychological disorder concepts occur. In addition to highlighting the purpose or shortcomings of behavior, the provision of such contextual information provides a more useful framework for discriminating what might constitute "abnormal" forms of behavior from more functional and appropriate forms. For example, the topography "commonly responds quickly and without deliberation" can be a very adaptive and effective response in some contexts (e.g., many athletes strive for this in the context of participation in their sport). When such behavior routinely results in unfavorable outcomes, however, then it is not effective (and in this sense, is truly "dysfunctional").

In the next chapter, we discuss specific behavioral intervention strategies, and in so doing, we note the common response topographies and functions that are particularly responsive to these techniques.

6

THE TECHNIQUES OF BEHAVIOR THERAPY

Unlike many other approaches to therapy, in behavior therapy there is no assumption that a standard treatment or "packaged" approach is appropriate for all clients. Furthermore, there is no assumption that clients who have similar problems would benefit equally from the same form of therapy. Rather, in behavior therapy, there is a presumption that each person lives in a unique context and has a unique learning history and set of biological attributes and properties. For these reasons, a principal tenant of behavior therapy is that treatment approaches should be designed specifically for the individual client and should take into account the factors that maintain that person's problem areas, his or her needs and goals, as well as the range of behavioral repertoires and skills that the individual currently has available. Indeed, the idiographic approach used in behavior therapy is one of its hallmarks. Nomothetic observations about what is generally true for persons with similar behavior patterns can, however, guide behavior therapists during pretreatment assessments and also be of use in decisions about which treatment approaches may be most useful for a given individual.

The goals of this chapter are twofold. First, we describe examples of behavior therapy techniques that are often used in clinical contexts, either as core features within a therapy program or as treatment components within a larger treatment program. Second, we highlight where within a functional domain the particular technique may be most relevant or beneficial. In so doing, we recognize that many of these functional response domains are overlapping and not mutually exclusive. Also, consistent with the idiographic approach of behavior therapy, we recognize that the potential applicability of the techniques described within this nomothetic framework would need to be established for each individual case.

General Assessment and Treatment Guidelines

Behavior therapy is unique from other therapeutic approaches as behavior therapy (a) views problematic or clinically relevant behavior as sets of actions that take place within behavior–context transactions, (b) regards life problems as understandable given the history of the individual and the context within which he or she lives, and (c) discounts the notion that individuals with emotional or behavioral difficulties are defective in some way (Martell et al., 2001). With these general philosophical assumptions as background, we briefly review general assessment and treatment guidelines associated with behavior therapy.

General Assessment Guidelines

In the initial stages of assessment, a goal is to establish the functional context within which problems occur, because each client exists in a different context and has a different life history, the cumulative effect of which uniquely affects one's current behavior. As a result, a functional analysis (chap. 3) to establish the context of a client's problem areas should be undertaken first to establish the suitability and appropriateness of various behavioral interventions. In conducting such an analysis, a behavior therapist might ask questions such as, "What function or purpose does this behavior have for the person in this context?" and "What is the advantage in this behavior being selected for this particular environment at this time?" (Sturmey, 1996). Findings from a clinical functional analysis should not only specify relevant target behaviors and the contexts within which they occur, but should also indicate appropriate replacement behaviors that have some functional equivalence to the target behaviors selected for change (Sturmey, 1996).

General Treatment Guidelines

Response classes maintained by reinforcement can often be addressed by interventions that facilitate behavioral inhibition strategies or promote the substitution of problematic behaviors with other behavioral repertoires that provide similar functions. Wulfert et al. (1996) suggested that some behavioral problems maintained by positive reinforcement should be treated, in part, with therapeutic strategies that specifically target a client's verbal behavioral repertoire that reveals ambivalence or a desire to change problematic behaviors. Strategies for accomplishing this might include motivational interviewing (Miller & Rollnick, 1991) or aspects of acceptance and commitment therapy (ACT; Hayes, Strosahl, & Wilson, 1999).

For problematic response classes that are maintained by negative reinforcement processes, exposure-based interventions may be implemented that seek to block behavioral avoidance while promoting habituation to stimuli that are associated with negative emotional states. Alternatively, skills training work may be undertaken to promote behavioral skills that can effectively counter aversive contexts, such as problem-solving skills training or social skills training.

A related consideration is the degree of alternative sources of reinforcement available to the individual. Some studies suggest that problematic forms of behavior become more frequent and entrenched if (a) they produce a positive or negative reinforcing consequence and (b) there are limits on alternative sources of reinforcement for other behaviors (Wulfert et al., 1996). As a result, in the context of ongoing client assessment, it is often important to evaluate a client's degree of satisfaction with other life areas (e.g., quality of interpersonal and romantic relations, occupational satisfaction, quality of leisure activities) and to consider these areas for strengthening if deficient (Wulfert et al., 1996). Within a behavioral therapy program, it is also useful to consider the development of behavioral repertoires that lessen the likelihood for relapse or slipping back into problematic behavioral routines (Marlatt & Gordon, 1985).

Examples of the Techniques of Behavior Therapy

The techniques delineated in this chapter are examples of the types of strategies that behaviorally oriented therapists use for client problem areas. In no way is this list comprehensive; rather, the techniques described represent only a small sampling. Additional descriptions of behavior therapy techniques and their applications can be found in Barlow (2001); Davis et al. (2000); Goldfried and Davison (1976); Hayes, Barlow, and Nelson-Gray (1999); Kazdin (2001); Leahy and Holland (2000); Mallot et al. (2000); McKay, Davis, and Fanning (1997); O'Donohue, Fisher, and Hayes (2003); and Plaud and Eifert (1998).

Following Follette and colleagues (e.g., Follette & Hayes, 2000; Follette et al., 2000), this chapter is organized within the framework of functional response domains presented in chapter 5. That is, we highlight examples of specific behavior therapy techniques that may be especially appropriate and effective based on where problems occur within the functional context.

PROBLEMS WITH STIMULUS CONTROL AND THE PROBLEMATIC INFLUENCE OF ESTABLISHING OPERATIONS

Therapeutic strategies related to contexts or events that occasion problematic behavior are discussed in this section. Two general classes of setting occasions are described, inappropriate stimulus control and establishing operations, along with interventions that might be used to reduce the influence of these events on problematic behavior.

Inappropriate Stimulus Control

Stimulus Control Procedures

The consequences of behavior exert a substantial influence on the likelihood that a given behavior will be displayed on future occasions. Antecedent conditions that set the occasion for behavior can also influence whether a behavior is displayed. A central concept related to this process, as discussed in greater detail in chapter 3, is *discriminative stimulus*. Discriminative stimuli were defined as antecedent setting conditions that influence behavior through their previous association with reinforcement contingencies, specifically whether reinforcement or punishment has typically followed (S^D) or not followed (S^Δ) behavior in the presence of these antecedent conditions. The influence that discriminative stimuli have on behavior is referred to as *stimulus control.*

Inappropriate stimulus control refers to behaviors that are appropriate in form and in some contexts, but not within contexts where they are often displayed. That is, an individual has the skills to display a particular form of behavior but may not have the skills to discriminate when the enactment of such behavior is acceptable, appropriate, or desirable. Alternatively, an individual may have difficulty inhibiting undesirable behaviors in the presence of such stimuli. A goal of stimulus control procedures, then, is to make behavior more likely in the presence of one class of stimuli and less likely in the presence of other stimulus classes.

Stimulus control techniques are often used in a variety of behavior therapy programs. For example, stimulus control techniques are often used in obesity reduction programs, particularly for individuals whose eating behavior is less influenced by internal cues associated with hunger than by a broad range of external stimuli or contexts (e.g., the sight of food, when television viewing). Stimulus control procedures in these programs often attempt to reduce the influence that the sight of food has on eating behavior, or to limit eating to a narrow range of environmental contexts. Examples of such stimulus control techniques include the following:

- Preparing one food portion at a time (e.g., if a person is preparing to eat potato chips, one might pour a small amount into a dish rather than eat out of a bag)

- Preparing food over an extended time period so as to reduce the association between the sight of food and immediate eating
- Increasing the availability of healthy foods and reducing or eliminating the availability of unhealthy foods
- Consuming all food in the same place to associate eating with specific environments
- Leaving the table immediately after eating so as to eliminate a cue that is associated with eating
- Using small plates, bowls, and utensils when eating so as to reduce the influence that these cues have on the quantity of food consumed

The provision of rules that specify relations between behavior and events is another example of a general approach to stimulus control (Poling & Gaynor, 2003). For example, in motivational enhancement therapy for alcohol abuse (Miller, Zweben, DiClemente, & Rychtarik, 1995), a component of therapy involves the provision of information to the client about the longer term effects of excessive alcohol use. The message imparted to the client, whether or not explicitly stated, is something like, "If you continue to drink at your current level, you can expect to experience a number or serious physical, social, and psychological problems in the future." The provision of information about the longer term detrimental effects of alcohol misuse can establish or make more salient connections between excessive drinking behavior and probable associated negative consequences. If this information, expressed in the form of rule statements concerning the effects of alcohol misuse, contributes to a reduction in alcohol consumption, then one might conclude that drinking behavior has come under some degree of rule control.

Cue Elimination

Cue elimination is another example of a stimulus control technique. The basic premise of cue elimination is that behavior will become less likely if the cues that have historically signaled the availability of reward for engagement in problematic behavior are removed. A goal of this procedure, then, would be to eliminate as many stimuli as possible that have become associated with the problematic behavior. In the case of substance misuse or abuse, therapeutic tasks in relation to cue elimination would include the removal of all drug-associated stimuli from the client's environment or to remove the drug user from those environments (Cunningham, 1998). Because delinquent behavior among teenagers often occurs in the presence of particular peers (who function as S^Ds for such behavior), some therapists suggest a change in peer group as a way to reduce or eliminate conduct behavior problems (Poling & Gaynor, 2003).

Discrimination Difficulties Among Environmental Contexts

As noted in chapter 5, the tendency to experience environmental contexts as functionally similar when they are not can result in rigid and inflexible behavior patterns that are inappropriate or ineffective for their given context. In this section, we describe discrimination training as a therapeutic intervention to promote behavior flexibility and effectiveness across situations.

Discrimination Training

Discrimination training is another type of stimulus control procedure and involves the provision of reinforcement for a set of responses to a given stimulus situation and to withhold reinforcement (both positive and negative) for the same set of responses to a different (and inappropriate) stimulus situation. When an individual has learned to discriminate, his or her behavior will likely occur in the presence of an S^D but not in the presence of an S^Δ. Once this learning has occurred, the individual will be more likely to pay attention to relevant aspects of the situation (S^Ds) while learning to ignore irrelevant aspects (S^Δs).

In day-to-day situations, individuals respond differently to others on the basis of various features that these other persons display. For example, one would likely interact differently with a bartender in a bar setting than one would with a police officer who is considering whether to write a ticket for speeding. When driving a car, most people (thankfully) drive differently when driving toward a green light than they do when driving toward a red one. These stimulus cues (bartender in a bar, police officer with a ticket book in hand, red light versus green light) signal that some forms of behavior are likely to be reinforced, whereas other behaviors are unlikely to produce reinforcement.

Discrimination training procedures can be particularly helpful in cases where there is inappropriate stimulus generalization. Stimulus generalization is evident when a response that is reinforced in one context increases in frequency in other contexts where the response has not been reinforced. Should an individual discriminate among environmental contexts where behavior is and is not appropriate, relevant responses will become more specific to those environments where they are appropriate and less likely in those environments where they are not. As a result, stimulus generalization will be reduced.

Some clinical conditions are defined, in part, by discrimination deficits, inappropriate stimulus generalization, or both. For example, a *Diagnostic and Statistical Manual of Mental Disorders* (4th ed., Text Revision; *DSM–IV–TR*) criterion feature of histrionic personality disorder is "considers relationships to be more intimate than they actually are" (p. 714). A possible unfortunate consequence of this failure to discriminate features that distinguish intimate from nonintimate relations would be displays of behavior that are inappropriate given the context and perhaps aversive to others (e.g., inappropriate self-disclosure, excessive demands on others, seductiveness, engagement in relationship-related risk-taking behaviors that may be punished rather than reinforced).

Therapist and researchers who work with people who have posttraumatic stress disorder (PTSD) have noted the stimulus generalization of trauma-related cues, even though they may conceptualize this phenomenon in nonbehavioral terms (e.g., Foa & Rothbaum, 1998). For example, a rape survivor who was raped at gunpoint in her suburban home by a tall, bald man may, as a result of this experience, overgeneralize some stimulus–stimulus relations. That is, "bald man" may become strongly associated with gun and rape and hence become feared and avoided even though bald men are no more likely to carry guns or to rape than any other men (Foa & Rothbaum, 1998, pp. 76–77). "Home" and "suburbs," too, may become associated with rape and hence experienced as dangerous or threatening environmental contexts and as an ongoing source of anxiety. The numbers of stimuli that become associated with trauma among those with PTSD are often large and contribute to the experience of several environmental contexts as dangerous and to be avoided.

Therapy for PTSD often involves some sort of discrimination training to lessen the stimulus generalization that has occurred subsequent to the trauma. In so doing, common environmental cues that, in actuality, are not associated with an increased risk of a subsequent traumatic event eventually become responded to as S^{Δ}s rather than S^{D}s.

Discrimination Deficits of Private Events

Just as discrimination deficits for relevant features of environmental contexts can occasion rigid and ineffective behavior, so too can deficits in the ability to discriminate private events such as thoughts, emotions, or sensations. This section describes basic behavioral intervention strategies for enhancing self-observation and for promoting a contextual understanding of one's experience.

Self-Labeling Training

Emotions can have at least two functions: to communicate to others and to motivate one's own behavior (Linehan, 1993a). The functional potentials of emotions cannot be fully realized, however, among individuals who display deficits in their ability to identify and accurately label their emotional experiences. Furthermore, in relation to emotion regulation, many behavior therapists (e.g., Linehan, 1993a) have suggested that a necessary first step in the process of emotion regulation is the ability to identify and label ongoing current emotions. To this end, Linehan (1993a) suggested that the identification of an emotional response is aided if one can observe and describe the following:

- The events that prompted the emotion
- The interpretations of the events that prompted the emotion
- The phenomenological experience of the emotion (e.g., quality of the emotion, associated physical sensations)
- The expressive behaviors associated with the emotion
- The aftereffects of the emotion on one's own functioning

At the most basic level, the identification and accurate labeling of emotion involves the ability to observe the presence of physical sensations, feelings, and thoughts that have a strong emotional component, as well as behavioral tendencies associated with particular emotion experiences (Linehan, 1993a). With these skills developed, it becomes easier to identify one's emotional experience, to communicate this experience to others, and to engage in effective action related to this experience.

Validation and Acceptance Strategies

In recent years, validation and acceptance strategies have become core elements within a variety of behavior therapies (e.g., Hayes, Strosahl, & Wilson, 1999; Linehan, 1993a; Wheeler, Christensen, & Jacobson, 2001). One factor that has contributed to this trend is recognition by behavior therapists that the historical emphasis on behavior change processes in behavior therapy has resulted in an imbalance in the acceptance and change therapy dialectic (Linehan, 1994). That is, because of its origins in learning theory, behavior therapy has primarily been concerned with behavior change. The incorporation of acceptance-based principles and strategies into behavioral approaches represents an attempt to strike a better balance between emphasis on change processes and the therapeutic acceptance of the client as a person (Linehan, 1994). A second factor that has facilitated this shift is the recognition that many clients who seek psychological services have had the experience of being raised in invalidating environments (Linehan, 1993a). Clients with histories of invalidation by others are less inclined to trust others or to accept or value themselves. Therefore, validation strategies are used by behavior therapists to help promote client self-valuation and validation. In addition, if the therapist is experienced as valuing, accepting, and supportive, the client is more likely to take risks in therapy, to open up, and to work collaboratively with the therapist. Clients who experience the therapeutic environment as a safe place to engage in self-examination and exploration are often more willing to contact fully the range of their private experiences and, therefore, develop greater skill in discriminating among them.

At the most basic level, validation from the therapist communicates to the client that his or her behavior makes sense and is understandable in the current context. In assisting the client to understand his or her actions, emotions, thoughts, or implicit rules, the therapist not only helps the client feel validated, but also helps teach a strategy for self-validation (Linehan, 1993a). A specific group of validation strategies, emotion validation strategies (Linehan, 1993a), are premised on the notion that unhealthy forms of responding are often connected with valid responses to events. When a client is in a state of emotional crisis, the therapist may elect to simply listen, identify, clarify, and directly validate the client's feelings in a nonjudgmental fashion. On the other hand, when clients are emotionally inhibited, sessions can be structured to facilitate the communications of emotions (Linehan, 1993a). This could involve asking questions about emotional reactions and leaving enough silence for the client to respond. Other therapist validation strategies outlined by Linehan (1993a) include the following:

- *Active observing*: With this strategy, the therapist conveys that he or she is interested in and engaged with the client by actively observing the client's thoughts, feelings, and actions.
- *Reflection*: With reflection, the therapist accurately reflects back to the client his or her own feelings, thoughts, and behaviors.
- *Direct validation*: With direct validation, the therapist looks for and reflects the wisdom or validity of the client's emotions, thoughts, and behaviors and communicates that these are understandable because all behavior is caused by current events and past learning.

Ineffective Arrangement of Contingencies

Problematic behavior often arises because environments support (reinforce) such behavior. To change problematic behavior that has been historically supported in multiple contexts requires an alteration in the consequences that follow such behavior. Contingency management procedures, such as those described in this section, attempt to change behavior by changing the environmental context, whereby features of the environment are made salient which signal that inappropriate or problematic behavior will not be reinforced. Additionally, alternative behaviors that result in reinforcement are clearly identified and, if necessary, subjected to a shaping process that supports their development and expression.

Contingency Management Procedures

Contingency management procedures involve the direct influence of behavior by the immediate environmental consequences that follow behavior. These procedures involve the delivery of rewards or incentives for positive or desired behaviors and the withholding or removal of rewards or incentives for undesirable or problematic behavior (Boyce & Roman, 2003). Therefore, behavior that is most likely to be affected by contingency management procedures are those influenced by immediate or short-term consequences. Boyce and Roman (2003) have provided useful general guidelines for designing effective contingency management programs.

One example of a contingency management procedure is the *token economy*. Token economy systems are typically used in institutional or residential settings and are most appropriate for shaping and sustaining therapeutically desirable behaviors. When such behaviors are displayed, tokens are earned that are, in turn, exchangeable for a variety of commodities, privileges, or activities (Stahl & Leitenberg, 1976). Tokens represent an intermediate step between behavioral activation and long-term behavior maintenance. In such systems, it is recognized that behavior, once established through token economy programs, will need to be sustained by naturally occurring contingencies if it is to generalize outside of the therapeutic setting.

Stahl and Leitenberg (1976, p. 212) identified four necessary features of token economy systems:

1. They must specify beneficial or adaptive behaviors that can be directly observed.
2. Tokens should be delivered contingent on the occurrence of these behaviors.
3. Effective reinforcers that can be exchanged for tokens need to be identified.
4. A balance between the number of tokens that can be earned and the number of tokens that can be exchanged for tangible reinforcers needs to be found.

Token economies have been used in a wide variety of settings with different populations and have often been observed to produce therapeutically desirable effects when implemented within residential settings (Kazdin, 2001; Stahl & Leitenberg, 1976). Although the extent to which behavior change observed in such settings generalizes to other settings has not been well researched, Stahl and Leitenberg (1976) offered suggestions for facilitating generalization of training outside of residential settings.

Some behavior therapists regard the therapeutic environment as a potent one for bringing about change in problematic social behaviors. An assumption underlying this notion is that the therapeutic environment is an important interpersonal environment and that any changes made in this context are likely to generalize to social environments outside of therapy. For example, Kohlenberg and Tsai (1991) described a therapeutic approach called *functional analytic psychotherapy* (FAP), which emphasizes the use of continuous in-clinic observations of client behavior. Basic elements of this approach include the continuous functional analysis of the ongoing interpersonal process present in the psychotherapy environment and immediate therapist reactions to client behavior that function to shape and reinforce improvements in the client's behavioral repertoire.

Initial behavioral assessments in FAP involve the identification of clinically relevant behaviors for reduction or promotion. In this phase of therapy, emphasis is placed on the identification of observable behaviors related to the client's problem areas that also occur in his or her natural environment and can be evoked in the context of the therapy. Examples of clinically relevant behaviors include the following: (a) displays of behaviors during the session that represent occurrences of the client's problematic behavior, with the therapeutic goal to decrease such behavior (e.g., excessive demands for reassurance, self-punitive statements); (b) the absence of behaviors related to the clinical problem, with the therapeutic goal to increase such behavior (e.g., awareness and verbalization of emotional experiences in an "emotion phobic" individual, assertive behaviors among a socially avoidant person); and (c) the client's verbal behavior as it relates to his or her own clinically relevant behavior and associated influencing variables (e.g., identification of situations that evoke problematic behavior, positive and negative consequences that follow problematic behavior).

As noted by Kohlenberg and Tsai (1991), therapy will likely be more effective if the client's problem behaviors or improvements occur within the session, when the therapist can immediately respond to them. As a result, FAP therapists' intervention strategies include evocation and observation of clinically relevant behaviors, and the immediate and natural reinforcement of client improvements. Natural reinforcers in therapeutic settings often include expressions by the therapist that communicate approval, care, concern, interest, liking or admiring the client, or therapist behaviors that reassure the client that the therapist is dependable and the therapy is secure (Linehan, 1993a).

Within sessions, contingency management procedures can also be used to decrease the occurrence of inappropriate or aversive client behaviors. For example, the therapist must first determine which reinforcers are maintaining a particular maladaptive behavior pattern and then systematically withhold those reinforcers following behavior. This can be an especially difficult thing for a therapist to do because behavior that is put under an extinction schedule often demonstrates an "extinction burst" in which the behavior initially becomes more intense, salient, or frequent prior to a reduction in frequency or intensity. Once a client's behavior is placed on an extinction schedule, the therapist must continue to withhold reinforcement of such behavior, even when behavior frequency or intensity initially escalates (Linehan, 1993a).

For behavior under extinction, it is often useful to find another behavior to reinforce, particularly one that is incompatible with the behavior undergoing extinction. With a client on an extinction schedule, it is often important for the therapist to validate the client's communications about what he or she wants and needs and to assist the client in finding more appropriate ways to have these wants and needs met.

Overly Rigid Rule Governance

One possible negative consequence of overly rigid rule governance is that excessive rule influence may result in an individual becoming relatively insensitive to changing contingencies in the immediate environment (Follette & Hayes, 2000). The end result is likely to be behavior that is excessively inflexible and not optimally effective because the individual is primary concerned about rule following, not with what actually works in the current environment. In this section, strategies for relaxing rigid rule governance are described

Shift From Rule-Control to Contingency Control

Hayes, Strosahl, and Wilson (1999) suggested that some individuals who exhibit overly rigid and inflexible behaviors or who display obsessive characteristics do so in the larger services of wanting to be good, to please others, or not to offend. Other such individuals may engage in a variety of time-consuming, if not harmful, behaviors (e.g., obsessive ruminations, compulsions, self-injury) in an effort to avoid private experiences regarded as "bad," "intolerable," "consuming," and the like. ACT, in part, attempts to undermine the role that verbal functions play in the nonadaptive regulation of behavior. In particular, ACT is concerned with the client's avoidance of private events (e.g., thoughts, feelings, and sensations) as well as the environmental contexts that may occasion such events. Aversive private events can be avoided through a variety of means, including active or passive behavioral avoidance (e.g., physically leaving the shopping mall when one initially feels anxious, avoidance of intimate relationships for a person with a sexual abuse history), substance use (e.g., alcohol misuse to "numb the pain"), or a variety of covert avoidance strategies (e.g., thought suppression, dissociation). A paradox associated with such avoidance is that it tends to have only short-term benefits and often results in the avoided experiences becoming more common or predominant in the future (Hayes, Strosahl, & Wilson, 1999). In ACT, special attention is given to verbal functions that contribute to the avoidance of private experiences, such as reason giving (e.g., "My depression prevented me from going to the party"), evaluation (e.g., "Anxiety is bad and should be avoided"), and literality (e.g., "I feel worthless so I must be worthless").

Cognitive Therapy Techniques to Promote Rule Evaluation and Appraisal

At the most basic level, traditional cognitive therapy is concerned with the identification and modification of unhealthy modes of thinking so as to influence beneficially emotion and behavior. In relation to depression specifically, depressed persons are presumed to have a depressogenic cognitive style or schema that consists of negative views about self, world, and future, with thought processes and perceptions systematically distorted in a negative way so as to maintain these negative views (Beck et al., 1979). In cognitive therapy, then, the focus of therapy is on the modification of automatic thoughts and schemas to effect change in mood and behavior.

From a behavioral perspective, thinking is the same as behaving (Hayes & Ju, 1998). One aspect of thinking involves the formation and subsequent adherence to self-rules, which can be construed as verbal stimuli that come about as a result of ongoing interactions with the social environment (Hayes & Ju, 1998). Prepositional forms of logic that clients may use (as illustrated in "if . . . , then . . . " statements, such as "If I am nice, bad things won't happen to me") and other beliefs about their behavior often take the form of reasons or rules (Zettle & Hayes, 1982). Following Skinner, behavior therapists such as Hayes suggest that unproductive rules clients hold can be modified through the arrangement of situations in which the natural consequences of rules can be contacted, often resulting in a modification of that rule. Behavioral experiments, reviewed in the following section, are one such method for modifying inaccurate rule or reason statements.

Behavioral Experiments

When beliefs or rules are identified in therapy that function to influence behavior, the therapist, in collaboration with the client, can develop an experiment that tests validity of the assumptions that underlie the client's belief or rule (Beck et al., 1979). With this technique, the client is first encouraged to view beliefs as hypotheses to be tested. The therapist and client then work together in collaboration to devise a meaningful test of these beliefs. Once the experiment has been undertaken, the client is encouraged to evaluate whether the assumptions associated with the tested belief were supported or disconfirmed.

For example, a client may say something such as, "Nothing makes a difference. I feel equally terrible all day" (Beck et al., 1979, p. 125). A behavior therapist may first work with the client to help him or her view this belief as a hypothesis to be tested. Once this has been achieved, a test of this belief can be arranged, such as a self-monitoring exercise whereby the client is instructed to record the following over a period of several days: (a) the time of day in hour-long intervals, (b) activities that were engaged in during that interval, and (c) average mood rating (from 0 = *worst I ever felt* to 10 = *best I ever felt*) for that interval. Many clients who engage in this type of self-monitoring exercise often discover that activities and events do make a difference and that mood quality varies over the course of the day and usually in relation to the type of activity that one performs.

Behavioral experiments can also be particularly helpful when clients demonstrate low self-efficacy. Bandura (1986) defined self-efficacy as a set of beliefs or expectations about one's ability to perform behaviors. Low self-efficacy would be evident when the client expresses the view that he or she does not have the ability to enact a particular behavior. From a cognitive perspective, Bandura suggested that positive self-efficacy expectations function as incentives for behavior, whereas negative efficacy expectations tend to function as disincentives for behavior.

Person ———————→ Behavior
(efficacy expectations)

Although behavior therapists may conceptualize this process differently (e.g., skills deficits, inadequate learning, verbal functions associated with derived stimulus relations), therapists from various theoretical perspectives generally agree that clients are unlikely to enact behaviors that are (a) not in their repertoire, (b) relatively underdeveloped or deficient in their associated skill level, or (c) strongly influenced by inaccurate reason or rule statements (e.g., "My anxiety prevents me from going into the grocery store").

Behavioral experiments may be particularly helpful when clients display ideas concerning negative outcomes for behavior, sometimes referred to as *outcome expectancies*. Bandura, from a cognitive perspective, suggested that rewards for behavior from the environment function to provide information about the relationship between behavior and environmental outcomes. Positive outcome expectations function as incentives for behavior, whereas negative outcome expectations tend to function as disincentives.

Behavior ———————→ Outcome or Consequence
(outcome expectations)

Behavior therapists, in contrast, would place greater emphasis on the actual consequences that follow behavior as determinants of its future probability or on the information about behavior–consequence relations provided by discriminative stimuli or rule statements. From either perspective, however, behavior is less likely to occur if the outcomes associated with it are apt to be ineffective or undesirable. Behavioral experiments can be used to determine whether behavior can produce desirable or effective outcomes in particular environments.

Tacting Environment–Behavior Relations

A *tact* is a verbal behavior (spoken, written) that is influenced by a nonverbal discriminative stimulus (Mallott et al., 2000). For example, if a child points to a red, round object and states, "that is an apple," and if the child is correct, then he or she has accurately tacted a verbal relation (the word "apple") to a nonverbal stimulus (the object "apple").

The tacting of environment–behavior associations involves the process of establishing an accurate verbal relation that describes the effect that behavior has on the environment. Some clients display only minimal awareness of the effects of their behavior. This lack of awareness may be evident by verbal rule statements that inaccurately characterize the relationships between behavior and outcomes (e.g., following the revocation of a driver's license because of a third DUI, a person states in an incredulous manner, "My drinking hasn't caused me any problems before!").

In behavior therapy, self-monitoring strategies are often used to facilitate the establishment of connections between behavior and consequences. For example, in dialectical behavior therapy (DBT; Linehan, 1993a), clients are encouraged to complete a diary card each day that asks about a number of clinically relevant behaviors (e.g., drug use, suicidal ideation, self-harm behavior). The DBT diary card also asks clients to monitor the use of coping skills and whether these skills were effective if used. By keeping track of this information, clients are more likely to develop accurate statements concerning the associations between their coping behavior and resultant outcomes.

Psychoeducation

Sometimes, clients and their families have erroneous beliefs related to psychological conditions. For example, among some family members, there may be a tendency to blame a family member with schizophrenia for his or her negative symptoms rather than to see these symptoms as part of the schizophrenia condition. It has become widely recognized that the simple provision of information to clients and their families about psychological conditions can in itself be an important treatment component (Hogarty, 2002; Miklowitz, 2001). As observed by Hogarty (2002), the provision of accurate information can help clients and their families gain better understanding about the etiological and maintaining factors associated with a psychological condition and perhaps alleviate guilt, hopelessness, or blame. Such information can also clarify the rationale for any treatment plan that is offered and make more apparent the potential utility of various treatment components.

Establishing Operations Associated With Substance Intoxication

As we noted in chapter 3, several events can function as establishing operations (or motivating events) for substance use. These include social conflict and associated negative feeling states, the presence of conditioned stimuli that have been previously associated with substance intoxication (and the associated "high"), states of physiological withdrawal (i.e., reduced tissue concentrations of the substance), and drug cravings following an interval of nonuse. These events, when present, can establish a motivation for substance use (Wulfert et al., 1996). Furthermore, once a substance has been consumed, the intoxicated state can act as an additional establishing operation for disinhibited behavior (Gray, 1987a).

Because of space limitations, we cannot offer a comprehensive review of the various behavior therapies for substance abuse disorders, particularly those that are well suited for countering establishing operations associated with substance use. The following represents a small sample of such approaches.

Cue Exposure

Cue exposure involves the presentation of substance cues (e.g., sight and smell) without allowing consumption to take place. This procedure is generally thought to be an extinction-based approach that facilitates the attenuation of emotional and physiological reactions associated with drug craving.

Cue exposure can be carried out in a variety of ways. In the case of cue exposure for alcohol misuse, a client may be seated in front of a glass of his or her most frequently consumed alcoholic beverage. The clients may then be directed to sniff the beverage and look at the glass for a prolonged period and to note the various thoughts, feelings, and physiological sensations that arise during the exposure.

Cue exposure can alternatively involve the continuous exposure to an open beverage throughout the session, with portions of the session focused on the sight and smell of the beverage. When the sight and smell of the beverage is the object of the client's attention, he or she may also be asked to imagine himself or herself in situations previously identified as trigger situations for drinking. A guided practice component could also be added in which the client is encouraged to use coping skills to reduce the urge to drink during the imaginal or in vivo exposure. There is some indication that this procedure in combination with other treatment elements is effective for reducing alcohol consumption among persons who abuse or are dependent on alcohol (e.g., Sitharthan, Sitharthan, Hough, & Kavanagh, 1997).

Urge Surfing

Among persons who misuse substances, urges associated with substance use are commonly experienced following prolonged periods of substance nonuse or during periods of negative emotional arousal (Lloyd, 2003). Urges and the events that give rise to them are often potent establishing operations for further substance use, as they function to potentiate the reinforcing properties of intoxication.

As a therapeutic technique, urge surfing challenges the client to experience and cope with urges to use while refraining from substance use. Four basic components are associated with this technique (Lloyd, 2003; Marlatt & Gordon, 1985). First, clients are provided with a description of the technique and its associated rationale. In the course of this description, urges are conceptualized as a natural feature of habit disorders and addictive behaviors. Urge surfing is presented as a skill that can be developed with practice and that can be applied to counter urges that typically precede episodes of substance misuse. Second, time is taken to develop an awareness of substance abuse situations. The therapist and client work together to identify the typical antecedents and consequences of substance abuse, especially those associated with high-risk situations. Coping plans for responding to these situations might also be developed, such as strategies for avoiding high-risk situations or coping strategies (including urge surfing) that can be used when such situations are unavoidable. Third, the therapist clarifies with the client how urges are experienced (e.g., where is it experienced, what does it feel like, what thoughts and feelings typically accompany the urge, how does the nature of the urge change over time?). Once the nature of these experiences is clarified, the client is taught the urge surfing skill. In this approach, the urge is portrayed as an ocean wave that slowly and gradually builds until the time when it crests and then gradually subsides. The crest of the wave is analogous to the peak of the urge, the point at which the tendency to act on the urge through substance use is at its greatest strength. Clients are instructed that it is possible to be an observer of the rise and fall of these urges, or to surf these urges, without becoming "wiped out" by them. Fourth, after the client has had practice with urge surfing, it is important to evaluate how skillful he or she is in applying the behavior and the degree to which it serves as an effective coping strategy. In the course of this review, the effects of urge surfing in relation to how the client regards his or her urges should be assessed. For example, has the client come to view urges as state conditions that will eventually pass on their own? Is the discomfort associated with not acting on urges tolerable? Is the client able to apply this skill in high-risk situations, and, if so, to what degree does it work? If urge surfing is effective, does this have implications for the client's longer term goals in relation to substance use (e.g., abstinence, controlled drinking)?

Motivational Enhancement or Motivational Interviewing

Motivational enhancement as an approach to therapy is based on principles from motivational psychology and is designed to produce rapid, internally motivated change (Miller & Rollnick, 1991). With this approach, motivational strategies are used to mobilize the client's own change resources.

Motivational enhancement therapy (MET) as applied in the Project MATCH treatment study (Miller et al., 1995) involved three primary treatment phases that included elements common among brief interventions that attempt to facilitate a change motivation (Miller & Rollnick, 1991). These are summarized in the FRAMES acronym:

- Feedback of personal risk or impairment
- Emphasis on personal Responsibility for change
- Clear Advice to client to make a change
- A Menu of alternative change options
- Therapist Empathy
- Facilitation of client Self-efficacy, hope, or optimism

The first phase involves building a motivation for change. Primary therapeutic interventions used in this stage consisted of the elicitation of self-motivational statements, empathic listening, questioning, feeding back pretreatment assessment information concerning alcohol use and its effects, client affirmation and validation, responding to client resistance, and reframing (the facilitation of the client's reexamination of his or her perceptions as they relate to drinking in light of new information or perspectives). The second stage involves the strengthening of the commitment to change. Component features of this phase include recognition of a readiness for change, planning for change, client choice in decisions to make change, anticipation of consequences associated with action and inaction, therapist provision of information and advice (including the rationale for abstinence as a personal goal), and the involvement of a significant other. The third phase involves the use of follow-through strategies as a means of capitalizing on an established motivation for change from the first two phases. This latter phase involves a review of progress, a renewal of motivation, and a reaffirmation of commitment.

Elimination of Establishing Operations Associated With Aversive States of Physiological Arousal or Activation

Several events can function as establishing operations (or motivating events) for aversive states of physiological arousal and activation. Operations that produce such states of arousal or activation can, in turn, alter the reinforcing properties of a variety of behaviors.

Following are some behavioral intervention strategies that are particularly well suited for countering establishing operations that lead to aversive states of arousal or activation or that may lessen these states once they have been produced.

Relaxation Training

A number of therapeutic techniques have been developed to reduce unpleasant physiological states (most notably anxiety or fear) through the facilitation of a state of activation or arousal that is incompatible with these aversive states. *Progressive muscle relaxation* (PMR) is one such technique. This technique involves the sequential tensing of isolated muscles to about three quarters of their potential tension for about 5 to 10 seconds, followed by a release of the muscle tension for about 20 seconds. This process is often repeated twice for each muscle group. While tensing and relaxing, the client is challenged to study the tension or to contrast the experience of tension with the experience associated with the release of muscle tension.

Clients who participate in a PMR treatment component are often asked to practice this one or twice a day for 20 minutes each session. Typically, a large number (e.g., 16) of muscle groups are initially targeted for tensing and relaxation, with this number subsequently halved (e.g., 8) and then halved again (e.g., 4). As the number of muscle groups is reduced, two other related techniques are typically introduced. *Relaxation by recall* involves the recall of the relaxed state achieved during progressive muscle relaxation. Once clients have had several different sessions of PMR, they will be able to recall what the experience of relaxation feels like. The recall of this experience can subsequently be used in anxiety-associated situations to decrease anxiety through promotion of the relaxed state. *Cue-controlled relaxation* involves the repetitive association of a word label with the letting go of tension in muscles during PMR. That is, in the moment the client lets go of muscle tension in the PMR exercises, he or she can covertly state a word such as "relax." Through both operant and classical conditioning processes, the word "relax" over time will serve as a potent verbal stimulus that can be used most anywhere for the facilitation of a relaxed state.

There is a good deal of evidence available indicating that muscle relaxation strategies are effective for reducing anxiety or aversive arousal states (Goldfried & Davison, 1976). Detailed descriptions of PMR can be found in Goldfried and Davison (1976).

Imagery techniques have also been used to produce changes in physiological states through the development of internal images that correspond to contexts historically associated with feeling states that are incompatible with aversive states. For example, a client might imagine a scene that is experienced as pleasant—perhaps related to some favored place that has previously been associated with feelings of calm, relaxation, or peace.

A few cautions related to the use of relaxation training for some clients. First, a small subset of clients find states of relaxation to be aversive, to the extent that such states may trigger intense anxiety or a panic attack. This intense anxiety or panic may be related to a sense of losing control. To reduce the likelihood of such outcomes, clients should be assured in advance that they are in control of this process, and that they may terminate relaxation proceedings at any time (Goldfried & Davison, 1976). Relaxation procedures based on muscle tensing, closed eyes, or imagery may also be contraindicated for persons with psychotic or seizure disorders.

Breathing Exercises and Meditation Practices

Breathing retraining is often useful for teaching clients to slow down and control their breathing and to breath from the abdomen rather than from the upper chest. This latter aspect of breathing retraining may be particularly useful for persons who experience panic attacks, because breathing from the abdomen will produce improved carbon dioxide exchange, which is sometimes disrupted during periods of hyperventilation common during panic episodes. Hazlett-Stevens and Craske (2003) described various approaches for breathing retraining.

Meditation practice, particularly in the form of mindfulness meditation, is primarily concerned with training the individual to focus on the present (not the past or hypothetical future). Mindfulness meditation practices promote a quality of attention characterized by noticing without choosing or without preference. In the context of practice, the person is challenged to become aware of and accept the constantly changing nature of life itself on a moment-to-moment basis.

Linehan (1993a, 1993b) has incorporated mindfulness practices into her multicomponent DBT treatment package. In DBT, Linehan differentiates between two types of mindfulness skills. One set of skills is characterized as the "what" skills, and these are central to what one does when being mindful. The three skills that belong to this group include observing, describing, and participating without self-consciousness. In DBT, an overarching goal associated with these skills is the facilitation of a lifestyle characterized by participation with awareness, because participation without awareness is presumed to be a key feature of impulsive and mood-dependent behaviors. The second set of mindfulness skills, or "how" skills, has to do with how one observes, describes, and participates. The three skills associated with this group of skills are taking a nonjudgmental stance, focusing on one thing in the moment, and being effective.

Alteration of Establishing Operations That Potentiate Reinforcing Properties Associated With Problematic Behavior Maintenance

Establishing operations refer to the motivational effect that certain environmental conditions have on behavior by altering the reinforcing or punishing qualities of events. Intervention strategies described in this section seek to alter or undermine the establishing operations that make problematic behavior more likely.

Satiation Therapy

As we noted in chapter 3, environmental events such as deprivation and satiation can alter the reinforcing properties of other events that follow behavior. When a person is deprived of water, for example, the reinforcing properties of water and similar substances become greater. As a result, under conditions of deprivation, the individual would likely exhibit frequent, persistent, and intense behavioral displays directed toward the attainment of water.

Behavior therapists have long recognized that some inappropriate or problematic behaviors are directly influenced by the power of the reinforcers that follow such behaviors. In some of these instances, reinforcers for problematic behaviors gain their influence because they are associated with the environmental deprivation of other related events.

Satiation therapy seeks to reduce the reinforcing properties of problematic behavior by satiating the individual with the reinforcers that problematic behavior produces. The provision of reinforcing events is done noncontingently, however, in relation to displays of the target behavior. One of the first applications of satiation therapy was focused on the hoarding behavior of an institutionalized client (Ayllon, 1963). This particular client hoarded towels and continued to do so despite verbal reprimands by hospital staff. When satiation procedures were implemented, the hospital staff noncontingently provided the client with towels over a several-week period, with an increasing number of towels delivered to her room each week during the intervention period. After awhile, not only did the client's towel hoarding behavior become substantially less frequent relative to pretreatment levels, she also actually removed towels from her room that the hospital staff previously delivered. Bowers (2003) has reviewed more contemporary applications of satiation therapy, most notably in the area of sexual deviance, as well as some of the basic procedures and ethical considerations associated with this approach.

RESPONSE PROBLEMS

In this section, we describe intervention strategies for developing, refining, or strengthening behavioral repertoires. As will become evident, the teaching of new behaviors can be regarded as analogous to providing the individual with the tools needed to respond flexibly and effectively to a variety of situations and scenarios, or to cope effectively with various demands or challenges.

Behavioral Deficits

Shaping

Shaping is one type of contingency management technique and is especially well suited to the development of new behavioral repertoires. This procedure involves the gradual development of complex behavior or behavior sequences through the reinforcement of closer and closer approximations to the final form of the behavior (Goldfried & Davison, 1976). With shaping procedures, a behavioral sequence is first broken down into smaller elements. Behavioral elements, when enacted, are reinforced on the basis of successive approximations to the final target behavior. As behavioral elements early in the sequence become established, reinforcement for those behaviors is faded while the next behavior in the sequence is prompted. When emitted following the display of earlier established behaviors in the sequence, this next behavior in the sequence becomes the object of reinforcement. This process of fading, prompting, and reinforcement is continued until which time the final form of behavior is established.

For young and old alike, shaping processes are involved in the acquisition of new and complex behavioral sequences or repertoires. One of the authors of this book is in the initial stages of learning a new language. Because he has had no previous exposure to this language, the shaping processes involved in developing the most rudimentary skills related to the use of this new language are very elemental, very basic, and often require several trials to learn.

Therapy in the most general sense often represents a shaping process, as therapy typically involves instruction in new and effective coping behaviors and the application of such behaviors in contexts where they are potentially most useful. Explicit shaping procedures have been used for a wide variety of clinical conditions, such as the facilitation of verbal expression among persons with schizophrenia who were electively mute (Isaacs, Thomas, & Goldiamond, 1960) and training in social skills among those with schizophrenia (Pratt & Mueser, 2002). Shaping processes are often involved in the development of any new skill or behavioral repertoire.

Self-Reinforcement

Self-reinforcement involves the establishment of a reinforcement contingency for the enactment of certain behaviors. The basic principle that underlies this technique is the notion that reinforced behaviors will become more frequent or probable.

One common self-reinforcement technique for increasing behavior frequency is called *Premacking*, named after David Premack, who suggested the approach. The basic idea here is that the engagement in frequent behavioral activities (that are presumed to be reinforcing) can be used to reinforce engagement in less frequent activities. If, for example, a person frequently watches movies but infrequently studies for school exams, the act of watching a movie can be made contingent on (or reinforce) studying for school exams. That is, only until an individual studies for some number of hours can she then follow that activity with viewing a movie.

Premack's approach is a bit different from that used in traditional behavior theory, as he conceptualizes behaviors as reinforcing events. Although there are some controversial aspects associated with this conceptualization, and some basic unanswered questions (e.g., "why do activities that occur more often reinforce other activities?"; Mallot et al., 2000, p. 166), the Premack procedure has been applied in a number of behavior change interventions. For example, this procedure has been used to facilitate attention to in-class instructional tasks among preschool children (Homme, DeBaca, Devine, Steinhorst, & Rickert, 1963), to increase ambulatory behavior in a person with conversion disorder (Kallman, Hersen, & O'Toole, 1975), and to increase behavior activity among people with schizophrenia (Mitchell & Stoffelmayr, 1973).

Behavioral Rehearsal/Role-Playing

The principle use of behavioral rehearsal or role-playing in behavior therapy is to help clients learn new ways of responding in specific situations, or *how* to do a particular behavior (Goldfried & Davison, 1976). As delineated by Goldfried and Davison (1976), there are four primary stages in behavioral rehearsal:

- client preparation, which involves clients' recognition of the relevant behavioral deficit and willingness to learn a new and relevant behavior through rehearsal processes;
- selection of a target situation, specifically an example of a situation in which effective behavioral responses are absent that, in turn, results in distress or impairment;
- behavioral rehearsal in the clinical setting, which involves the production of behavioral enactments coupled with direct instruction, modeling, shaping processes, and feedback as delivered by the therapist; and
- enactment of rehearsed behaviors in real-life situations, with attention given to how effective the behavior was in these situations (e.g., did it produce the desired consequences?).

Direct Instruction, Coaching, and Cheerleading Strategies

Direct instruction and coaching procedures involve telling or physically showing a client how to perform a certain behavior or sequence of behaviors and to provide the client with information about contexts within which such behavior would or would not be appropriate. In contrast to behavioral rehearsal and role-play, which are concerned with *how* to execute a behavior, direct instruction and coaching involve telling the client *what* to do (Goldfried & Davison, 1976).

From time to time, coaching strategies may give way to *cheerleading strategies* (Linehan, 1993a). With such strategies, the therapist validates the client's ability to overcome difficulties and to improve his or her quality of life. As noted by Linehan, the task here is to balance an appreciation of the difficulties associated with making progress with realistic assurances of hope and confidence that the client can develop the behavioral patterns that he or she associates with positive change.

Observational Learning

In observational learning or modeling procedures, the therapist will enact a series of behavior sequences and note to the client what he or she is doing and how the behavior is being enacted. While the therapist is modeling behavior, the client observes and discriminates the components of the therapist's behavior.

Observational learning approaches are particularly useful for teaching new behavior patterns that combine sets of existing behavioral repertoires. In addition to teaching new behaviors, models can also demonstrate coping efforts. If the coping behavior is effective and the observer is able to discriminate that the behavior was effective, then it is more likely that the observer will enact the model's coping behavior in similar future circumstances (Bandura, 1986).

Social Skills Training

Social skills are particularly important skills because individuals are more likely to experience reinforcement from the social environment if they have learned the requisite social behaviors for obtaining such reinforcers. Social skills training programs are carried out in much the same way as any other form of skills training, and typically involve (a) skills acquisition (e.g., instructions, modeling), (b) skills strengthening (e.g., behavioral rehearsal, feedback), and (c) skills generalization (e.g., homework assignments to practice skills in relevant contexts in between sessions, discussions of similarities and differences associated with target situations).

In social skills training, emphasis is usually placed on the shaping of response topographies or patterns associated with social behavior. As some (e.g., Follette & Hayes, 2000) have noted, however, there are drawbacks associated with such an approach, because many forms of behavior in a given social context can produce similar and effective outcomes. In addition to shaping up new behaviors based on form, therapists who embark on social skills training should also emphasize response effectiveness in the evaluation of behavior skill.

Social skills training programs are often done in the context of a multicomponent treatment package. Behavioral rehearsal, modeling, and direct instruction and coaching are typically components in such training programs. Twentyman and Zimering (1979) outlined the components of social skills training that involves the following elements:

- Behavioral rehearsal of target responses;
- Modeling on the part of the therapist;
- Instructing clients in appropriate behaviors (coaching);
- Feedback and reinforcements;
- Homework assignments to engage in social behaviors;
- Projected positive consequences (e.g., client imagines positive ;outcomes associated with assertive responses); and
- Cognitive modifications, such as self-statement training.

Assertiveness training is a specific form of social skills training that has as its goal the removal of barriers to open self-expression, including instruction in behavioral skills consistent with this goal (Alberti & Emmons, 1990). Assertiveness can be defined as an interpersonal interaction pattern whereby the individual expresses his or her needs, feelings, and desires and does so in a manner that does not violate the rights of other persons (Alberti & Emmons, 1990; Dow, 1994). Because many clients have passive or aggressive tendencies (or both), assertiveness training has become a widely used component in social skills training programs.

Coping Skills Training

Coping skills vary considerably in terms of their complexity and generalizability across situations or contexts. When assisting a client to develop healthy forms of coping, attention should be given to situations in which coping is difficult as evident by the use of maladaptive coping strategies in such settings.

Although coping skills vary in form and application, the following constitutes a general framework for teaching coping skills, whereby the therapist provides

- a definition of the coping skill;
- a rationale for the coping skill;
- an explanation of the mechanism by which the skill works;
- a physical demonstration of the skill;
- guidelines for the application and practice the skill;
- guidelines for the evaluation of the efficacy of the skill; and
- instruction in how the skill can be applied in a variety of real-life situations.

Problem Solving

Problem solving represents a specific coping skill that is often relevant for a variety of challenging situations. Goldfried and Davison (1976) and Linehan (1993a) noted that problem-solving skills are often deficient among some clinical populations. The difficulty that some people have in coming up with solutions to the problems of life no doubt contributes to their distress, despair, and hopelessness.

There are five main components of problem solving, which can be subsumed under the acronym "SOLVE" (McKay et al., 1997):

- S (State the problem): In this step, the client attempts to discriminate the features of the problem or situation at hand. These may be related to some external situation or challenge or may be associated with internal events, such as problematic thoughts or feelings (Goldfried & Davison, 1976).
- O (Outline your goals): Once the problem has been identified, the client should try to identify what the desired goals are in this situation, that is, what needs to occur for the problem to be resolved. The more specific a person can be in this regard, the better.
- L (List the alternatives): In this step, the client is challenged to come up with a list of possible solutions to the problem at hand, that is, things that he or she can do to produce a desirable effect. In this stage, self-censoring is discouraged. Rather, the person is encouraged to come up with as many novel responses

as possible and to consider ways in which separate ideas can be combined.

- **V** (View the consequences): In this step, the client considers the list of possible solutions in terms of the likelihood that they will be effective in helping him or her realize goals in this situation. Once considered, the person selects the approach or approaches deemed most likely to succeed and develops a plan for putting this alternative into action.
- **E** (Evaluate the outcome): Once the client has tried an alternative approach to responding, he or she then considers whether this response has produced the desired effect. If so, the problem has been resolved. If not, the person may reenter this process at the third step ("L") and try something different to produce the desired goal.

Graded Task Assignments

Graded tasks assignments involve the breaking down of more complex forms of behavior into smaller elements. As Martell et al. (2001) noted, for persons who are depressed, the thought of carrying out the smallest activity can seem overwhelming. By breaking up an activity into smaller units, an activity that was once experienced as overwhelming can become more manageable because the person can focus on one small unit at a time rather than the activity as a whole.

Martell et al. (2001) further suggested that graded task assignments can be especially helpful for those who engage in avoidance behavior. Through the use of graded task assignments, the client can be encouraged to expose himself or herself to a series of feared situations that gradually increase in relation to the amount of fear and avoidance they typically evoke.

Self-Instruction

Self-instructions, or verbally stating behavioral instructions or rules either overtly or covertly, can be a method for guiding behavior. Stress inoculation training (SIT), a treatment approach developed by Donald Meichenbaum (1994), has as a centerpiece the use of self-instruction methods. These consist of three components administered sequentially: (a) an educational phase during which the client is provided with an explanation of how some thinking patterns influence ineffective behavior or negative emotions, (b) a rehearsal phase during which the client generates coping self-statements that can be applied in difficult situations, and (c) an implementation phase during which the client uses these coping self-statements in problematic situations.

Coping self-statements are divided into four categories: (a) preparing for a stressor (e.g., "What do I have to do?"), (b) confronting and responding to a stressor (e.g., "Don't make more out of this than I have to"), (c) coping with feelings of being overwhelmed (e.g., "Time to take a slow, deep breath"), and (d) self-reinforcement for effective coping (e.g., "I can be pleased with the progress I'm making").

Experiential and Behavioral Avoidance

Experiential and behavioral avoidance are thought to be instrumental in the maintenance of many forms of problematic behavior (e.g., Hayes, Strosahl, & Wilson 1999), most notably those that define the various anxiety disorders. With experiential and behavioral avoidance, the person engages in actions that function to terminate contact with contexts or events experienced as aversive. Avoidance and escape behaviors are often maintained by their associated short-term (negatively) reinforcing effects (i.e., the termination of something aversive). However, when used frequently and inflexibly over time, avoidance and escape behaviors will often result in impairments and a host of other associated problems. Therapeutic strategies reviewed in this section seek to promote a range of behaviors responses and reactions to aversive contexts as a means to promote effective and adaptive coping.

Exposure Therapy–Exposure and Response Prevention

Exposure-based therapies have largely been influenced by Mowrer's (1947) two-factor theory of fear conditioning and maintenance. The two factors in this model are classical conditioning and operant conditioning. Classical conditioning processes are thought to underlie fear acquisition. That is, classical conditioning processes were proposed to account for the high levels of fear and anxiety found among individuals exposed to traumatic events. In this process, the unconditional stimuli (US) would be the aversive or traumatic event that, in turn, evokes unlearned or unconditional responses (UR), such as fear or anxiety. As a result of conditioning, previously neutral cues become conditional stimuli (CS) as a result of their association with the US, and these CS acquire the property of eliciting fear and anxiety (i.e., conditional emotional responses, or CRs), responses that are topographically similar to the URs.

For example, Figure 6.1 depicts the classical conditioning processes associated with a physical assault (US) committed by a man at night who used a wooden stick in the assault. Also, during the assault, the assault survivor detected the smell of a common aftershave lotion on the man and heard him speak with a British accent.

Weeks after the assault, the assault survivor displayed fear and panic (CRs) to a variety of trauma-related stimuli (e.g., outdoors at night, men with British accents, smell of a particular aftershave, wooden sticks). These environmental contexts, or situations in which these cues could be present, were subsequently experienced as anxiety evoking.

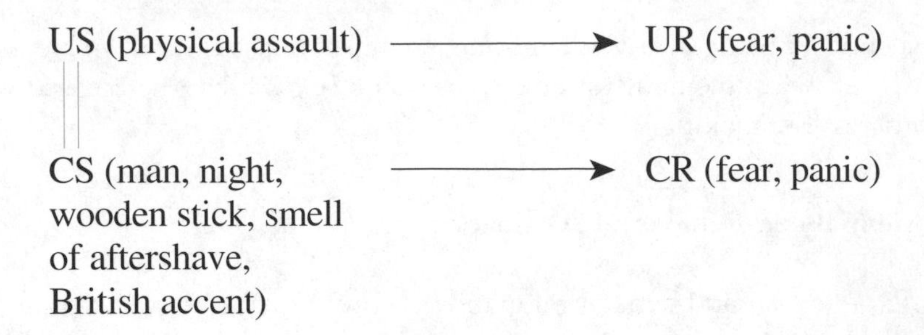

Figure 6.1. Classical conditioning process associated with acquired fear responses. The parallel vertical lines that link the unconditional stimulus (US) and conditional stimulus (CS) indicate that a conditioned association has been established. CR = conditional response; UR = unconditional response.

The operant conditioning process in Mowrer's two-factor model is associated with fear maintenance through escape and avoidance coping. That is, presentation of CS in the absence of the US would not produce extinction of fear (CR) related to conditioned trauma cues so long as the individual sought to avoid or escape from the conditional stimuli (CS). Negatively reinforced behavioral avoidance of CS, in turn, functions to maintain the conditional response (CR) of fear to the CS.

According to the principles associated with Mowrer's two-factor model, a variety of exposure therapies have been applied to the treatment of acquired fears or avoidance behaviors (e.g., prolonged exposure, systematic desensitization, flooding). These exposure therapies seek to weaken the association between the conditional fear response (CR) and trauma-related cues (CS) through deliberate exposure to CS cues in the absence of US cues until habituation occurs. Through exposure, the client learns that anxiety linked to the CS will reduce on its own in the absence of any avoidance or escape response. Also through exposure, the conditioned UC–CS pairing is weakened as the individual is exposed for prolonged periods to the CS in the absence of the US.

With PTSD as an example, the following is an outline of the procedure that might be used for conducting exposure-based therapy. The first step would involve an assessment of trauma-related stimuli (CS) and their associated level of fear or anxiety (CR). Trauma-related stimuli can include objects such as weapons, situations such as being alone at night, or internal images or thoughts that might have been present during the traumatizing event. An anxiety rating system is devised whereby the client can assign a numerical value to indicate the degree of anxiety or fear associated with each stimulus situation (e.g., 0 = *no fear at all*, 100 = *most fear ever experienced*).

The second step involves the development of a trauma-related exposure hierarchy (for either imaginal or in vivo exposure). For each item in the hierarchy, a scene should be developed that can be subsequently imagined or to which the individual can be directly exposed. These trauma-related scenes or stimuli should then be hierarchically arranged from lowest to highest according to their associated fear rating.

The third step involves gradual prolonged exposure. Gradual exposure is characterized by exposure to situations that evoke minimal anxiety, followed by gradual progress toward those that are more difficult. A therapist would typically begin with the item in the exposure hierarchy that is associated with the least amount of fear and work upward from there. In the case of imaginal exposure, a scene is described, and the client is asked to imagine it vividly. As an alternative, the client can describe the scene in as much detail as possible if it is a scene that he or she personally experienced. In the case of in vivo exposure, or direct exposure to the feared stimulus of event, the client may be encouraged to focus directly on the feared stimulus cues (without accompanying distraction or other avoidance strategies) and to report continuously his or her experiences while focusing on these cues.

During either the imaginal or in vivo exposure, the therapist regularly (e.g., every 2–3 minutes) samples the client's anxiety level according to the rating system previously used. Anxiety ratings are taken repeatedly throughout the exposure period to monitor anxiety levels and to assess the effects of habituation processes. Exposure to a given fear-evoking scene should continue until anxiety associated with the scene has significantly attenuated for a sustained period (e.g., at least 50% below baseline or preexposure levels). Because a good deal of time may be required for habituation to occur, sessions might be scheduled for 90 minutes or more.

The last step involves exposure-based homework assignments. Clients can expose themselves to feared items in between sessions. For this to be effective, clients must fully understand the procedures for exposure. By the end of treatment, ideally, clients should make efforts almost every day to expose themselves systematically to fear-eliciting stimuli.

Exposure sessions also often involve a response prevention component. The response that is prevented could be behavioral or covert avoidance, or it could be mental or behavioral rituals or compulsions that have an avoidance function. Before embarking on an exposure and response prevention intervention, the therapist and client often work collaboratively to develop guidelines for the response prevention procedure. Such guidelines might include a provision that stipulates a limitation on reassurance seeking from client (e.g., "is this safe?"). During response prevention in the context of exposure, the client is not permitted to engage in rituals to decrease distress following exposure to feared stimuli. During the exposure, the therapist should assess for use of "mini rituals" or mental rituals by the client that could attenuate the effects of exposure. "Cold turkey" abandonment of rituals is more effective than gradual abandonment. For more information on the use of exposure therapy for anxiety conditions, the reader is referred to the work of Edna Foa and Gail Steketee (e.g., Foa & Rothbaum, 1998; Steketee, 1993).

The key mechanism that promotes therapeutic change in exposure therapy appears to be the exposure to the fear-eliciting stimuli in the absence of any negative or aversive consequences (Follette & Hayes, 2000). Because exposure is an evocative therapy, and because avoidant, fearful, or traumatized individuals also often display other clinically relevant behaviors (e.g., self-injury, substance abuse), there are number of considerations that should be entertained before conducting exposure-based therapies with clients. Exposure should not be undertaken with those with psychosis, severe depression, low IQ, or current substance dependence, or with those who engage in self-injury or have suicidal ideation with some degree of accompanying intent.

Inappropriate Conditioned Emotional Response

Many emotional disorders and some behavioral disorders are characterized by strong emotional reactions to environmental cues or events. Depending on the nature of the emotional reaction, approach or avoidance behaviors may become more likely in the presence of these cues or events. Therapeutic interventions such as those described in this section can be used to reduce or eliminate conditioned emotional reactions that accompany problematic approach or avoidance behaviors.

Covert Sensitization (or Covert Conditioning)

Covert sensitization is a procedure that has been used to decrease the likelihood of a response as a result of pairing an imagined response with an imagined aversive consequence. This approach combines the use of imagery with basic operant learning and classical conditioning principles. Covert behaviors (thoughts, images, feelings) are the targets for this procedure, and it is believed that the modification of these covert behaviors through their association with imagined aversive consequences can facilitate positive change in other domains (e.g., result in the decrease in targeted overt behaviors or physiological responses; Upper & Cautela, 1979).

When using this method to facilitate a decrease in an unwanted behavior, the therapist and client will work together to develop an imaginal situation or context within which the problematic behavior will be displayed and immediately followed by an unpleasant image of an associated consequence (often nausea or fear). These imaginal scenes also typically include a negative reinforcement aspect in which the person is encouraged to imagine feeling better once he or she escapes the context within which the problematic behavior took place.

One area in which covert sensitization has been used is to decrease inappropriate behaviors. Exhibitionism has been one behavior treated successfully with this method, as have habit disorders such as smoking (Upper & Cautela, 1979).

Behavioral Excesses

Positive or negative reinforcement processes, or the simultaneous influence of both processes, invariably maintain behavioral excesses. As a result, behavioral interventions for reducing problematic behavioral excesses, such as those described below, often involve changing the reinforcing properties associated with such behavior.

Removal of Reinforcers Following Inappropriate Behavior Excesses

This procedure involves the contingent removal of reinforcers (e.g., attention, privileges, a favored toy) following an undesirable behavior. The general term for this procedure is *response cost,* because this negative punishment procedure involves the loss of something that is valued or reinforcing following the occurrence of a problematic behavior. One common response cost procedure is *time-out.* With this procedure, a child's misbehavior is immediately responded to with a short verbal reprimand and placement in a time-out setting (i.e., a setting that is free of any potential reinforcers that may support the child's misbehavior—ideally a place that the child finds boring). Clark (1985) suggested that the amount of time spent in time-out should be 1 minute for each year of age. Detailed guidelines for time-out are presented in Clark (1985).

Response cost procedures can also be used for adult misbehavior or excesses. For example, an individual who wants to decrease and eventually stop cigarette smoking may set up a "donation jar," to which he or she makes a financial contribution (say $3) for every cigarette consumed above and beyond the target number for that day. At the end of the intervention period, any monies in the donation jar would then be donated to a charitable organization that the person finds particularly offensive (e.g., a political party that holds views opposite to those held by the person who is attempting to reduce his or her behavior).

Extinction and Differential Reinforcement

Extinction involves the attenuation or elimination of a behavior as a result of the removal of either positive or negative reinforcement following behavior. As such, procedures used to promote extinction should only be used if the goal is to reduce substantially or eliminate a particular behavior that was previously reinforced.

Differential reinforcement involves the replacement of an inappropriate response with another response. This goal is accomplished through the reinforcement of one set of responses while another set of responses (i.e., the inappropriate ones) is placed under an extinction schedule. *Differential reinforcement of an alternative behavior* occurs when the replacement response that is reinforced functions to produce the same outcome as the inappropriate behavior. *Differential reinforcement of an incompatible behavior* occurs when a behavior is reinforced that is incompatible with another behavior.

A first step in the use of extinction procedures is to identify the reinforcer that maintains excessive behavioral displays. For escape and avoidance behavior, one would assume that such behavior is maintained because it functions to terminate something aversive. For other behaviors, positive reinforcement processes are likely involved. A second step would be to reinforce a different response or a response that is either an alternative to or incompatible with the response that is being extinguished (Goldfried & Davison, 1976). Reinforcement of either an alternative or incompatible behavior will often facilitate the extinction process while at the same time strengthening a different, and perhaps more appropriate, behavior.

Habit Reversal

Habit reversal techniques are particularly well suited for repetitive problem behaviors. To date, this technique has been most commonly applied in the treatment of tic disorders and trichotillomania, although it has been used to eliminate or reduce other repetitive behaviors such as stuttering, nail biting, skin picking and scratching, and teeth grinding (Adams, Adams, & Miltenberger, 2003).

Two components of the habit reversal procedure appear to be primarily responsible for positive treatment effects when observed: awareness training and competing response training (Adams et al., 2003). *Awareness training* first involves an assessment of the degree to which the client is aware that the problematic behavior is occurring each time he or she performs it. The component features and different manifestations of the habit are also clarified, as are the antecedent conditions that typically set the occasion for the behavior's occurrence. In *competing response training,* the client attempts to stop the problematic behavior immediately as soon as he or she is aware of its occurrence and to perform a response that competes with the target behavior. With this procedure, the competing behavior serves as a replacement for the habit. In the case of nail biting, for example, the client might instead put on hand lotion or gloves, or engage in an activity such as squeezing a small ball. The activity that is selected should make hands unavailable for nail biting and should be appropriate or unremarkable for the environments within which it is displayed. Adams et al. (2003) described other applications of the habit reversal procedure.

PROBLEMS WITH REINFORCING CONTINGENCIES

A central thesis of this book is that the consequences that follow behavior have a substantial influence on its subsequent occurrence. For this reason, behaviorally oriented clinicians are concerned about what happens following displays of problematic behavior. The variety of ways that an environment responds (or does not respond) to behavior is frequently examined in behavior therapy because, as this section indicates, problems can occur in any number of areas.

Behavior Ineffectively Controlled

Self-Control Training

Within behavior theory and therapy, *self-control* has been defined as "behavior that leads to alterations in the probability of selecting one outcome, or end state, over another" (Karoly, 1995, p. 263). Self-control training procedures involve the self-administration of consequences following behavior to facilitate the movement toward a desired outcome. This occurs when an individual deliberately alters the contingencies associated with problematic behaviors in an effort to change those behaviors. Because an absence of self-control often implies behavior under the influence of immediate environmental rewards, such behavior often has an associated impulsive quality (Logue, 1995). Component processes associated with this behavior change method include self-monitoring of target behaviors, self-evaluation of behavior in relation to goals or objectives, and self-administration of consequences.

One form of self-control involves delay of gratification. Some behaviors become problematic because their associated short-term effects are gratifying or reinforcing, although the longer term effects of reward-seeking behavior can be deleterious. For example, some consume excessive amounts of alcohol for its immediate effects, even though long-term excessive use can lead to liver and brain damage. Likewise, the selection of food items for consumption based on immediate taste qualities can be quite gratifying. If these food items do not have health-sustaining or promoting properties, however, then adverse long-term effects may follow (e.g., diabetes, obesity, high blood pressure, coronary heart disease).

There is some suggestion that self-control procedures are most likely to be effective if the behavioral goal is publicly stated (Follette & Hayes, 2000). That is, the act of making the goal public brings to bear a number of proximal social contingencies, because people in the social environment will respond in varying ways depending on whether the person is or is not successful in realizing personal goals, or even exerting effort toward the realization of these goals.

The potential effectiveness of self-control procedures can also be enhanced if individuals attend to features other than specific outcomes or goals. For example, someone who wishes to lose weight might have more to gain by focusing on the development and maintenance of healthy eating habits and behaviors rather than the specific goal of losing 2 pounds per week.

Another strategy is to consider cost–benefit outcomes. When presented with a choice, a client can weigh the costs versus benefits or pros versus cons of acting in a particular way. When persons engage in the consequence-weighing process, self-control becomes more likely, perhaps because the process increases the salience of possible aversive outcomes associated with less controlled behavior. Modeling of self-control might likewise be beneficial. When persons can observe a model display choice behavior that emphasizes a more distal outcome and experience benefit as a result, there is an increased likelihood of self-control (Logue, 1995).

Another form of self-control involves overcoming established patterns of behavior (or habits) as well as behavior that may be influenced by our evolutionary history (or phylogenetic contingencies). Baumeister et al. (1994) have proposed a model that conceptualizes self-regulation as the inhibition of this normal or natural response and the substitution of another response (or no response) in its place. By "normal and natural response," these authors suggest that in the absence of self-regulation, people would respond to situations according to their learning history, habit, inclination, or innate tendencies. In their model, consequently, self-regulation is evident when an effort is made to alter one's own responses, including behaviors, thoughts, and feelings. As such, self-regulation involves the process of behavior change.

In their nonbehavioral model of self-regulation, Baumeister et al. (1994) emphasized three component features associated with self-regulation. *Standards* refer to abstract concepts as to how things should be and include social norms, personal goals, and expectations of others. From a behavioral perspective, standards often take the form of rule statements that, in turn, exert influence on behavior (i.e., rule-governed behavior). Baumeister and colleagues suggested that when standards are unclear or absent, or if standards are conflicting, self-regulation failure becomes more probable. *Monitoring* in their model involves paying attention to one's own actions and comparing one's actions against standards. In behavior therapy, this process would be called *self-monitoring*. They suggest that the less persons monitor their behavior, the more likely that efforts at self-regulation will fail. The last component in their model is *self-regulation strength* or *willpower*. Baumeister and colleagues proposed that willpower is a mechanism by which individuals muster the strength to alter normal or natural responses to bring responses more in line with standards. Behavior theorists and therapists have a difficult time accepting autonomous internal mechanisms or forces as sources of behavior and would eschew attempts to explain behavior through the use of such mentalistic concepts. It would be fully compatible in behavior theory, however, to discuss persistence as a response repertoire that can be shaped and otherwise influenced by environmental contingencies just like any other behavioral repertoire. Viewed in this way, persistence is a skill that can be developed or strengthened.

One application of self-control theory has been in the area of food consumption. Overeating relative to the expenditure of energy, or taking in more calories than are burned off, is one of the primary reasons for the epidemic of obesity noted in many cultures. For many individuals, instances of overeating are impulsive acts that involve an inability to delay immediate gratification in the service of more distal and desirable goals (e.g., greater physical health and fitness, more attractive body, decreased likelihood for illness or disease; Logue, 1995; see also Farmer, Nash, & Field, 2001). A good deal of evidence suggests that people who overeat impulsively tend to have their eating behavior guided by external environmental cues rather than by states of food deprivation and resultant hunger. These environmental cues include the sights or smells of food, the degree to which food is easily available, the nature of food available (with sweet, salty, and highly caloric foods more strongly associated with unrestrained eating), social situations associated with eating, and those that indicate an upcoming period of food deprivation (Logue, 1995). In addition, exposure to stressful environments and substance intoxication has also been associated with overeating (Logue, 1995).

To reduce vulnerability to acts of overeating, a number of self-control procedures can be used (Baumeister et al., 1994; Logue, 1995). One such set of procedures is *precommitment* strategies. Precommitment strategies in relation to overeating might include the avoidance of or limited exposure to situations that have been associated with overeating. The reduction or elimination of these cues will likely result in markedly reduced contexts associated with temptation. Public statements to commit to reducing overeating may also be helpful, as might written contracts specifying that a set of identifiable pleasurable activities will be pursued only after a specified period of engagement in healthy eating behavior (i.e., the Premacking approach that we described earlier).

Another factor that may increase vulnerability to periods of overeating is *counterregulation* (Baumeister et al., 1994). A good deal of available evidence suggests that persons who engage in somewhat radical diets that involve excessive food deprivation are more likely to engage in unrestrained eating when the diet has been broken (e.g., "I've blown my diet, so what the hell—might as well go for it!"). As a result, the goals that one sets for oneself in a self-control program associated with overeating may, somewhat paradoxically, contribute to episodes of overeating if the goal is unrealistic or increases one's vulnerability to overeating. In other words, it's better to have a dietary goal of three regular and healthy meals and occasional snacks than to abstain from eating altogether for prolonged periods.

In the event that overeating functions as a form of *escape or avoidance behavior* (e.g., avoidance of unpleasant thoughts or feelings), self-control strategies may include a provision of reinforcement for nonescape from these experiences through food consumption, perhaps through self-reinforcement of more adaptive forms of coping. If overeating has an escape from self-awareness function (Baumeister et al., 1994), then an associated self-control strategy might similarly be to reinforce the engagement in incompatible behaviors, such as mindfulness practice that facilitates greater ongoing awareness of experience. Greater awareness of food consumption, or the self-monitoring of food intake, can also facilitate reductions in food consumption.

Finally, self-control strategies that function to reduce establishing operations for overeating may be helpful. We have already noted that the relaxation of extreme dietary restraint will similarly reduce the establishing operation of food deprivation. Procedures that also counter sleep deprivation or alcohol intoxication, both of which have been associated with overeating (Baumeister et al., 1994; Logue, 1995), may be similarly helpful.

Insufficient Environmental Reinforcement

Behavioral activation (BA) is a therapeutic approach that attempts to increase behavior that has become less frequent because of a reduction in or loss of one's social network (an important source of social reinforcement for social behaviors), a loss of reinforcer availability for other (nonsocial) behaviors, an increased rate of punishment for behavior, or habitual engagement in escape and avoidance behaviors or behaviors that result in inactivity (e.g., rumination, seclusion).

As a therapy approach, BA has a few essential elements (Martell et al., 2001). First, a therapist who works within this framework adopts a functional analytic perspective and constantly looks for and evaluates the role that environmental factors play in the maintenance of negative mood or in the suppression of behavior. Second, the client is taught to become behaviorally active even when mood states are negative. One aspect of this feature involves identifying activities to try and then resolving any issues that make it difficult to carry out these activities. All of this is done in the context of assisting the client in achieving his or her life goals. Third, a BA therapist seeks to identify environmental factors and patterns of responding that function to maintain depressed mood. In this regard, BA discourages the use of avoidant coping strategies and instead encourages reentering into experiences or situations that are currently avoided but were previously reinforced. Finally, BA aims to teach clients to be astute observers of their own behaviors and to make connections between behavior and variations in mood. In relation to this aspect of therapy, a client would be encouraged to notice the types of situations that either set the occasion for behavior to occur or inhibit a behavior's occurrence. Clients are also instructed in how to identify the consequences that follow their behavior and how such consequences are related to variability in mood.

When applied to the treatment of depression, BA has been found to be as effective as cognitive therapy (Jacobson et al., 1996). Related behavior therapies that have similar therapeutic goals have likewise been found to be effective in reducing depression. One example is Lewinsohn's coping with depression course (Lewinsohn, Antonuccio, Steinmetz-Breckenridge, & Teri, 1984), which emphasizes pleasant-events scheduling to increase engagement in behaviors that have historically been pleasurable and rewarding.

Restricted Range of Reinforcement

A behaviorally oriented therapist who is working with a client who displays behavioral excesses in certain areas that are harmful or cause distress (e.g., substance abuse, promiscuous sex, gambling) may, as a part of his or her pretreatment assessment, establish what, if any, other sources of reinforcement exist for behavior other than the problematic behavior. For many individuals who have excessive behavioral habits, a good deal of the person's time is spent either engaging in the problematic behavior, recovering from the problematic behavior, getting the financial resources to support the problematic behavior, or establishing the context for the behavior itself. In short, much of one's activities are geared toward the problematic behavior and the attainment of the positive reinforcers it occasions.

If the goal of therapy is to decrease such behaviors, the therapist may consider looking for other potential reinforcers that would support behavior incompatible with the problematic behavior. To this end, during pretreatment assessments a therapist may assess other types of activities that the client has previously engaged in that were pleasurable. Because therapy seeks to reduce the frequency of the problematic behavior, the client's behavior can be shifted to alternative activities that the individual finds rewarding or pleasing.

Overly Punitive Environment

As noted in chapter 5, environments that are overly punitive tend to be characterized by excessive use of aversive consequences or coercive practices to influence behavior. Although such strategies may indeed influence behavior, they often do so at a significant cost. Those who are frequently on the receiving end of aversive control practices often experience feelings of mistrust, fear, and anger when among those who are punitive and controlling. When aversive control practices are modeled, they are also more likely to be subsequently adopted and displayed by those subjected to them. Intervention strategies reviewed in this section are examples of approaches that therapists might use to reduce the aversive control of behavior.

Parent Training

There is an indication of an association between child behavior problems and parental discipline strategies that involve the use of strong aversives or harsh physical punishments. In particular, children who display physically aggressive acts against others are more likely than others to have parents who use harsh punishments in response to problematic behavior (Moore & Arthur, 1983; Sears, Maccoby, & Levin, 1957). The use of harsh punishments is also associated with emotional upset in children, as well as avoidance of persons who administer punishments.

Parent training approaches are used to address and resolve significant childhood behavior problems (Clark, 1985). One aspect of this approach is to teach parents the use of effective methods of responding to child behavior problems other than those that are aversive or punitive. At the most basic level, parent training involves instruction in learning and behavioral principles, instruction in new parenting-related skills, behavior management, problem solving, and communication.

Involvement of Significant Others in Therapy

Relationship distress has been associated with a number of clinical concerns, such as depression (Prince & Jacobson, 1995). In fact, some evidence suggests that therapies targeting relationship distress, when present, positively affect other client problem areas such as depression (Beach, Fincham, & Katz, 1998).

Coercion theory (Patterson & Hops, 1972) has been used to explain how some behavioral patterns become reinforced and contribute to couple distress. In coercion theory, partners provide aversive stimuli that control the behavior of the other. Negative reinforcement results from the termination of the aversive stimuli and serves to strengthen the behavior of both partners. The following example from Patterson and Hops (1972, pp. 424–425) illustrates the basic principle:

> *Wife:* You still haven't fixed that screen door.
>
> *Husband:* (Makes no observable response, continues to read the newspaper)
>
> *W:* A lot of thanks I get for all I do. You said three weeks ago . . .
>
> *H:* Damn it, stop nagging at me. As soon as I walk in here and try to read the paper I get yelling and bitching.
>
> *W:* You're so damn lazy.
> *H:* Alright, damn it, I'll fix it later! Now leave me alone.

In this scenario, the wife has learned that shouting and insults lead to a change in what she regards as an aversive behavior of her husband's, namely, acts that fall under the general category of laziness (e.g., sitting and reading the newspaper). Also in this scenario, the husband has learned that vague promises will get the wife to stop the insults and the shouting. These types of coercive interaction styles coupled with aversive verbal behaviors (e.g., putdowns, criticisms, disagreements, disapproval, blaming) are commonly observed among distressed couples and often result in an aversive relationship. For these reasons, communication training constitutes an important part of most behaviorally oriented marital therapies (Wheeler et al., 2001).

Family environments that are characterized by high expressed emotion, most notably anger and hostility, are associated with higher rates of relapse for a variety of conditions, including schizophrenia, bulimia, and depression (Butzlaff & Hooley, 1998). Research indicates that treatments that are effective in moving families from high to low on the expressed emotion construct significantly reduce the likelihood of future relapse.

Excessively Stringent Self-Reinforcement Strategies

Individuals who display excessively high standards for performance are prone to experience dissatisfaction, disappointment and frustration because only exceptional, if not impossible, behavioral displays are evaluated as worthy of praise or reward. As a result, the range of potential reinforcers for behavior is often substantially diminished among those with high self-standards. Intervention strategies such as those described below target excessively high or unrealistic rules or standards for behavior in an effort to reduce disappointment and self-criticism and to increase self-acceptance and life satisfaction.

Modification in Self-Standards

Self-standards can arise through experience with immediate contingencies (i.e., reinforcement or punishment), rules or direct instruction, prescriptions from other cultural influences, or acquired through the observations of others (Bandura, 1986). At the most basic level, relevant environments are pleased (i.e., rewarding) when high standards for behavior are met, whereas they are disappointed when behavior falls short of these standards. As a result, persons exposed to such environmental contexts similarly come to respond to their own behavior in self-approving or self-critical ways (Bandura, 1986).

If a person has a learning history whereby displays of behavior that meet or surpass high standards set by the social environment are the only behaviors generally reinforced, it is likely that such experiences will become translated into rules for behavior (e.g., "to be worthwhile, I must succeed at the highest levels"). The adoption of dysfunctional rules related to high standards for performance can serve as a source of disappointment, self-criticism, or self-loathing. Excessively high standards result in the pursuit of unattainable goals (Bandura, 1986) and negate the possibility of an evaluation of behavior in any other way, such as in terms of degree or effectiveness. Excessively high self-standards are particularly relevant among those who have strong perfectionistic strivings, a common feature of some psychological conditions (e.g., obsessive–compulsive personality disorder, Type A personality, anorexia nervosa, depression).

Cognitive therapy techniques, particularly those that specifically target dichotomous thinking patterns and work toward the establishment of realistic goals, can be useful for altering self-standards and associated self-reinforcement contingencies (Burns, 1980, chap. 14). Another approach is to shift the emphasis away from the striving to realize high self-standards and toward indices of behavioral effectiveness, a topic discussed next.

Shift Focus to Emphasize Behavioral Effectiveness

Attention to the outcomes of behavior shifts the focus away from the form or topography of behavior as well as unrealistic rules that influence the evaluation of behavior. With such a shift comes less concern about getting the form of the behavior correct (mimicking some response) or being right or doing what one is supposed to do. Rather, the focus becomes how one can realize positive outcomes through one's behavior. As such, the measure of behavior is based on the effect or outcome it produces (Follette & Hayes, 2000). This may be an especially useful approach for persons with perfectionistic tendencies, because many of their concerns tend to center on getting the form of behavior just right or perfect, not on being effective.

Excessive Schedule Dependence

Some individuals' behavior tends to be most strongly affected by the immediate consequences that follow it. As a result, behavior from such persons will often appear to have a more erratic or inconsistent quality because behavior is largely stimulus driven and subject to the changing contingencies for behavior across different contexts. The shift away from short-term contingency control to rule control may result in behavior patterns that are less impulsive and less influenced by immediate environmental events and may facilitate the development of behavior patterns that have a greater likelihood of being sustained as one begins to act in a manner consistent with the realization of more distal goals or values. In this section, examples of intervention strategies are reviewed that seek to lessen the influence that immediate consequences have on behavior.

Shift From Contingency Control to Rule Control

An approach for facilitating a shift away from short-term contingency control to full control has been variously named "acting toward a goal" (Martell et al., 2001) or "committed action" (Hayes, Strosahl, & Wilson, 1999). With this approach, a client is encouraged to act in a manner consistent with a personal goal. For example, clients may elect to behave in a manner that is consistent with how they would like to feel, how they would like to be perceived, or how they would like to see themselves. Such an approach may make more salient distal consequences that the client seeks and as such reduce the salience of the more immediate contingencies that surround behavior.

As Hayes, Strosahl, and Wilson (1999) noted, the pursuit of longer term goals through action is often fraught with contacting immediate and aversive outcomes associated with such action. In the case of an individual who seeks no longer to escape from situations associated with fear, for example, committed action would involve exposure to the situation and experiences associated with such situations (e.g., marked fear). As such, for committed action to be potentially effective, the action taken must be strongly tied to highly valued ends or outcomes for the client.

Values-Based Intervention Strategies

Values clarification and the development of a commitment to lead a valued life have been central features of various forms of therapy that have arisen from the human potential movement. Various forms of behavior therapy have recently incorporated these approaches in a manner that remains true to behavioral principles and a contextual understanding of behavior. For example, in the last stage of ACT (Hayes, Strosahl, & Wilson, 1999), behavioral goals and commitments become a central focus of attention in therapy. This is done though an analysis of clinically relevant situations in terms of values, goals, actions, and barriers. Clients are encouraged to resolve these situations through consideration of the following questions (Follette & Hayes, 2000, p. 403):

- What values do you intend to make manifest?
- What concrete, achievable events are on this path?
- What could you do now to produce those achievements?
- What stands in the way of engaging in these actions?

Attention to such values and goals may sustain behaviors over time, even if the more immediate contingencies associated with valued or goal-directed behaviors are not immediately reinforced.

Relapse Prevention

The main feature of relapse prevention is to help the individual anticipate and cope with relapse situations. Although relapse prevention procedures were initially applied to substance abuse-related problems (e.g., Marlatt & Gordon, 1985), they are now a common feature across a wide range of behavior therapies for a multitude of problem areas (Brunswig, Sbraga, & Harris, 2003). When applied to substance abuse, there are five basic components associated with relapse prevention procedures:

1. *Development of awareness of substance abuse situations.* This involves identification of antecedents and consequences of

substance abuse, high-risk situations, and the discriminative stimuli associated with these situations. Within this component, clients are taught to first recognize the stimuli or cues that trigger the urge to drink or the craving for a substance.

2. *Skills training*. Cues associated with high-risk situations for substance abuse are used as cues to implement coping skills (e.g., assertiveness, alternative activity, leaving situation).
3. *Establishment of a commitment to change*. This component includes a commitment to abstinence or a commitment to reduce harm associated with substance misuse.
4. *Anticipation of behavior lapses*. Lapses are viewed as a natural part of the habit change process. For some clients, there is a danger that a mild loss in self-regulation (i.e., a lapse) becomes an occasion for wholesale loss in self-regulation (i.e., a relapse). This would be analogous to a person who abused alcohol on one occasion to conclude that he or she will always be a drunk and on the basis of that rule statement abandon all efforts at behavioral regulation (i.e., resume excessive drinking patterns without any attempts at restraint). Because of such possible outcomes, lapses are anticipated, with an effort made to create a context of acceptance when lapses do occur, in an effort to reduce the likelihood of a full-blown relapse. To this end, a lapse is regarded as both a danger sign and an opportunity for new learning of coping responses.
5. *Promotion of lifestyle changes*. This involves avoiding risk situations, improving social networks, and using meditation, relaxation, and exercise for self- and emotion-regulation purposes.

SUMMARY

In this section, we reviewed some examples of behavioral intervention strategies that can be used to alter behavior in desirable ways. In so doing, we noted where within functional response domains such strategies could be particularly appropriate. In the following two chapters, we expand on this discussion by describing behavioral intervention approaches that are often suitable for a wide variety of Axis I and II clinical conditions.

7

BEHAVIORAL TREATMENT OF AXIS I DISORDERS

According to the *Diagnostic and Statistical Manual of Mental Disorders, Text Revision* (*DSM–IV–TR*; American Psychiatric Association, 2000), Axis I disorders are "clinical disorders" or "other conditions that may be the focus of clinical attention." A first strategy that many behavioral clinicians follow in treating Axis I disorders is consulting and using the list of empirically validated treatments (EVTs), initially developed by a task force within Division 12 (the clinical division) of the American Psychological Association. There are many exceptions, problems, and issues, however, in applying this strategy and these treatments universally to clients. One issue, related to the focus of this book, is that there is relatively little mention of personality variables or individual characteristics in the application of these treatments. Alternative strategies, such as modifying EVTs for particular types of clients, assessing and treating individual response classes, and the use of the functional analysis are described in this chapter.

THE USE OF EMPIRICALLY VALIDATED TREATMENTS

Division 12 of the American Psychological Association created the Task Force on Psychological Interventions. Members of the task force have published a series of papers, listing the therapies that have been found to be "well established" or "probably efficacious" in treating persons with particular diagnoses (Chambless & Ollendick, 2001; Chambless et al., 1998; Chambless et al., 1996). Nathan and Gorman (1998) and Barlow (2001) have edited books that review empirically supported treatments. Ollendick and King (2000) have written a chapter summarizing EVTs for children and adolescents.

These papers also contain the criteria used to include a therapy technique on these lists (e.g., Chambless et al., 1998). To be considered a "well-established treatment," treatment efficacy must have been demonstrated by at least two good between-subject group designs or by a large series of single-case-design experiments ($n > 9$), which show that the treatment is superior to pill or psychological placebo or to another treatment, or equivalent to another well-established treatment. Moreover, the experiments must have been conducted with treatment manuals, characteristics of the client samples must have been clearly specified, and the effects must have been demonstrated by at least two investigating teams. To be considered a "probably efficacious treatment," two experiments must have demonstrated that the treatment is superior to a waiting-list control, or there must have been one or more experiments meeting the criteria for a well-established treatment, with the exception that replication was not attempted by an independent group of investigators or that a small series of single-case-design experiments ($n \geq 3$) was used to establish treatment effectiveness. The cited articles contain lists of well-established and probably efficacious treatments and also citations of the articles that demonstrate the efficacy of the treatments.

The lists of EVTs are accessed by diagnostic category. Not all diagnostic categories are included in these lists of EVTs. The major categories of disorders included are anxiety and stress, depression, health problems, problems of childhood, marital discord, chemical abuse and dependence, sexual dysfunction, and a small category called "other." Within the probably efficacious "other" category is dialectical behavior therapy for borderline personality disorder (efficacy established by Linehan, Armstrong, Suarez, Allmon, & Heard, 1991). Several diagnostic categories are *not* included in the EVT lists. Among these nonincluded categories are all remaining personality disorders, somatoform disorders, and dissociative disorders.

The majority of the EVTs are based on behavioral or cognitive–behavioral strategies. An example of a behavioral strategy is exposure and response prevention, a well-established effective treatment for obsessive–compulsive disorder (efficacy established by van Oppen et al., 1995). Foa (1996; Franklin & Foa, 1998) provided a summary of the treatment and outcome data related to exposure and response prevention. According to these articles, this treatment is based on learning theory that views obsessions as evoking anxiety and compulsions as reducing that anxiety. In the treatment program, patients are confronted with situations that provoke obsessional distress, with the anxiety being maintained sufficiently long to allow habituation or extinction to occur, while at the same time preventing the patient from carrying out any compulsions that would reduce the distress. According to Foa (1996), treatment in her clinic consists of 15 exposure sessions, each of 2-hour duration, delivered over 3 weeks. This exposure and response prevention treatment for obsessive–compulsive disorder is clearly based on the basic behavioral principle that nonreinforced exposure to the conditioned aversive stimulus produces extinction.

Other EVTs are considered to be cognitive or cognitive–behavioral strategies. One example is Beck's cognitive therapy for depression (efficacy, described by Dobson, 1989). Both of the Beck books that narrate cognitive therapy for depression describe not only the cognitive components, but also describe more behavioral components (Beck, 1995; Beck et al., 1979). In chapter 12 of Beck's (1995) book, for example, nearly a dozen behavioral components are described (e.g., problem solving, distracting and refocusing, relaxation, and role-playing). One of these components is activity scheduling or activity monitoring, during which clients schedule and carry out pleasurable activities or components of overwhelming or large tasks. Thus, because cognitive therapy includes both cognitive and behavioral components, it is difficult to attribute the efficacy data for cognitive therapy (e.g., Dobson, 1989) solely to its cognitive components. In fact, Jacobson et al. (1996) found that the behavioral activation component of cognitive therapy is the most effective ingredient in the treatment. Thus, although this chapter focuses on behavioral treatments for Axis I disorders, it is sometimes difficult to distinguish behavioral treatments from cognitive treatments or cognitive–behavioral treatments.

BEHAVIOR THERAPY AND THE USE OF DIAGNOSIS

At this point, the reader may be wondering how and why behaviorally oriented clinicians would be making and using diagnoses, albeit to access an EVT list. It is true that behavioral assessment and therapy developed on a parallel track from diagnoses, which are psychiatrically derived. Nelson-Gray and Paulson (2003) described in detail the relationship between behavioral assessment and diagnoses. Some of this history is also described in chapter 2 of this volume.

Despite very different historical traditions, the *DSM* system of diagnosis (currently *DSM–IV–TR*) has become more acceptable, as well as more useful, to behavior therapists over the years. Despite its beginnings as a revolutionary and radical new therapeutic approach, behavior therapy is currently considered to be a mainstream approach to psychological problems (Nelson-Gray et al., 1997). Not only do many cognitive–behavioral therapy techniques appear on the EVT list, but also behavioral outcome measures are required to demonstrate the efficacy of these therapies. Not only has behavior therapy become more widely accepted by scientist–practitioners of various theoretical persuasions, but behavior therapists have also become more tolerant of at least some mainstream assessment and therapy practices, including the use of *DSM* diagnosis, with the implicit proviso that these practices have an empirical basis.

In the early days of behavior therapy, a popular term was "target behavior," indicating an emphasis on identifying and modifying one specific behavior for each client. Individual behaviors were typically selected as treatment goals, with no consideration that the behaviors might be part of a larger constellation of behaviors. One example is Ayllon's approach to the treatment of psychotic patients. Using different interventions, these specific target behaviors were modified in individual patients: eating problems, stealing food, towel hoarding, and the wearing of excessive clothing (Ayllon, 1963, 1965). Another example was the choice of a very slow speech rate as the target behavior in a chronically depressed man (Robinson & Lewinsohn, 1973). Linehan (e.g., 1981) initially discussed women with parasuicidal behavior before considering that parasuidical behavior was part of the constellation of borderline personality disorder. Gradually over the years, there was increasing recognition in behavioral circles that behaviors occurred in response clusters and that diagnoses were one way of recognizing the repeated co-occurrence of groups of psychopathological behaviors (Nelson-Gray & Paulson, 2003).

As mainstream scientist–practitioners, behavior therapists have much to gain by using *DSM* diagnoses (as reviewed in chap. 5). Despite these various advantages, most behaviorally oriented clinicians would view a diagnosis as an adjunct to and not a replacement for behavioral assessment. The main reason is that the *DSM* is nomothetic, and behavioral assessment is idiographic. Behavioral assessment is necessary to make an idiographic determination of treatment goals, controlling variables, treatment choice, and treatment outcome measures for an individual client. Individual treatment goals and appropriate treatment outcome measures must be established in the context of the client's presenting problems and values. Even though the *DSM* does indeed suggest environmental or organismic controlling variables for each disorder (Nelson & Barlow, 1981), a behavioral assessment must be conducted to determine which of these controlling variables or additional controlling variables is applicable for the specific client. Even the assumption that behavior assessment must be done on an idiographic basis usually does not imply a behavioral assessment of personality variables. In chapter 8, more is written about the consideration of personality and other idiographic variables in the context of EVTs and alternative ways to select treatment strategies.

Critiques of EVT Strategies in Treatment Selection

It is our opinion that the EVT lists have greatly advanced psychological treatment. The era in which all forms of psychotherapy are assumed to be of comparable efficacy is over (Luborsky, Singer, & Luborsky, 1976; Smith & Glass, 1977). All therapies are not created equal. Therapies do indeed differ in their effectiveness in treating specific disorders.

Despite the demonstrated efficacy of many treatments for specific disorders, the EVT movement is not without its critics. Ollendick (1999) summarized three main criticisms of the EVT movement: (a) controversies regarding the criteria used to classify treatments as "well established," "probably efficacious," and "experimental"; (b) discomfort with the use of manualized treatments, which is a requirement for a therapy to be placed on the EVT list; and (c) the inadequacy of evidence that these EVTs, the efficacy of which has been established through clinical research, will work in everyday clinical settings. In addition, a gap exists between clinical researchers and clinical practitioners, so that many of these effective treatments are not made available to the public who could benefit from them (Barlow, Levitt, & Bufka, 1999).

CONSIDERATION OF INDIVIDUAL DIFFERENCES IN EVT TREATMENT SELECTION

As noted at the beginning of this chapter, one typical strategy used by behavioral clinicians is to determine the client's diagnosis and then identify a treatment that is likely to work based on the EVT lists. Although a good first step, this strategy is not universally successful for all clients. Some exceptions are described next.

Multiple EVTs for a Specific Disorder

In a few instances, disorders may have more than one EVT. One notable example is unipolar depression. There are at least three therapeutic approaches (among others) that have been shown to be effective with unipolar depression: cognitive therapy (e.g., Sacco & Beck, 1995), behavior therapy (e.g., Lewinsohn & Gotlib, 1995), and interpersonal psychotherapy (e.g., Markowitz & Weissman, 1995).

With several effective treatments for unipolar depression from which to choose, the question arises as to which of these treatments to try with a particular client. There are currently no guidelines within the EVT literature regarding which treatment to select for an individual client when there is more than one EVT for a particular disorder. A response class strategy, described by Nelson (1988), may be useful in selecting between the EVTs for depression. Nelson (1988) described three strategies for linking assessment and treatment. In addition to the use of diagnosis (discussed earlier) and the functional analysis (discussed subsequently), a third strategy that she outlined is the identification and treatment of specific response classes that are thought to comprise particular disorders. Response classes, as used here, refer to groups of behavior that covary together and nomothetically across a group of individuals with a particular disorder or problematic behavior pattern. Sometimes, but not always, useful response classes overlap with the *DSM* diagnostic criteria for a particular disorder (Nelson & Barlow, 1981).

In unipolar depression, problematic response classes that may be assessed and targeted for treatment include dysfunctional thoughts, the ratio of pleasant and unpleasant events, and social skills. These response classes correspond to the three treatment approaches noted earlier (i.e., cognitive, behavior, and interpersonal therapies) that have been shown to be effective with unipolar depression.

One approach in selecting among several alternative effective treatments for an individual client is a treatment-matching approach. In this approach, an individual's weakest or most problematic response class is identified in assessment and then targeted in treatment through the use of the matching therapy. Treatment selection based on response classes is a way to individualize treatment selection, even though it is not based on traditional personality variables. A study by McKnight et al. (1984) provided some empirical support for this treatment-matching approach. In this study, a single-subject-design that combined a multiple baseline across subjects with an alternating-treatments design (ATD) was used. The ATD involves a random or semirandom alternation, usually once weekly, of two or more conditions, along with weekly measurements. Differential effectiveness of the two treatments can then be determined within the same individual (Hayes, Barlow, & Nelson-Gray, 1999). McKnight et al. (1984), for example, compared the effectiveness of treatments for reducing depression that were directly matched to or not matched to initial assessment findings. Depressed women were divided into two types based on assessment data (i.e., predominant problem area associated with irrational cognitions or social skills deficits). Each client participated in an ATD, with weekly sessions of either social skills training or cognitive therapy. Depressed clients with assessed problems in social skills significantly improved more in both social skills and depression after receiving the related treatment of social skills training compared with the unrelated treatment of cognitive therapy. Depressed clients with assessed problems in irrational cognitions significantly improved more in both cognitions and depression after receiving the related treatment of cognitive therapy compared with the unrelated treatment of social skills training. These results provide some support for treatment matching within unipolar depression, that is, choosing among effective treatments, based on which treatment appears to address the client's problematic response class.

Rude and Rehm (1991) have published a review article on the effectiveness of selecting treatment matched to specific response classes in unipolar depression. Their article reviewed therapy outcome studies in which measures of cognitive or behavioral deficits were used as predictors of response to related therapy. Contrary to expectation, there was no relationship between deficit scores and outcome in many studies, and, in several, a finding opposite to prediction was obtained. That is, subjects with more functional scores on the cognitive or behavioral measures did better in therapy than those with less functional scores. These results are consistent with those of a post hoc study designed to seek the identity of treatment responders versus nonresponders. Keller (1983) found that a group of depressed community volunteers with low pretreatment scores on the Dysfunctional Attitude Scale (DAS; Weissman & Beck, 1978) showed a greater response to cognitive therapy than did their counterparts with high scores, contradicting the notion in cognitive therapy that participants with high DAS scores would benefit more from cognitive therapy. Rude and Rehm noted that "It is unclear whether the advantage seen in these studies is a response to a particular type of treatment or whether it represents general prognosis" (1991, p. 493).

The disorder of unipolar depression is obviously ripe for more treatment utility studies. Several distinct forms of therapy have been shown to be effective for this disorder. For each client, the therapist must choose among these effective treatments, raising the issue of whether treatment should be matched to a client's presenting problem or if a randomly selected treatment is as effective. The treatment-matching procedure uses individual differences in the selection of effective treatments even though it is not based on traditional personality variables.

Clients Without Obvious Empirically Validated Treatments (EVTs)

For many types of clients, there is no obvious matching EVT. These types of clients include the following.

Diagnoses Not Included on the EVT Lists

Many *DSM* disorders do not have an associated empirically validated treatment. This could mean that there is no effective treatment for a particular disorder or that appropriate research is underway to determine whether a particular treatment is effective or not for a particular condition. Among the *DSM* disorders for which there is no listed EVT are the somatoform disorders and the dissociative disorders, which are somewhat rare in day-to-day practice. Another much more common set of disorders without EVTs are the personality disorders (excepting borderline personality disorder, which has the probably efficacious EVT of dialectical behavior therapy).

Clients Without Clear-Cut Diagnoses

Despite attempts to use structured and nonstructured assessment devices, all clinicians have encountered clients with whom it is impossible to achieve diagnostic clarity. Some of these clients have severe but undifferentiated psychopathology. These are the clients who score high on many or most scales of an assessment device. We are reminded of a case in one of our training clinics in which a female client who was difficult to diagnose was very resistant to completing a semistructured diagnostic interview. The client said, "Why are you asking me all these questions? I don't belong in any pigeonhole. Don't you know that I am just plain crazy?" It is quite possible that the client was correct in her evaluation of the breadth and severity of her experience. Alternatively, the *DSM* system may not have sufficient discriminant validity in all cases.

Other clients may have more diffuse problems in living that cause them suffering but that do not merit a *DSM* diagnosis. In the words of Thompson and Williams (1985):

> These are the individuals that behavior therapy *must* learn to treat because they will become the dominant problems for clinical psychology in the coming years. We are talking about those large numbers of individuals who suffer from clinical signs of malaise, apathy, despondency, lethargy, general discontent, and lack of symptomatology—although depression may result in some persons—and for whom no discipline has an adequate treatment. (p. 49)

As an example of this, we are reminded of a client who had different problems in living that caused her suffering. She manifested mild anxiety and depression and faithfully attended therapy on a weekly basis. Her vague presenting problems changed from session to session (no friends, unhappy marriage, choice of majors at a community college, indecision about attending Narcotic Anonymous meetings, seeing strange patterns, a historical negative view of her by her mother, etc.). After the first several meetings, we had no firm treatment goals.

Clients With Diagnoses With Heterogeneous Membership

Another type of *DSM* disorders for which there are no listed EVTs are those with heterogeneous membership, such as personality disorders (other than borderline), mental retardation, and pervasive developmental disorders. Diagnostic categories vary in their within-category variability. Haynes (1986) noted that for heterogeneous diagnostic categories, a more individualized assessment might be required, in addition to a diagnosis. The treatment goals for each individual with a diagnosis noted for its associated heterogeneity may vary markedly. A more individualized assessment appears to be necessary to establish treatment goals and outcome measures, as well as to select a treatment. The diagnosis by itself is unable to suggest an efficacious treatment.

Alternatives to Matching Diagnosis and the EVT Lists

A useful first strategy with many clients is to determine their diagnoses and then consult the EVT lists for a treatment that may work with that client. As described earlier, however, there are several categories of clients for whom this strategy is not helpful, namely, clients who have diagnoses that are not included on the EVT lists, clients who are difficult to diagnose, and clients with diagnoses that have heterogeneous group membership. The following sections discuss alternative ways to approach treatment planning for these individuals.

Using Strategies That Are on the EVT List of Other Disorders

Among the diagnostic categories that do not yet appear on EVT lists are the somatoform disorders, including hypochondriasis. One of us recently supervised a student therapist at our training clinic whose client presented with moderately severe hypochondriasis. The client was intelligent and worked part time at a bookstore, but he spent countless hours inspecting parts of his body looking for signs of a fatal disease, worrying that he had a fatal disease, and surfing the Internet for information about various fatal diseases. His behavior was of such concern that his roommates hid his computer modem. Because there is no listed EVT for hypochondrias, the student therapist researched alternative treatments and found a chapter that described cognitive therapy for hypochondrias (Wells, 1997). The student therapist discarded this option, however, because the client argued intelligently and vehemently with each challenge to his dysfunctional thoughts. The hypochondriacal thoughts continued to occur at baseline high levels. The student therapist then decided to try putting his hypochondriacal worries under stimulus control or worrying in a concentrated fashion at a certain time of the day and in a certain place (Borkovec, Wilkinson, Folensbee, & Lerman, 1983). It remains to be seen how effective this treatment will be with this client. Thus, when there is no known EVT for a disorder, one strategy is to try treatments that have been shown to be effective for other disorders and to determine whether they are also helpful with the disorder that is the focus of treatment. Client individual differences, however, must be taken into account. In this example, the client was too intelligent and too verbal to respond well to cognitive therapy that challenged his well-established hypochondriacal cognitions.

Given that Linehan's Dialectical Behavior Therapy (DBT; Linehan, 1993a) is an EVT for borderline personality disorder, DBT could also be an effective treatment for other related disorders. In one of our research programs, we have attempted to apply DBT skills training to middle-school children who are diagnosed with a minimum of oppositional–defiant disorder (ODD). This DBT skills training has been effective in reducing ODD symptom count, in reducing both internalizing and externalizing disorders, in reducing depression, and in increasing interpersonal strength (Warburton, Hurst, Topor, Nelson-Gray, & Keane, 2003). Other efficacious treatments for ODD children include variations of parent training programs (summarized by Ollendick & King, 2000). The advantage of DBT skills training is that the children learn to control and manage their own behavior rather than relying on external control through parent training. Thus, an EVT found to be effective for one disorder, namely, DBT for borderline personality disorder, has also been found to be effective, at least in this preliminary study, with children with ODD.

Use of Functional Analysis

A tried-and-true behavioral strategy that individualizes assessment and treatment is the functional analysis, a classic strategy that links behavioral assessment and behavioral treatment. The variables presently controlling the target behavior are identified in assessment and are subsequently modified in treatment (Goldfried & Pomeranz, 1968). The assumption is that if these maintaining variables are altered in treatment, then the problem behavior will improve. In Ferster's (1965, p. 11) words, "Such a functional analysis of behavior has the advantage that it specified the causes of behavior in the form of explicit environmental events that can be objectively identified and that are potentially manipulable." The following terms are usually used interchangeably: *functional analysis*, *functional behavioral assessment*, and *functional assessment*. A recent definition of functional behavioral assessment was provided by Sugai et al. (2000): "a systematic process of identifying problem behaviors and the events that (a) reliably predict occurrences and non-occurrences of those behaviors and (b) maintain the behaviors across time" (p. 137). A current description of the components of the functional analysis, as well as more highly elaborated versions of the functional analysis that are known as behavioral case formulation strategies, was presented by Haynes, Nelson, Thacher, and Kaholokula (2002). Another contemporary presentation of the issues surrounding functional analysis is provided by Haynes and O'Brien (1990). Nelson-Gray (2003) summarized research that has examined the utility of the functional analysis in individualizing treatment.

One category of disorders that presents with heterogeneity is autistic disorder, one of the pervasive developmental disorders. Because the category is heterogeneous in its membership, treatment for people with autism must be individualized. Even though Lovaas's intensive behavioral treatment program has been cited as an EVT for autism (see review by Ollendick & King, 2000), it also must be individualized in terms of choice of treatment goals. A good example is provided by Carr and Durand (1985), who used behavioral assessment to differentiate the controlling variables in tantrums in different children with autism. Some children were observed to display tantrums because their work was too hard for them, others because they sought more adult attention. The two sets of controlling variables suggested different treatments for different autistic children.

To conclude, there are several diagnostic categories with heterogeneous membership and no known EVT. For individuals seeking treatment who bear these diagnoses, an individualized treatment plan is necessary. Also, for other clients, it is nearly impossible to establish diagnostic clarity. An individualized treatment plan must be formed according to specific presenting problems. The functional analysis often forms the basis of this individualized treatment plan.

Effective Treatments That Are Not Linked to a Specific Diagnosis

Another alternative in selecting treatment when there is no obvious diagnosis–EVT match is to use a treatment that has been shown to be effective but is not linked to a specific disorder.

An interesting example is provided by the token economy (Kazdin, 1977). The token economy has been found to be effective with a wide variety of individuals, including psychiatric patients, persons with mental retardation, individuals in classroom settings, and delinquents and adult offenders. It has also been found to be effective in a variety of settings, including mental hospitals, classrooms, group homes, work settings, and community settings. The 1998 EVT list by Chambless et al. contains an interesting footnote:

> Two treatments have been deleted (compared with the EVT list of Chambless et al., 1996), not because of negative evidence, but because, unlike the other treatments, we do not have specific target problems identified yet for these approaches: token economy (target problem not specified) and behavior modification for people with developmental disabilities (target unspecified). (p. 12)

Thus, token economies are effective, but are not linked to a specific diagnosis and hence no longer appear on the EVT list. Nonetheless, for clients for whom there is no ready link between a diagnosis and an EVT, a token economy could be considered a treatment option. In our training clinic, many children diagnosed with ODD or conduct disorder (CD) are placed on point systems or token economies in their homes or school settings (or both).

As described in chapter 2, the last decade has seen the development of some new behavior therapy techniques (e.g., DBT, functional analytic psychotherapy, acceptance and commitment therapy). At the present time, these techniques show promise in terms of effectiveness, but they have not been linked to a specific disorder. Thus, if there is no obvious EVT for a particular client based on his or her diagnosis, an alternative is to try one of these newer strategies.

IMPACT OF AXIS II DISORDERS ON EVT TREATMENT OF AXIS I DISORDERS

According to *DSM–IV–TR*, Axis I disorders are clinical disorders or other conditions that may be a focus of clinical attention. Axis II disorders are personality disorders and mental retardation. There is often a high rate of personality disorders among those with Axis I disorders, and a consistent indication that the presence of personality disorders has an adverse impact on the effectiveness of treatment of co-occurring Axis I disorders (Costello, 1996a). Apart from this general observation concerning treatment effectiveness, few empirical studies have investigated the nature of the relations shared among personality disorders and Axis I conditions or how and why some personality characteristics adversely affect treatments of clinical disorders.

Farmer and Nelson-Gray (1990) have summarized the various hypothesized relationships between the Axis I and Axis II disorders, using the example of the co-occurrence of depression with one or more personality disorders (see Exhibit 7.1). One hypothesis is the *characterological predisposition hypothesis*, which states that characterological disorders are primary, with depression being a secondary feature of character pathology. Depression is seen as a product of difficulties that the individual experiences as a result of a personality disorder. A second hypothesis is the *complication hypothesis*, which notes that personality disorders are the product or aftermath of depressive episodes. These personality modifications can be limited to the duration of the depressive episode, or they can become chronic. A third hypothesis is the *attenuation hypothesis*, which presumes that personality disorders are an attenuated or alternative expression of the disease process that underlies the depressive disorder. Both depressive and personality disorders are seen as arising from the same genetic or constitutional origin. A fourth hypothesis is the *coeffect hypothesis*, which states that both depression and personality arise together from a common third factor, such as traumatic childhood experiences. A fifth hypothesis, the *heterogeneity hypothesis*, postulates that signs and symptoms of depression and personality disorders arise from several sources, including genetic vulnerabilities and environmental influences. These sources produce individuals with heterogeneous psychopathology, a subset of whom manifest both depression and one or more personality disorders.

The five hypotheses reviewed thus far posit causal directional relations between depression and personality disorders, or the causal effect that some alternative factor has on the production of personality disorder and depressive features. The remaining two hypotheses have been used to account for the comorbidity of personality disorders and depression, but are largely descriptive in nature. One of these is the *orthogonal hypothesis*, which suggests that personality disorders and depression are independent constructs but are frequently observed as occurring together because they are both common in the general population. The comorbidity of these two conditions, then, is the result of chance occurrence. Of the models reviewed, this one is most consistent with the structure of *DSM*, in which Axis I and II conditions are regarded as relatively independent. Finally, the *overlapping symptomatology* hypothesis posits that the observed comorbidity of personality disorders

EXHIBIT 7.1

Theoretical Accounts of the Relationship Between Personality Disorders and Axis I Conditions (With Depression as the Example)

Characterological predisposition hypothesis

Personality disorders → depression

Complication hypothesis

Depression → personality disorders

Attenuation hypothesis

Biological vulnerability (e.g., disease, genetics)	→ depression → personality disorder

Coeffect hypothesis

Common environmental etiological determinant (e.g., child abuse)	→ depression → personality disorder

Heterogeneity hypothesis

Variety of etiological determinants (e.g., genetic, environment)	→	vulnerability Factor	→ depression → personality disorder

Orthogonal hypothesis

Personality disorders and depression are independent of each other ($r = .0$)

Overlapping symptomatology

Criteria that define personality disorders and depression are not distinct, and share several common features.

and depression is largely an artifact of overlapping criteria sets used to define each of the disorders.

Regardless of these varying and sometimes competing hypotheses about the relationships between Axis I and Axis II disorders, a large number of clients who seek treatment are diagnosed with both Axis I and Axis II disorders. The next section describes the impact of Axis II disorders on the treatment of Axis I disorders.

Impact of Axis II Disorders on Treating Axis I Disorders

A reasonable amount of research exists on the impact of the presence of Axis II personality disorders on the effectiveness of an EVT treatment applied to an Axis I disorder. Although there is a fair amount of evidence to suggest that Axis I treatments are generally less effective for those with co-occurring Axis II conditions (Costello, 1996a), some studies suggest that individuals benefit in a comparable manner from an Axis I treatment whether or not they have a co-occurring personality disorder. Simun (1999), for example, reported that depressed clients with and without co-occurring personality disorders benefited equally from the Coping with Depression Course, which is an EVT behavioral treatment for depression (Lewinsohn et al., 1984). Comer (1998), who used an EVT cognitive–behavioral treatment for bulimia, reported that Axis II psychopathology failed to demonstrate any relationship to treatment outcome. Dreessen, Hoekstra, and Arntz (1997) also found that neither categorical nor dimensional personality disorder variables affected treatment outcome in 52 participants diagnosed with obsessive–compulsive disorder who followed a standardized cognitive–behavioral therapy program. Even the inclusion of dropouts did not change the results that neither categorical nor dimensional personality disorder variables significantly affected treatment outcome. Van Velzen, Emmelkamp, and Scholing (1997) demonstrated that exposure treatment conducted in vivo benefited all three of these groups of social phobics: social phobics without a personality disorder, social phobics with a single diagnosis of avoidant personality disorder, and social phobics with several personality disorders. Finally, Sanderson, Beck, and McGinn (2002) noted that there was no difference in posttreatment outcome in persons with generalized anxiety disorder who were treated by cognitive therapy, regardless of whether they had a comorbid personality disorder. Those persons with comorbid personality disorder, however, were more likely to drop out of treatment: 7 of the 10 dropouts had a comorbid personality disorder compared with only 9 of the 22 completers.

Personality psychopathology was conversely found to have a detrimental effect on the outcome of an EVT cognitive–behavioral treatment for panic disorder, whereas the impact of comorbid depression produces more mixed findings (Mennin & Heimberg, 2000). Marlowe, Kirby, Festinger, Husband, and Platt (1997) found no significant difference in response to a behaviorally oriented treatment in urban, poor, cocaine abusers with and without various categorical personality disorders. Dimensional analyses of personality disorder symptoms generated from a semistructured interview accounted for substantial proportions of variance in treatment outcomes, however. Mavissakalian and Hamann (1987) reported that 75% of patients with low initial personality traits responded to a pharmacological and behavioral treatment for agoraphobia, whereas only 25% of patients with high personality traits responded. A different strategy was used by Nelson-Gray, Johnson, Foyle, Daniel, and Harmon (1996). In this study, cognitive therapy was used to address both depression and co-occurring Axis II disorders in 9 adult clients. Overall, cognitive therapy was more effective in treating depression than in treating the co-occurring personality disorder.

Impact of Axis II Disorders on the Treatment Process

McGinn, Young, and Sanderson (1995) noted that short-term cognitive therapies often are insufficient for patients with personality disorders. These authors contend that a longer term therapy, schema-focused therapy that combines cognitive, behavioral, interpersonal, and experiential techniques is needed to provide optimal treatment to patients with personality disorders. In the studies just described that show no differential outcome in Axis I disorders whether the person also has an Axis II disorder, it should be noted that generally outcome measures specific to the Axis I disorder were used. Perhaps more general measures of life satisfaction might have shown more differential results. That is, even though the Axis I disorder may have improved, patients with co-occurring Axis II disorders may have not shown improvement in general life satisfaction.

Why might it be more difficult to treat Axis I disorders if the client also has a personality disorder? First, according to the *DSM–IV–TR* (p. 686), personality disorders are ego-syntonic, that is, "the characteristics that define a Personality Disorder may not be considered problematic by the individual." We are reminded of a clinical case of a young man who often found himself in legal trouble (e.g., for a hit-and-run driving accident, for fracturing the nose of his girlfriend during an argument, for driving while intoxicated and resisting arrest). He also had repeated difficulties in relationships, with his family, girlfriend, acquaintances, and office coworkers. His Axis II diagnosis was Personality Disorder Not Otherwise Specified, with antisocial, dependent, and narcissistic traits. Multiple treatment goals were suggested to him, as well as multiple treatment options. Despite his clear personal suffering, legal difficulties, and faithfulness in attending therapy sessions, he maintained that he did not want to change and must remain "true to himself." His way of living was clearly ego-syntonic, even though it created great unhappiness in himself and in others around him.

Another reason it is difficult to treat individuals with co-occurring Axis I and Axis II disorders is that the clinical research literature does not provide guidelines of where to begin treatment. Should both types of disorders be address simultaneously? Should the Axis I or Axis II disorder be addressed first? Without guidelines, each clinician uses his or her best judgment, with surely variable outcomes.

Persons with personality disorders appear to be more likely to drop out of treatment. As noted by Sanderson et al. (2002), persons with comorbid personality disorders were more likely to drop out of treatment for generalized anxiety disorder.

Finally, many clients with personality disorders have difficulty complying with manualized treatments, which is a requirement of EVT status for a treatment. The EVTs are each described in a treatment manual that allows replication of the treatment across clinicians. The intent is to implement the treatment manual with a particular client, on a session-by-session basis. Many clients, however, poorly tolerate such structured treatment, despite its previous demonstrations of efficacy with other clients.

In our experience, and somewhat contrary to the literature reviewed here, many of the clients who react negatively to such manualized or structured treatments are clients who not only have an Axis I disorder, but who also have a co-occurring personality disorder. For example, persons diagnosed with borderline personality disorder are characterized by a pattern of unstable interpersonal relationships and marked affective impulsivity (e.g., irritability, anxiety, anger episodes). People with borderline personality disorder are often in a state of crisis, involving mostly life outside of therapy, but perhaps also involving their therapist. These individuals are often too crisis-ridden and emotionally labile to participate in structured or manualized treatment for a co-occurring Axis I disorder on a week-to-week basis. For example, the individual might benefit from an EVT for depression, such as cognitive therapy (e.g., Sacco & Beck, 1995), behavior therapy (e.g., Lewinsohn & Gotlib, 1995), or interpersonal psychotherapy (e.g., Markowitz & Weissman, 1995). Nonetheless, their regular crises and labile affect interfere with any systematic application of a manualized treatment.

We also have experienced some difficulties in applying the skills training portion of DBT (Linehan, 1993b), an empirically validated treatment for persons with borderline personality disorder, to the typical problems of clients with the disorder because of either constant life crises or resistance to structured treatments. One woman with borderline personality disorder in our training clinic was a student who had very negative interpersonal interactions with her teachers because she believed they were not being of sufficient help to her. In our opinion, she would have benefited especially from the DBT module on interpersonal effectiveness to obtain what she wanted interpersonally in a more effective manner. In every session that DBT skills training for interpersonal effectiveness was undertaken, she displayed somatic complaints (e.g., "I need to leave this session because my back is hurting" or "I have a headache and can't do this type of session").

CLIENT RESISTANCE TO THERAPY

The problems described here are not limited to clients with personality disorders. Others may present similar challenges during assessment and therapy. In clinical terms, this phenomenon has been termed "client resistance." Although this term is usually associated with the psychodynamic treatment literature, some behavioral clinicians have described and attempted to explain "client resistance," namely, Jahn and Lichstein (1980) and Newman (1994).

Treatment Failures With EVTs

A strong example of client resistance might be treatment failures for individual clients even though an EVT was competently provided. An example of an EVT is Foa's exposure and response prevention (e.g., Foa, Steketee, Grayson, Turner, & Latimer, 1984) for obsessive–compulsive disorder (OCD). With this approach, the client is exposed to the obsession-related stimuli and prevented from making the usual compulsive responses. The intervention, however, appears to be effective in only about 60% to 70% of treated cases (Salkovskis, 1995). Moreover, attrition rates are approximately 20%. Approximately 50% of clients demonstrate a reduction in symptoms of 30%

of more (Salkovskis, 1998), and many continue to display OCD symptoms below this threshold (Kasviskis & Marks, 1988).

For those who dropped out of treatment, some other approach may have been necessary, but there is no other EVT for OCD. For those with minimal treatment responsiveness, some adjunct treatments may be required, but there is little guidance in the clinical literature about adjusting treatment for individual differences.

Client Noncompliance With EVT Treatments

In another example of "client resistance," many clients simply cannot comply with the manualized treatments that characterize the empirically validated treatments. This situation was described earlier in the case of clients with personality disorders, but even clients without co-occurring personality disorders sometimes object to manualized treatment. One client in our training clinic presented with panic disorder, for which there is a well-known EVT, Barlow's cognitive–behavioral therapy for panic disorder (e.g., Barlow, Craske, Cerny, & Klosko, 1989). When asked whether he had previously been in treatment, the client replied that he had been, but left the other therapist because the therapist had wanted to focus on "a single treatment goal," that is, increasing his ability to cope with panic attacks. The client reported that he also wanted to talk about his job and relationships with his daughter and with his mother.

Suggestions for Working With Resistant Clients

Behavioral assessment and behavioral principles have been useful in suggesting how to modify the application of EVTs to clients who resist manualized treatments. For example, using the Premack principle (see chap. 6), the session agenda can be arranged so that the first portion of the session is spent on structured treatment and the second on the client's crisis.

The same issue as discussed earlier, how to apply an EVT effectively with an individual client, may occur when clients have not only a personality disorder, but also normal variations in personality. To illustrate, many of the manualized or structured treatments require completion of weekly therapy homework assignments. A client who is low in conscientiousness (which is a normal variation of personality) may be unlikely to complete weekly therapy homework assignments and may also be unlikely even to attend therapy sessions on a regular basis.

Many suggestions for increasing compliance with behavioral homework assignments have been provided by Shelton and Levy (1981). Examples of suggestions offered by Shelton and Levy for facilitating client compliance include the following. In each instance, the therapist should

- be sure assignments contain specific detail regarding response and stimulus elements relevant to the desired behavior (that is, provide specific instructions);
- give direct skill training when necessary;
- begin with small homework requests and gradually increase assignments;
- reinforce compliance;
- provide cuing to remind the client to carry out the homework assignments;
- help the client develop a commitment to compliance;
- use cognitive rehearsal strategies to improve success with assignments;
- try to anticipate and reduce the negative effects of compliance; and
- closely monitor compliance with as many sources as possible.

One modification that we have tried ourselves is "informal cognitive therapy." Instead of requiring clients to complete forms monitoring their thoughts in specific situations outside of sessions, we have asked clients in session to recall their most recent incident of being negatively aroused and have used this instance to identify environmental antecedents and consequent automatic thoughts.

As reviewed in this section, behavioral principles provide useful suggestions for how to modify the application of EVTs to clients who show "resistance," possibly related to a personality disorder or to normal personality variations.

Personality Variables and Treatment Selection for Axis I Disorders

EVT treatments are available for many Axis I disorders. As described earlier, however, many Axis I disorders have no EVT, many clients have unclear or no diagnoses, and many clients cannot or will not comply with an Axis I EVT. In these situations, behavioral principles can be used to develop treatments based on a functional analysis or on response class selection or to modify the application of an EVT. In these situations, nomothetic treatments are applied idiographically through the use of behavioral principles.

As described earlier, behavior therapists of late have been much more accepting of the utility of psychiatric diagnoses (Nelson-Gray & Paulson, 2003). Thompson and Williams (1985, p. 47) noted that "it is doubtful that many behavioral persons would discount the phenomenon of a personality entirely. People vary in the way they approach phenomena and the disposition that they bring to a situation." Along the same vein, there have been attempts to relate the outcomes of behavior therapy techniques to personality variables as they have been traditionally conceived. Rathus, Sanderson, Miller, and Wetzler (1995), for example, examined the effects of personality characteristics on the outcomes of 18 clients with panic disorder who were treated with cognitive–behavioral therapy. Significant scale elevations on the Millon Clinical Multiaxial Inventory—II (MCMI–II; Millon, 1987) yielded no outcome differences. Nonetheless, treatment responders showed a different personality profile: lower initial scores on borderline, histrionic, schizoid, schizotypal, antisocial, aggressive/sadistic, and self-defeating scales, and higher initial scores on the compulsive scale. Keutzer (1968) examined the relationship between success in smoking cessation and various personality variables. The relationship between treatment outcome and personality variables was significant for only one such variable, the effective cognitive dissonance score. Darlington (1995) examined the relationship between success in weight loss treatment and personality variables. Field independence, as measured by the Group Embedded Figures Tests (Witkin, Oltman, Raskin, & Karp, 1971), was significantly related to weight loss, whereas Vocabulary IQ predicted continuing in treatment. Vassend, Willumsen, and Hoffart (2000) examined the relationships between dental fear, treatment success for dental fear, and personality variables. Using the five-factor model (discussed in chap. 4) of personality dimensions, there were significant correlations between neuroticism, extraversion, and agreeableness with emotional distress symptoms. When initial symptom level was controlled for in multiple regression analysis, however, the statistical effects of personality variables disappeared. Hudzinski and Levenson (1985) reported that a biofeedback program for the treatment of headaches was most successful for clients under 40 years and those with an internal locus of control.

The reports described here show that it is certainly possible to relate the outcomes of various behavioral techniques with personality variables. There could be an endless array of such studies, given that there are many current and valid measures of personality and many effective behavioral techniques. As clinicians, we experience the differential responses of clients to manualized treatments in general and to specific treatments in particular. It would be convenient to be able to predict which clients would stay in therapy, and which clients would respond well to which treatments. It is questionable, however, if correlational studies relating personality variables and treatment outcomes are the most efficient route to identify these predictor variables. Measures of personality variables are responses, as are responses to treatment. These response–response relationships are descriptive or structural; they are not functional. They do not provide a description of stimuli that can be used to then modify treatment. Personality variables generally do not provide suggestions on how to modify treatment so that it will be more effective for a particular individual.

It is the spirit of this book that behavior therapists do well to acknowledge individual differences while remaining true to behavioral principles.

Treatments for Axis I disorders can be selected first on the basis of diagnoses and the EVT list. When this strategy is not applicable, we recommend that individual differences be conceptualized within a behavioral perspective and that treatment strategies incorporate behavioral principles.

8

BEHAVIORAL TREATMENT OF PERSONALITY DISORDERS

The behavior therapy movement has a long and distinguished history of developing and evaluating psychosocial treatments to address the needs of persons for whom other treatments were largely unavailable. The advances made in behavior therapy for the treatment of autism, schizophrenia, and self-injurious behavior among the intellectually handicapped are exemplars of this history. Consistent with this tradition, available research suggests that behavior therapy also has a good deal to offer to the treatment of persons with personality disorders (Piper & Joyce, 2001; Robins, Ivanoff, & Linehan, 2001). As we note later, however, there is surprisingly little research on the effectiveness of therapies for personality disorders, including behavior therapy for these conditions.

In the sections that follow, we discuss possible behavioral treatment approaches for problem areas common among persons with personality disorders. Prior to this review, we discuss some of the descriptive aspects of the *Diagnostic and Statistical Manual of Mental Disorders (DSM)*-defined personality disorders, as well as issues related to the assessment and treatment of personality disorders from a behavioral perspective.

DSM PERSONALITY DISORDERS: DESCRIPTIVE FEATURES

Personality disorders represent a special challenge to behavior therapy because the multiple problem areas that define these conditions are typically long-standing and usually reflect deeply entrenched and inflexible behavioral repertoires. Even when other conditions are the focus of therapy, such as mood or anxiety disorders, therapy for those conditions tends to be less effective or to take longer to produce significant therapeutic change when the client also has a co-occurring personality disorder (Costello, 1996a; Pilkonis, 2001).

In the *Diagnostic and Statistical Manual of Mental Disorders, Text Revision* (*DSM–IV–TR*; American Psychiatric Association, 2000, p. 685), a personality disorder is defined as "an enduring pattern of inner experience and behavior that deviates markedly from expectations of the individual's culture, is pervasive and inflexible, has an onset in adolescence or early adulthood, is stable over time, and leads to distress or impairment." The 10 personality disorders of *DSM–IV–TR* are organized into three intuitively derived symptom-based clusters. Cluster A consists of the "odd–eccentric" personality disorders (paranoid, schizoid, schizotypal), Cluster B the "erratic–emotional–dramatic" personality disorders (histrionic, narcissistic, borderline, antisocial), and Cluster C "anxious–fearful" personality disorders (avoidant, dependent, and obsessive–compulsive).

In the multiaxial system of *DSM*, personality disorders are distinguished from "syndrome disorders," with each general class of disorders coded on separate axes of clinical description. *DSM* structurally regards syndrome disorders (Axis I) as "quasi-independent" of personality disorders (Axis II). Notably absent in *DSM* is any discussion of the rationale that led to the representation of syndromal and personality disorders on separate axes. Livesley, Schroeder, Jackson, and Jang (1994) suggested that the architects of *DSM–III* (American Psychiatric Association, 1980), where the Axis II designation first appeared, assumed that Axis I and II disorders had different etiologies, whereby clinical syndromes were considered to have a biological origin and personality disorders a psychosocial origin. On the basis of available research, Livesley et al. (1994) questioned the validity of the assumptions that gave rise to the distinction because their research review suggested the importance of both biological–genetic and psychosocial components in the development of disorders within both of these classes.

Other problems with the Axis I and II distinction have been noted (Farmer, 2000; Livesley et al., 1994). For example, the assumption that Axis II conditions consist of enduring and lifelong patterns whereas Axis I concepts represent more transient and variable conditions in terms of severity and duration is not supported by the existing data. Long-term stability studies generally suggest modest to poor stability of personality disorder diagnoses as evident by test–retest kappa coefficients generally less than .60 (Zimmerman, 1994). Findings from research conducted by Ferro, Klein, Schwartz, Kasch, and Leader (1998) and Loranger et al. (1991) exemplify those commonly reported on the temporal stability of personality disorder concepts. These studies suggested that although diagnoses of personality disorders over time were moderately unstable, there was a good deal of consistency in the level of personality disorder symptoms experienced over time. That is, whereas behavioral patterns consistent with personality disorder concepts were moderately to highly correlated among persons evaluated on two separate occasions, personality disorder status (i.e., disorder present versus disorder absent) was susceptible to change, even within relatively short time intervals.

Another conceptual problem associated with the Axis I and II distinction is the considerable degree of comorbidity associated with these conditions. About 75% of persons with an Axis II diagnosis will also meet criteria for at least one Axis I diagnosis, whereas 13% to 81% of persons with an Axis I condition will also meet criteria for at least one Axis II condition (Dolan-Sewell, Krueger, & Shea, 2001). Personality disorders concepts do not appear to be well distinguished among themselves, as evident by their moderate to high comorbidity. For example, if a mental health client is diagnosed with a personality disorder, there is about a 25% (Drake & Vaillant, 1985) to 50% (Maier, Lichterman, Klingler, Heun, & Hallmayer, 1992; Zimmerman & Coryell, 1989) chance that the person will have at least one other personality disorder. On average, if a mental health client meets criteria for one personality disorder, he or she likely will meet criteria for four personality disorders (Widiger et al., 1991). The degree of comorbidity of personality disorders among nonpatient or community samples may be somewhat less, however (Farmer & Chapman, 2002; Farmer & Nelson-Gray, 1995; Zimmerman & Coryell, 1989).

Finally, there is a question of just how abnormal or deviant features of personality disorder are. Available data suggest that individuals with personality disorders are fairly common in the general population. One recent review by Mattia and Zimmerman (2001) placed the median prevalence of any *DSM*-defined personality disorder in the general population at 12.9%. If, in fact, one of eight people meet diagnostic criteria for at least one *DSM*-defined personality disorder, then these conditions would be rather normative. Given this and other significant conceptual problems noted here, we address in greater detail in the section that follows notions of normality and abnormality from a behavioral perspective, after which we present an alternative framework for considering personality disorder–related pathology from a behavior therapy perspective.

ISSUES IN THE ASSESSMENT AND TREATMENT OF PERSONALITY DISORDERS FROM A BEHAVIORAL PERSPECTIVE

Behavioral conceptualizations of personality disorder pathology differ from other approaches in a variety of ways. In this section, we discuss behavioral notions of abnormality, and then describe how behaviorally oriented clinicians might view personality disorders from their theoretical perspective.

Behavioral Perspectives on Normality Versus Abnormality in Relation to Personality Disorders: The Culture Is Context

The term *normal* is derived from the Latin term *norma*, which referred to a carpenter's square—a standard measure or reference. Over time, the term "normal" has come to mean a standard, pattern, or rule by which events or things might be measured or judged. The prefix *ab* means "away from." *Abnormal*, then, refers to a deviation from what is normal, or a deviation from what is regarded as an accepted standard.

What is the standard that someone with a personality disorder deviates from? That is, what is the context for defining "abnormal" or "disordered" as it relates to personality? Cognitive, psychodynamic, and medical model perspectives all presuppose that there is something inherently deviant about individuals with personality disorders. Furthermore, the deviant source is presumed to reside within the individual and that this internal anomaly must be modified, changed, or removed for the person no longer to be disordered. In the cognitive realm, schemas are viewed as etiologically relevant and as maintaining factors, and thus targeted for change in therapy (Beck et al., 1990; Young, 1994). In psychodynamic therapies, poorly developed and integrated mental representations of self and others coupled with maladaptive inner defensive coping mechanisms are viewed as causal and are the focus of therapy (Kernberg, Selzer, Koenigsberg, Carr, & Appelbaum, 1989). In the medical model approach, the presence of an underlying disease process or biological anomaly such as abnormal neurochemistry (Markovitz, 2001) is regarded as causal of personality disorder–related behaviors. Thus, the disease itself or its associated effects (e.g., neurochemical levels) are targeted for change.

Behavior theory defines the concept of abnormality in terms of cultural values; that is, what is regarded as normal or abnormal is the result of cultural views or practices. Culture is the context within which judgments about normality are made, whereby normality is a standard approved by the majority of people within a culture. In this respect, there is no "absolute truth" for what defines normality or abnormality; each culture has guidelines for making this distinction according to cultural beliefs, values, mores, and norms. From a behavioral perspective, then, there is nothing inherently defective about a person who has a personality disorder. Rather, the label "personality disorder" as it relates to a constellation of covarying behaviors represents a societal value judgment about those behaviors. Furthermore, the behavioral perspective would also expect that there would be considerable variability in terms of how cultures define personality disorders, and there is accumulating evidence that this is the case (Alarcon, Foulks, & Vakkur, 1998).

Another consideration in the definition of abnormality from a behavioral perspective is the degree of impairment or distress associated with behavior patterns for both the person who exhibits such behaviors as well as the social environment that is subjected to them. From this perspective, "behavior disorders" would only be designated for behavioral patterns associated with subjective distress or impairment in occupational or social functioning. That is, the condition or disorder must be associated with harm or some loss of benefit to the person. Often, the concepts of harm or loss of benefit are judged with reference to the standards or values of a person's culture.

A Behavioral Perspective on the Personality Disorder Concept

From the perspective of behavioral assessment and behavioral case formulation, the term "personality disorder" is problematic. Traditional views conceptualize personality as something within the individual (e.g., personality structure, personality dynamic, internalized representations, ego, cognitive schema) that guides behavior largely independent of the context in which behavior occurs. From a behavioral perspective, such an emphasis on hypothesized internal causal entities shifts the focus of interventions away from the context within which clinically relevant behavior occurs to the modification of hypothetical constructs that do not exist in any tangible form.

A behavioral account of personality disorder–related behaviors is no different from that of other behaviors. That is, the etiological, causal, or maintaining factors associated with behavior generally also apply to the response tendencies that define each of the personality disorders. Therefore, personality disorder–related behavior is viewed as the combined result of phylogenetic selection contingencies (i.e., heritable attributes) and other biological variables, faulty or deficient environmental learning during one's lifetime, and current problematic environmental contingencies. The behaviors that define personality disorders may be regarded as more extreme variants of common forms of related behavior, however, a perspective that is consistent with available research (Livesley, 2001a). As such, we see the dichotomous representation of personality disorder pathology into "diagnosis present" or "diagnosis absent" as arbitrary and a significant departure from current scientific understandings.

From this basic behavioral formulation of personality disorder–related behaviors, the primary goals of behavior therapy for personality disorders are to (a) modify existing environmental contingencies that maintain problematic behaviors, (b) modify inaccurate or problematic rules that ineffectively govern current behavior, or (c) teach new skills to expand the client's behavioral repertoire so that he or she has more behavioral options for responding effectively in different situations.

GENERAL THERAPY PRINCIPLES AND GUIDELINES IN THE BEHAVIOR THERAPY OF PERSONS WITH PERSONALITY DISORDERS

Behavioral approaches to the treatment of personality disorders share many common features with traditional therapeutic practices. There are, however, a number of characteristic features that distinguish a behavioral approach from other approaches. In the sections that follow, a general behavioral approach to the treatment of personality disorder pathology is outlined.

Therapeutic Relationship Factors

Among persons with personality disorders, a majority of the core problem areas tend to be manifest in interpersonal contexts. Therefore, it is critical for therapists who work with persons with personality disorders to facilitate the development and maintenance of a trusting, empathic, allied, and collaborative relationship. Livesley (2001b) provided several useful suggestions for accomplishing these goals:

- The therapist should continuously communicate respect, understanding, acceptance, and support of the client.
- The therapist and client should work collaboratively together during all stages of the therapeutic process.
- The therapist should maintain realistic optimism for therapy, even in the face of what appear to be overwhelming obstacles to change.
- The therapist should acknowledge client progress and emerging competencies, particularly those related to the effective use of skills targeted for development or refinement in therapy.
- The therapist in conjunction with the client should seek to develop and maintain a therapeutic context whereby relationship issues can be constructively addressed as they emerge in therapy.

Establishment of a Therapy Focus and Framework

The collaborative establishment of a therapy focus and framework is among the first tasks in a behavior therapy for personality disorders. In the following two sections, we describe basic considerations related to the selection of therapeutic targets and goals, and to the overall emphasis and structure of therapy.

Agreement on the Focus of Therapy

When individuals with personality disorders come to therapy, it is often for some other problem area such as substance abuse, depression, social phobia, or trauma-related symptoms. Less common are individuals who come to therapy explicitly for treatment of Axis II–related pathology, even though associated behaviors may contribute to ongoing distress or impairment. For example, it has been our experience that the majority of people who habitually self-injure as a form of coping do not experience that behavior as particularly problematic and are often initially reluctant to make that behavior a high-priority treatment target. A responsible therapist, however, will negotiate with a client to make such behavior a primary focus of treatment and will explain the rationale for doing so. Because therapist and client perspectives on what represents problematic behavior can differ, it is important within the first few meetings to get a clear perspective on why the client is coming to therapy and his or her therapeutic goals. Additional treatment goals may be negotiated with the client in the event the therapist becomes aware of other problematic behaviors that place either the client or others at risk or behaviors that could complicate the therapy of other conditions.

Establishment of a General Therapeutic Framework

As Livesley (2001b) noted, personality disorders involve multiple domains of problematic behaviors, and any treatment of personality disorders will necessarily need to be tailored to the unique clinical presentation that each client displays. Furthermore, Livesley suggested that a general therapeutic framework or strategy is necessary to organize and provide conceptual clarity to the therapeutic work. A therapeutic framework can be considered at three levels: (a) the framework of therapy with a client as it unfolds over time, (b) the structural framework within which different treatment modalities are embedded, and (c) the framework that guides the work of individual sessions. Linehan's (1993a) dialectical behavior therapy (DBT) provides a useful example of each of these therapeutic frameworks.

In DBT, the *format of therapy as it unfolds over time* follows a sequential stage model. In the first stage, emphasis is placed on the attainment of basic capacities. Therapeutic goals within this first stage include decreasing suicidal and therapy interfering behaviors, reducing or eliminating factors that detract from the quality of life, and the development and appropriate use of behavioral skills. This first stage typically takes place within the first year of therapy. The second stage of therapy involves reducing posttraumatic stress. This phase of therapy is initiated only when first-stage target behaviors are under control. When dealing with issues related to posttraumatic stress, treatment often involves an exposure component to trauma-related cues. In the third stage, emphasis is placed on increasing self-respect and achieving individual goals. This involves the development of the ability to trust and respect oneself; to validate one's opinions, emotions, and actions; and the development of plans for realizing goals and for overcoming potential obstacles to goal attainment.

In DBT, there is also a *framework for the various treatment modalities*. There are four such treatment modalities in DBT. Individual outpatient therapy typically involves one or two weekly sessions that last between 1 to 1.5 hours each. The primary focus of these sessions is on target problems (e.g., self-injury, suicidal ideation, therapy interfering behaviors, substance misuse, factors that interfere with quality of life), whether efforts were made to engage in adaptive coping, and the degree to which coping methods were effective if used. The skills training group is another treatment modality and involves instruction in coping skills. The skills training group is typically composed of 6 to 8 clients, and group meetings last for about 2 hours and take place weekly during the first year of therapy. Telephone consultation is a third treatment modality and involves the opportunity for the therapist or client to contact one another in between sessions. This component is intended to provide an opportunity for (a) the client to consult with the therapist in between sessions about ways to cope with difficult situations other than through self-injury or suicidal behaviors; (b) the promotion of skills generalization to everyday situations; and (c) the repair of the therapeutic relationship, if damaged or disrupted, prior to the next session. The fourth treatment modality is case consultation meetings for therapists. These meetings typically occur on a weekly basis and are attended by therapists who use DBT in their work with clients. The nature and purpose of this consultation group is described more fully in the section on therapist supervision that follows.

Finally, in the individual therapy component of DBT, there is a *within session framework* that prioritizes treatment targets in terms of their potential for damage to the client or the therapeutic process. Within the first year of therapy, these targets, hierarchically arranged in order of importance, are as follows:

- *Suicidal and parasuicidal behaviors*. These include suicide crisis behaviors, parasuicidal acts, suicidal ideation and communication, suicide-related expectancies and beliefs, and suicide-related affect.
- *Therapy-interfering behaviors*. Examples of behaviors that would fall within this category are frequent missed sessions, behaviors that interfere with the therapeutic process, and within-session client behaviors that are similar to targeted problem behaviors that routinely occur outside of the therapeutic context.
- *Quality of life–interfering behaviors*. Examples of such behaviors include substance abuse, unprotected sexual behavior, financial problems, criminal behaviors, and dysfunctional interpersonal behaviors.
- *Behavioral skills*. Although skills training is the primary focus of the skills training group, individual therapy sessions facilitate the integration of these skills into the client's daily life.

This hierarchical arrangement of treatment targets within sessions gives the therapist guidance in determining which of the client's problematic behaviors should be attended to, and in what order, within individual therapy sessions. For example, if suicidal or parasuicidal acts occur between sessions, these would be discussed in the next individual therapy session. This discussion would include a detailed behavioral analysis of the situation in which these acts occurred, what if any skills other than parasuicidal or suicidal behavior were used to cope with this situation, and a review of possible effective alternatives to parasuicidal and suicidal behavior for coping that can be used in similar future situations.

Establishment of a Motivation to Change

As persons with personality disorders infrequently present for therapy to address specifically personality disorder–related behaviors, motivational enhancement strategies (Miller & Rollnick, 1991) are often required in the early stages of therapy to facilitate an awareness of the problematic nature of certain behaviors, and of how the repetitive engagement in such behaviors may be inconsistent with the realization of one's values or longer term goals. The therapist might also work with the client to develop a commitment to change and a plan for carrying out committed action. Ideas that come from this process, in turn, can establish the foundation for subsequent therapeutic work.

Development of a Functional Understanding of the Client's Problem Behaviors

As noted in chapter 3, the cornerstone of a behavioral formulation of a client's problem behavior is the functional analysis. Functional analyses identify the context within which behavior occurs and, in so doing, isolate potential variables that influence or maintain problematic behavior. Such an analysis may also reveal behavioral repertoires that warrant development, reduction, or refinement. A functional understanding of a client's behaviors can also suggest relevant treatment interventions.

Behavior and Environmental Change

Behavior therapy is often geared toward the development or refinement of new behaviors as well as the modification of environments that make problematic behavior more likely. During the process of behavior change, it is important to carry out change procedures in such a way that the client's views of personal competency are enhanced as he or she acquires new skills (Livesley, 2001b). As such, behavior change should often be undertaken in a gradual or stepwise manner, beginning with change strategies that are likely to produce success and, consequently, aid in the modification of self-rules that suggest "nothing works" or "I'll never change." In addition, as change is promoted through the teaching of new behaviors or through environmental modification, it is important for the therapist and client to work together to develop strategies for inhibiting deeply entrenched problematic responses.

As new learning occurs, it is important to facilitate the application of new skills, behaviors, and modes of coping to new situations (Livesley, 2001b). Such generalization of training makes it more likely that new adaptive behavioral skills will be used flexibly in a wide variety of situations and contexts rather than in narrowly focused situational contexts. Such broad application of new skills will also increase the likelihood that these skills will be maintained over time, because more frequent behavioral displays in a variety of contexts increases the likelihood that naturally occurring contingencies will maintain these behaviors over time.

Client Acceptance and Validation

Clients with personality disorders were often raised in environments that were invalidating, nonaccepting, neglectful, or abusive (Linehan, 1993a). Given such histories, it is of little wonder that many clients struggle with issues of self-trust, self-acceptance, and self-valuation.

When therapists overtly demonstrate acceptance and valuation of their clients, they convey understanding and respect for the individual and his or her experience. They also model an alternative way to regard the self. Such modeling coupled with skills training in self-acceptance and validation strategies facilitates the movement away from self-invalidating behavior patterns that are highly common among persons with personality disorders and toward behavior patterns that reflect respect and caring for the self.

It is also important for therapists who work with individuals with personality disorders to acknowledge to themselves and to their clients that seemingly "dysfunctional" behavior is often quite functional. That is, problematic behavior serves a purpose because it generally produces a consequence that is desirable, which accounts for its maintenance over time. As the client contemplates and works toward change, he or she will be continuously confronted with the dilemma of whether to hold onto or give up behaviors that previously worked in some beneficial way, at least in the short term. The therapist, in turn, must find the optimal balance between pushing for adaptive and healthy change and accepting and valuing the client for who he or she is (Linehan, 1993a).

Enhancement of Client Awareness of the Context of Behavior

Teaching clients to be good observers of their behavior and evaluators of the contexts within which their behavior occurs are core features of behavioral interventions. Self-monitoring is a central assessment and therapeutic modality in behavior therapy (Nelson, 1977). In behavior therapy programs for personality disorders, self-monitoring is often used (a) to record occurrences of the target behavior, (b) to note the conditions under which the behavior occurred (including the consequence that the behavior was intended to produce), and (c) as a vehicle for developing behavioral alternatives to the target behavior that are potentially effective in producing desired outcomes without the associated negative side effects.

Promoting the Maintenance of Therapeutic Gains

During therapy, the therapist provides instruction in therapeutic strategies that can be applied to the client's problem areas. Over the course of therapy, the client learns these methods, and it is the continual application of this learning once therapy ends that is critical for the maintenance of therapeutic gains and for additional future growth (Livesley, 2001b). To facilitate this, the therapist and client can work together to develop plans for handling difficult life circumstances in the latter stages of therapy.

Relapse prevention procedures (see chap. 6) can also be included in the final stages of therapy to assist the client in anticipating and coping with problematic situations that are likely to arise in the future. This would include an identification of high-risk situations for problematic behavior, a review of skills that can be effectively applied in these situations, an anticipation of future lapses, and a review of what such lapses might mean for the client when they occur. The overarching goal of relapse prevention is to reduce the likelihood that future lapses would serve as occasions for a full-blown relapse and, consequently, as a buffer against hopelessness and demoralization.

An establishment of a commitment to maintain therapeutic gains is also often useful. As part of this commitment, a client may commit to making lifestyle changes to reduce the likelihood of entering into high-risk situations. The client may similarly commit to developing new habits that are incompatible with problematic behaviors, such as a commitment to self-care, exercise, and good nutrition. To facilitate the client's commitment, his or her values and goals should first be clarified. In the context of this analysis, plans for achieving these distal outcomes can be developed, as well as ideas for navigating potential obstacles that may arise.

Therapist Supervision and Consultation

It is generally good practice for therapists who routinely work with persons who have personality disorders to have peer supervision. Linehan (1993a), for example, has included the consultation team as a component in DBT for borderline personality disorder. One of the functions of the consultation group is to evaluate the treatment plan and its implementation with reference to the idiographic needs of the client. The consultation group also promotes treatment adherence, ensures that the therapist remains engaged in the therapeutic relationship, and reduces the likelihood of therapist burnout through the provision of support and supervisory assistance (Robins et al., 2001).

CORE BEHAVIOR PATTERNS AND REPERTOIRES AMONG PERSONS WITH PERSONALITY DISORDERS

In the sections that follow, we provide overviews of therapeutic strategies or interventions that are potentially helpful in the modification of behaviors associated with personality disorders. Following Costello (1996b) and Widiger and Shea (1991), we describe the treatment of Axis II conditions in terms of core response topographies or behavior patterns rather than with reference to specific personality disorder concepts (see Table 8.1). We do this for several reasons. First, many of the behavioral features that define personality disorder concepts are heterogeneous. For example, in the case of borderline personality disorder, *DSM* diagnostic criteria variously refer to the experience of negative affects or states, problems in affect regulation, impulsivity, self-harm or suicidal tendencies, dissociation, paranoid modes of thinking, pervasive interpersonal difficulties, and self-identity problems. Each of these behavioral features is different in form and also likely different in associated functions. As a result, various therapeutic interventions might be indicated for the various behavior patterns included among the diagnostic criteria for this condition. The "borderline" diagnostic label is similarly not especially helpful for identifying which of the possible behavioral features is present for the client because only a subset of these need to be present for a person to receive the diagnosis.

Second, given that there are significant commonalities and covariations among personality disorder features, even among those associated with different diagnostic concepts, we felt that the following approach taken would be less redundant and would more effectively highlight meaningful similarities across concepts.

Third, some behaviors that define personality constructs highlighted in this section have similar functional properties across persons. In fact, it may be that common functions associated with diverse behavioral topographies account for the high degree of comorbidity within Axis II conditions as well as between Axis I and II conditions. Although we note common general functions associated with such topographies and repertoires, it is important to keep in mind that any given form of behavior may have several associated functions for a given individual or among individuals. Thus, it is important to evaluate the unique function(s) that clinically relevant behaviors have for each client.

TABLE 8.1
Core Behavior Patterns and Repertoires Common Among Persons With Personality Disorders

Personality disorder	Anxiety	Anger/ hostility/ aggression	Emotional reactivity/ intensity/ dysregulation	Behavioral/ experiential avoidance	Impulsivity/ disinhibition	Conduct problems/ behavioral acting out	Obsessiveness	Suspiciousness/ paranoia	Odd thinking/ perceptual anomalies	Detached	Dependency	Entitlement/ grandiosity/ egocentricity
Paranoid	*	**	**	*	*	*	**	**	**	*		**
Schizoid	*			**			*	*	*	**		
Schizotypal	*	*	*	**		*	**	**	**	**		*
Histrionic			*	*	**	*					*	**
Narcissistic		*	*		**	*	*	*				**
Borderline	**	**	**	**	**	*	**	**	*		**	*
Antisocial		**			**	**		*		*		**
Avoidant	**		**	**			*	*		*	*	
Dependent	**		**	**			**	*			**	
Obsessive–compulsive	**			**			**			*		

Note. ** predominant feature; * common correlated feature

Finally, the behavior patterns described here share many features with Axis I disorders (Dolan-Sewell et al., 2001; Livesley, 2001a); therefore, treatment considerations outlined here may also be appropriate for those conditions. We, like several other researchers and theorists, do not find the Axis I and Axis II distinction to be especially useful, particularly because there is a good deal of research available that is inconsistent with many of the assumptions that initially gave rise to the distinction (Farmer, 2000).

Our presentation of treatments for core response topographies and repertoires is divided up into four sections: emotional features (anxiety, anger–hostility–aggression, emotional reactivity–intensity–dysregulation), overt behavioral features (behavioral–experiential avoidance, impulsivity–disinhibtion, conduct problems–behavioral acting out), cognitive features (obsessiveness, suspiciousness–paranoia, odd thinking–perceptual anomalies), and interpersonal features (detached, dependency, entitlement–grandiosity–egocentricity).

EMOTIONAL FEATURES

Anxiety

Anxiety is a common emotional experience among persons with anxious–fearful personality disorders and borderline personality disorder (Dolan-Sewell et al., 2001; Farmer & Nelson-Gray, 1995). Anxiety also has moderate covariations with features associated with each of the odd–eccentric personality disorders (Farmer et al., 2004). It is the experience of anxiety, however, that appears to differentiate maximally the anxious–fearful personality disorders from others (Farmer et al., 2004; Farmer & Nelson-Gray, 1995).

Anxiety, when present, is associated with heightened sensitivity and responsiveness to stimuli or contexts associated with punishment, threat, or danger (Gray, 1987a). Responses to such stimuli often involve escape or avoidance, examples of which include both active avoidance (e.g., flee situation, worry, substance abuse, dissociation) and passive avoidance (e.g., behavioral avoidance and inhibition). These responses, in turn, are often negatively reinforced because they function to terminate or prevent exposure to aversive states and situations, thus making these coping responses more likely in similar future circumstances.

Because anxious individuals are inclined to avoid or escape from situations that evoke anxiety, skills associated with effective behavior in avoided situations are often deficient. For example, if an individual avoids social situations and the anxiety that they occasion, then social skills deficits become more likely because of restricted opportunities to learn effective social behavior. That is, if one avoids entry into environments where social behavior is typically enacted and responded to by the social environment, then one does not have access to relevant shaping and modeling experiences that are critical for the development of complex forms of behavior such as social behavior. If a person routinely avoids situations that evoke anxiety, then he or she is unlikely to develop effective anxiety-coping skills.

Treatment Considerations and Approaches

Research on the behavioral treatment of anxiety and related behaviors among people who have anxious–fearful personality disorders is limited. Behavior therapy, however, has been demonstrated to be helpful for reducing anxiety and associated behaviors in general, including those subsumed under the diagnoses of simple phobia (McGlynn, 1994), social phobia (Heimberg et al., 1998), panic disorder with agoraphobia (Craske & Barlow, 2001), obsessive–compulsive disorder (Steketee, 1993), and posttraumatic stress disorder (Foa & Rothbaum, 1998). A common element to many of these therapies is exposure and response prevention. The procedures associated with this treatment approach are summarized in chapter 6.

Much of the research on behavior therapy for anxiety-related personality disorder features has been done on clients with avoidant personality disorder (Alden, 1989; Renneberg, Goldstein, Phillips, & Chambless, 1990; Turner, Beidel, Dancu, & Keys, 1986). These therapies typically include skills training and exposure elements. Therapeutic changes observed following therapy include reductions in social anxiety, increases in social functioning, improvements in mood, and enhanced self-esteem. Given the considerable diagnostic comorbidity between avoidant personality disorder and social phobia (Bernstein & Travaglini, 1999), it is possible that behavioral interventions found to be effective for social phobia (e.g., Heimberg et al., 1998) may also be helpful for producing change in clients with avoidant personality disorder. Therapeutic gains may not be as great or could require more time to realize, however (Bernstein & Travaglini, 1999).

Because many individuals with anxious–fearful personality disorder features experience depressed mood, behavioral activation approaches (Martell et al., 2001) can facilitate improvements in mood (Jacobson et al., 1996). Behavioral activation may have additional benefits because this approach challenges clients to engage in behaviors that are incompatible with avoidance, passivity, and seclusion.

Many researchers have also observed that individuals with anxious–fearful personality disorders experience negative views of themselves (Millon, 1999). Some of these negative views often comprise sets of rule statements that connote an inability to effectively carry out desired behaviors. Other negative self-views are related to perceptions of oneself as defective or not worthwhile. To address these, behavioral interventions that promote mastery experiences and self-efficacy might be used (Bandura, 1986). Such strategies include behavioral experiments, skills training, and traditional cognitive therapy techniques.

Anger–Hostility–Aggression

Overt expressions of anger and aggression tend to be most commonly observed among the erratic–dramatic (impulsive) personality disorders, most notably borderline and antisocial (Lish, Kavoussi, & Coccaro, 1996). Anger and anger expression are also predominant features of paranoid personality disorder.

From a behavioral perspective, anger, hostility, and aggression are examples of response patterns that are likely to be observed in contexts where one experiences frustration. Frustration is perhaps most commonly experienced when behavior does not produce desired consequences from the environment (extinction) or when the opportunity for reinforcement is removed as a result on one's behavior (negative punishment). Behaviors that have an angry or aggressive quality may be used to obtain the reinforcers that have been denied or are not otherwise available. For example, bullying, intimidation, and threats of use of physical force might be used to obtain tangible reinforcers, such as money. Angry displays may similarly be used coercively to get another to comply with behavioral demands (e.g., "if you do what I want you to do, then I will stop yelling and throwing things"). In such a scenario, the cessation of angry displays is contingent on meeting the demands of the person who is expressing anger. The expression of inappropriate anger is unfortunately often effective in getting others to comply with demands. As a result, angry displays become more likely in the future because of their effectiveness in producing desired outcomes.

Treatment Considerations and Approaches

Among clients with borderline personality disorder, DBT has been shown to decrease the subjective experience of anger and suicidal behavior (Linehan, Heard, & Armstrong, 1993). It is unclear, however, what aspects of DBT are most strongly associated with reductions in anger and self-directed aggression.

There is some indication that exposure and response prevention treatment in conjunction with other behavior therapy techniques are also of benefit for reducing the subjective experience of anger and overt anger episodes. Brondolo et al. (1997) described an exposure-centered treatment approach for anger that, in many respects, is quite similar to exposure-based approaches for anxiety disorders.

Emotional Reactivity–Intensity–Dysregulation

Spoont (1996) conceptualized the construct of emotional instability in terms of four component features: (a) unpredictable emotional responses to a variety of stimuli (e.g., lower response thresholds), (b) increased baseline mood lability, (c) propensity to experience moods more intensely, and

(d) atypical response tendencies that co-occur with emotional activation (e.g., suicide, self-mutilation, outwardly directed anger outbursts). A stable pattern of one or more of these characteristics over time could be evidence of general mood or emotion instability.

Research has suggested an association between emotional instability and child abuse history, as well as an association between child abuse and two of the personality disorders, borderline and antisocial (Spoont, 1996). Traumatic stress reactions to such abuses have been further linked to modifications in biological systems and structures associated with emotion and emotion regulation (Spoont, 1996).

Prolonged child abuse has also been observed to result in the conditioning of traumatic reactions to a variety of stimuli. Given the many associations that abusive experiences have with a variety of stimulus cues, it is not surprising that many individuals with significant trauma histories experience a wide variety of internal and external cues as potentially threatening or dangerous and, consequently, react with strong emotional intensity to them (Spoont, 1996). For many, abusive histories also give rise to a variety of rule statements about response–consequence relations, such as "people will use me if I give them the chance" and "people that I get close to will only harm me in the end."

Although emotional instability may be correlated with child abuse histories, an individualized assessment to establish such histories and their potential associations to current clinically relevant behaviors would need to be undertaken. Persons may display emotional instability for other reasons, and these possible factors must also be assessed and ruled out. Among some persons, for example, displays of intense negative emotions are instrumental in terminating aversive aspects of another's behavior and are maintained by this negative reinforcement process (Patterson & Hops, 1972).

Treatment Considerations and Approaches

In the event an individual does have a history of trauma, and if aftereffects of trauma include inappropriately excessive, intense, and reactive emotional displays, then therapy might focus on trauma-related issues. As we noted in chapter 6, however, any work around trauma-related issues is best undertaken once the individual has acquired adaptive emotion and behavior coping skills and demonstrated significant and sustained reductions in any harmful behaviors directed toward the self or others.

For some individuals, intense emotional displays may also represent attempts to solve current problems, particularly if the individual does not have other skills for addressing these. That is, displays of intense emotions may be intended to mobilize others to take action to solve some difficulty. Both Turkat (1990) and Linehan (1993a) have noted that persons with borderline personality disorder often have deficient problem-solving skills. Instruction in these skills might provide such persons with alternative means for addressing life problems.

Excessive emotional displays may also have a communication function. Individuals who are emotionally demonstrative for this purpose may seek acknowledgment and validation for their experience from the social environment through their behavior. In the therapy context, the provision of acceptance and validation of the client's experience noncontingent with inappropriate displays may reduce the emergence of such behaviors during therapy sessions. Instruction in skills for appropriately eliciting support and validation from others may also be beneficial.

Finally, therapeutic strategies that involve the development of coping skills related to negative emotions may prove fruitful. Among the suggestions Linehan (1993a, 1993b) advocated for this purpose are mindfulness, emotion regulation, and distress tolerance skills.

OVERT BEHAVIORAL FEATURES

Behavioral–Experiential Avoidance

Avoidance can be construed as an effort to avoid proximity or contact with external events (e.g., certain environmental contexts, specific stimulus cues) and internal events (e.g., thoughts, feelings, sensations, recollections) that are experienced as unpleasant in some way. Behavioral and experiential avoidance have many different expressions and manifestations (Hayes et al., 1996). Avoidant acts, however, are often maintained by their short-term consequences (relief from aversive events), with the primary associated reinforcement process being negative reinforcement.

Individuals who experience excess anxiety often display coping behaviors that have an experiential avoidance function. Given that anxiety is a central defining feature of the *DSM–IV–TR* anxious–fearful personality disorders and borderline personality disorder, one might expect that the use of avoidant coping strategies would be especially common among persons with these conditions. An examination of the symptom criteria for these disorders reveals several avoidant–related behaviors, among which are the following:

- "avoids occupational activities that involve significant interpersonal contact, because of fears of criticism, disapproval, or rejection" (Avoidant Criterion 1);
- "has difficulty making everyday decisions without an excessive amount of advice and reassurance from others" (Dependent Criterion 1);
- "shows perfectionism that interferes with task completion (e.g., is unable to complete a project because his or her own overly strict standards are not met)" (Obsessive–Compulsive Criterion 2); and

- "frantic efforts to avoid real or imagined abandonment" (Borderline Criterion 1).

Experiential and behavioral avoidance are also common among people with other personality disorders, including schizoid and schizotypal personality disorders and, to a lesser extent, paranoid and histrionic personality disorders.

Suicide is perhaps the ultimate form of escape or avoidance. In the United States in 2001, the rate of suicide was 10.7 per 100,000, with suicide constituting the 11th leading cause of death for all ages (Centers for Disease Control, 2004). Men commit suicide at a rate 4 to 5 times higher than women across the age span, with the highest risk groups consisting of men between the ages of 15 and 24 and those over 65. Much more common are suicide attempts. It has been estimated that up to 12% of persons from the general population attempt suicide during their lifetime and that up to 40% of persons have at some point seriously considered suicide (Chiles & Strosahl, 1995).

Suicidal acts and intentional self-injurious behavior are common among those with personality disorders, particularly borderline personality disorder (BPD). Between two thirds to three quarters of those with BPD have a history of at least one suicide attempt, and about 6% to 9% persons with BPD ultimately suicide (Davis, Gunderson, & Myers, 1999; Tanney, 2000). More generally, personality disorders are relatively common among people who completed suicide. It has been estimated that 31% to 57% of persons who suicide would have met criteria for at least one *DSM* personality disorder (Tanney, 2000).

Treatment Considerations and Approaches

Behavioral and experiential avoidance coping strategies are often enacted for one of two primary, and related, reasons: as a form of coping and as a mode of problem solving. As a *method of coping*, avoidance strategies often work, at least in the short term, because they function to reduce contact with aversive internal events or external events or situations. The effectiveness of such coping strategies only makes them more entrenched and contributes to a narrowing of the range of response options for responding to various life adversities. Thus, substance use to cope with acutely stressful environments or unpleasant moods can evolve into substance dependence. Sporadic avoidance of anxiety-evoking environments can transform into avoidance of most contexts that elicit anxiety and perhaps eventually evolve into full-blown agoraphobia. Occasional acts of mild self-cutting for emotion regulation purposes can evolve into habitual, severe, and potentially lethal acts of self-harm or eventuate in an act of suicide. Because the effects of avoidance are immediate and relieving, for many it becomes a way of life that results in marked impairment, distress, or even death.

Behavioral therapies for experiential and behavioral avoidance often include an exposure and response prevention (avoidance blocking) component. Depending on the degree to which other adaptive coping skills are part of a client's behavioral repertoire, skills training (e.g., instruction in problem solving, emotion regulation skills, breathing retraining) may be undertaken prior to any exposure work. If the individual displays frequent, severe, risky, or impairing forms of avoidant coping (e.g., moderate to severe substance use, self-injurious behavior), these might also be dealt with prior to engagement in an exposure therapy component.

A primary objective associated with exposure techniques is to reduce or eliminate phobic reactions to avoided events or experiences. To accomplish this, an individual will typically be exposed to avoided events or experiences in graduated form (see chap. 6), starting with those that evoke mild to moderate distress. Clients who undergo exposure therapy are encouraged to use coping skills other than avoidance during exposure sessions, to increase the likelihood of successful coping while simultaneously remaining in the presence of the distressing stimuli. As a result of exposure process, clients often learn that (a) they can use effective coping strategies other than avoidance during stressful situations, (b) distress experienced in certain situations will diminish in time on its own and that anticipated aversive consequences will not occur as a result of remaining in the situation, (c) prolonged exposures to previously avoided events or contexts make it easier to remain in contact with these events in the future, and (d) it is possible to masterfully cope with difficult and challenging situations.

If experiential and behavioral avoidance is used as a *form of problem solving* and proves effective in addressing problems, then avoidant behaviors are likely to become more entrenched and resistant to change. For example, dependent persons may avoid dealing with life problems by displaying a number of behaviors that result in others making decisions for them. Persons with avoidant personality disorder may avoid the problem of social anxiety by avoiding social contexts altogether. Individuals with obsessive–compulsive personality disorder may avoid the problem of potential failure though prolonged procrastination or perfectionistic strivings that interfere with task completion.

Following Linehan (1993a), we see parasuicidal and suicidal behavior as attempts to solve life's problems. According to Chiles and Strosahl (1995), when suicide is seen as an effective means of problem solving among clients who cannot tolerate emotional discomfort, the risk for suicide is especially high. Chiles and Strosahl suggested that questions such as the following can be used to evaluate risk on the basis of these indicators (p. 40):

- "On a scale from 0 to 5, how effective is suicidal behavior in solving these problems"?
- "If your situation did not improve in the next 24 hours, on a scale from 0 to 5, to what extent could you tolerate the emotional pain?"

On the basis of the recognition that suicidal and parasuicidal behavior often have associated distress avoidance and problem-solving functions and that distress tolerance and problem–solving skills are often deficient among those who engage in such behavior, a number of therapeutic approaches that target suicidal or self-injurious behavior include skills training in these areas (Chiles & Strosahl, 1995; Linehan, 1993a; Rotheram-Borus, Goldstein, & Elkavich, 2002).

In the application of problem-solving approaches to suicidal or parasuicidal behavior, it is important to identify the triggers that occasion associated urges, thoughts, or behaviors. That is, the therapist should seek to clarify contexts within which these acts occur and the function that such acts are intended to serve. From the client's perspective, is there an alternative to suicide for solving a specific life problem? Are there alternative skills or coping strategies that can be used when the urge to self-harm or commit suicide is high? The therapist should work with the client to generate possible solutions to such problems, to mobilize the client's behavior to take action, and to reduce hopelessness. Means and methods for committing suicide or intentional self-injury should also be removed from the client's environment whenever possible. Chapter 6 outlines the procedure for problem solving, and the reader is referred to Chiles and Strosahl (1995) and Linehan (1993a) for additional details concerning the application of this procedure to suicidal and parasuicidal persons.

Another ongoing treatment strategy is to develop a reward system that is different from or incompatible with parasuicidal and suicidal behaviors (Chiles & Strosahl, 1995; Linehan, 1993a). General strategies for accomplishing this include (a) therapist provision of attention and caring that is noncontingent with self-harm or suicidal acts and (b) the initiation of contact with the client at random times in between sessions to show support when he or she is not suicidal. Both of these approaches can be particularly useful when suicidal behavior operates as a reinforced, problem-solving behavior for reducing emotional distress.

During particularly acute episodes of distress, the therapist may consider the involvement of a significant other; for example, the client might stay at a significant other's house for a brief period. Doing so must be countered with the possibility of reinforcing suicidal behavior with companionship, however. As a general rule, such approaches are perhaps best instituted if the client asks for help before engagement in parasuicidal or suicidal acts. In the event that none of these approaches is likely to be effective and if suicidal action is eminent, time-limited voluntary or involuntary hospitalization should be considered.

Impulsivity–Disinhibition

Impulsivity has been conceptualized as a higher order personality dimension that subsumes "action-oriented" personality features such as sensation seeking, novelty seeking, reward seeking, extraversion, risk taking, and poor behavioral control (Barrett & Stanford, 1996; Zuckerman, 1996). A common feature to all of these related concepts is that impulsive behavior is often appetitive in nature; that is, impulsive behavior is enacted to produce some desirable consequence such as a tangible reward or pleasant experience. Indeed, many theories of impulsivity have suggested that this personality dimension is strongly associated with sensitivity and responsiveness to rewarding stimuli (e.g., Cloninger, 1987; Gray, 1987a). Herein lies an important distinction. Some individuals who display what appears to be impulsive behavior are actually enacting behavior that functions to terminate an aversive experience (e.g., self-injurious behavior to terminate aversive inner states). Behaviors that appear to be impulsive but are enacted to terminate something aversive might better be conceptualized as avoidance or escape behaviors that are primarily influenced by negative reinforcement processes rather than positive reinforcement processes. When both positive and negative reinforcement processes are operative for the same behavior, then that behavior may have both appetitive and escape functions. Substance abuse is often maintained by both of these processes for the same individual, as are habit disorders such as compulsive sexual behavior and gambling.

Impulsiveness is a central, if not defining, feature to the erratic–dramatic personality disorders (Farmer et al., 2004; Farmer & Nelson-Gray, 1995; Svrakic et al., 1993) and a correlated feature of paranoid personality disorder. It is interesting to note that impulsivity is unrelated to negative emotional experiences and moods (Emmons & Diener, 1986; Farmer et al., 2004) with the possible exception of anger (Barrett & Stanford, 1996; Siever & Davis, 1991). Given our conceptualization of impulsivity as unregulated behavior in the pursuit of rewarding consequences, the experience of anger can be explained within this framework as a result of the inability of behavior to produce reinforcing consequences (i.e., extinction or punishment). In support of this, Patterson et al. (1987) found that impulsive individuals who were responding for reward became disinhibited and less effective in their behavior immediately following instances when behavior was punished rather than rewarded.

Treatment Considerations and Approaches

Self-control strategies such as those described in chapter 6 could potentially be useful for modifying impulsive behavior patterns. “Premacking,” public statements related to behavioral goals, cost–benefit analyses, and counterregulation methods are among those that can be used to bring such behavior under the influence of alternative reinforcement contingencies that are incompatible with disinhibited behavior.

Turkat (1990) proposed that impulsivity can also be treated through basic exposure therapy procedures. For example, he suggested that situations in which impulse control is difficult could be hierarchically organized according to the degree of behavioral control typically evident. Once accomplished, the client is then taught competing or incompatible responses to impulsive action. During the actual exposure process, the therapist facilitates the urge for impulsive action in a given situation and then challenges the client to enact coping strategies for responding to the situation and associated urges. Treatment progress with this method is indexed by the latency to respond during exposure sessions or by the substitution of impulsive action with more deliberate forms of behavior.

From a cognitive perspective, Daruna and Barnes (1993) proposed that impulsivity could reflect inadequately detailed cognitive representations of situations traceable, in part, to low arousal. They went on to suggest that cognitive–behavioral interventions that promote cognitive efficiency could be beneficial. In relation to this suggestion, behavioral interventions that involve training individuals to be more aware of the richness and variety of internal and external stimuli present may result in actions that are based on a greater amount and range of information and, consequently, result in more deliberate and effective action. Self-monitoring, discrimination training, and mindfulness practice represent examples of approaches that can facilitate greater awareness of internal and external events. Other examples include the use of mirrors in situations where impulsive behavior may be problematic, to increase the salience of stimulus cues that potentially function to inhibit behavior. For example, Pliner and Iuppa (1978) found that the presence of a mirror reduced food consumption among obese participants.

Conduct Problems–Behavioral Acting Out

Conduct problems or frequent behavioral acting out may occur for a variety of reasons. Such behavior may have a predominant impulsive (reward seeking) or avoidant quality, for example. In this section, however, we are primarily concerned with stable patterns of behavior that are enacted with the knowledge that they are in conflict with society's formal or informal rules or that they demonstrate disregard for the rights or welfare of others.

Conduct problems and behavioral acting out as defined here are most common among those with antisocial personality disorder, although such behavior is not that uncommon among those with paranoid and schizotypal personality disorders, as well as among members with other erratic–dramatic personality disorders (i.e., histrionic, narcissistic, and borderline). Perhaps the greatest concentration of individuals with personality disorders, and antisocial personality disorder in particular, is found in society's correctional settings. Among incarcerated adult offenders, 50% to 80% meet criteria for antisocial personality disorder, and about 90% meet criteria for any personality disorder (Hart, 2001).

Lykken (1995) noted that individuals who meet criteria for the antisocial personality disorder diagnosis represent a heterogeneous group. Important discriminators of future adjustment within this group are (a) early onset of delinquent behaviors (i.e., preteen versus teen), (b) degree of socialization, and (c) degree of neurotic adjustment (or the degree to which negative emotions are experienced; Lykken, 1995). Early onset of delinquent behaviors, poor socialization, and low neuroticism represents a particularly malignant form of adjustment, referred to by some as *primary psychopathy* (Blackburn, 1987), which is notably resistant to therapeutic change.

From a behavioral perspective, the socialization process requires that behavior be brought under the partial influence of long-term, socially mediated contingencies (rules, laws, values, morals, etc.) that function to reinforce prosocial forms of behavior and to punish behaviors that substantially deviate from society's interests or welfare. Some persons, however, may not follow socially prescribed rules because rule following in the past may have been weakly or inconsistently reinforced, or perhaps even punished. At least two possible outcomes would be associated with such histories: (a) disregard of rules set up by the social community (i.e., culture) that function to regulate the behavior of its members and (b) an increased likelihood to experience aversive consequences for rule noncompliance provided that the rule accurately represented behavioral contingencies for instances where the rule was not followed (Follette et al., 2000). In relation to this latter outcome, the resultant aversive consequences could have been avoided had the rule been followed.

Treatment Considerations and Approaches

Persons with long-standing conduct problems and histories of acting out are generally not disturbed by their behavior. If such persons come to therapy at all, it is usually done at the request of others (e.g., family members, parole boards). Under these circumstances, the likelihood for meaningful change is low. If there is a genuine desire to change, then change is possible.

Perhaps a starting point in any therapy for persons with conduct problems is motivational interviewing, whereby the pros versus cons of continuing problematic behavior patterns versus change in the service of longer term goals can be evaluated. For many individuals with problems in these areas, notions of longer term goals or aspirations are, unfortunately, often absent or vague. Perhaps it is no wonder, then, that immediate contingencies or rule statements such as "live for today because who knows what tomorrow will bring" often exert greater influence on behavior for such persons. A motivational interview with such clients may reveal the extent to which goals or values are developed and the degree to which behavior is influenced by these.

A number of theorists have suggested that individual therapy for some antisocial types is unlikely to produce significant therapeutic change, in part because these individuals do not have learning histories whereby strong attachments to others have been experienced (e.g., Benjamin, 1993). For such individuals, milieu forms of treatment may be of greater benefit. In residential and inpatient settings, there is also an indication that institutionally based contingency management and token economy procedures reduce inappropriate behaviors and aggressive outbursts (Piper & Joyce, 2001). Group therapy programs for antisocial behavior in correctional settings also have some demonstrated effectiveness (MacKenzie, 2001). These programs generally include skills training components (e.g., anger management, communication skills, empathy training), information provision, analyses of the context of criminal behavior, and relapse prevention strategies.

In prison settings, there is also some indication that therapeutic communities may have some benefit, particularly in reducing psychological symptoms and disciplinary offences within the prison setting. The data are mixed in terms of reduced recidivism. In general, recidivism appears to be lower among men who received longer courses of therapeutic community living. There is an indication that psychopathic inmates as defined in Hare's model (Harpur, Hare, & Hakstian, 1989) show less improvement in therapeutic community interventions (Ogloff, Wong, & Greenwood, 1990), however, and are perhaps more likely to reoffend violently than psychopathic inmates who do not participate in the therapeutic community experience (Harris, Rice, & Cormier, 1994). One account offered for this latter observation is that psychopathic individuals may use the process group experience to further develop and refine their manipulative skills.

COGNITIVE FEATURES

Obsessiveness

A number of features often accompany obsessive tendencies. These include rigidity, preoccupation with orderliness, strong sense of right and wrong, stubbornness, parsimony, restraint, preoccupation, worry, overconscientiousness, perfectionistic strivings, planfulness, excessive devotion to work at the expense of engagement in fun or rewarding activities unrelated to work, behavioral inhibition, and hypersensitivity to potential threats or punishments (Pfohl, 1996). The *DSM* personality disorder concept that most strongly corresponds to these descriptions is obsessive–compulsive personality disorder. Other personality disorders that are defined, in part, by obsessional tendencies include dependent, borderline, paranoid, and schizotypal personality disorders and, to a lesser extent, schizoid, narcissistic, and avoidant personality disorders.

A common element to most obsessional features is an overemphasis on rational thought and a de-emphasis of emotional experience. Many features correlated with obsessional tendencies also suggest avoidant coping. For example, procrastination, frequent self-censoring and inhibition, compulsive doubting and indecisiveness, and protracted ambivalence can be regarded as avoidant behaviors, perhaps used to avoid negative judgments or evaluations from others (Salzman, 1985). Salzman further suggested that obsessional individuals tend to be oriented toward the future and anticipate potential problems to guarantee that future life will be free of anxiety or tension.

Two other related features are also common to obsessional presentations. One is that the behavior of obsessional persons is highly rule governed and relatively less influenced by immediate environmental contingencies. The *DSM–IV–TR* obsessive–compulsive personality disorder (OCPD) criterion, "is excessively devoted to work and productivity to the exclusion of leisure activities and friendships," captures this tendency. The obsessional individual lives life in accordance with presumed distal consequences (e.g., works hard toward some distant and nebulous goal) and, in so doing, fails to experience fully the potential of his or her current environment in terms of the various rewards it can offer.

Other dominant features among obsessional individuals include the tendency to see the world in black or white terms and, correspondingly, marked rigidity in behavior. Rigidity in behavior and thinking patterns is common among persons with other personality disorders in which obsessional tendencies are common, perhaps most notably among those with paranoid personality disorder. This rigid form of rule governance can result in the formation of faulty, inaccurate, or incomplete rules that, if followed, result in less effective or inappropriate forms of behavior.

Treatment Considerations and Approaches

The therapist should be cognizant that obsessional clients will often wish to engage in intellectual or irrelevant discussions that have an avoidant quality. Such conversations should be limited or minimized. Because a premium is placed on the intellectual over the emotional among obsessional clients, therapists may also wish to reinforce naturally any displays of emotional expression. In the course of doing so, the therapist can formally or informally pursue the strengthening of emotion labeling skills in the event that such skills are deficient.

Three other general behavioral intervention strategies may be particularly appropriate with this population: (a) strengthening the influence of immediate reinforcement contingencies on behavior, (b) weakening rule control of behavior, and (c) using exposure therapy in the form of behavioral experiments to counter maladaptive avoidant coping.

If a person avoids pleasurable activities, then there is little chance for the individual to directly experience the naturally occurring rewarding consequences associated with their engagement. For obsessional clients who have the tendency to forgo opportunities for fun and pleasure in the service of work-related activities maintained by more distal consequences, a therapeutic goal might be to *increase participation in valued or rewarding activities*. To this end, behavioral activation procedures might be used (Lewinsohn et al., 1984; Martell et al., 2001).

Because the behavior of obsessional individuals is often under strong rule governance, therapy might also be geared toward the *weakening of rules that are particularly inflexible and maladaptive*, and contributors to distress and impairment. Traditional cognitive therapy interventions might be used to promote flexibility in thinking, particularly if dichotomous, all-or-nothing, modes of thought are present. Burns (1980, chap. 14) outlined cognitive therapy strategies for addressing dichotomous thinking patterns related to excessive perfectionistic strivings. In the case of perfectionism, a starting point might be the acknowledgment that perfection as an outcome is not tangible. That is, persons with strong perfectionist strivings will often acknowledge that if they meet a performance standard, a reevaluation of the standard ensues along with what constitutes "perfect." As succinctly summarized by Burns (1980, p. 310):

> Everything can be improved if you look at it closely and critically enough—every person, every idea, every work of art, every experience, everything. So if you are a perfectionist, you are guaranteed to be a loser in whatever you do.

Techniques outlined by Burns to address such rigid forms of thought as perfectionistic thinking include:

- *An evaluation of the effectiveness associated with perfectionistic thinking.* Does such thinking help in any way, or is it more strongly associated with hopelessness, demoralization, and negative self-views?
- *Engagement in behavioral experiments associated with the exploration of outcomes related to lower standards.* As a result of such experiments, one might come to notice that when personal standards for performance are lowered, there is often an associated increase in personal satisfaction, performance satisfaction, and effectiveness. Practically this might mean that rather than striving to give a 110%, one might experiment with giving 80% or 75% and noticing what outcomes follow.
- *Engagement in behavioral experiments that involve the intentional making of mistakes to experience associated outcomes.* Obsessional individuals often fear making mistakes because of rule statements that predict highly negative consequences for such actions. When an individual actually discovers that outcomes are not consistent with catastrophic rules, new learning results. A variant of this procedure might involve appropriately disclosing to others weakness, flaws, imperfections, or inadequacies, and to notice the consequences that occur as a result. Clients

will often learn that appropriate personal disclosure, particularly as it relates to one's vulnerabilities or shortcomings, will actually result in the deepening of relationships.

- *Increase awareness that dichotomous categories do not adequately capture or represent naturally occurring events.* To facilitate this discovery, clients may be encouraged to notice actively if certain events, situations, or persons are all one way. For example, is the best looking apple in the fruit section at the store perfectly symmetrical, uniformly colored, and completely free of blemishes or other imperfections? Is a person who is regarded calm and confident *always* this way? Is a person who is regarded as attractive flawless in all respects? Does a very professional coworker always behave professionally at work?

Among obsessional individuals there is a tendency to measure one's own behavior in relation to its associated (and more distal) outcomes than in terms of associated processes that eventuate in such outcomes (Salzman, 1985). For example, in a competitive group activity, an individual may be more focused on what to do in order ultimately to win than on the pleasurable aspects associated with the more intermediate acts that contribute to this outcome. In other words, the fun of the ongoing activity takes a back seat to the outcome and whether outcome goals were achieved. To facilitate an orientation that promotes the discovery of value or reward in one's moment-to-moment actions, mindfulness practices (Kabat-Zinn, 1990) may be beneficial. Other behavioral interventions such as those included within acceptance and commitment therapy (ACT; Hayes, Strosahl, & Wilson, 1999) similarly promote a more process-oriented approach to everyday living.

Suspiciousness–Paranoia

Paranoid thinking or excessive suspiciousness is a feature common to many of the *DSM* personality disorder concepts, most notably paranoid, schizotypal, and borderline personality disorders and, to a lesser extent, schizoid, narcissistic, antisocial, avoidant, and dependent personality disorders.

As defined by Fenigstein (1996, p. 242), paranoia is "a disordered mode of thought that is dominated by an intense, irrational, but persistent mistrust or suspicion of people, and a corresponding tendency to interpret the actions of others as deliberately threatening or demeaning." As evident in this definition, paranoid thinking patterns tend to be rigid and inflexible and not easily modifiable even when the individual has experiences that are inconsistent with the content of his or her beliefs.

Given the persistence of such modes of thinking, even in the face of evidence to the contrary, one may conclude that paranoid thoughts are more readily influenced by maladaptive and rigidly held rules rather than actual current environmental contingencies. In fact, relevant environmental stimuli may be minimally attended to whereas irrelevant stimuli that can be conceptualized in accordance with paranoid-themed rules may exert a greater influence on one's attention and subsequent behavior. As paranoid ideation tends to involve the presumed intentions or actions of others, interpersonal contexts may represent situations in which a potentially large number of environmental cues can be construed as in agreement with firmly embraced rule statements. Thus, the behavior of the paranoid individual may, in part, be under a combination of faulty, overgeneralized rules and inappropriate stimulus control.

Paranoid thinking may also reflect the effects of response generalization. For example, many individuals with personality disorders who display paranoid forms of thought often have abuse histories. Such forms of thought may have been accurate, appropriate, and adaptive in these historical environments. In contemporary environments that are nonabusive, however, such thoughts could be maladaptive and contribute to social isolation and psychological distress.

Suspicious or paranoid modes of thought may also have an experiential avoidance function. As Fenigstein (1996) noted, theorists have long proposed that the primary maladaptive mode of coping among persons with paranoid thinking is the projection of unacceptable inner experiences (e.g., thoughts of helplessness, feelings of anger or frustration) onto others in an effort to reduce guilt or distress or to manage ambivalence or conflicts. Although a behavioral view would eschew reference to autonomous inner causal processes such as defense mechanisms to account for behavior, the observation among traditional theorists that paranoid thought has an associated experiential avoidance quality suggests that behaviorally oriented clinicians may look for similar functional properties when seeking a contextual understanding of such thought.

Paranoid thinking may also represent a more intense form of thinking commonly seen among individuals who experience marked social anxiety or fear of negative evaluation. The jump from "people are evaluating me negatively and seeing all of my faults" to "people are aware of my vulnerabilities and seek to exploit them" is not that great. Fenigstein (1996) reviewed several studies suggesting that the act of seeing oneself as the object of others' attention makes one more vulnerable to the development of paranoid thoughts. Such an explanation may account for the moderate diagnostic comorbidity observed between *DSM–IV*-defined avoidant and paranoid personality disorders (about 25%) and moderate correlation shared among symptom features that define these disorders ($r = .42$; Farmer & Chapman, 2002). One implication of such research is that excessive self-attention and hypersensitivity to the judgments of others may be learned, particularly because the behavior displayed in the presence of such thoughts often results in impaired interpersonal relations and social isolation. For a paranoid person, the absence of potentially malevolent persons and the ensuing social isolation may actually be relieving (negatively reinforcing), although such social isolation will do little to help the individual overcome faulty thinking patterns that resulted in such maladaptive relief-seeking behaviors.

Finally, it has also been suggested that paranoid thinking may reflect attempts to account for aberrant sensory experiences (Fenigstein, 1996). For example, persons who are losing the capacity for hearing because of normal aging may incorrectly perceive others as whispering or intentionally speaking in a low tone and then conclude that others are whispering about them and planning to exploit them in some way. Disruptions in other cognitive functions such as memory may similarly occasion the occurrence of paranoid thinking in some. For example, a person who cannot remember where he or she placed his wallet may incorrectly conclude that the wallet has been stolen (Fenigstein, 1996).

Treatment Considerations and Approaches

Many commentators have noted that therapy with suspicious or paranoid persons is difficult (e.g., Fenigstein, 1996). The combination of mistrust of persons (including the therapist), extreme rigidity in thinking, strong need for control, and the tendency to externalize problems significantly challenge efforts to establish a trusting therapeutic relationship. For persons with extreme suspiciousness, however, therapeutic rapport and a strong therapeutic alliance are necessary elements for successful therapy. The provision of acceptance and validation (e.g., looking for the "kernel of truth") in the early stages of therapy is essential (Fenigstein, 1996). "Tagging the feeling" (Meissner, 1986), or observing to the client the *emotional* content of a disclosure, may be a useful strategy for validating the client's experience while simultaneously avoiding protracted and unhelpful discussions concerning the validity of the content of a client's thoughts.

Orienting the client to other aspects of his or her situation may gently challenge inaccurate yet firmly held rules. Therapist queries such as, "Are there other possible explanations for ____?" may be especially useful in this regard. Magaro (1980) similarly suggested that paranoid individuals should be challenged to engage in hypothesis generation related to relevant environmental stimuli. Such approaches can promote response flexibility to stimulus cues that are typically responded to in rigid and maladaptive ways.

Magaro (1980) further suggested that because paranoid individuals largely respond to environmental features that fit into their conceptual framework or learning history, treatment should attempt to extend clients' perceptual input to relevant, yet unattended, stimuli. One approach for accomplishing this would be to increase the recognition of a greater number of relevant stimulus cues though stimulus discrimination and cue attendance tasks. Studies suggest that cue attendance training facilitates greater awareness of and focus on relevant stimuli, while at the same time blocking stimulus shifting or scanning to less relevant stimuli (Magaro, 1980).

Suspicious forms of thought may arise as a result of the individual not knowing all of the details of an event or situation. As a result, the person "invents" explanations or reasons that often have a suspicious content, and accepts these as real. This may be particularly true for individuals who have diminished sensory (e.g., hearing) or cognitive (e.g., memory) functions. A therapeutic goal for such clients might be to explore the factual basis of conclusions, with an eye toward reinforcing disclosures associated with not knowing or uncertainty (Meissner, 1986).

As noted by Fenigstein (1996), therapy for suspicious persons may involve standard anxiety management techniques (e.g., diaphragmatic breathing) and instruction in skills for effectively responding to actual or perceived criticism. If paranoid thinking is associated with avoidance behavior, such avoidance can also be a target for treatment through graduated exposure. Graded exposure may also be helpful among clients with avoidant personality disorder who also have difficulties in the areas of trust and anger (Alden & Capreol, 1993)

Therapy may also involve teaching the client more effective ways to respond to perceived or actual threats, or to instances of criticism or negative evaluation. Assertiveness training may be especially useful for reducing aggressive displays and for facilitating the use of more constructive approaches to resolving disagreements or conflicts. Finally, some of the techniques described earlier for all-or-none thinking may be especially relevant for this population for reducing rigidity in thinking.

Odd Thinking–Perceptual Anomalies

The types of experiences emphasized in this section include peculiar perceptions (e.g., reoccurring illusions) and unusual forms of thinking (e.g., magical thinking, delusional beliefs). Frequent co-occurring features among those with odd thinking and anomalous perceptional experiences include marked social anxiety, hypersensitivity to social evaluation, social skills deficits, poor stress coping skills, and problem-solving deficits. These types of experiences are most common among those with schizotypal personality disorder and are occasionally observed during acutely stressful periods among those with paranoid, schizoid, and borderline personality disorders.

Peculiarities of thought and experience are frequently characterized by heightened awareness and responsiveness to irrelevant stimuli that are often imbued with personal significance (Berenbaum, 1996). From a behavioral perspective, such thought peculiarities may, in part, reflect the influence of any number of processes, including inappropriate stimulus control, poor stimulus discrimination, inappropriate response generalization, faulty rules coupled with strong rule governance, and inappropriate tacting of events (e.g., incorrect labeling of anomalous experiences).

Unusual thoughts and experiences among some serve an avoidance function (Berenbaum, 1996). That is, such thoughts may serve as distracters from sources of physical, emotional, or psychological pain or as a way to impose understanding of or control over events that are uncontrollable or within which the person experiences himself or herself as helpless. Given the tenuous functioning of persons with thought disturbance, skills training interventions are often preferred over emotionally evocative exposure-based treatments to address maladaptive avoidant coping behaviors.

Treatment Considerations and Approaches

Research on nonpharmacological therapies for personality disorders characterized by odd thinking and perceptual anomalies such as schizotypal personality disorder is sparse (Piper & Joyce, 2001). There is, however, an indication that schizotypal personality disorder is related to the schizophrenia spectrum of disorders (Dolan-Sewell et al., 2001). Thus, psychosocial interventions for schizophrenia may have some relevance for treatment of personality disorder features (primarily schizotypal) that have in common peculiarities in thought and perception.

When available and interested in assisting the client in his or her care, the client's family or social network can be a potent component to any therapeutic regimen. A primary goal of family therapy for psychotic disorders is to provide family members or significant others with information about the condition and to teach strategies for managing common problems. Techniques typically used in such family therapy interventions include the identification of stressors associated with relapse, advice giving, setting realistic expectations, social and vocational homework, stress management, and training in communication and problem-solving skills (Hogarty, 2002).

In general, family therapies for persons with schizophrenia and psychotic disorders are effective when used in combination with standard treatments (e.g., pharmacological, case management). Most studies indicate that the addition of family therapy to standard treatment is associated with a lower rate of relapse and improved social functioning over a 1- to 2-year interval when compared with the standard treatment alone. This effect is mediated by the length of the intervention, however, with brief interventions (3 months or less) associated with fewer positive outcomes compared with those interventions that lasted 9 months or more (Hogarty, 2002).

In Falloon's (2002) family-focused problem-solving approach, initial assessments are geared toward the evaluation of family stress, family vulnerability, and the problem-solving capacity of the family unit as a whole. Assessments include interviews with the family as a group as well as separate interviews with each family member. If specific problems are identified within the family, a functional analysis associated with the problem area is performed in an effort to gain a greater understanding of the context within which it occurs. Particular attention is given to how family members go about solving family-based problems, including an evaluation of whether effective problem-solving methods are used (e.g., development of a consensual view of the problem, provision of mutual assistance, family collaboration and cooperation in working toward the resolution of stressors) or whether problems are addressed by other means (e.g., passive avoidance, blaming, coercion, hostile verbal exchanges). Another feature of this assessment is to evaluate the degree of knowledge members have about the client's condition, as well as each family member's impressions about factors that seem to make the client's condition better or worse.

Routinely within this approach, families are provided with information about the nature of the condition and its treatment. Personal goals for each family member are also evaluated, as are any obstacles that may make the realization of such goals difficult. Communication training may be undertaken to facilitate problem-solving discussions among family members, and family members may be instructed in an explicit framework for solving problems (similar to that outlined in chap. 6). Basic behavioral intervention strategies (e.g., contingency management, social skills training, relaxation training) may be used to address specific problems within the family. Home-based crisis intervention strategies are also taught, with these grounded within a general problem-solving framework. This intervention has been shown to decrease major relapses, reduce positive symptoms, and result in fewer hospital admissions and hospital treatment days at 9- and 24-month follow-up periods (Falloon, 2002).

Hogarty's personal therapy (2002) has as its primary goals of intervention the realization and maintenance of clinical stability. Treatment components are organized in phases and tailored to the client's needs with consideration given to his or her clinical state, deficits, and strengths. In this model, therapy is divided up into three sequential phases (i.e., basic, intermediate, and advanced) that assume some degree of hierarchical learning or skills acquisition. Common features of each of the therapeutic phases include the following:

- *Psychoeducation.* This component addresses a number of issues related to the person's condition, such as possible etiological factors associated with the development of the disorder, education in symptom constellations and expressions, and the provision of information about medication action, associated side effects, and the importance of medication adherence.
- *Instruction in coping skills.* Examples of skills taught within this area include the identification of prodromal signs, identification of antecedent conditions associated with stress, awareness of internal cues that accompany stress, deep breathing and re-

laxation exercises, development of autonomous choice skills, and discrimination training related to the identification of coping skills that are most appropriate when considered in relation to the nature of stressful antecedent conditions and accompanying internal states.

- *Social skills training*. Examples of skills taught within this component include role restructuring, basic communication skills, conflict avoidance and resolution strategies, assertion skills, social perception training, and criticism management skills.
- *Resumption of daily tasks*. Examples of daily task skills include those related to hygiene and nutrition, home responsibilities, and any vocational-related activities.

Some treatment features are unique to each phase. For example, during the basic phase, treatment is also geared toward the establishment of a therapeutic alliance and development of an individualized treatment plan. Within the intermediate phase, factors that can potentially enhance clinical stability are a focus of attention (e.g., possible modifications in medication regimen, medication adherence, alcohol and drug misuse), as are any difficulties associated with the client's adjustment to his or her disability (e.g., overcoming denial, working with grief). During the advanced phase, attention is also given to the identification of events or activities that might compromise recovery and the exploration of means by which treatment gains can be maintained following treatment.

Finally, outpatient milieu treatment programs (e.g., day hospital and day treatment programs) or inpatient services may be indicated for individuals who have rather severe behavioral deficits or excesses (Azim, 2001; Piper & Joyce, 2001). Common features among milieu programs include the opportunity to interact with other persons in a communal, structured setting where problematic behaviors are targeted in the context of ongoing therapy groups and community meetings.

INTERPERSONAL FEATURES

Detachment

Personality disorder concepts most strongly associated with interpersonal detachment include schizoid, schizotypal, and obsessive–compulsive personality disorders, and, to a lesser extent paranoid, antisocial, and avoidant personality disorders. Schizoid and schizotypal individuals, in particular, have a profound difficulty in forming and maintaining relationships with others. Avoidant persons, on the other hand, very much want to have close relationships, but largely do not pursue these out of fear of potential painful consequences, such as rejection. In the case of antisocial personality disorder, relationships are often multiple, transient, and superficial and commonly have an exploitive quality (Birtchnell, 1996).

Interpersonal detachment may be related to lack of interest in others, the objectification of others into "things" that have no special status beyond that afforded to other physical objects, problems in trust, and feelings of being overwhelmed in the context of relations with others (Birtchnell, 1996). Poor social skills are also quite common among individuals who are interpersonally detached. Such persons may demonstrate verbal and nonverbal expression deficits, be emotionally flat and nonreactive, and have difficulty initiating social encounters. There is an indication, too, that interpersonally detached persons may be somewhat unresponsive to the naturally occurring consequences of behavior (American Psychiatric Association, 2000). For example, among persons with schizoid personality disorder, few events are experienced as rewarding or pleasurable. Such insensitivity to the effects of behavior can produce a situation that is analogous to a chronic extinction schedule, which may account for the low rate of behavior among such persons. Other research suggests that persons who are interpersonally detached and have psychotic features may be relatively poor in operant learning (Corr et al., 1997), thus providing further evidence that the behavior of such individuals is relatively unaffected by the consequences it produces.

Treatment Considerations and Approaches

Millon (1999) suggested that intervention strategies that enhance the experience of pleasure and facilitate greater activity and action may be beneficial for persons with these characteristics. We concur; however, a challenge in pursuing therapeutic goals such as these is the difficulty associated with identifying events that are rewarding for the individual. When the degree of interpersonal detachment is profound and long-standing, therapy will need to be gradual, with modest initial goals.

Behavioral activation strategies may be undertaken to identify the types of goals or activities that the person wishes to pursue but currently does not. If these situations are social in nature, the client's level of social skill should be evaluated first. If deficits are noted, skills training in these areas should be undertaken before or concurrently with entry into social situations. Skills that might be of an initial therapeutic focus include basic conversation skills (e.g., how to initiate a conversation, appropriate personal disclosure, appropriate nonverbal behavior) and listening skills (e.g., active listening). As the client experiences progress in these domains, more complex social skills such as assertiveness skills might be taught. During the skills training phase, it may be useful periodically to videotape the client carrying out role-plays with the therapist. This can facilitate client awareness of his or her interpersonal behavior, including the identification of behaviors that are either effective or ineffective in social contexts. Videotapes of models can also be reviewed by the client and therapist, with attention given to the components of social discourse and the associated functions that specific behaviors have within interpersonal transactions.

If social anxiety is a problem, skills for coping with such anxiety can be developed. Once basic skills have been established and somewhat refined, the client can begin gradual and graded exposure to social situations. Social situations selected for exposure therapy should include (a) those that the client is likely to frequent in the future, (b) those in which the client is able to perform effectively given current skills levels and thus more likely to have a mastery experience as a result, and (c) those situations in which the client is able to engage in ongoing skill rehearsal and refinement and receive support for such efforts.

Dependency

Features associated with the dependency construct include passivity, suggestibility, compliance to the demands of others, conflict avoidance, pessimism, self-doubt, excessive help seeking, perception of self as low in social competence, and strong need for approval (Bornstein, 1993). Among the *DSM* personality disorders, dependency-related issues are most strongly associated with dependent and borderline personality disorders and to a lesser extent histrionic and avoidant personality disorders.

From a developmental perspective, dependency is a part of a normal developmental sequence through which all people pass as they mature (Bornstein, 1993). Dependency-related behaviors in adulthood can become interpersonally problematic, however, while being functional in producing short-term desired consequences. At the most basic level, dependent behavior can function to produce assistance, attention or approval, or guidance from others (Livesley, Schroeder, & Jackson, 1990). Submission to and compliance with others are often experienced as functional in maintaining important relationships, with self-effacing comments frequently offered in the service of securing reassurance from others. If dependent behaviors are responded to with rewarding outcomes such as these, then they will likely become more probable in future situations in which such outcomes are desired. Dependent behaviors may also be maintained by negatively reinforcing outcomes. For example, Bornstein's (1996) review suggests that among dependent persons, the physical presence of others who offer nurturance and protection acts as a stress reducer.

There is some indication that mothers of dependent boys display greater protective tendencies and are more inclined to reinforce dependent behavior in their children (Bornstein, 1993). Authoritarian parental practices have similarly been associated with adolescent or adult dependency, with the use of such practices statistically unrelated to the use of overprotection practices (Bornstein, 1993). As Bornstein (1993, p. 44) noted,

> just as parental overprotectiveness and authoritarianism prevent the child from engaging in the kind of trial-and-error learning that are critical for the development of a sense of autonomy and self-confidence, unrealistic independence and achievement expectations on the part of the parents can result in the child's continuing to display high levels of passive, dependent behavior during middle and late childhood.

There is some indication that dependency-related affiliative needs are frequently expressed in maladaptive ways, such as through clinging behavior, the adoption of passive and helpless stances in relationships, and intense expressions of concern related to possible abandonment (Bornstein, 1996). Such actions compel others to enter into a caretaking role, which may paradoxically result in impaired social relationships when others experience these behaviors as aversive.

Treatment Considerations and Approaches

As noted by Bornstein (1993), when dependent persons seek psychological treatment, they will often assume a compliant, advice-seeking, reassurance-needing, and help-seeking stance. Therapists should acknowledge these behaviors when observed and place limitations on their expression.

Dependent behaviors, by definition, are interpersonal in nature. Thus, in initial assessments, current social relations should be evaluated to determine how and to what degree dependent behaviors are being maintained. Questions that therapists might explore include the following:

- Are intimate relations characterized by overprotectiveness or authoritarian practices?
- Are helpless behaviors positively reinforced? If so, how and by whom?
- Is the client able to establish and maintain social relationships? If not, are there social skills deficits or does clinging behavior drive others away?
- If there are dependent-like behaviors that are experienced as aversive by others, what are they (e.g., excessive reassurance seeking, constant pleas for remaining physically present)? In what types of situations are these aversive behaviors more likely to be expressed? What short-term consequences follow?
- Can the individual appropriately elicit social support from others?

Such questions will establish whether maladaptive environmental contingencies or social skills deficits are present that, in turn, can be targeted in therapy.

For those with social skills deficits, treatment might initially be geared toward the development of behavioral skills that result in the more adaptive expression of affiliative interests and dependency needs. This would include direct instruction in behavioral topographies that are potentially effective and appropriate for eliciting support or caring from others, as well as in behaviors that are important for sustaining and maintaining intimate relationships (Bornstein, 1996). Relevant behaviors or skills might include those related to the detection of and appropriate response to interpersonal cues (see Bornstein 1996, p. 136) and the inhibition of more maladaptive forms of dependent behavior in contexts where dependency-related anxieties are aroused. Related to this, the client may need to learn skills that promote tolerance of dependency-related emotions as a means to facilitate the inhibition of dependent behaviors.

Bornstein (1993) also suggested that persons with dependent features become anxious or fearful when required to perform independently and particularly in contexts in which the social evaluation of performance is possible. The presence of anxiety and fear is likely to result in behavioral avoidance. To address this, a combination of anxiety-management techniques, skills training, and graded exposure around independent decision making and action can be used in targeted social contexts (see also Turkat, 1990).

Therapy might also target individuals' beliefs or self-rules about their own efficacy as well as beliefs associated with the notion that others must be looked to for protection and support (Bornstein, 1996). To facilitate the emergence of autonomy and the promotion of mastery experiences, therapeutic tasks such as behavioral experiments might be used. If such experiments prove effective, resultant change may be apparent in efficacy and outcome expectations related to behavior. In the event that such skills are deficient, direct instruction in daily living skills may also be beneficial.

Finally, dependent-related behaviors are often emitted in the context of life problems (e.g., when making decisions, feeling alone, or when immediate relationships are tenuous or threatened). To promote effective responding in such situations, problem-solving skills should be evaluated and targeted for treatment in the event of excessive reliance on others to solve life's problems.

Entitlement–Grandiosity–Egocentricity

For individuals who are grandiose or who have a strong sense of entitlement, interpersonal relationships are often experienced as vehicles to some end, whether it be the fulfillment of one's own needs or as a source of interpersonal or tangible reinforcers, such as attention, admiration, affirmation, comfort, or goods and services.

Attention, approval, and validation are potent sources of short-term reinforcement for grandiose or entitled persons. When reinforcement is forthcoming, this may contribute to a sense of being special. The effects of such reinforcement are often short-lived, however. In addition, the attention-seeking behavior of such individuals is likely to undergo extinction quickly in specific situations if reinforcement is not forthcoming. Evidence of extinction in such contexts includes the experience of boredom and an associated desire to leave the situation, disparaging statements made about aspects of the current environment, and irritable or angry displays.

Another feature of entitled and grandiose individuals is strong reactivity to negative social evaluation (Beck et al., 1990). Negative evaluation by others, even if constructively offered, will often lead to disproportionate and inappropriate aggressive behaviors that demean or attack. One possible explanation for this tendency is that grandiose and egocentric individuals have a strong tendency to equate "behavior" with "self." That is, feedback on a specific behavior is regarded not as a comment on the behavior in isolation, but rather as an evaluation of the self as a whole. In other words, the part is experienced as the whole and, from the perspective of the client, there is functional equivalence between the two.

Personality disorders in which issues of entitlement, grandiosity, or egocentricity are predominant include narcissistic, histrionic, paranoid, and antisocial, and, to a lesser extent, schizotypal and borderline personality disorders.

Treatment Considerations and Approaches

Clients who are grandiose, entitled, and egocentric often emit behaviors that are geared toward the attainment of attention, admiration, and respect from others. As a result, it would be important in the initial stages of therapy for therapists to emphasize acceptance and validation strategies in their work rather than behavior change strategies. Empathic mirroring is a technique many therapists have suggested for such persons during the early stages of therapy (e.g., Kohut, 1977; Millon, 1999). Because egocentric individuals tend to externalize blame and come to therapy for reasons other than those related to their personality disorder, time should similarly be dedicated during the initial assessment phase to clarify what these clients want from therapy. To facilitate such discussions, motivational interviewing techniques might be used, as might the clarification of life goals and values, particularly as they relate to the issues that brought the client to therapy.

As a firm and allied therapeutic relationship becomes established, therapeutic change strategies can be introduced into therapy. As empathy deficits are often apparent among persons with histrionic, narcissistic, antisocial, and paranoid personality disorders, empathy training can be a useful change-oriented therapeutic approach for persons with these conditions. Such training would involve the further development of basic listening and attending skills in interpersonal contexts. Instruction in reflection skills related to the emotional content of another's speech may also be particularly useful because it challenges the client to pay greater attention to the inner life of others, specifically to others' feelings (Turkat, 1990). A caution must be offered here, however. For a subset of individuals who are grandiose and egocentric, particularly those who have several features consistent with Hare's concept of psychopathy (e.g., Harpur et al., 1989), empathy training may be contraindicated because it could facilitate the development of more effective skills that can be used in the exploitation of others (e.g., Harris et al., 1994).

Difficulties with anger and frustration tolerance are common among a subset of individuals who are grandiose or entitled. This may be particularly evident when sought after reinforcers (praise or admiration from others, assistance from others in realizing personal goals of objectives) are not forthcoming, and particularly during periods of prolonged nonreinforcement for previously reinforced behavior (i.e., extinction). In such instances, anger management training, assertiveness training, and training in distress tolerance skills may be indicated. Problem-solving training may also be useful in the event the client has an overly restricted or maladaptive behavioral repertoire for producing instrumental outcomes.

Discrimination training can also be useful in at least two respects. For those individuals who exploit others for their own personal gain, discrimination training can be used to help such individuals identify alternative and appropriate sources of reinforcement. For those with histrionic personality disorder, discrimination training procedures can similarly be used to help individuals distinguish features that, when present, signal the degree of intimacy present in relationships. Traditional cognitive therapy techniques that target dichotomous thinking might be used for those persons who tend to see events or others in terms of discrete, black-and-white categories.

Finally, Johnson (1987, p. 67) suggested that a central focus of therapy with narcissistic individuals is "the discovery and enhancement of natural self-expression." This would include the awareness and expression of one's needs. The facilitation of awareness of such needs can be accomplished through self-monitoring strategies, and behavioral experiments can be used in the event that need expression is inhibited as a result of inaccurate or rigid rule statements (e.g., "I never get what I want"). Johnson (1987) further suggested that therapy should encourage and support the realistic appraisal of the client's abilities and achievements, as well as limitations, weaknesses, and vulnerabilities. If underlying self-esteem deficits or negative self-views are apparent, consideration should be given to the use of therapeutic strategies that enhance self-efficacy.

SUMMARY

In this chapter, we briefly summarized examples of therapeutic approaches and interventions that are potentially appropriate for core features related to personality disorder pathology. Because personality disorders are defined by heterogeneous sets of behavior patterns that are deeply engrained and inflexible, therapy is necessarily broad-based and often of longer duration. In addition, because much of the behavior described in the personality disorder criterion sets occurs in interpersonal contexts, and because the therapeutic context is distinctly interpersonal, it is often the case that problematic behavior patterns will arise within sessions. For these reasons, it is especially important for therapists who work with persons with significant personality disorder features to be attuned to the ongoing interpersonal exchanges within therapy, to structure the therapeutic environment in a way that allows for the nonthreatening examination of interpersonal processes, and to seize opportunities to promote behavior change by immediately responding appropriately and therapeutically to problematic behavior when it occurs.

Many of the therapeutic strategies described in this chapter involve a skills training component. This is because many of the behaviors that define the personality disorders represent efforts at coping with stressful life circumstances that are often at the same time both effective in the short term (i.e., produce desired effects) and ineffectual or maladaptive in the long term (e.g., result in strained or severely impaired interpersonal relations). Skills training is used to teach new behaviors, often coping behaviors, that are potentially effective and adaptive in both the short and long term. Furthermore, the addition of new behaviors to a client's behavioral repertoire facilitates response flexibility because the client who has more behavioral options available has a greater likelihood of effectively responding to a wide range of unique or difficult situations that might subsequently arise. Consistent with the general practice of behavior therapy, other interventions summarized in this chapter involve the modification of existing environmental contingencies that maintain problematic behaviors, as well as the modification of faulty or inaccurate rules that ineffectively influence behavior. Following Linehan (1993a) and others, we further noted that the use of these change strategies (i.e., skills training, environmental change, modification of faulty rules) should be balanced with acceptance and validation strategies, particularly in light of the histories of persons with personality disorders, which are so often characterized by marked invalidation and nonacceptance. The push for adaptive and healthy change ideally occurs in a context that is simultaneously valuing and accepting.

REFERENCES

Adams, A. N., Adams, M. A., & Miltenberger, R. G. (2003). Habit reversal. In W. O'Donohue, J. E. Fisher, & S. C. Hayes (Eds.), *Cognitive behavior therapy: Applying empirically supported techniques in your practice* (pp. 189–195). Hoboken, NJ: Wiley.

Adams, H. E., & Sutker, P. B. (Eds.). (2001). *Comprehensive handbook of psychopathology* (3rd ed.). New York: Kluwer Academic/Plenum.

Agras, W. S., & Apple, R. F. (1997). *Overcoming eating disorders: A cognitive–behavioral treatment for bulimia nervosa and binge-eating disorder: Therapist guide.* San Antonio, TX: Graywind/Psychological Corporation.

Agras, W. S., Schneider, J. A., Arnow, B., Raeburn, S. D., & Telch, C. F. (1989). Cognitive–behavioral and response-prevention treatments for bulimia nervosa. *Journal of Consulting and Clinical Psychology, 57,* 215–221.

Alarcon, R. D., Foulks, E. F., & Vakkur, M. (1998). *Personality disorders and culture.* New York: Wiley.

Alberti, R., & Emmons, M. (1990). *Your perfect right: A guide to assertive living* (6th ed.). San Luis Obispo, CA: Impact.

Alden, L. (1989). Short-term structured treatment for avoidant personality disorder. *Journal of Consulting and Clinical Psychology, 57,* 756–764.

Alden, L. E., & Capreol, M. J. (1993). Avoidant personality disorder: Interpersonal problems as predictors of treatment response. *Behavior Therapy, 24,* 357–376.

Alessi, G. (1992). Models of proximate and ultimate causation. *American Psychologist, 47,* 1359–1370.

American Psychiatric Association. (1980). *Diagnostic and statistical manual of mental disorders* (3rd ed.). Washington, DC: Author.

American Psychiatric Association. (1994). *Diagnostic and statistical manual of mental disorders* (4th ed.). Washington, DC: Author.

American Psychiatric Association. (1997). Practice guideline for the treatment of patients with schizophrenia. *American Journal of Psychiatry, 154*(Suppl.), 1–63.

American Psychiatric Association. (1998). Practice guideline for the treatment of patients with panic disorder. *American Journal of Psychiatry, 155*(Suppl.), 1–34.

American Psychiatric Association. (2000). *Diagnostic and statistical manual of mental disorders* (4th ed., text rev.). Washington, DC: Author.

American Psychiatric Association. (2002). Practice guideline for the treatment of patients with bipolar disorder (revision). *American Journal of Psychiatry, 159*(Suppl.), 1–50.

Anderson, C. M., Hawkins, R. P., Freeman, K. A., & Scotti, J. R. (2000). Private events: Do they belong in a science of human behavior? *The Behavior Analyst, 23,* 1–10.

Anderson, C. M., Hawkins, R. P., & Scotti, J. R. (1997). Private events in behavior analysis: Conceptual basis and clinical relevance. *Behavior Therapy, 28*, 157–179.

Anderson, C. M., Hawkins, R. P., & Scotti, J. R. (1999). Private events in behavior analysis: Conceptual basis and clinical relevance. *Behavior Therapy, 28*, 157–179.

Angleitner, A., & Ostendorf, F. (1994). Temperament and the big five factors of personality. In C. F. Halverson, G. A. Kohnstamm, & R. P. Martin (Eds.), *The developing structure of temperament and personality from infancy to adulthood* (pp. 69–90). Hillsdale, NJ: Erlbaum.

Arnett, P. A. (1997). Autonomic responsivity in psychopaths: A critical review and theoretical proposal. *Clinical Psychology Review, 17*, 903–936.

Avila, C., Moltó, J., Segarra, P., & Torrubia, R. (1995). Sensitivity to conditioned or unconditioned stimuli: What is the mechanism underlying passive avoidance deficits in extraverts? *Journal of Research in Personality, 29*, 273–294.

Ayala, F. (1985). Reduction in biology: A recent challenge. In D. Depew & B. Weber (Eds.), *Evolution at a crossroad: The new biology and a new philosophy of science* (pp. 65–79). Cambridge, MA: MIT Press.

Ayllon, T. (1963). Intensive treatment of psychotic behaviour by stimulus satiation and food reinforcement. *Behaviour Research and Therapy, 1*, 53–61.

Ayllon, T. (1965). Some behavior problems associated with eating in chronic schizophrenic patients. In L. P. Ullmann & L. Krasner (Eds.), *Case studies in behavior modification* (pp. 73–77). New York: Holt, Rinehart, & Winston.

Ayllon, T., & Michael, J. (1959). The psychiatric nurse as a behavioral engineer. *Journal of the Experimental Analysis of Behavior, 2*, 323–334.

Azim, H. F. (2001). Partial hospitalization programs. In W. J. Livesley (Ed.), *Handbook of personality disorders: Theory, research, and treatment* (pp. 527–540). New York: Guilford Press.

Bandura, A. (1969). *Principles of behavior modification*. New York: Holt, Rinehart, & Winston.

Bandura, A. (1977). *Social learning theory*. Englewood Cliffs, NJ: Prentice Hall.

Bandura, A. (1986). *Social foundations of thought and action: A social cognitive theory*. Englewood Cliffs, NJ: Prentice Hall.

Barlow, D. H. (Ed.). (2001). *Clinical handbook of psychological disorders* (3rd ed.). New York: Guilford Press.

Barlow, D. H., & Craske, M. G. (2000). *Mastery of your anxiety and panic: Client workbook for anxiety and panic (MAP-3)*. San Antonio, TX: Graywind/Psychological Corporation.

Barlow, D. H., Craske, M. G., Cerny, J. A., & Klosko, J. S. (1989). Behavioral treatment of panic disorder. *Behavior Therapy, 20*, 261–282.

Barlow, D. H., & Durand, V. M. (2002). *Abnormal psychology: An integrative approach* (3rd ed.). Belmont, CA: Wadsworth.

Barlow, D. H., Levitt, J. T., & Bufka, L. F. (1999). The dissemination of empirically supported treatments: A view to the future. *Behaviour Research and Therapy, 37*(Suppl. 1), S147–S162.

Barnes-Holmes, D., O'Hora, D., Roche, B., Hayes, S. C., Bissett, R. T., & Lyddy, F. (2001). Understanding and verbal regulation. In S. C. Hayes, D. Barnes-Holmes, & B. Roche (Eds.), *Relational frame theory: A post-Skinnerian account of human language and cognition* (pp. 103–117). New York: Kluwer Academic/Plenum.

Barrett, E. S., & Stanford, M. S. (1996). Impulsiveness. In C. G. Costello (Ed.), *Personality characteristics of the personality disordered* (pp. 91–119). New York: Wiley.

Barrios, B., & Hartmann, D. P. (1986). The contributions of traditional assessment: Concepts, issues, and methodologies. In R. O. Nelson & S. C. Hayes (Eds.), *Conceptual foundations of behavioral assessment* (pp. 81–110). New York: Guilford.

Baum, W. M. (1994). *Understanding behaviorism: Science, behavior, culture.* New York: HarperCollins.

Baumeister, R. F., Heatherton, T. F., & Tice, D. M. (1994). *Losing control: How and why people fail at self-regulation.* San Diego, CA: Academic Press.

Beach, S. R. H., Fincham, F. D., & Katz, J. (1998). Marital therapy in the treatment of depression: Toward a third generation of therapy and research. *Clinical Psychology Review, 18,* 635–661.

Beck, A. T., Freeman, A., Pretzer, J., Davis, D., Fleming, B., Ottaviani, R., et al. (1990). *Cognitive therapy for personality disorders.* New York: Guilford Press.

Beck, A. T., Rush, A. J., Shaw, B. F., & Emery, G. (1979). *Cognitive therapy of depression.* New York: Guilford Press.

Beck, J. S. (1995). *Cognitive therapy: Basics and beyond.* New York: Guilford Press.

Beitman, B. D., Goldfried, M. R., & Norcross, J. C. (1989). The movement toward integrating the psychotherapies: An overview. *American Journal of Psychiatry, 146,* 138–147.

Benjamin, L. S. (1993). *Interpersonal diagnosis and treatment of personality disorders.* New York: Guilford Press.

Berenbaum, H. (1996). Peculiarity. In C. G. Costello (Ed.), *Personality characteristics of the personality disordered* (pp. 206–241). New York: Wiley.

Bernstein, D. P., & Travaglini, L. (1999). Schizoid and avoidant personality disorders. In T. Millon, P. H. Blaney, & R. D. Davis (Eds.), *Oxford textbook of psychopathology* (pp. 523–534). New York: Oxford University Press.

Beyts, J., Frcka, G., Martin, I., & Levey, A. (1983). The influence of psychoticism and extraversion on classical eyeblink conditioning using paraorbital shock UCS. *Personality and Individual Differences, 4,* 275–283.

Bijou, S. W., Birnbrauer, J. S., Kidder, J. D., & Tague, C. (1966). Programmed instruction as an approach to teaching of reading, writing, and arithmetic to retarded children. *The Psychological Record, 16,* 505–522.

Birtchnell, J. (1996). Detachment. In C. G. Costello (Ed.), *Personality characteristics of the personality disordered* (pp. 173–205). New York: Wiley.

Bissett, R. T., & Hayes, S. C. (1999). The likely success of functional analysis tied to the *DSM*. *Behaviour Research and Therapy, 37*, 379–383.

Blackburn, R. (1987). Two scales for the assessment of personality disorder in antisocial populations. *Personality and Individual Differences*, 8, 81–93.

Blackmore, S. (1999). *The meme machine*. Oxford: Oxford University Press.

Blais, M. (1997). Clinician ratings of the five-factor model of personality and the *DSM–IV* personality disorders. *Journal of Nervous and Mental Disease, 185*, 388–393.

Blake, M. J. F. (1967). Relationship between circadian rhythm of body temperature and introversion–extraversion. *Nature, 215*, 896–897.

Block, J. (1977a). P scale and psychosis: Continued concerns. *Journal of Abnormal Psychology*, 4, 431–434.

Block, J. (1977b). The Eysencks and psychoticism. *Journal of Abnormal Psychology*, 86, 653–654.

Bo-Linn, G. W., Santa Ana, C. A., Morawski, S. G., & Fordtran, J. S. (1983). Purging and calorie absorption in bulimic patients and normal women. *Annals of Internal Medicine*, 99, 14–17.

Borkovec, T. D., Wilkinson, L., Folensbee, R., & Lerman, C. T. (1983). Stimulus control applications to the treatment of worry. *Behaviour Research and Therapy, 21*,

Bornstein, R. F. (1993). *The dependent personality*. New York: Guilford Press.

Bornstein, R. F. (1996). Dependency. In C. G. Costello (Ed.), *Personality characteristics of the personality disordered* (pp. 120–145). New York: Wiley.

Bowers, A. H. (2003). Satiation therapy. In W. O'Donohue, J. E. Fisher, & S. C. Hayes (Eds.), *Cognitive behavior therapy: Applying empirically supported techniques in your practice* (pp. 349–353). Hoboken, NJ: Wiley.

Boyce, T. E., & Roman, H. R. (2003). Contingency management interventions. In W. O'Donohue, J. E. Fisher, & S. C. Hayes (Eds.), *Cognitive behavior therapy: Applying empirically supported techniques in your practice* (pp. 109–113). Hoboken, NJ: Wiley.

Brondolo, E., DiGiuseppe, R., & Tafrate, R. C. (1997). Exposure-based treatment for anger problems: Focus on the feeling. *Cognitive and Behavioral Practice, 4*, 75–98.

Brown, M. Z., Comtois, K. A., & Linehan, M. M. (2002). Reasons for suicide attempts and nonsuicidal self-injury in women with borderline personality disorder. *Journal of Abnormal Psychology, 111*, 198–202.

Brown, T. A., Chorpita, B. F., & Barlow, D. H. (1998). Structural relationships among dimensions of the *DSM–IV* anxiety and mood disorders and dimensions of negative affect, positive affect, and autonomic arousal. *Journal of Abnormal Psychology, 107*, 179–192.

Brunswig, K. A., Sbraga, T. P., & Harris, C. D. (2003). Relapse prevention. In W. O'Donohue, J. E. Fisher, & S. C. Hayes (Eds.), *Cognitive behavior therapy: Applying empirically supported techniques in your practice* (pp. 321–329). Hoboken, NJ: Wiley.

Burns, D. D. (1980). *Feeling good: The new mood therapy*. New York: Signet.

Buss, D. M. (1996). Social adaptation and five major factors of personality. In J. S. Wiggins (Ed.), *The five factor model of personality: Theoretical perspectives* (pp. 180–207). New York: Guilford Press.

Buss, D. M. (1999). *Evolutionary psychology: The new science of the mind.* Boston: Allyn and Bacon.

Butzlaff, R. L., & Hooley, J. M. (1998). Expressed emotion and psychiatric relapse: A meta-analysis. *Archives of General Psychiatry, 55*, 547–552.

Carr, E. G. (1977). The motivation of self-injurious behavior: A review of some hypotheses. *Psychological Bulletin, 84*, 800–816.

Carr, E. G., & Durand, V. M. (1985). The social–communicative basis of severe behavior problems in children. In S. Reiss & R. R. Bootzin (Eds.), *Theoretical issues in behavior therapy* (pp. 220–254). New York: Academic.

Caspi, A. (2000). The child is father of the man: Personality continuities from childhood to adulthood. *Journal of Personality and Social Psychology, 78*, 158–172.

Catania, A. C. (1994). The natural and artificial selection of verbal behavior. In S. C. Hayes, L. J. Hayes, M. Sato, & K. Ono (Eds.), *Behavioral analysis of language and cognition: The Fourth International Institute on Verbal Relations* (pp. 31–49). Reno, NV: Context Press.

Centers for Disease Control. (2004). *2001, United States suicide injury death and rates per 100,000*. Retrieved January 14, 2004 from webapp.cdc.gov/sasweb/ncipc/mortrate10_fy.html

Chambless, D. L., Baker, M. J., Baucom, D. H., Beutler, L. E., Calhoun, K. S., Crits-Christoph, P., et al. (1998). Update on empirically validated treatments II. *The Clinical Psychologist, 51*, 3–18.

Chambless, D. L., & Ollendick, T. H. (2001). Empirically supported psychological interventions: Controversies and evidence. *Annual Review of Psychology, 52*, 685–716.

Chambless, D. L., Sanderson, W. C., Shoham, V., Bennett Johnson, S., Pope, K. S., Crits-Cristoph, P., et al. (1996). An update on empirically validated therapies. *The Clinical Pssychologist, 49*, 5–18.

Chapman, A. L., Mayer, J. L., Specht, M. W., Farmer, R. F., & Field, C. E. (2003). Passive avoidance learning as a function of Cloninger's temperament typology: An extension to male undergraduates. *Personality and Individual Differences, 35*, 1571–1584.

Chesney, M. A., & Tasto, D. L. (1975). The effectiveness of behavior modification with spasmodic and congestive dysmenorrhea. *Behaviour Research and Therapy, 13*, 245–253.

Chiles, J. A., & Strosahl, K. D. (1995). *The suicidal patient: Principles of assessment, treatment, and case management.* Washington, DC: American Psychiatric Press.

Claridge, G., & Davis, C. (2003). *Personality and psychological disorders.* London: Arnold.

Clark, L. (1985). *SOS! Help for parents.* Bowling Green, KY: Parents Press.

Cloitre, M., Scarvalone, P., & Difede, J. (1997). Post-traumatic stress disorder, self and interpersonal dysfunction among sexually revictimized women. *Journal of Traumatic Stress, 10,* 435–450.

Cloninger, C. R. (1986). A unified biosocial theory of personality and its role in the development of anxiety states. *Psychiatric Developments, 3,* 167–226.

Cloninger, C. R. (1987). A systematic method for clinical description and classification of personality variants: A proposal. *Archives of General Psychiatry, 44,* 573–588.

Cloninger, C. R. (1992). *The Temperament and Character Inventory.* (Available from C. R. Cloninger, Washington University School of Medicine, Department of Psychiatry, PO Box 8134, St. Louis, MO, 63110).

Cloninger, C. R. (2003). Completing the psychobiological architecture of human personality development: Temperament, character, and coherence. In U. Staudinger & U. Lindenberger (Eds.), *Understanding human development: Dialogues with lifespan psychology* (pp. 159–181). Boston: Kluwer Academic.

Cloninger, C. R., Svrakic, D. M., & Przybeck, T. R. (1993). A psychobiological model of temperament and character. *Archives of General Psychiatry, 50,* 975–990.

Comer, S. L. (1998). Cognitive–behavioral treatment outcome in bulimia: The impact of comorbid personality disorders. *Dissertation Abstracts International, 58,* 10-B, 5638. Abstract obtained from *PsycINFO* database.

Corr, P. J., Pickering, A. D., & Gray, J. A. (1997). Personality, punishment, and procedural learning: A test of J. A. Gray's anxiety theory. *Journal of Personality and Social Psychology, 73,* 337–344.

Cosmides, L., & Tooby, J. (1992). Cognitive adaptations for social exchange. In J. H. Barkow, L. Cosmides, & J. Tooby (Eds.), *The adapted mind: Evolutionary psychology and the generation of culture* (pp. 163–228). Oxford, England: Oxford University Press.

Costa, P. T., Jr., & McCrae, R. R. (1992). *Revised NEO Personality Inventory (NEO-PI-R) and NEO Five Factor Inventory (NEO-FFI): Professional manual.* Odessa, FL: Psychological Assessment Resources.

Costa, P. T., Jr., McCrae, R. R., & Siegler, I. C. (1999). Continuity and change over the adult life cycle: Personality and personality disorders. In C. R. Cloninger (Ed.), *Personality and psychopathology* (pp. 129–154). Washington, DC: American Psychiatric Press.

Costa, P. T., Jr., & Widiger, T. A. (Eds.). (2002). *Personality disorders and the five-factor model of personality* (2nd ed.). Washington, DC: American Psychological Association.

Costello, C. G. (1996a). The advantages of focusing on the personality characteristics of the personality disordered. In C. G. Costello (Ed.), *Personality characteristics of the personality disordered* (pp. 1–23). New York: Wiley.

Costello, C. G. (Ed.). (1996b). *Personality characteristics of the personality disordered.* New York: Wiley.

Coyne, J. C. (1989). Thinking positive-cognitively about depression. In A. Freeman, K. M. Simon, L. E. Beutler, & H. Arkowitz (Eds.), *Comprehensive handbook of cognitive therapy* (pp. 227–244). New York: Plenum Press.

Craske, M. G., & Barlow, D. H. (2001). Panic disorder and agoraphobia. In D. H. Barlow (Ed.), *Clinical handbook of psychological disorders* (3rd ed., pp. 1–59). New York: Guilford Press.

Cunningham, C. L. (1998). Drug conditioning and drug-seeking behavior. In W. O'Donohue (Ed.), *Learning and behavior therapy* (pp. 518–544). Boston: Allyn and Bacon.

DaCosta, M., & Halmi, K. A. (1992). Classification of anorexia nervosa: Question of subtypes. *International Journal of Eating Disorders, 11*, 305–313.

Darlington, D. A. (1995). Weight loss as a function of treatment and personality variables. *Dissertation Abstracts International, 56*, 3-B, 1732. Abstract obtained from *PsycINFO* database.

Daruna, J. H., & Barnes, P. A. (1993). A neurodevelopmental view of impulsivity. In W. G. McCown, J. L. Johnson, & M. B. Shure (Eds.), *The impulsive client: Theory, research, and treatment* (pp. 23–37). Washington, DC: American Psychological Association.

Davis, M., Eshelman, E. R., & McKay, M. (2000). *The relaxation & stress reduction workbook* (5th ed.). Oakland, CA: New Harbinger.

Davis, T., Gunderson, J. G., & Myers, M. (1999). Borderline personality disorder. In D. G. Jacobs (Ed.), *Guide to suicide assessment and intervention* (pp. 311–331). San Francisco: Jossey-Bass.

Dawkins, R. (1976). *The selfish gene*. Oxford, England: Oxford University Press.

De Fruyt, F., Van De Wiele, L., & Van Herringen, C. (2000). Cloninger's psychobiological model of temperament and character and the five-factor model of personality. *Personality and Individual Differences, 29*, 441–452.

Delprato, D. J., & Midgley, B. D. (1992). Some fundamentals of B. F. Skinner's behaviorism. *American Psychologist, 47*, 1507–1520.

Derryberry, D., & Rothbart, M. K. (1984). Emotion, attention, and temperament. In C. E. Izard, J. Kagan, & R. B. Zajonc (Eds.), *Emotions, cognition, and behavior* (pp. 132–166). New York: Cambridge University Press.

Digman, J. M., & Shmelyov, A. G. (1996). The structure of temperament and personality in Russian children. *Journal of Personality and Social Psychology, 71*, 341–351.

Dobson, K. S. (1989). A meta-analysis of the efficacy of cognitive therapy for depression. *Journal of Consulting and Clinical Psychology, 57*, 414–419.

Dolan-Sewell, R. T., Krueger, R. F., & Shea, M. T. (2001). Co-occurrence with syndrome disorders. In W. J. Livesley (Ed.), *Handbook of personality disorders: Theory, research, and treatment* (pp. 84–104). New York: Guilford Press.

Dougher, M. J. (1993). On the advantages and implications of a radical behavioral treatment of private events. *The Behavior Therapist, 16*, 204–206.

Dougher, M. J., & Hayes, S. C. (2000). Clinical behavior analysis. In M. J. Dougher (Ed.), *Clinical behavior analysis* (pp. 11–25). Reno, NV: Context Press.

Dow, M. G. (1994). Social inadequacy and social skill. In L. W. Craighead, W. E. Craighead, A. E. Kazdin, & M. J. Mahoney (Eds.), *Cognitive and behavioral interventions: An empirical approach to mental health problems* (pp. 123–140). Boston: Allyn and Bacon.

Drake, R. E., & Vaillant, G. E. (1985). A validity study of Axis II of *DSM–III. American Journal of Psychiatry, 142*, 553–558.

Dreessen, L., Hoekstra, R., & Arntz, A. (1997). Personality disorders do not influence the results of cognitive and behavior therapy for obsessive compulsive disorder. *Journal of Anxiety Disorders, 11*, 503–521.

Duijsens, I. J., & Diekstra, R. F. W. (1996). *DSM–III–R* and ICD-10 personality disorders and their relationship with the big five dimensions of personality. *Personality and Individual Differences, 21*, 119–133.

Emmons, R. A., & Diener, E. (1986). Influence of impulsivity and sociability on subjective well-being. *Journal of Personality and Social Psychology, 50*, 1211–1215.

Evans, I. M. (1986). Response structure and the triple-response-mode concept. In R. O. Nelson & S. C. Hayes (Eds.), *Conceptual foundations of behavioral assessment* (pp. 131–155). New York: Guilford Press.

Eysenck, H. J. (1952). The effects of psychotherapy: An evaluation. *Journal of Consulting Psychology, 16*, 319–324.

Eysenck, H. J. (1957). *The dynamics of anxiety and hysteria.* London: Routledge & Kegan Paul.

Eysenck, H. J. (1959). Learning theory and behaviour therapy. *Journal of Mental Science, 105*, 61–75.

Eysenck, H. J. (Ed.). (1960). *Behavior therapy and the neuroses*. New York: Pergamon.

Eysenck, H. J. (Ed.). (1964). *Experiments in behaviour therapy*. London: Pergamon.

Eysenck, H. J. (1967). *The biological basis of personality*. Springfield, IL: Charles C Thomas.

Eysenck, H. J. (1969a). The biological basis of personality. In H. J. Eysenck & S. B. G. Eysenck (Eds.), *Personality structure and measurement*. San Diego, CA: Knapp.

Eysenck, H. J. (1969b). Factor analytic studies of personality. In H. J. Eysenck & S. B. G. Eysenck (Eds.), *Personality structure and measurement*. San Diego, CA: Knapp.

Eysenck, H. J. (1970). *The structure of human personality* (3rd ed.). London: Methuen.

Eysenck, H. J. (1983). A biometrical–genetic analysis of impulsive and sensation seeking behavior. In M. Zuckerman (Ed.), *Biological bases of sensation seeking, impulsivity, and anxiety* (pp. 1–27). Hillsdale, NJ: Erlbaum.

Eysenck, H. J. (1987). The definition of personality disorders and the criteria appropriate for their description. *Journal of Personality Disorders, 1*, 211–219.

Eysenck, H. J., & Eysenck, M. W. (1985). Personality and individual differences: A natural science approach. New York: Plenum Press.

Eysenck, H. J., & Eysenck, S. B. G. (1968). *Manual for the Eysenck Personality Inventory*. San Diego, CA: Educational and Industrial Testing Service.

Eysenck, H. J., & Eysenck, S. B. G. (1975). *Manual for the Eysenck Personality Questionnaire*. San Diego, CA: Educational and Industrial Testing Service.

Eysenck, H. J., & Rachman, S. (1965). *The causes and cures of neurosis*. San Diego, CA: Knapp.

Eysenck, M. W., & Folkard, S. (1980). Personality, time of day, and caffeine: Some theoretical and conceptual problems in Revelle et al. *Journal of Experimental Psychology: General, 109*, 32–41.

Falloon, I. R. H. (2002). Cognitive–behavioral family and educational interventions for schizophrenic disorders. In S. G. Hoffman & M. C. Tompson (Eds.), *Treating chronic and severe mental disorders* (pp. 3–17). New York: Guilford Press.

Farmer, R. F. (1998). Depressive symptoms as a function of trait anxiety and impulsivity. *Journal of Clinical Psychology, 54*, 129–135.

Farmer, R. F. (2000). Issues in the assessment and conceptualization of personality disorders. *Clinical Psychology Review, 20*, 823–851.

Farmer, R. F., & Chapman, A. L. (2002). Evaluation of *DSM–IV* personality disorder criteria as assessed by the Structured Clinical Interview for *DSM–IV* Personality Disorders. *Comprehensive Psychiatry, 43*, 285–300.

Farmer, R. F., Field, C. E., Gremore, T. M., Chapman, A. L., Nash, H. M., & Mayer, J. L. (2003). Passive avoidance learning among females as a function of Cloninger's temperament typology. *Personality and Individual Differences, 34*, 983–997.

Farmer, R. F., Nash, H. M., & Dance, D. (2004). Mood patterns and variations associated with personality disorder pathology. *Comprehensive Psychiatry, 45*, 289–303.

Farmer, R. F., Nash, H. M., & Field, C. E. (2001). Disordered eating behaviors and reward sensitivity. *Journal of Behavior Therapy and Experimental Psychiatry, 32*, 211–219.

Farmer, R., & Nelson-Gray, R. O. (1990). Personality disorders and depression: Hypothetical relations, empirical findings, and methodological considerations. *Clinical Psychology Review, 10*, 453–476.

Farmer, R. F., & Nelson-Gray, R. O. (1995). Anxiety, impulsivity, and the anxious–fearful and erratic–dramatic personality disorders. *Journal of Research in Personality, 29*, 189–207.

Farmer, R. F., & Nelson-Gray, R. O. (1999). Functional analysis and response covariation in the assessment of personality disorders: A reply to Staats and to Bissett and Hayes. *Behaviour Research and Therapy, 37*, 385–394.

Fenigstein, A. (1996). Paranoia. In C. G. Costello (Ed.), *Personality characteristics of the personality disordered* (pp. 242–275). New York: Wiley.

Ferro, T., Klein, D., Schwartz, J., Kasch, K., & Leader, J. (1998). 30-month stability of personality disorder diagnoses in depressed outpatients. *American Journal of Psychiatry, 155*, 653–659.

Ferster, C. B. (1965). Classification of behavioral pathology. In L. Krasner & L. P. Ullman (Eds.), *Research in behavior modification* (pp. 6–26). New York: Holt, Rinehart, & Winston.

Ferster, C. B. (1973). A functional analysis of depression. *American Psychologist, 28*, 857–870.

Foa, E. B. (1996). The efficacy of behavioral therapy with obsessive–compulsives. *The Clinical Psychologist, 49*, 19–22.

Foa, E. B., & Rothbaum, B. O. (1998). *Treating the trauma of rape: Cognitive–behavior therapy for PTSD*. New York: Guilford Press.

Foa, E. B., Stekete, G., Grayson, J. B., Turner, R. M., & Latimer, P. (1984). Deliberate exposure and blocking of obsessive–compulsive rituals: Immediate and long-term effects. *Behavior Therapy, 15*, 450–472.

Follette, W. C., Bach, P. A., & Follette, V. M. (1993). A behavior-analytic view of psychological health. *Behavior Analyst, 16*, 303–316.

Follette, W. C., & Hayes, S. C. (2000). Contemporary behavior therapy. In C. R. Snyder & R. E. Ingram (Eds.), *Handbook of psychological change: Psychotherapy process and practices for the 21st century* (pp. 381–408). New York: Wiley.

Follette, W. C., & Houts, A. C. (1996). Models of scientific progress and the role of theory in taxonomy development: A case study of the *DSM*. *Journal of Consulting and Clinical Psychology, 64*, 1120–1132.

Follette, W. C., Houts, A. C., & Hayes, S. C. (1992). Behavior therapy and the new medical model. *Behavioral Assessment, 14*, 323–343.

Follette, W. C., Naugle, A. E., & Linnerooth, P. J. N. (2000). Functional alternatives to traditional assessment and diagnosis. In M. J. Dougher (Ed.), *Clinical behavior analysis* (pp. 99–125). Reno, NV: Context Press.

Forsyth, J. P., & Eifert, G. H. (1996). Cleaning up "cognition" in triple-response fear assessment. *Journal of Behavior Therapy and Experimental Psychiatry, 27*, 87–98.

Fowles, D. C. (1980). The three arousal model: Implications of Gray's two-factor learning theory for heart rate, electrodermal activity, and psychopathy. *Psychophysiology, 17*, 87–104.

Fowles, D. C. (2001). Biological variables in psychopathology: A psychobiological perspective. In P. B. Sutker & H. E. Adams (Eds.), *Comprehensive handbook of psychopathology* (3rd ed., pp. 85–104). New York: Kluwer Academic/Plenum.

Frankel, A. J. (1975). Beyond the simple functional analysis—The chain: A conceptual framework for assessment with a case example. *Behavior Therapy, 6*, 254–260.

Franklin, M. E., & Foa, E. B. (1998). Cognitive–behavioral treatments for obsessive–compulsive disorder. In P. E. Nathan & J. M. Gorman (Eds.), *A guide to treatments that work* (pp. 339–357). New York: Oxford University Press.

Glenn, S. S., Ellis, J., & Greenspoon, J. (1992). On the revolutionary nature of the operant as a unit of behavioral selection. *American Psychologist, 47*, 1329–1336.

Goldberg, L. R. (1993). The structure of phenotypic personality traits. *American Psychologist, 48*, 26–34.

Goldfried, M. R., & Castonguay, L. G. (1992). The future of psychotherapy integration. *Psychotherapy, 29,* 4–20.

Goldfried, M. R., & Davison, G. C. (1976). *Clinical behavior therapy.* New York: Holt, Rinehard & Winston.

Goldfried, M. R., & Kent, R. N. (1972). Traditional versus behavioral assessment: A comparison of methodological and theoretical assumptions. *Psychological Bulletin, 77,* 409–420.

Goldfried, M. R., & Pomeranz, D. M. (1968). Role of assessment in behavior modification. *Psychological Reports, 23,* 75–87.

Goldfried, M. R., & Sprafkin, J. N. (1976). Behavioral personality assessment. In J. T. Spence, R. C., Carson, & J. W. Thibaut (Eds.), *Behavioral approaches to therapy* (pp. 295–321). Morristown, NJ: General Learning Press.

Goodenough, F. L. (1949). *Mental testing.* New York: Rinehart.

Gould, S. J. (1980). *The panda's thumb.* New York: Norton.

Gray, J. A. (1970). The psychophysiological basis of introversion–extraversion. *Behavior Research and Therapy, 8,* 249–266.

Gray, J. A. (1973). Causal theories of personality and how to test them. In J. R. Royce (Ed.), *Multivariate analysis and psychological theory* (pp. 409–451). New York: Academic Press.

Gray, J. A. (1981). A critique of Eysenck's theory of personality. In H. Eysenck (Ed.), *A model for personality* (pp. 264–276). New York: Springer-Verlag.

Gray, J. A. (1987a). *The psychology of fear and stress* (2nd ed.). New York: Cambridge University Press.

Gray, J. A. (1987b). Perspectives on anxiety and impulsivity: A commentary. *Journal of Research in Personality, 21,* 493–509.

Gray, J. A. (1987c). Discussions arising from "A unified biosocial theory of personality and its role in the development of anxiety states." *Psychiatric Developments, 4,* 377–385.

Gray, J. A. (1999). Cognition, emotion, conscious experience and the brain. In T. Dalgleish & M. Power (Eds.), *Handbook of cognition and emotion* (pp. 83–102). New York: Wiley.

Gray, J. A., & McNaughton, N. (1996). The neuropsychology of anxiety: Reprise. In D. A. Hope (Ed.), *Perspectives on anxiety, panic, and fear. Nebraska Symposium on Motivation* (Vol. 43, pp. 61–134). Lincoln: University of Nebraska Press.

Gremore, T. M., Chapman, A. L., & Farmer, R. F. (in press). Passive avoidance learning among female inmates as a function of behavioral inhibition and activation. *Personality and Individual Differences.*

Gresswell, D. M., & Hollin, C. R. (1992). Toward a new methodology of making sense of case material: An illustrative case involving attempted multiple murder. *Clinical Behaviour and Mental Health, 2,* 329–341.

Hare, R. D. (1998). Psychopathy, affect, and behavior. In D. J. Cooke, A. E. Forth, & R. D. Hare (Eds.), *Psychopathy: Theory, research, and implications for society* (pp. 105–137). Dordrecht, the Netherlands: Kluwer Academic.

Harkness, A. R., & Hogan, R. (1995). The theory and measurement of traits: Two views. In J. N. Butcher (Ed.), *Clinical personality assessment: Practical approaches* (pp. 28–41). New York: Oxford University Press.

Harpur, T. J., Hare, R. D., & Hakstian, A. R. (1989). Two-factor conceptualization of psychopathy: Construct validity and assessment implications. *Psychological Assessment, 1*, 6–17.

Harris, G., Rice, M. E., & Cormier, C. (1994). Psychopaths: Is the therapeutic community therapeutic? *Therapeutic Communities, 15*, 283–300.

Hart, S. D. (2001). Forensic issues. In W. J. Livesley (Ed.), *Handbook of personality disorders: Theory, research, and treatment* (pp. 555–569). New York: Guilford Press.

Harter, S. (1999). *The construction of the self: A developmental perspective*. New York: Guildford Press.

Hathaway, S. R., & McKinley, J. C. (1943). *Minnesota Multiphasic Personality Inventory Manual.* New York: Psychological Corporation.

Hawkins, R. P. (1997). Can behavior therapy be saved from triviality? Commentary on "Thirty years of behavior therapy." *Behavior Therapy, 28*, 637–645.

Hayes, S. C., Barlow, D. H., & Nelson-Gray, R. O. (1999). *The scientist–practitioner: Research and accountability in the age of managed care* (2nd ed.). Boston: Allyn and Bacon.

Hayes, S. C., & Brownstein, A. J. (1986). Mentalism, behavior–behavior relations, and a behavior–analytic view of the purpose of science. *The Behavior Analyst, 9*, 175–190.

Hayes, S. C., Brownstein, A. J., Zettle, R. D., Rosenfarb, I. S., & Korn, Z. (1986). Rule-governed behavior and sensitivity to changing consequences of responding. *Journal of the Experimental Analysis of Behavior, 45*, 237–256.

Hayes, S. C., & Follette, W. C. (1992). Can functional analysis provide a substitute for syndromal classification? *Behavioral Assessment, 14*, 345–365.

Hayes, S. C., & Follette, W. C. (1993). The challenge faced by behavioral assessment. *European Journal of Psychological Assessment, 9*, 182–188.

Hayes, S. C., Hayes, L. J., Reese, H. W., & Sarbin, T. R. (Eds.). (1993). *Analytic goals and the varieties of scientific contextualism.* Reno, NV: Context Press.

Hayes, S. C., & Ju, W. (1998). Rule-governed behavior. In W. O'Donohue (Ed.), *Learning and behavior therapy* (pp. 374–391). Boston: Allyn and Bacon.

Hayes, S. C., Nelson, R. O., & Jarrett, R. B. (1987). Treatment utility of assessment: A functional approach to evaluating the quality of assessment. *American Psychologist, 42*, 963–974.

Hayes, S. C., Strosahl, K. D., & Wilson, K. G. (1999). *Acceptance and commitment therapy: An experiential approach to behavior change.* New York: Guilford Press.

Hayes, S. C., Wilson, K. G., Gifford, E. V., Follette, V. M., & Strosahl, K. (1996). Experiential avoidance and behavioral disorders: A functional dimensional approach to diagnosis and treatment. *Journal of Consulting and Clinical Psychology, 64*, 1152–1168.

Haynes, S. N. (1986). The design of intervention programs. In R. O. Nelson & S. C. Hayes (Eds.), *Conceptual foundations of behavioral assessment* (pp. 386–429). New York: Guilford Press.

Haynes, S. N., Kaholokula, J. K., & Nelson, K. (1999). The idiographic application of nomothetic, empirically based treatments. *Clinical Psychology: Science and Practice*, 6, 456–461.

Haynes, S. N., Nelson, K. G., Thacher, I., & Kaholokula, J. K. (2002). Outpatient behavioral assessment and treatment target selection. In M. Hersen & L. K. Porzelius (Eds.), *Diagnosis, conceptualization, and treatment planning for adults: A step-by-step guide* (pp. 35–70). Mahwah, NJ: Erlbaum.

Haynes, S. N., & O'Brien, W. H. (1990). Functional analysis in behavior therapy. *Clinical Psychology Review*, *10*, 649–668.

Haynes, S. N., & O'Brien, W. H. (2000). *Principles and practice of behavioral assessment*. New York: Kluwer Academic/Plenum.

Hazlett-Stevens, H., & Craske, M. G. (2003). Breathing retraining and diaphragmatic breathing techniques. In W. O'Donohue, J. E. Fisher, & S. C. Hayes (Eds.), *Cognitive behavior therapy: Applying empirically supported techniques in your practice* (pp. 59–64). Hoboken, NJ: Wiley.

Heatherton, T. F., & Baumeister, R. F. (1991). Binge eating as escape from self-awareness. *Psychological Bulletin*, *110*, 86–108.

Heimberg, R. G., Liebowitz, M. R., Hope, D. A., Schneier, F. R., Holt, C. S., Welkowitz, et al. (1998). Cognitive behavioral group therapy vs. phenelzine therapy for social phobia: 12-week outcome. *Archives of General Psychiatry*, *55*, 1133–1141.

Hersen, M. (1988). Behavioral and psychiatric diagnosis. *Behavioral Assessment*, *10*, 107–121

Hoage, C. M. (1989). The use of in-session structured eating in the outpatient treatment of bulimia nervosa. In L. M. Hornyak & E. K. Baker (Eds.), *Experiential therapies for eating disorders* (pp. 60–77). New York: Guilford Press.

Hoes, M. J. A. J. M. (1986). Biological markers in psychiatry. *Acta Psychiatrica Belgica*, 86, 220–241.

Hogarty, G. E. (2002). *Personal therapy for schizophrenia and related disorders*. New York: Guilford Press.

Homme, L. E., DeBaca, P. C., Devine, J. V., Steinhorst, R., & Rickert, E. J. (1963). The use of the Premack principle in controlling the behavior of nursery school children. *Journal of the Experimental Analysis of Behavior*, 6, 544.

Howe, H., & Lyne, J. (1992). Gene talk in sociobiology. *Social Epistemology*, 6, 109–163.

Hudzinski, L. G., & Levenson, H. (1985). Biofeedback behavioral treatment of headache with locus of control pain analysis: A 20-month retrospective study. *Headache*, *25*, 380–386.

Hull, C. L. (1943). *Principles of behavior*. New York: Appleton-Century-Crofts.

Hull, D. L., Langman, R. E., & Glenn, S. S. (2001). A general account of selection: Biology, immunology, and behavior. *Behavioral and Brain Sciences, 24,* 511–573.

Hyler, S. E., & Lyons, S. E. (1988). Factor structure of the *DSM–III* personality disorder clusters: A replication. *Comprehensive Psychiatry, 29,* 304–308.

Hyler, S. E., Lyons, S. E., Rieder, R. O., Young, L., Williams, J. B. W., & Spitzer, R. L. (1990). The factor structure of self-report inventories *DSM–III* Axis II symptoms and their relationship to clinician's ratings. *American Journal of Psychiatry, 147,* 751–757.

Isaacs, W., Thomas, J., & Goldiamond, I. (1960). Application of operant conditioning to reinstate verbal behavior in psychotics. *Journal of Speech and Hearing Disorders, 25,* 8–12.

Iwata, B. A., Pace, G. M., Dorsey, M. F., Zarcone, J. R., Vollmer, T. R., Smith, R. G., et al. (1994). The functions of self-injurious behavior: An experimental–epidemiological analysis. *Journal of Applied Behavior Analysis, 27,* 215–240.

Jacobson, N. S., & Christensen, A. (1996). *Acceptance and change in couple therapy: A therapist's guide to transforming relationships.* New York: Norton.

Jacobson, N. S., Dobson, K. S., Truax, P. A., Addis, M. E., Koerner, K., Gollan, J. K., et al. (1996). A component analysis of cognitive–behavioral treatment for depression. *Journal of Consulting and Clinical Psychology, 64,* 295–304.

Jahn, D. L., & Lichstein, K. L. (1980). The resistive client: A neglected phenomenon in behavior therapy. *Behavior Modification, 4,* 303–320.

Jimerson, D. C., Wolfe, B. E., Metzger, E. D., Finkelstein, D. M., Cooper, T. B., & Levine, J. M. (1997). Decreased serotonin function in bulimia nervosa. *Archives of General Psychiatry, 54,* 529–534.

John, O. P., & Srivastava, S. (1999). The big five trait taxonomy: History, measurement, and theoretical perspectives. In L. A. Pervin & O. P. John (Eds.), *Handbook of personality: Theory and research* (pp. 102–138). New York: Guilford Press.

Johnson, S. M. (1987). *Humanizing the narcissistic style.* New York: Norton.

Johnson, W. G., Schlundt, D. G., Barclay, D. R., Carr-Nangle, R. E., & Engler, L. B. (1995). A naturalistic functional analysis of binge eating. *Behavior Therapy, 26,* 101–118.

Johnston, J. M., & Pennypacker, H. S. (1993). *Strategies and tactics of behavioral research* (2nd ed.). Hillsdale, NJ: Erlbaum.

Jones, M. C. (1924). The elimination of children's fears. *Journal of Experimental Psychology, 7,* 382–390.

Kabat-Zinn, J. (1990). *Full catastrophe living: Using the wisdom of your body and mind to face stress, pain, and illness.* New York: Dell.

Kagan, J., Reznick, J. S., Clarke, C., Snidman, N., & Garcia-Coll, C. (1984). Behavioral inhibition to the unfamiliar. *Child Development, 55,* 2212–2225.

Kagan, J., & Snidman, N. (1991). Temperamental factors in human development. *American Psychologist, 46,* 856–862.

Kallman, W. M., Hersen, M., & O'Toole, D. H. (1975). The use of social reinforcement in a case of conversion reaction. *Behavior Therapy, 6,* 411–413.

Kandel, E. R. (1998). A new intellectual framework for psychiatry. *American Journal of Psychiatry, 155,* 457–469.

Kanfer, F. H., & Saslow, G. (1969). Behavioral diagnosis. In C. M. Franks (Ed.), *Behavior therapy: Appraisal and status* (pp. 417–444). New York: McGraw-Hill.

Kantor, J. R. (1958). *Interbehavioral psychology*. Chicago: Principia Press.

Karoly, P. (1995). Self-control theory. In W. O'Donohue & L. Krasner (Eds.), *Theories of behavior therapy: Exploring behavior change* (pp. 259–285). Washington, DC: American Psychological Association.

Kass, F., Skodol, A. E., Charles, E., Spitzer, R. L., & Williams, J. B. W. (1985). Scaled ratings of *DSM–III* personality disorders. *American Journal of Psychiatry, 142,* 627–630.

Kasviskis, Y., & Marks, I. M. (1988). Clomipramine, self-exposure, and therapist-accompanied exposure in obsessive–compulsive ritualizers: Two year follow-up. *Journal of Anxiety Disorders, 2,* 291–298.

Kaye, W. H., Weltzin, T. E., Hsu, G., McConaha, C. W., & Bolton, B. (1993). Amount of calories retained after binge eating and vomiting. *American Journal of Psychiatry, 150,* 969–971.

Kazdin, A. E. (1977). *The token economy*. New York: Plenum Press.

Kazdin, A. E. (1978). *History of behavior modification: Experimental foundations of contemporary research*. Baltimore: University Park Press.

Kazdin, A. E. (1982). Symptom substitution, generalization, and response covariation: Implications for psychotherapy outcome. *Psychological Bulletin, 91,* 349–365.

Kazdin, A. E. (1983). Psychiatric diagnosis, dimensions of dysfunction, and child behavior therapy. *Behavior Therapy, 14,* 73–99.

Kazdin, A. E. (2001). *Behavior modification in applied settings* (6th ed.). Homewood, IL: Dorsey.

Keel, P. K., & Mitchell, J. E. (1997). Outcome in bulimia nervosa. *American Journal of Psychiatry, 154,* 313–321.

Keller, K. E. (1983). Dysfunctional attitudes and cognitive therapy for depression. *Cognitive Therapy and Research, 7,* 437–444.

Kendler, K. S., McGuire, M., Gruenberg, A. M., & Walsh, D. (1995). Schizotypal symptoms and signs in the Roscommon family study: Their factor structure and familial relationship with psychotic and affective disorders. *Archives of General Psychiatry, 52,* 296–303.

Kepley, H. O. (2003). *AD/HD subtypes in adults: Differences in personality dimensions and comorbid internalizing disorders*. Unpublished doctoral dissertation, University of North Carolina at Greensboro.

Kernberg, O. F., Selzer, M. A., Koenigsberg, H. W., Carr, A. C., & Appelbaum, A. H. (1989). *Psychodynamic psychotherapy of borderline patients*. New York: Basic Books.

Keutzer, C. S. (1968). Behavior modification of smoking: The experimental investigation of diverse techniques. *Behaviour Research and Therapy, 6*, 137–157.

Kirk, K. S. (1999). Functional analysis and selection of intervention strategies for people with attention-deficit/hyperactivity disorder. In J. R. Scotti & L. H. Meyer (Eds.), *Behavioral intervention: Principles, models, and practices* (pp. 71–99). Baltimore: Brookes.

Kirkpatrick, L. A. (1999). Toward an evolutionary psychology of religion and personality. *Journal of Personality, 67*, 921–952.

Klerman, G. L. (1986). Historical perspectives on contemporary schools of psychopathology. In T. Millon & G. L. Klerman (Eds.), *Contemporary directions in psychopathology: Towards DSM–IV* (pp. 3–28). New York: Guilford Press.

Koerner, K., Kohlenberg, R. J., & Parker, C. R. (1996). Diagnosis of personality disorder: A radical behavioral alternative. *Journal of Consulting and Clinical Psychology, 64*, 1169–1176.

Kohlenberg, R. J., & Tsai, M. (1991). *Functional analytic psychotherapy: Creative intense and curative therapeutic relationships*. New York: Plenum Press.

Kohut, H. (1977). *The restoration of the self*. New York: International Universities Press.

Kosson, D. S., Smith, S. S., & Newman, J. P. (1990). Evaluation of the construct validity of psychopathy in black and white male inmates: Three preliminary studies. *Journal of Abnormal Psychology, 99*, 250–259.

Kozak, M. J., & Miller, G. A. (1982). Hypothetical constructs versus intervening variables: A re-appraisal of the three-systems model of anxiety assessment. *Behavioral Assessment, 4*, 347–358.

Krasner, L. (1992). The concepts of syndrome and functional analysis: Compatible or incompatible? *Behavioral Assessment, 14*, 307–321.

Lacey, J. H. (1992). Long-term follow-up of bulimic patients treated in integrated behavioural and psychodynamic treatment programmes. In W. Herzog, H. C. Deter, & W. Vandereycken (Eds.), *The course of eating disorders: Long-term follow-up studies of anorexia and bulimia nervosa* (pp. 150–173). New York: Springer-Verlag.

Lacey, J. H., & Evans, C. D. H. (1986). The impulsivist: A multi-impulsive personality disorder. *British Journal of Addictions, 81*, 641–649.

Lang, P. J. (1968). Fear reduction and fear behavior: Problems in treating a construct. In J. M. Schlien (Ed.), *Research in psychotherapy* (Vol. 3, pp. 90–102). Washington, DC: American Psychological Association.

Laraway, S., Snycerski, S., Michael, J., & Poling, A. (2003). Motivating operations and terms to describe them: Some further refinements. *Journal of Applied Behavior Analysis, 36*, 407–414.

Last, C. G., Hersen, M., Kazdin, A. E., Francis, G., & Grubb, H. J. (1987). Psychiatric illness in the mothers of anxious children. *American Journal of Psychiatry, 144*, 1580–1583.

Latimer, P. R., & Sweet, A. A. (1984). Cognitive versus behavioral procedures in cognitive behavior therapy: Critical review of the evidence. *Journal of Behavior Therapy and Experimental Psychiatry, 15*, 9–22.

Leahy, R. L., & Holland, S. J. (2000). *Treatment plans and interventions for depression and anxiety disorders*. New York: Guilford Press.

Leitenberg, H., Rosen, J. C., Gross, J., Nudelman, S., & Vara, L. S. (1988). Exposure plus response–prevention treatment of bulimia nervosa. *Journal of Consulting and Clinical Psychology, 56*, 535–541.

Lewinsohn, P. M., Antonuccio, D. O., Steinmetz-Breckenridge, J., & Teri, L. (1984). *The coping with depression course*. Eugene, OR: Castalia.

Lewinsohn, P. M., & Gotlib, I. H. (1995). Behavioral theory and treatment of depression. In E. E. Beckham & W. R. Leber (Eds.), *Handbook of depression* (2nd ed., pp. 352–375). New York: Guilford Press.

Lickliter, R., & Honeycutt, H. (2003a). Developmental dynamics: Toward a biologically plausible evolutionary psychology. *Psychological Bulletin, 129*, 819–835.

Lickliter, R., & Honeycutt, H. (2003b). Developmental dynamics and contemporary evolutionary psychology: Status quo or irreconcilable views? Reply to Bjorklund (2003), Krebs (2003), Buss and Reeve (2003), Crawford (2003), and Tooby et al. (2003). *Psychological Bulletin, 129*, 866–872.

Lilenfeld, L., Kaye, W., Greeno, C., Merkiangas, K., Plotnicov, K., Pollice, C., et al. (1997). Psychiatric disorders in women with bulimia nervosa and their first degree relatives: Effects of comorbid substance dependence. *International Journal of Eating Disorders, 22*, 253–264.

Linehan, M. M. (1981). A social–behavioral analysis of suicide and parasuicide: Implications for clinical assessment and treatment. In J. F. Clarkin & H. I. Glazer (Eds.), *Depression: Behavioral and directive intervention strategies* (pp. 229–294). New York: Garland.

Linehan, M. M. (1993a). *Cognitive–behavioral treatment of borderline personality disorder*. New York: Guilford Press.

Linehan, M. M. (1993b). *Skills training manual for treating borderline personality disorder*. New York: Guilford Press.

Linehan, M. M. (1994). Acceptance and change: The central dialectic in psychotherapy. In S. C. Hayes, N. S. Jacobson, V. M. Follette, & M. J. Dougher (Eds.), *Acceptance and change: Content and context in psychotherapy* (pp. 73–86). Reno, NV: Context Press.

Linehan, M. M., Armstrong, H. E., Suarez, A., Allmon, D., & Heard, H. L. (1991). Cognitive–behavioral treatment of chronically parasuicidal borderline patients. *Archives of General Psychiatry, 48*, 1060–1064.

Linehan, M. M., Heard, H., & Armstrong, H. (1993). Naturalistic follow-up of a behavioral treatment for chronically parasuicidal borderline patients. *Archives of General Psychiatry, 50*, 971–974.

Lish, J. D., Kavoussi, R. J., & Coccaro, E. F. (1996). Aggressiveness. In C. G. Costello (Ed.), *Personality characteristics of the personality disordered* (pp. 24–47). New York: Wiley.

Livesley, W. J. (2001a). Conceptual and taxonomic issues. In W. J. Livesley (Ed.), *Handbook of personality disorders: Theory, research, and treatment* (pp. 3–38). New York: Guilford Press.

Livesley, W. J. (2001b). A framework for an integrated approach to treatment. In W. J. Livesley (Ed.), *Handbook of personality disorders: Theory, research, and treatment* (pp. 570–600). New York: Guilford Press.

Livesley, W. J., & Jackson, D. N. (1986). The internal consistency and factorial structure of behaviors judged to be associated with *DSM–III* personality disorders. *American Journal of Psychiatry, 143,* 1473–1474.

Livesley, W. J., Jackson, D. N., & Schroeder, M. L. (1989). A study of the factorial structure of personality pathology. *Journal of Personality Disorders, 3,* 292–306.

Livesley, W. J., Schroeder, M. L., & Jackson, D. N. (1990). Dependent personality disorder and attachment problems. *Journal of Personality Disorders, 4,* 131–140.

Livesley, W. J., Schroeder, M. L., Jackson, D. N., & Jang, K. L. (1994). Categorical distinctions in the study of personality disorder: Implications for classification. *Journal of Abnormal Psychology, 103,* 6–17.

Lloyd, A. (2003). Urge surfing. In W. O'Donohue, J. E. Fisher, & S. C. Hayes (Eds.), *Cognitive behavior therapy: Applying empirically supported techniques in your practice* (pp. 451–455). Hoboken, NJ: Wiley.

Loehlin, J. C., McCrae, R. R., Costa, P. T., Jr., & John, O. P. (1998). Heritabilities of common and measure-specific components of the Big Five personality factors. *Journal of Research in Personality, 32,* 431–453.

Loevinger, J. (1957). Objective tests as instruments of psychological theory. *Psychological Reports, 3* (Monograph No. 9), 635–694.

Logue, A. W. (1995). *Self-control: Waiting until tomorrow for what you want today.* Englewood Cliffs, NJ: Prentice Hall.

Loranger, A., Lenzenweger, M., Gartner, A., Sussman, V., Herzig, J., Zammit, G., et al. (1991). Trait-state artifacts and the diagnosis of personality disorder. *Archives of General Psychiatry, 48,* 720–728.

Lovaas, O. I., Freitag, G., Gold, V. J., & Kassorla, I. C. (1965). Experimental studies in childhood schizophrenia. I. Analysis of self-destructive behavior. *Journal of Experimental Child Psychology, 2,* 67–84.

Lowe, M. R., & Eldredge, K. L. (1993). The role of impulsiveness in normal and disordered eating. In W. G. McCown, J. L. Johnson, & M. B. Shure (Eds.), *The impulsive client: Theory, research, and treatment* (pp. 185–224). Washington, DC: American Psychological Association

Lubinski, D., & Thompson, T. (1986). Functional units of human behavior and their integration: A dispositional analysis. In T. Thompson & M. D. Zeiler (Eds.), *Analysis and integration of behavioral units* (pp. 275–314). Hillsdale, NJ: Erlbaum.

Luborsky, L., Singer, B., & Luborsky, L. (1975). Comparative studies of psychotherapies: Is it true that "everybody has won and all must have prizes?" *Archives of General Psychiatry, 32,* 995–1008.

Lykken, D. T. (1957). A study of anxiety in the sociopathic personality. *Journal of Abnormal and Social Psychology, 55,* 6–10.

Lykken, D. T. (1995). *The antisocial personalities.* Hillsdale, NJ: Erlbaum.

MacCorquodale, K., & Meehl, P. E. (1948). On a distinction between hypothetical constructs and intervening variables. *Psychological Review, 55,* 95–107.

MacKenzie, K. R. (2001). Group psychotherapy. In W. J. Livesley (Ed.), *Handbook of personality disorders: Theory, research, and treatment* (pp. 497–526). New York: Guilford Press.

Magaro, P. A. (1980). *Cognition in schizophrenia and paranoia: The integration of cognitive processes*. Hillsdale, NJ: Erlbaum.

Mahoney, M. J. (1974). *Cognition and behavior modification*. Cambridge, MA: Ballinger.

Maier, W., Lichterman, D., Klingler, T., Heun, R., & Hallmayer, J. (1992). Prevalences of personality disorders in the community. *Journal of Personality Disorders, 6*, 187–196.

Malott, R. W. (1989). The achievement of evasive goals: Control by rules describing contingencies that are not direct acting. In S. C. Hayes (Ed.), *Rule-governed behavior: Cognition, contingencies, and instructional control* (pp. 269–322). New York: Plenum Press.

Malott, R. W., Malott, M. E., & Trojan, E. A. (2000). *Elementary principles of behavior* (4th ed.). Upper Saddle River, NJ: Prentice Hall.

Markovitz, P. (2001). Pharmacotherapy. In W. J. Livesley (Ed.), *Handbook of personality disorders: Theory, research, and treatment* (pp. 475–493). New York: Guilford Press.

Markowitz, J. C., & Weissman, M. M. (1995). Interpersonal psychotherapy. In E. E. Beckham & W. R. Leber (Eds.), *Handbook of depression* (2nd ed., pp. 376–390). New York: Guilford Press.

Markus, H. (1977). Self-schemata and processing information about the self. *Journal of Personality and Social Psychology, 35*, 63–78.

Marlatt, G. A., & Gordon, J. R. (Eds.). (1985). *Relapse prevention: Maintenance strategies in the treatment of addictive behaviors*. New York: Guilford Press.

Marlowe, D. B., Kirby, K. C., Festinger, D. S., Husband, S. D., & Platt, J. J. (1997). Impact of comorbid personality disorders and personality disorder symptoms on outcomes of behavioral treatment for cocaine dependence. *Journal of Nervous and Mental Disease, 185*, 483–490.

Martell, C. R., Addis, M. E., & Jacobson, N. S. (2001). *Depression in context: Strategies for guided action*. New York: Norton.

Mattia, J. I., & Zimmerman, M. (2001). Epidemiology. In W. J. Livesley (Ed.), *Handbook of personality disorders: Theory, research, and treatment* (pp. 107–123). New York: Guilford Press.

Mavissakalian, M., & Hamann, M. S. (1987). *DSM–III* personality disorder in agoraphobia: II. Changes with treatment. *Comprehensive Psychiatry, 28*, 356–361.

McCrae, R. R., & Costa, P. T., Jr. (1996). Toward a new generation of personality theories: Theoretical contexts for the five-factor model. In J. S. Wiggins (Ed.), *The five factor model of personality: Theoretical perspectives* (pp. 51–87). New York: Guilford Press.

McCrae, R. R., & Costa, P. T., Jr. (1997). Personality trait structure as a human universal. *American Psychologist, 52*, 509–516.

McCrae, R. R., & Costa, P. T., Jr. (1990). *Personality in adulthood.* New York: Guilford Press.

McDonald, D. A., & Holland, D. (2002). Examination of the relations between the NEO Personality Inventory-Revised and the Temperament and Character Inventory. *Psychological Reports, 91,* 921–930.

McFarlane, A. C., Weber, D. L., & Clark, C. R. (1993). Abnormal stimulus processing in PTSD. *Biological Psychiatry, 34,* 311–320.

McFarlane, A. C., & Yehuda, R. (1996). Resilience, vulnerability, and the course of posttraumatic reactions. In B. A. van der Kolk, A. C. McFarlane, & L. Weisaeth (Eds.), *Traumatic stress: The effects of overwhelming experience on the mind, body, and society* (pp. 155–181). New York: Guilford Press.

McGinn, L. K., Young, J. E., & Sanderson, W. C. (1995). When and how to do longer term therapy. *Cognitive and Behavioral Practice, 2,* 187–212.

McGlynn, F. D. (1994). Simple phobia. In M. Hersen & R. T. Ammerman (Eds.), *Handbook of prescriptive treatments for adults* (pp. 179–196). New York: Plenum Press.

McKay, M., Davis, M., & Fanning, P. (1997). *Thoughts and feelings: Taking control of your moods and your life.* Oakland, CA: New Harbinger

McKnight, D. L., Nelson, R. O., Hayes, S. C., & Jarrett, R. B. (1984). Importance of treating individually-assessed response classes in the amelioration of depression. *Behavior Therapy, 15,* 315–335.

McManus, F., & Waller, G. (1995). A functional analysis of binge eating. *Clinical Psychology Review, 15,* 845–863.

McNally, R. J. (1999). Posttraumatic stress disorder. In T. Millon, P. H. Blaney, & R. D. Davis (Eds.), *Oxford textbook of psychopathology* (pp. 144–165). New York: Oxford University Press.

McNaughton, N., & Gray, J. A. (2000). Anxiolytic action on the behavioural inhibition system implies multiple types of arousal contribute to anxiety. *Journal of Affective Disorders, 61,* 161–176.

Mealey, L. (2001). "La plus ça change . . . ": Response to a critique of evolutionary psychology. *Evolution and Cognition, 7,* 14–19.

Meichenbaum, D. (1994). *A clinical handbook/practical therapist manual for assessing and treating adults with post-traumatic stress disorder (PTSD).* Waterloo, Ontario, Canada: Institute Press.

Meichenbaum, D., & Cameron, R. (1982). Cognitive behavior modification: Current issues. In G. T. Wilson & C. M. Franks (Eds.), *Contemporary behavior therapy: Conceptual and empirical foundations.* New York: Guilford Press.

Meissner, W. W. (1986). *Psychotherapy and the paranoid processes.* Northvale, NJ: Aronson.

Mennin, D. S., & Heimberg, R. G. (2000). The impact of comorbid mood and personality disorders in the cognitive–behavioral treatment of panic disorder. *Clinical Psychology Review, 20,* 339–357.

Meyer, V. (1960). The treatment of two phobic patients on the basis of learning principles. In H. J. Eysenck (Ed.), *Behavior therapy and the neuroses* (pp. 135–143). New York: Pergamon.

Michael, J. (1982). Distinguishing between the discriminative and motivational functions of stimuli. *Journal of the Experimental Analysis of Behavior, 37*, 149–158.

Michael, J. (1993). Establishing operations. *The Behavior Analyst, 16*, 191–206.

Michael, J. (2000). Implications and refinements of the establishing operation concept. *Journal of Applied Behavior Analysis, 33*, 401–410.

Miklowitz, D. J. (2001). Bipolar disorder. In D. H. Barlow (Ed.), *Clinical handbook of psychological disorders* (3rd ed., pp. 523–561). New York: Guilford Press.

Miller, W. R., & Rollnick, S. (1991). *Motivational interviewing: Preparing people to change addictive behavior*. New York: Guilford Press.

Miller, W. R., Zweben, A., DiClemente, C. C., & Rychtarik, R. G. (1995). *Motivational enhancement therapy manual: A clinical research guide for therapists treating individuals with alcohol abuse and dependence*. Rockville, MD: U.S. Department of Health and Human Services.

Millon, T. (1969). *Modern psychopathology: A biosocial approach to maladaptive learning and functioning*. Philadelphia: Saunders.

Millon, T. (1981). *Disorders of personality: DSM–III: Axis II*. New York: Wiley.

Millon, T. (1983). The *DSM–III*: An insider's perspective. *American Psychologist, 38*, 804–814.

Millon, T. (1986). On the past and future of the *DSM–III*: Personal recollections and projections. In T. Millon & G. L. Klerman (Eds.), *Contemporary directions in psychopathology: Towards DSM-IV* (pp. 29–70). New York: Guilford Press.

Millon, T. (1987). *Manual for the Millon Clinical Multiaxial Inventory—II*. Minneapolis, MN : National Computer Systems.

Millon, T. (1990). *Toward a new personology: An evolutionary model*. New York: Wiley.

Millon, T. (1999). *Personality-guided therapy*. New York: Wiley.

Millon, T., & Davis, R. D (1996). An evolutionary model of personality disorders. In J. F. Clarkin & M. F. Lenzenweger (Eds.), *Major theories of personality disorders* (pp. 221–346). New York: Guilford Press.

Millon, T., & Everly, G. S., Jr. (1985). *Personality and its disorders*. New York: Wiley.

Mischel, W. (1968). *Personality and assessment*. New York: Wiley.

Mitchell, W. S., & Stoffelmayr, B. E. (1973). Application of the Premack principle to the behavioral control of extremely inactive schizophrenics. *Journal of Applied Behavior Analysis*, 6, 419–423.

Moore, D. R., & Arthur, J. L. (1983). Juvenile delinquency. In T. H. Ollendick & M. Hersen (Eds.), *Handbook of child psychopathology* (pp. 357–387). New York: Plenum.

Morey, L. C. (1988). The categorical representation of personality disorder. A cluster analysis of *DSM–III–R* personality features. *Journal of Abnormal Psychology, 97*, 314–321.

Morey, L. C. (1991). Classification of mental disorder as a collection of hypothetical constructs. *Journal of Abnormal Psychology, 100,* 289–293.

Morey, L. C., Skinner, H. A., & Blashfield, R. K. (1986). Trends in the classification of abnormal behavior. In A. R. Ciminero, K. S. Calhoun, & H. E. Adams (Eds.), *Handbook of behavioral assessment* (2nd ed., pp. 47–75). New York: Wiley.

Morin, C. M. (1993). *Insomnia: Psychological assessment and management.* New York: Guilford Press.

Mowrer, O. H. (1947). On the dual nature of learning: A re-interpretation of "conditioning" and "problem–solving." *Harvard Educational Review, 17,* 102–148.

Mowrer, O. H., & Mowrer, W. M. (1938). Enuresis—a method for its study and treatment. *American Journal of Orthopsychiatry, 8,* 436–439.

Narine, J. S. (2000). *Psychology: The adaptive mind* (2nd ed.) Belmont, CA: Wadsworth/Thompson.

Nathan, P. E., & Gorman, J. M. (1998). (Eds.). *A guide to treatments that work.* New York: Oxford University Press.

Naugle, A. E., & Follette, W. C. (1998). A functional analysis of trauma symptoms. In V. M. Follette, J. I. Ruzek, & F. R. Abueg (Eds.), *Cognitive–behavioral therapies for trauma* (pp. 48–73). New York: Guilford Press.

Nelson, R. O. (1977). Assessment and therapeutic functions of self-monitoring. In M. Hersen, R. Eisler, & P. Miller (Eds.), *Progress in behavior modification: Vol. 5* (pp. 236–308). New York: Academic Press.

Nelson, R. O. (1988). Relationships between assessment and treatment within a behavioral perspective. *Journal of Psychopathology and Behavioral Assessment, 10,* 155–170.

Nelson, R. O., & Barlow, D. H. (1981). Behavioral assessment: Basic strategies and initial procedures. In D. H. Barlow (Ed.), *Behavioral assessment of adult disorders* (pp. 13–43). New York: Guilford Press.

Nelson, R. O., & Hayes, S. C. (1986). Nature of behavioral assessment. In R. O. Nelson & S. C. Hayes (Eds.), *Conceptual foundations of behavioral assessment* (pp. 3–41). New York: Guilford Press.

Nelson, R. O., Hayes, S. C., Jarrett, R. B., Sigmon, S. T., & McKnight, D. L. (1987). Effectiveness of matched, mismatched, and package treatments for depression. *Psychological Reports, 61,* 816–818.

Nelson-Gray, R. O. (2003). Treatment utility of psychological assessment. *Psychological Assessment, 15,* 521–531.

Nelson-Gray, R. O., & Farmer, R. F. (1999). Behavioral assessment of personality disorders. *Behaviour Research and Therapy, 37,* 347–368.

Nelson-Gray, R. O., Gaynor, S. T., & Korotitsch, W. J. (1997). Behavior therapy: Distinct but acculturated. *Behavior Therapy, 28,* 563–572.

Nelson-Gray, R. O., Johnson, D., Foyle, L. W., Daniel, S. S., & Harmon, R. (1996). The effectiveness of cognitive therapy tailored to depressives with personality disorders. *Journal of Personality Disorders, 10,* 132–152.

Nelson-Gray, R. O., & Paulson, J. F. (2003). Behavioral assessment and the *DSM* system. In S. N. Haynes & E. M. Heiby (Eds.), *Behavioral assessment* (pp. 470–486). Volume 3 of M. Hersen (Ed.), *Comprehensive handbook of psychological assessment*. New York: Wiley.

Newman, C. F. (1994). Understanding client resistance: Methods for enhancing motivation to change. *Cognitive and Behavioral Practice, 1*, 47–69.

Newman, J. P. (1987). Reaction to punishment in extraverts and psychopaths: Implications for the impulsive behavior of disinhibited individuals. *Journal of Research in Personality, 21*, 464–480.

Newman, J. P., & Kosson, D. S. (1986). Passive avoidance learning in psychopathic and non-psychopathic offenders. *Journal of Abnormal Psychology, 95*, 252–256.

Newman, J. P., Patterson, C. M., Howland, E., & Nichols, S. L. (1990). Passive avoidance in psychopaths: The effects of reward. *Personality and Individual Differences, 11*, 1101–1114.

Newman, J. P., Patterson, C. M., & Kosson, D. S. (1987). Response perseveration in psychopaths. *Journal of Abnormal Psychology, 96*, 145–148.

Newman, J. P., & Schmitt, W. A. (1998). Passive avoidance in psychopathic offenders: A replication and extension. *Journal of Abnormal Psychology, 107*, 527–532.

Newman, J. P., Widom, C. S., & Nathan, S. (1985). Passive avoidance in syndromes of disinhibition: Psychopathy and extraversion. *Journal of Personality and Social Psychology, 48*, 1316–1327.

O'Connor, B. P., & Dyce, J. A. (1998). A test of models of personality disorder configuration. *Journal of Abnormal Psychology, 107*, 3–16.

O'Donohue, W., Fisher, J. E., & Hayes, S. C. (Eds.). (2003). *Cognitive behavior therapy: Applying empirically supported techniques in your practice*. Hoboken, NJ: Wiley.

Ogloff, J. R. P., Wong, S., & Greenwood, A. (1990). Treating criminal psychopaths in a therapeutic community program. *Behavioral Sciences and the Law, 8*, 181–190.

O'Leary, K. D., & Wilson, G. T. (1987). *Behavior therapy: Application and outcome* (2nd ed.). Englewood Cliffs, NJ: Prentice Hall.

Ollendick, T. H. (1999). Empirically supported treatments: Promises and pitfalls. *The Clinical Psychologist, 52*, 1–3.

Ollendick, T. H., & King, N. J. (2000). Empirically supported treatments for children and adolescents. In P. C. Kendall (Ed.), *Child and adolescent therapy* (2nd ed., pp. 386–425). New York: Guilford Press.

Ost, L. G., Jerremalm, A., & Johansson, J. (1981). Individual response patterns and the effects of different behavioral methods in the treatment of social phobia. *Behaviour Research and Therapy, 19*, 1–16.

Palmer, D. C., & Donahoe, J. W. (1992). Essentialism and selectionism in cognitive science and behavior analysis. *American Psychologist, 47*, 1344–1358.

Panksepp, J., & Panksepp, J. B. (2000). The seven sins of evolutionary psychology. *Evolution and Cognition, 6*, 108–131.

Panksepp, J., & Panksepp, J. B. (2001). A continuing critique of evolutionary psychology: Seven sins for seven sinners, plus or minus two. *Evolution and Cognition, 7*, 56–80.

Patterson, C. M., Kosson, D. S., & Newman, J. P. (1987). Reaction to punishment, reflectivity, and passive avoidance learning in extroverts. *Journal of Personality and Social Psychology, 52*, 565–575.

Patterson, C. M., & Newman, J. P. (1993). Reflectivity and learning from aversive events: Towards a psychological mechanism for the syndromes of disinhibition. *Psychological Review, 100*, 716–736.

Patterson, G. R., & Hops, H. (1972). Coercion, a game for two: Intervention techniques for marital conflict. In R. Ulrich & P. Mountjoy (Eds.), *The experimental analysis of social behavior* (pp. 424–440). New York: Appleton-Century-Crofts.

Paul, G. L. (1969a). Outcome of systematic desensitization. I: Background procedures, and uncontrolled reports of individual treatment. In C. M. Franks (Ed.), *Behavior therapy: Appraisal and status* (pp. 63–104). New York: McGraw-Hill.

Paul, G. L. (1969b). Outcome of systematic desensitization. II: Controlled investigations of individual treatment, technique variations, and current status. In C. M. Franks (Ed.), *Behavior therapy: Appraisal and status* (pp. 105–159). New York: McGraw-Hill.

Pavlov, I. (1927). *Conditioned reflexes*. Oxford, England: Oxford University Press.

Persons, J. B. (2003). The Association for Behavioral and Cognitive Therapies: An idea whose time has come. *The Behavior Therapist, 26*, 225.

Pfohl, B. (1996). Obsessiveness. In C. G. Costello (Ed.), *Personality characteristics of the personality disordered* (pp. 276–288). New York: Wiley.

Pickering, A. D., Corr, P. J., Powell, J. H., Kumari, V., Thornton, J. C., & Gray, J. A. (1997). Individual differences in reactions to reinforcing stimuli are neither black or white: To what extent are they Gray? In H. Nyborg (Ed.), *The scientific study of human nature: Tribute to Hans Eysenck at eighty* (pp. 36–67). New York: Elsevier.

Pickering, A. D., Díaz, A., & Gray, J. A. (1995). Personality and reinforcement: An exploration using a maze learning task. *Personality and Individual Differences, 18*, 541–558.

Pickering, A. D., & Gray, J. A. (1999). The neuroscience of personality. In L. A. Pervin & O. P. John (Eds.), *Handbook of personality: Theory and research* (2nd ed., pp. 277–299). New York: Guilford Press.

Pilkonis, P. A. (2001). Treatment of personality disorders in association with symptom disorders. In W. J. Livesley (Ed.), *Handbook of personality disorders: Theory, research, and treatment* (pp. 541–554). New York: Guilford.

Piper, W. E., & Joyce, A. S. (2001). Psychosocial treatment outcome. In W. J. Livesley (Ed.), *Handbook of personality disorders: Theory, research, and treatment* (pp. 323–343). New York: Guilford Press.

Pittenger, D. J., Pavlik, W. B., Flora, S. R., & Kontos, J. M. (1988). The persistence of learned behaviors in humans as a function of changes in reinforcement schedule and response. *Learning and Motivation, 19*, 300–316.

Plaud, J. J., & Eifert, G. H. (Eds.). (1998). *From behavior theory to behavior therapy*. Boston: Allyn & Bacon.

Pliner, P., & Iuppa, G. (1978). Effects of increasing awareness of food consumption in obese and normal weight subjects. *Addictive Behaviors, 3,* 19–24.

Poling, A., & Gaynor, S. T. (2003). Stimulus control. In W. O'Donohue, J. E. Fisher, & S. C. Hayes (Eds.), *Cognitive behavior therapy: Applying empirically supported techniques in your practice* (pp. 396–401). Hoboken, NJ: Wiley.

Powell, D. H. (1996). Behavior therapy-generated insight. In J. R. Cautela & W. Ishaq (Eds.), *Contemporary issues in behavior therapy: Improving the human condition* (pp. 301–314). New York: Plenum Press.

Pratt, S., & Mueser, K. T. (2002). Social skills training for schizophrenia. In S. G. Hoffman & M. C. Tompson (Eds.), *Treating chronic and severe mental disorders* (pp. 18–52). New York: Guilford Press.

Prince, S. E., & Jacobson, N. S. (1995). Couple and family therapy for depression. In E. E. Beckham & W. R. Leber (Eds.), *Handbook of depression* (2nd ed., pp. 404–424). New York: Guilford Press.

Rachlin, H. (1976). *Introduction to modern behaviorism* (2nd ed.). San Francisco: Freeman.

Rachlin, H. (1999). Teleological behaviorism. In W. O'Donohue & R. Kitchner (Eds.), *Handbook of behaviorism* (pp. 195–215). San Diego, CA: Academic Press.

Rachlin, H. (2000). *The science of self-control.* Cambridge, MA: Harvard University Press.

Rachman, S., & Hodgson, R. (1974). Synchrony and desynchrony in fear and avoidance. *Behaviour Research and Therapy, 12,* 311–318.

Ramanaiah, N. V., Rielage, J. K., & Cheng, Y. (2002). Cloninger's Temperament and Character Inventory and the NEO Five-Factor Inventory. *Psychological Reports, 90,* 1059–1063.

Rapee, R. M., & Barlow, D. H. (2001). Generalized anxiety disorders, panic disorders, and phobias. In P. B. Sutker & H. E. Adams (Eds.), *Comprehensive handbook of psychopathology* (3rd ed., pp. 131–154). New York: Kluwer Academic/Plenum.

Rathus, J. H., Sanderson, W. C., Miller, A. L., & Wetzler, S. (1995). Impact of personality functioning on cognitive behavioral treatment of panic disorder: A preliminary report. *Journal of Personality Disorders, 9,* 160–168.

Reeves, J. C., Werry, J. S., Elkind, G. S., & Zametkin, A. (1987). Attention deficit, conduct, oppositional, and anxiety disorders in children: Clinical characteristics. *Journal of the American Academy of Child and Adolescent Psychiatry, 26,* 144–155.

Renneberg, B., Goldstein, A. J., Phillips, D., & Chambless, D. L. (1990). Intensive behavioral group treatment of avoidant personality disorder. *Behavior Therapy, 21,* 363–377.

Repp, A. C., Felce, D., & Barton, L. E. (1988). Basing the treatment of stereotypic and self-injurious behaviors on hypotheses of their causes. *Journal of Applied Behavior Analysis, 21,* 281–289.

Rescorla, R. A. (1988). Pavlovian conditioning: It's not what you think it is. *American Psychologist, 43*, 151–160.

Revelle, W., Humphreys, M. S., Simon, L., & Gilliland, K. (1980). The interactive effect of personality, time of day, and caffeine: A test of the arousal model. *Journal of Experimental Psychology: General, 109*, 1–31.

Rhee, S. H., Feigon, S. A., Bar, J. L., Hadeishi, Y., & Waldman, I. D. (2001). Behavior genetic approaches to the study of psychopathology. In P. B. Sutker & H. E. Adams (Eds.), *Comprehensive handbook of psychopathology* (3rd ed., pp. 53–84). New York: Kluwer Academic/Plenum.

Richards, J. R. (2000). *Human nature after Darwin: A philosophical introduction.* New York: Routledge.

Robins, C. J., Ivanoff, A. M., & Linehan, M. M. (2001). Dialectical behavior therapy. In W. J. Livesley (Ed.), *Handbook of personality disorders: Theory, research, and treatment* (pp. 437–459). New York: Guilford Press.

Robinson, J. C., & Lewinsohn, P. M. (1973). Behavior modification of speech characteristics in a chronically depressed man. *Behavior Therapy, 4*, 150–152.

Rose, H., & Rose, S. (Eds.). (2000). *Alas, poor Darwin: Arguments against evolutionary psychology.* London: Jonathan Cape.

Rosen, J. C., & Leitenberg, H. (1988). The anxiety model of bulimia nervosa and treatment with exposure plus response prevention. In K. M. Pirke, W. Vandereycken, & D. Ploog (Eds.), *The psychobiology of bulimia nervosa* (pp. 146–151). New York: Springer-Verlag.

Rosenbaum, J. F., Biederman, J., Gersten, M., Hirshfeld, D. R., Meminger, S., Herman, J. B., et al. (1988). Behavioral inhibition in children of parents with panic disorder and agoraphobia: A controlled study. *Archives of General Psychiatry, 45*, 463–470.

Rossiter, E., Agras, W. S., Telch, C., & Schneider, J. (1993). Cluster B personality disorder characteristics predict outcome in the treatment of bulimia nervosa. *International Journal of Eating Disorders, 13*, 349–357.

Rothbart, M. K., Ahadi, S. A., & Evans, D. E. (2000). Temperament and personality: Origins and outcomes. *Journal of Personality and Social Psychology, 78*, 122–135.

Rotheram-Borus, M. J., Goldstein, A. M., & Elkavich, A. S. (2002). Treatment of suicidality: A family intervention for adolescent suicide attempters. In S. G. Hoffman & M. C. Tompson (Eds.), *Treating chronic and severe mental disorders* (pp. 191–212). New York: Guilford Press.

Rude, S. S., & Rehm, L. P. (1991). Response to treatments for depression: The role of initial status on targeted cognitive and behavioral skills. *Clinical Psychology Review, 11*, 493–515.

Sacco, W. P., & Beck, A. T. (1995). Cognitive theory and therapy. In E. E. Beckham & W. R. Leber (Eds.), *Handbook of depression* (2nd ed., pp. 329–351). New York: Guilford Press.

Safer, D. L., Telch, C. F., & Agras, W. S. (2001). Dialectical behavior therapy for bulimia nervosa. *American Journal of Psychiatry, 158*, 632–634.

Salkovskis, P. M. (1995). Cognitive–behavioral approaches to the understanding of obsessional problems. In R. M. Rapee (Ed.), *Current controversies in the anxiety disorders* (pp. 103–133). New York: Guilford Press.

Salkovskis, P. M. (1998). Psychological approaches to the understanding of obsessional problems. In R. P. Swinson, M. M. Antony, S. Rachman, & M. A. Richter (Eds.), *Obsessive–compulsive disorder: Theory, research, and treatment*. New York: Guilford Press.

Salzman, L. (1985). *Treatment of the obsessive personality*. Northvale, NJ: Aronson.

Sanderson, W. D., Beck, A. T., & McGinn, L. K. (2002). Cognitive therapy for generalized anxiety disorder: Significance of comorbid personality disorders. In R. L. Leahy & E. T. Dowd (Eds.), *Clinical advances in cognitive psychotherapy: Theory and application* (pp. 287–293). New York: Springer Publishing Company.

Schneider, F., & Deldin, P. J. (2001). Genetics and schizophrenia. In P. B. Sutker & H. E. Adams (Eds.), *Comprehensive handbook of psychopathology* (3rd ed., pp. 371–402). New York: Kluwer Academic/Plenum.

Schwalberg, M. D., Barlow, D. H., Alger, S. A., & Howard, L. J. (1992). Comparison of bulimics, obese binge eaters, social phobics, and individuals with panic disorder on comorbidity across *DSM–III–R* anxiety disorders. *Journal of Abnormal Psychology, 101*, 675–681.

Schwartz, J. M., Stoessel, P. W., Baxter, L. R., Jr., Martin, K. M., & Phelps, M. E. (1996). Systematic changes in cerebral glucose metabolic rate after successful behavior modification treatment of obsessive–compulsive disorder. *Archives of General Psychiatry, 53*, 109–113.

Scotti, J. R., Morris, T. L., McNeil, C. B., & Hawkins, R. P. (1996). *DSM–IV* and disorders of childhood and adolescence: Can structural criteria be functional? *Journal of Consulting and Clinical Psychology, 64*, 1177–1191.

Sears, R. R., Maccoby, E. E., & Levin, H. (1957). *Patterns of child rearing*. Evanston, IL: Row, Peterson.

Segerstråle, U. (2000). *Defenders of the truth: The battle for science in the sociobiology debate and beyond*. Oxford, England: Oxford University Press.

Segerstråle, U. (2001). Minding the brain: The continuing conflict about models and reality. *Evolution and Cognition, 7*, 6–13.

Shapiro, S. K., Quay, H. C., Hogan, A. E., & Schwartz, K. P. (1988). Response preservation and delayed responding in undersocialized aggressive conduct disorder. *Journal of Abnormal Psychology, 97*, 371–373.

Shelton, J. L., & Levy, R. L. (1981). *Behavioral assignments and treatment compliance*. Champaign, IL: Research Press.

Siever, L. J., & Davis, K. L. (1991). A psychobiological perspective on the personality disorders. *American Journal of Psychiatry, 148*, 1647–1658.

Simun, A. E. (1999). Effects of the presence of personality disorders on the effectiveness of group cognitive–behavioral treatment of depression. *Dissertation Abstracts International, 60* (3-B), 1316. Abstract obtained from *PsycINFO* database.

Sitharthan, T., Sitharthan, G., Hough, M., & Kavanagh (1997). Cue exposure in moderation drinking: A comparison with cognitive–behavioral therapy. *Journal of Consulting and Clinical Psychology*, *65*, 878–882.

Skinner, B. F. (1938). *The behavior of organisms: An experimental analysis*. New York: Appleton-Century-Crofts.

Skinner, B. F. (1953). *Science and human behavior*. New York: Macmillan.

Skinner, B. F. (1957). *Verbal behavior*. New York: Appleton-Century-Crofts.

Skinner, B. F. (1969). *Contingencies of reinforcement: A theoretical analysis*. New York: Appleton-Century-Crofts.

Skinner, B. F. (1971). *Beyond freedom and dignity*. New York: Knopf.

Skinner, B. F. (1974). *About behaviorism*. New York: Vintage.

Skinner, B. F. (1981). Selection by consequences. *Science*, *213*, 501–504.

Skinner, B. F. (1984). The evolution of verbal behavior. *Journal of the Experimental Analysis of Behavior*, *45*, 115–122.

Skinner, B. F. (1989). *Recent issues in the analysis of behavior*. Columbus, OH: Merrill.

Smith, M. L., & Glass, G. V. (1977). Meta-analysis of psychotherapy outcome studies. *American Psychologist*, *32*, 752–760.

Spiegler, M. D. (1983). *Contemporary behavioral therapy*. Palo Alto, CA: Mayfield.

Spiegler, M. D., & Guevremont, D. C. (2003). *Contemporary behavior therapy* (4th ed.). Belmont, CA: Wadsworth/Thomson Learning.

Spitzer, R. L. (1991). An outsider-insider's views about revising the *DSMs*. *Journal of Abnormal Psychology*, *100*, 294–296.

Spoont, M. R. (1996). Emotional instability. In C. G. Costello (Ed.), *Personality characteristics of the personality disordered* (pp. 48–90). New York: Wiley.

Staats, A. W. (1963). *Complex human behavior*. New York: Holt, Rinehart, & Winston.

Staats, A. W. (1971). *Child learning, intelligence, and personality*. New York: Harper & Row.

Staats, A. W. (1986). Behaviorism with a personality: The paradigmatic behavioral assessment approach. In R. O. Nelson & S. C. Hayes (Eds.), *Conceptual foundations of behavioral assessment* (pp. 242–296). New York: Guilford Press.

Staats, A. W. (1996). *Behavior and personality: Psychological behaviorism*. New York: Springer Publishing Company.

Staats, A. W. (1999). Valuable, but not maximal: It's time behavior therapy attend to its theory. *Behaviour Research and Therapy*, *37*, 369–378.

Stahl, J. R., & Leitenberg, H. (1976). Behavioral treatment of the chronic mental hospital patient. In H. Leitenberg (Ed.), *Handbook of behavior modification and behavior therapy* (pp. 211–241). Englewood Cliffs, NJ: Prentice Hall.

Steketee, G. S. (1993). *Treatment of obsessive–compulsive disorder*. New York: Guilford Press.

Stunkard, A., Berkowitz, R., Tanrikut, C., Reiss, E., & Young, L. (1996). *d*-Fenfluramine treatment for binge eating disorder. *American Journal of Psychiatry*, *153*, 1455–1459.

Sturmey, P. (1996). *Functional analysis in clinical psychology*. New York: Wiley.

Sugai, G., Horner, R. H., Dunlap, G., Hieneman, M., Lewis, T. J., et al. (2000). Applying positive behavior support and functional behavioral assessment in schools. *Journal of Positive Behavior Intervention, 2*, 131–143.

Svrakic, D. M., Whitehead, C., Przybeck, T. R., & Cloninger, C. R. (1993). Differential diagnosis of personality disorders by the seven-factor model of temperament and character. *Archives of General Psychiatry, 50*, 991–999.

Sweet, A. A., & Loizeaux, A. L. (1991). Behavioral and cognitive treatment methods: A critical comparative review. *Journal of Behavior Therapy and Experimental Psychiatry, 22*, 159–185.

Tabakoff, B., & Hoffman, P. L. (1988). A neurobiological theory of alcoholism. In C. D. Chaudron & D. A. Wilkinson (Eds.), *Theories on alcoholism* (pp. 29–72). Toronto, Ontario, Canada: Addition Research Foundation.

Tanney, B. L. (2000). Psychiatric diagnoses and suicidal acts. In R. W. Maris, A. L. Berman, & M. M. Silverman (Eds.), *Comprehensive textbook of suicidology* (pp. 311–341). New York: Guilford Press.

Tarrier, N., & Calam, R. (2002). New developments in cognitive-behavioural case formulation. Epidemiological, systemic, and social context: An integrative approach. *Behavioural and Cognitive Psychotherapy, 30*, 311–328.

Thompson, J. K., & Williams, D. E. (1985). Behavior therapy in the 80's: Evolution, exploitation, and the existential issue. *The Behavior Therapist, 8*, 47–50.

Thorndike, E. L. (1911). *Animal intelligence: Experimental studies*. New York: Macmillan.

Thornquist, M. H., & Zuckerman, M. (1995). Psychopathy, passive–avoidance learning and basic dimensions of personality. *Personality and Individual Differences, 19*, 525–534.

Timberlake, W. (1999). Biological behaviorism. In W. O'Donohue & R. Kitchener (Eds.), *Handbook of behaviorism* (pp. 243–284). San Diego, CA: Academic Press.

Todd, J. T., & Morris, E. K. (1983). Misconception and miseducation: Presentations of racial behaviorism in psychology textbooks. *Behavior Analyst, 6*, 153–160.

Trower, P., Yardley, K., Bryant, B. M., & Shaw, P. (1978). The treatment of social failure: A comparison of anxiety-reduction and skills-acquisition procedures on two social problems. *Behavior Modification, 2*, 41–50.

Trull, T. J., Widiger, T. A., & Frances, A. J. (1987). Covariation of criteria sets for avoidant, schizoid, and dependent personality disorders. *American Journal of Psychiatry, 144*, 767–772.

Turkat, I. D. (1990). *The personality disorders: A psychological approach to clinical management*. New York: Pergamon.

Turner, S. M., Beidel, D. C., Dancu, C. V., & Keys, D. J. (1986). Psychopathology of social phobia and comparison. *Journal of Abnormal Psychology, 95*, 389–394.

Twentyman, C. T., & Zimering, R. T. (1979). Behavioral training of social skills: A critical review. In M. Hersen, R. M. Eisler, & P. M. Miller (Eds.), *Progress in behavior modification* (Vol. 7). New York: Academic Press.

Upper, D., & Cautela, J. R. (Eds.). (1979). *Covert conditioning*. New York: Pergamon.

van der Kolk, B. A. (1996). The body keeps the score: approaches to the psychobiology of posttraumatic stress disorder. In B. A. van der Kolk, A. C. McFarlane, & L. Weisaeth (Eds.), *Traumatic stress: The effects of overwhelming experience on the mind, body, and society* (pp. 214–241). New York: Guilford Press.

van Oppen, P., de Haan, E., van Balkom, A. J. L. M., Spinhoven, P., Hoogduin, K., & Van Dyck, R. (1995). Cognitive therapy and exposure in vivo in the treatment of obsessive-compulsive disorder. *Behaviour Research and Therapy, 33*, 379–390.

van Velzen, C. J. M., Emmelkamp, P. M. G., & Scholing, A. (1997). The impact of personality disorders on behavioral treatment outcome for social phobia. *Behaviour Research and Therapy, 35*, 889–900.

Vassend, O., Willumsen, T., & Hoffart, A. (2000). Effects of dental fear treatment on general distress: The role of personality variables and treatment method. *Behavior Modification, 24*, 580–599.

Wachtel, P. L. (1977). *Psychoanalysis and behavioral therapy: Toward an integration*. New York: Basic Books.

Wagner, A. W., & Linehan, M. M. (1998). Dissociative behavior. In V. M. Follette, J. I. Ruzek, & F. R. Abueg (Eds.), *Cognitive–behavioral therapies for trauma* (pp. 191–225). New York: Guilford Press.

Wallace, J. F., & Newman, J. P. (1990). Differential effects of reward and punishment cues on response speed in anxious and impulsive individuals. *Personality and Individual Differences, 11*, 999–1009.

Wallace, J. F., & Newman, J. P. (1997). Neuroticism and the attentional mediation of dysregulatory psychopathology. *Cognitive Therapy and Research, 27*, 135–156.

Walser, R. D., & Hayes, S. C. (1998). Acceptance and trauma survivors: Applied issues and problems. In V. M. Follette, J. I. Ruzek, & F. R. Abueg (Eds.), *Cognitive–behavioral therapies for trauma* (pp. 256–277). New York: Guilford Press.

Waltz, J., & Linehan, M. M. (1999). Functional analysis of borderline personality disorder behavioral criterion patterns. In J. Derksen, C. Maffei, & H. Groen (Eds.), *Treatment of personality disorders* (pp. 183–206). New York: Kluwer Academic/Plenum.

Warburton, J. B., Hurst, R. M., Topor, D., Nelson-Gray, R. O., & Keane, S. P. (2003, March). *DBT for aggressive adolescents: A preliminary evaluation of treatment efficacy*. Poster presented at the meeting of the North Carolina Psychological Association, Durham.

Watson, D. (2000). *Mood and temperament*. New York: Guilford Press.

Watson, J. B. (1919). *Psychology from the standpoint of a behaviorist*. Philadelphia: Lippincott.

Watson, J. B. (1925). *Behaviorism*. New York: Norton.

Watson, J. B., & Raynor, R. (1920). Conditioned emotional reactions. *Journal of Experimental Psychology, 3*, 1–14.

Weissman, A. N., & Beck, A. T. (1978, November). *Development and validation of the Dysfunctional Attitude Scale*. Paper presented at the annual meeting of the Association for Advancement of Behavior Therapy, Chicago.

Wells, A. (1997). *Cognitive therapy of anxiety disorders: A practice manual and conceptual guide*. New York: Wiley.

Welsh, G. S. (1956). Factor dimensions A and R. In G. S. Welsh & W. G. Dahlstrom (Eds.), *Basic readings on the MMPI in psychology and medicine* (pp. 264–281). Minneapolis: University of Minnesota Press.

Weltzin, T. E., Fernstrom, M. H., & Kaye, W. H. (1994). Serotonin and bulimia nervosa. *Nutritional Reviews, 52*, 399–408.

Wheeler, J. G., Christensen, A., & Jacobson, N. S. (2001). Couple distress. In D. H. Barlow (Ed.), *Clinical handbook of psychological disorders* (3rd ed., pp. 609–630). New York: Guilford Press.

Widiger, T. A., Frances, A., Harris, M., Jacobsberg, L., Fyer, M., & Manning, D. (1991). Comorbidity among Axis II disorders. In J. M. Oldham (Ed.), *Personality disorders: New perspectives on diagnostic validity*. Washington, DC: American Psychiatric Press.

Widiger, T. A., & Shea, M. T. (1991). Differentiation of Axis I and Axis II disorders. *Journal of Abnormal Psychology, 100*, 399–406.

Widiger, T. A., Trull, T. J., Clarkin, J. F., Sanderson, C., & Costa, P. T., Jr. (2002). A description of the *DSM–IV* personality disorders within the five-factor model of personality. In P. T. Costa, Jr., & T. A. Widiger (Eds.), *Personality disorders and the five-factor model of personality* (2nd ed., pp. 89–99). Washington, DC: American Psychological Association.

Wilson, G. T., Fairburn, C. G., & Agras, W. S. (1997). Cognitive–behavioral therapy for bulimia nervosa. In D. M. Garner & P. E. Garfinkel (Eds.), *Handbook of treatment for eating disorders* (2nd ed., pp. 67–93). New York: Guilford Press.

Witkin, H., Oltman, P. K., Raskin, E., & Karp, S. A. (1971). *A manual for the Embedded Figures Tests*. Palo Alto, CA: Consulting Psychologists Press.

Wolpe, J. (1958). *Psychotherapy by reciprocal inhibition*. Stanford, CA: Stanford University Press.

Wulfert, E., Greenway, D. E., & Dougher, M. J. (1996). A logical functional analysis of reinforcement-based disorders: Alcoholism and pedophilia. *Journal of Consulting and Clinical Psychology, 64*, 1140–1151.

Yeung, A., Lyons, M., Waternaux, C., Faraone, S., & Tsuang, M. (1993). The relationship between *DSM–III* personality disorders and the five-factor model of personality. *Comprehensive Psychiatry, 34*, 227–234.

Young, J. E. (1994). *Cognitive therapy for personality disorders: A schema-focused approach* (rev. ed.). Sarasota, FL: Professional Resource Press.

Zelenski, J. M., & Larsen, R. J. (1999). Susceptibility to affect: A comparison of three personality taxonomies. *Journal of Personality, 67*, 761–791.

Zettle, R. D., & Hayes, S. C. (1982). Rule-governed behavior: A potential theoretical framework for cognitive–behavioral therapy. In P. C. Kendall (Ed.), *Advances in cognitive behavioral research and therapy* (Vol. 1, pp. 73–118). New York: Academic Press.

Zimmerman, M. (1994). Diagnosing personality disorders: A review of issues and research methods. *Archives of General Psychiatry, 51,* 225–245.

Zimmerman, M., & Coryell, W. (1989). *DSM–III* personality disorder diagnoses in a nonpatient sample: Demographic correlates and comorbidity. *Archives of General Psychiatry, 46,* 682–689.

Zuber, I., & Ekehammar, B. (1988). Personality, time of day and visual perception: Preferences and selective attention. *Personality and Individual Differences, 9,* 345–352.

Zuckerman, M. (1996). Sensation seeking. In C. G. Costello (Ed.), *Personality characteristics of the personality disordered* (pp. 289–316). New York: Wiley.

AUTHOR INDEX

SUBJECT INDEX

ABOUT THE AUTHORS

Richard F. Farmer, PhD, is currently the senior lecturer in psychology at the University of Canterbury in Christchurch, New Zealand. After earning a PhD in clinical psychology from the University of North Carolina at Greensboro in 1993, he went on to serve as assistant and then associate professor of psychology at Idaho State University. His main areas of research and clinical interest include personality disorders, personality and behavioral assessment, behavior therapy, impulsivity and disinhibition, and experiential avoidance.

Rosemery O. Nelson-Gray, PhD, is currently a professor of psychology at the University of North Carolina at Greensboro and also served as Director of Clinical Training for over 20 years. She earned her PhD in clinical psychology from the State University of New York at Stony Brook in 1972, after studying under Hans Eysenck at the Institute of Psychiatry in London on a Fulbright Scholarship. She has published numerous empirical and theoretical articles, many book chapters, and four books on the topics of behavioral assessment (especially self-monitoring) and adult psychopathology (especially depression, personality disorders, and adult attention-deficit/hyperactivity disorder).